PHP
HACKS™

Other resources from O'Reilly

Related titles

Essential PHP Security
Learning PHP 5
MySQL in a Nutshell
Web Database
  Applications with PHP
  and MySQL

PHP Cookbook™
PHP in a Nutshell
PHPUnit Pocket Guide
Programming PHP
Upgrading to PHP 5

Hacks Series Home

hacks.oreilly.com is a community site for developers and power users of all stripes. Readers learn from each other as they share their favorite tips and tools for Mac OS X, Linux, Google, Windows XP, and more.

---

oreilly.com

oreilly.com is more than a complete catalog of O'Reilly books. You'll also find links to news, events, articles, weblogs, sample chapters, and code examples.

oreillynet.com is the essential portal for developers interested in open and emerging technologies, including new platforms, programming languages, and operating systems.

Conferences

O'Reilly brings diverse innovators together to nurture the ideas that spark revolutionary industries. We specialize in documenting the latest tools and systems, translating the innovator's knowledge into useful skills for those in the trenches. Visit *conferences.oreilly.com* for our upcoming events.

Safari Bookshelf (*safari.oreilly.com*) is the premier online reference library for programmers and IT professionals. Conduct searches across more than 1,000 books. Subscribers can zero in on answers to time-critical questions in a matter of seconds. Read the books on your Bookshelf from cover to cover or simply flip to the page you need. Try it today for free.

PHP
HACKS™

Jack D. Herrington

O'REILLY®

Beijing · Cambridge · Farnham · Köln · Paris · Sebastopol · Taipei · Tokyo

PHP Hacks™

by Jack D. Herrington

Copyright © 2006 O'Reilly Media, Inc. All rights reserved.
Printed in the United States of America.

Published by O'Reilly Media, Inc., 1005 Gravenstein Highway North,
Sebastopol, CA 95472.

O'Reilly books may be purchased for educational, business, or sales promotional use. Online editions are also available for most titles (*safari.oreilly.com*). For more information, contact our corporate/institutional sales department: (800) 998-9938 or *corporate@oreilly.com*.

Editor: Brett McLaughlin   **Cover Designer:**   Marcia Friedman
Production Editor: Reba Libby   **Interior Designer:**   David Futato

Printing History:

   December 2005:   First Edition.

 This book uses RepKover,™ a durable and flexible lay-flat binding.

ISBN: 0-596-10139-2
[M]

*This book is dedicated to
my wife, Lauren.*

*You have supported me in everything
I have done and said, and sometimes,
in spite of it.*

I love you.

Contents

Credits

About the Author

Jack D. Herrington is a programmer who has been developing applications since he was 13, almost 25 years ago. Over the years, he has written in every major programming language and for every environment.

He is the author of three books. *Code Generation in Action* (Manning, 2002) covers using code to write code automatically. Many of the elements from that book appear in the database section of this book. In *Podcasting Hacks* (O'Reilly, 2005), he encourages his readers to create a citizen's media through podcasting. His third book, *PHP Hacks*, is what you have in your hands.

He is the author of more than 30 articles ranging from PHP and code generation to podcasting, digital photography, and more. In one article for the O'Reilly Network, Jack had the audacity to propose that PHP was as apt at enterprise application development as Java or .NET. The ensuing comments battle extended onto Slashdot and continues to a small degree even today.

Jack lives with his wife Lori and daughter Megan in the San Francisco Bay Area. He works for a startup company named Leverage Software that specializes in social networking software. Before that, he was with Macromedia. He is an avid hiker, golfer, chef, woodworker, and (sometimes) origami artist when he isn't hacking on PHP.

Contributors

The following people contributed hacks to this book:

Ross Shannon

Ross Shannon is a student from Dublin, Ireland, currently studying for a Ph.D. in computer science at University College Dublin.

Ross is a part-time web designer with a great interest in web technologies. He is the webmaster of a web design tutorial site, HTMLSource, which you can find at *http://www.yourhtmlsource.com/*.

Matthew Terenzio

Matt Terenzio has more than 10 years of technology and media experience. He holds a master's degree in Internet engineering, and he has been lead architect on numerous projects for organizations, including The Berkman Center for Internet and Society at Harvard Law School.

He has held the position of senior web producer for GreenwichTime.com and StamfordAdvocate.com for nearly five years and has contributed to a number of high-profile news sites including NYNewsday.com and OrlandoSentinel.com.

Most recently, Matt founded BuddyBuilder LLC, which has launched a number of Web 2.0 services, among them BuddyBuilder.com, Skinny-Farm.com, and Newsmarks.com.

Michael Mulligan

Michael Mulligan (*mtm26@cornell.edu*) is a software engineer who earned his degree in computer science from the College of Engineering at Cornell University in 2005. He has worked in a variety of industries, ranging from small ventures to software engineering at Apple Computer. His main research interests lie in machine learning and vision.

In the summer of 2005, Mike married Dhipthi Devabose, his beautiful wife, and they settled in Florida. He now works full time as a software engineer at Lockheed Martin and is the author of myPhoto (*http://agent0068.dyndns.org/~mike/projects/myPhoto/*). For fun these days, he experiments with cooking new dishes and spends a lot of time with their new puppy, Siena.

Dru Nelson

Dru Nelson has been on the Internet since 1988. After starting an ISP in Florida, he moved to the San Francisco Bay Area and has been involved with large Internet infrastructure at companies like Four11 (Yahoo! Mail), Diva, eGroups (Yahoo! Groups), Danger, and Blue6. He is now at Plaxo.com doing Win32 software development. Dru has a blog at *http:// www.xxeo.com/*.

Tyler Mitchell

Tyler Mitchell is a geographer and open source enthusiast. The author of *Web Mapping Illustrated* (O'Reilly, 2005), Tyler works as a Geographic Information Systems (GIS) manager for Timberline Forest Inventory Consultants and lives in beautiful British Columbia, Canada. He also is a regular speaker, moderator, and workshop leader at GIS conferences. His foray into the open source world began while looking for alternatives to proprietary mapping tools. He is now a devoted open source GIS advocate.

Peter Lavin

Peter Lavin runs a web development firm in Toronto. He has been published in a number of magazines and online sites, including Unix-Review.com and Dr. Dobb's Journal. He is currently writing a book on object-oriented PHP, soon to be published by No Starch Press. For more information, see *http://softcoded.com/*.

Preface

PHP has earned its place as one of the premiere web scripting languages and is used in everything from small utility scripts to object-oriented enterprise applications. This book covers that entire spectrum, offering hacks focusing on everything from HTML and Ajax to code generation and database-driven message queuing.

We have written code and chosen authors from the cutting edge of web development, application development, graphics, and multimedia. Dynamic HTML is covered extensively, offering your users an interactive experience on the web page without having to watch a browser refresh; you'll learn how to generate Flash movies on the fly; you'll even see how to use PHP for database access, web services, and much more.

The book offers more than just canned solutions. It offers ideas and techniques that you can use in your own applications. And why stop there? We encourage you to take the ideas we've presented here and extend them, hacking our hacks, taking your scripts and classes even further.

Why PHP Hacks?

The term *hacking* has a bad reputation in the press. They use it to refer to someone who breaks into systems or wreaks havoc with computers as their weapon. Among people who write code, though, the term *hack* refers to a "quick-and-dirty" solution to a problem, or a clever way to get something done. And the term *hacker* is taken very much as a compliment, referring to someone as being *creative*, having the technical chops to get things done. The Hacks series is an attempt to reclaim the word, document the good ways people are hacking, and pass the hacker ethic of creative participation on to the uninitiated. Seeing how others approach systems and problems is often the quickest way to learn about a new technology.

How to Use This Book

You can read this book from cover to cover if you like, but each hack stands on its own, so feel free to browse and jump to the different sections that interest you most. If there's a prerequisite you need to know about, a cross-reference will guide you to the right hack.

How This Book Is Organized

The book is divided into several chapters, organized by subject:

Chapter 1, *Installation and Basics*

    This chapter walks you through the basics of installing PHP and MySQL, as well as using the excellent PEAR library.

Chapter 2, *Web Design*

    In this chapter, we cover how to use HTML tricks in conjunction with PHP to jazz up your interface.

Chapter 3, *DHTML*

    In this chapter, we use the powerful combination of HTML, CSS, and JavaScript known as Dynamic HTML (DHTML) in conjunction with PHP to show just what you can do in a web browser.

Chapter 4, *Graphics*

    This chapter shows a wide variety of methods that you can use to display data in a graphical form.

Chapter 5, *Databases and XML*

    Databases are critical to PHP applications. In this chapter, we show you how to make flexible database objects and even to build your database layer automatically using code generation.

Chapter 6, *Application Design*

    In this chapter, we take the coverage up a notch and discuss techniques that you can use to develop applications quickly and reliably.

Chapter 7, *Patterns*

    C++, C#, and Java programmers have used design patterns for years. Can you use them in PHP as well? You betcha. This chapter shows how to use several of the design patterns from the original *Design Patterns* book (Addison Wesley) to make better PHP applications.

Chapter 8, *Testing*

    Do you stay awake at night thinking about whether your PHP application is still running? This chapter covers testing techniques that will find bugs for you and continuously monitor the operation of your site.

Chapter 9, *Alternative UIs*

In this chapter, we show the use of different user interfaces to work with your PHP code. You can run PHP applications on the desktop, from your cell phone, and from your instant messaging application.

Chapter 10, *Fun Stuff*

In this chapter, we let it all hang out and use the fun stuff on the Web to monitor multiplayer games, use Google Maps in our applications, and much more.

Common Problems

I often see several problems with PHP applications, and this book helps address a number of these:

Bad database design

Most PHP applications work with a relational database, usually MySQL. Database design is not something that comes easily to most engineers trained in traditional programming languages. The first step in cleaning up an application is to make sure the database design is good [Hack #34].

Poor database use

PHP has provided several different variations on how to access databases, and doing this poorly can cause serious security problems. Fixing the database access layer can start with migrating to PEAR DB or PDO [Hack #35]. After that, you can see if it's possible to generate the SQL [Hack #41], the SELECT code [Hack #42], or the CRUD code [Hack #37].

Code embedded in the page

The next problem I see a lot is code that's embedded directly in the page. In particular, access to the database is embedded right in the code of the page. The code-generating hacks that build SELECT code [Hack #42] and CRUD code [Hack #37] show proper two-tier design with PHP. The SQL dynamic object hack [Hack #36] can also help factor SQL access code off the page.

Processing during the page build

Another issue I see is applications that attempt to do a lot of processing in the web server during the page fetch. An example is when an application needs to send out a lot of email in response to some user action. Often this is done in the page that responds to the user action—which leaves the user waiting for a page to come back while the system is sending out a bunch of mail. A message queue [Hack #50] is one elegant solution to this problem.

No testing

I hardly ever see test code in the applications that I look at, but automated testing is the first and best way to feel comfortable about going home at night, especially when your job is writing a 24/7 web application. This book contains information on unit tests [Hack #79] and how to generate them automatically [Hack #80]. It also contains code for checking the site through robots [Hack #83] and through the automation of Internet Explorer [Hack #82], which can even check your JavaScript code.

Provide better user security

Most people use the same password on most or all of their accounts. If your application stores passwords in the clear and your application is compromised, you are giving your users' passwords to the world. Use MD5 to scramble people's passwords [Hack #59]. And use a roles system [Hack #58] to make sure users don't see things they shouldn't see.

Make better use of patterns

I admit that the term *design patterns* has been overplayed. But there is a lot of good stuff there that has been underutilized in PHP applications. All of Chapter 7 is dedicated to showing how you can use design patterns pragmatically and effectively to make better PHP applications.

These are just a few ideas about how to upgrade your existing web application to something that is reliable and secure. But how about cool?

Making a Cool Web Application

You can do so much in browsers and with browser plug-ins, DHTML, and Ajax that it's not hard to have an application that is cool, is easy to use, and has cutting-edge features. Here are some ideas taken from various parts of the book:

Work from the desktop

Believe it or not, you can use PHP to make desktop applications [Hack #87] so that the same business logic code that runs on your web server can be used right on the desktop. Better yet, this code is portable between Mac OS X, Windows, and Linux, with little (and often no) code rewrite.

Use maps

Mapping has become really popular lately. There are two easy ways to handle mapping with PHP: first with MapServer [Hack #86] and second with Google Maps [Hack #95].

Graph it dynamically
> Graphics and graphing are always popular, and there are so many ways to do graphing in PHP. You can use basic HTML [Hack #8], SVG [Hack #28], Dynamic HTML [Hack #22], and the GD library [Hack #31]. I've also included information on how to build an object-oriented layer on top of the graphics library [Hack #29].

Work with your users' applications
> Another way to create a more compelling application is to reach out to your users. RSS [Hack #88] has become a very popular way to do that. I even take RSS to your PlayStation Portable [Hack #90]. And you can use more traditional routes like email [Hack #10]. I've also included some information on how to generate Word RTF documents [Hack #48] and Excel spreadsheets [Hack #49], as well as how to take Word [Hack #47] or Excel documents [Hack #45] as input.

Upgrade your web interface
> I also include some ideas for generating dynamic menus [Hack #17] and easily creating breadcrumb trails [Hack #4], tabs [Hack #6], skinnable interfaces [Hack #3], pop ups [Hack #12], stickies [Hack #16], drag-and-drop interfaces [Hack #13], calendars [Hack #25], link graphs [Hack #24], and more that will make your web interface the best it can be.

These are just a few ideas from the pages of this book. Dig right in and find out ways to take your PHP to the cutting edge.

Conventions Used in This Book

The following is a list of the typographical conventions used in this book:

Italics
> Used to indicate URLs, filenames and extensions, and directory/folder names. For example, a path in the filesystem would appear as */Developer/Applications*.

`Constant width`
> Used to show code examples, the contents of files, and console output, as well as the names of variables, commands, and other code excerpts.

`Constant width bold`
> Used to highlight portions of code, typically new additions to old code.

`Constant width italic`
> Used in code examples and tables to show sample text to be replaced with your own values.

Gray type
> Used to indicate a cross-reference within the text.

You should pay special attention to notes set apart from the text with the following icons:

This is a tip, suggestion, or general note. It contains useful supplementary information about the topic at hand.

This is a warning or note of caution, often indicating that your money or your privacy might be at risk.

The thermometer icons, found next to each hack, indicate the relative complexity of the hack:

 beginner   moderate   expert

Using Code Examples

This book is here to help you get your job done. In general, you may use the code in this book in your programs and documentation. You do not need to contact us for permission unless you're reproducing a significant portion of the code. For example, writing a program that uses several chunks of code from this book does not require permission. Selling or distributing a CD-ROM of examples from O'Reilly books *does* require permission. Answering a question by citing this book and quoting example code does not require permission. Incorporating a significant amount of example code from this book into your product's documentation *does* require permission.

We appreciate, but do not require, attribution. An attribution usually includes the title, author, publisher, and ISBN. For example: *PHP Hacks* by Jack D. Herrington. Copyright 2006 O'Reilly Media, Inc., 0-596-10139-2."

If you feel your use of code examples falls outside fair use or the permission given above, feel free to contact us at *permissions@oreilly.com*.

How to Contact Us

We have tested and verified the information in this book to the best of our ability, but you may find that features have changed (or even that we have made mistakes!). As a reader of this book, you can help us to improve future editions by sending us your feedback. Please let us know about any errors, inaccuracies, bugs, misleading or confusing statements, and typos that you find anywhere in this book.

Please also let us know what we can do to make this book more useful to you. We take your comments seriously and will try to incorporate reasonable suggestions into future editions. You can write to us at:

O'Reilly Media, Inc.
1005 Gravenstein Highway North
Sebastopol, CA 95472
(800) 998-9938 (in the U.S. or Canada)
(707) 829-0515 (international/local)
(707) 829-0104 (fax)

To ask technical questions or to comment on the book, send email to:

bookquestions@oreilly.com

The web site for *PHP Hacks* lists examples, errata, and plans for future editions. You can find this page at:

http://www.oreilly.com/catalog/phphks

For more information about this book and others, see the O'Reilly web site:

http://www.oreilly.com

Got a Hack?

To explore Hacks books online or to contribute a hack for future titles, visit:

http://hacks.oreilly.com

Safari Enabled

 When you see a Safari® Enabled icon on the cover of your favorite technology book, that means the book is available online through the O'Reilly Network Safari Bookshelf.

Safari offers a solution that's better than e-books. It's a virtual library that lets you easily search thousands of top tech books, cut and paste code samples, download chapters, and find quick answers when you need the most accurate, current information. Try it for free at *http://safari.oreilly.com.*

CHAPTER ONE

Installation and Basics

Hacks 1–2

Before you start hacking PHP, you have to either install PHP or get an account on a machine that has PHP already installed. This chapter covers the basics of installing PHP, as well as installing the critical second component, the MySQL database engine, that is so commonly used to provide data that drives PHP applications. The chapter also covers installing PEAR open source modules, which you can use for free in your own PHP applications.

HACK #1 Install PHP

Install the PHP language on Windows, Mac OS X, and Linux, and for both Apache and Internet Information Server.

Installing PHP is the first step in using this book, and on most operating systems, it's a very easy thing to do. PHP installation starts with going to the PHP web site (*http://www.php.net/*) and downloading either the source code or the binaries, along with documentation.

Installing PHP on Windows

On Windows, you need to start your PHP installation by downloading the PHP binaries for PHP Version 5. Use the *.msi* installer to make it easy on yourself, and specify the installation directory as *c:\php5*. With your PHP installation in place, you can run the PHP interpreter from a Windows DOS prompt:

```
C:\> php -v
PHP 5.0.4 (cli) (built: Mar 31 2005 02:45:00)
Copyright ¬© 1997-2004 The PHP Group
Zend Engine v2.0.4-dev, Copyright (c) 1998-2004 Zend Technologies
```

If the php executable is not found, you need to add *c:\php5\bin* to your path. Use the Advanced tab of the system control panel, and click on the Environ-ment Variables button. From there, edit the Path variable, adding *c:\php5\bin* to whatever path you already have in place.

> You will need to close any open command prompt windows and then open a new command prompt window to ensure that these changes take effect.

Command-line access to PHP is great, but you really want to have PHP installed in and integrated with your web server. On Windows, you have two options for this integration. The first is to install the Apache Web Server and configure it for PHP; the second is to install the Internet Information Services (IIS) web server and to install PHP into that environment.

In either case, you need to copy the *php.ini* file to your Windows directory, *c:\windows*. Edit the *c:\windows\php.ini* file and change the extension_dir line to read as follows:

```
extension_dir = "c:\php5\ext"
```

Further, uncomment lines such as this one:

```
extension=php_mysql.dll
```

This line enables access to the MySQL database.

> You might want to uncomment several other libraries in this file to enable access to other libraries; see the PHP documen-tation for more on specific libraries.

Now go back to the PHP site (*http://www.php.net/*) and download the collec-tion of PECL modules. Save these DLL files into the *c:\php5\ext* directory (the same directory you just referenced in *php.ini*). These extensions are required if you want access to SQL databases or if you want to use graphics functions (you *will* want to use both of these at some point).

Installing PHP in Apache. Go to the Apache web site (*http://www.apache.org/*) and download Version 1.3 of Apache, which is precompiled for Windows. This comes as an MSI installer, and that's the easiest way to install Apache. Once you've got Apache installed, the next step is to fix the *http.conf* file in the Apache *conf* directory (*c:\Program Files\Apache Group\Apache\conf* if you installed Apache in the default location).

Add the following lines to the end of the *httpd.conf* file:

```
LoadModule php5_module "c:/php5/php5apache.dll"
AddModule mod_php5.c
AddType application/x-httpd-php .php
AddType application/x-httpd-php-source .phps
```

Next, start the Apache server by running *apache.exe*:

```
C:\Program Files\Apache Group\Apache> apache
Apache/1.3.33 (Win32) PHP/5.0.4 running...
```

The documents directory for this installation is *htdocs* (making the complete path *c:\Program Files\Apache Group\Apache\htdocs*). To test it, create a *test.php* file in the *htdocs* directory and put this code in the file:

```
<?php
phpinfo( );
?>
```

Use your web browser to surf to the page; you should see something like Figure 1-1.

From here, you can use the code from all of the hacks in this book.

Installing PHP in IIS. After installing PHP to the *c:\php5* directory, you can integrate PHP into IIS through *php5isapi.dll*. Start by launching the IIS control panel. Then create a new virtual directory as shown in Figure 1-2.

Make sure to set the Execute permission correctly (detailed in Figure 1-3).

Next, right-click on the virtual directory and select Properties. Then, in the Properties dialog, click on the Configuration button. This will bring up the Application Mappings dialog, where you can associate the *.php* extension with *php5isapi.dll*. This dialog is shown in Figure 1-4.

Click on the Add button to create a new mapping, and set the executable to *c:\php5\php5isapi.dll*.

> If you use the Browse button when creating a new mapping, you will need to change the file type to the DLL setting so that you can see the file.

Set the extension to *.php*. The result should look like Figure 1-5.

Click OK (and confirm all the dialogs on the way out). Then navigate to the documents directory that you specified when you created the virtual directory. Create a new file called *test.php* with these contents:

```
<?php
phpinfo( );
?>
```

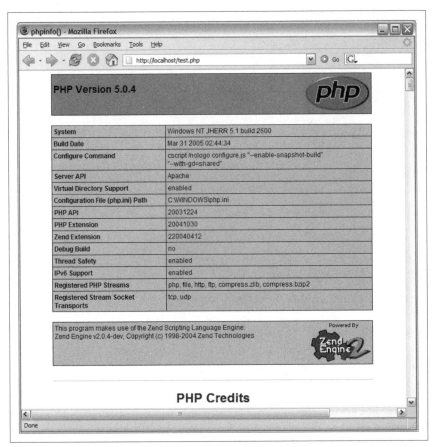

Figure 1-1. The PHP test page on an Apache/Windows install

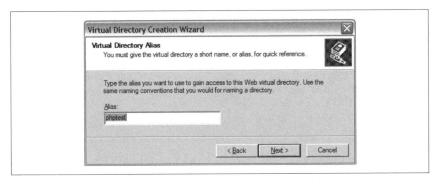

Figure 1-2. Creating a virtual directory

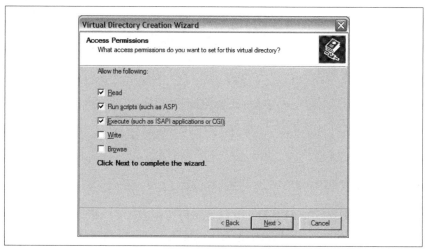

Figure 1-3. Setting the Execute permission of the virtual directory

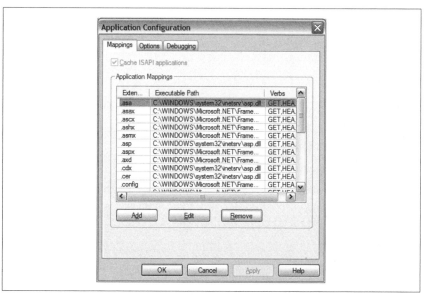

Figure 1-4. The Application Mappings dialog to set the .php file mapping

Then, navigate your browser to that file on *localhost*; you should see something like Figure 1-1.

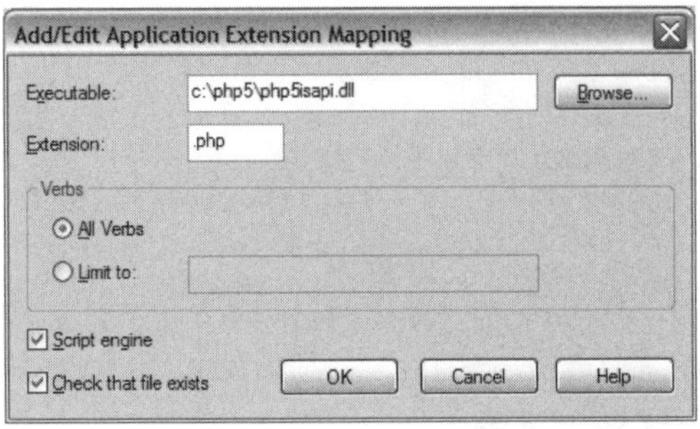

Figure 1-5. The mapping settings for PHP 5

Installing PHP on Mac OS X

PHP is preinstalled on all versions of OS X. All you need to do is enable it. That process starts with becoming the super user using the sudo command:

```
% sudo tcsh
```

In the super-user shell, you can modify system files. The next step is to edit the *httpd.conf* file in */etc/httpd* using your text editor of choice (vi, emacs, etc.). Find and uncomment this line:

```
LoadModule php4_module        libexec/httpd/libphp4.so
```

In addition, uncomment this line:

```
AddModule mod_php4.c
```

Then save the file and restart the built-in Apache server:

```
% apachectl restart
```

The default documents directory for the Apache Web Server on Mac OS X is */Library/WebServer/Documents*. To test that PHP is responding correctly, create a test script in the documents directory:

```
<?php
phpinfo( );
?>
```

Finally, surf to the test page so you can view the PHP status page (shown in Figure 1-6).

However, all is not well; the preinstalled version of PHP on Mac OS X is Version 4, which has a very limited set of modules. Notably missing are *any* graphics modules! To get Version 5 of PHP, you can either download the source and then compile and install it or find a precompiled binary package.

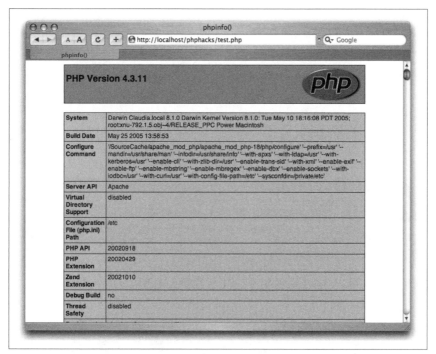

PHP Version 4.3.11

System	Darwin Claudia.local 8.1.0 Darwin Kernel Version 8.1.0: Tue May 10 18:16:08 PDT 2005; root:xnu-792.1.5.obj~4/RELEASE_PPC Power Macintosh
Build Date	May 25 2005 13:58:53
Configure Command	'/SourceCache/apache_mod_php/apache_mod_php-18/php/configure' '--prefix=/usr' '--mandir=/usr/share/man' '--infodir=/usr/share/info' '--with-apxs' '--with-ldap=/usr' '--with-kerberos=/usr' '--enable-cli' '--with-zlib-dir=/usr' '--enable-trans-sid' '--with-xml' '--enable-exif' '--enable-ftp' '--enable-mbstring' '--enable-mbregex' '--enable-dbx' '--enable-sockets' '--with-iodbc=/usr' '--with-curl=/usr' '--with-config-file-path=/etc' '--sysconfdir=/private/etc'
Server API	Apache
Virtual Directory Support	disabled
Configuration File (php.ini) Path	/etc
PHP API	20020918
PHP Extension	20020429
Zend Extension	20021010
Debug Build	no
Thread Safety	disabled

Figure 1-6. The test page on OS X

I recommend using a precompiled binary package since it's much easier. When you compile PHP from source, you need to also download, compile, and install a variety of other libraries that PHP uses, such as the graphics libraries. That can be a very time-consuming process.

Marc Liyanage has an OS X binary package of PHP 5 with a bunch of nice libraries preinstalled on his web site (*http://www.entropy.ch/software/macosx/php/*). To install it, simply download the package installer and launch it (don't you love Mac OS X sometimes?).

After installing the PHP 5 package, you will need to move the PHP 4 executables out of their default locations. Use these commands to move php and pear to php4 and pear4:

```
% sudo mv /usr/bin/php /usr/bin/php4
% sudo mv /usr/bin/pear /usr/bin/pear4
```

Now request the version information from the PHP interpreter to ensure that you have Version 5 installed:

```
% php -v
PHP 5.0.4 (cli) (built: Apr  4 2005 17:32:28)
Copyright (c) 1997-2004 The PHP Group
Zend Engine v2.0.4-dev, Copyright (c) 1998-2004 Zend Technologies
```

Verifying an Apache Web Server installation means going back to the test page we created earlier; Figure 1-7 shows the PHP page verifying that PHP 5 is running.

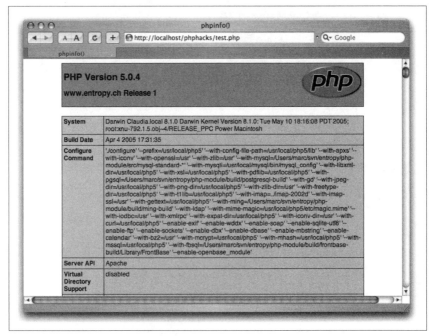

Figure 1-7. The test page after installing PHP 5

Installing PHP on Linux

The process of installing PHP on Linux actually begins with determining whether PHP is already installed (in many cases, it is). First, you should check for the presence of the Apache Web Server on your installation. Is the machine serving pages? If not, check for the presence of the Apache httpd executable:

```
my-host$ find / -name httpd
```

If you find the Apache binary, make sure it's run as part of your machine's startup process. If Apache is not installed, installing the web server is your first step toward installing PHP. Go to the Apache web site (*http://apache.org/*) and download and install the server.

> I strongly recommend installing Version 1.3 of the server, and not using Version 2.0. Most hosting sites on the Internet provide Apache 1.3, which is a stable and proven technology. Apache 2, while newly developed, has threading features that PHP doesn't use.

Once Apache is installed, the next step is to check for an existing PHP installation. Create a file called *index.php* and place it in the Apache documents directory. The contents of the file should be:

```
<?php
phpinfo( );
?>
```

Surf to the machine with your web browser and look at *index.php*. If you see something like Figure 1-7, you have a working PHP installation. If you see just the text of the *index.php* file, PHP is either not installed or not active.

Check your Apache *httpd.conf* configuration file. If you see lines like this:

```
# LoadModule php4_module        libexec/httpd/libphp4.so
```

enable those lines by removing the hash symbol at the start of the line. If the file contains no lines that are relevant to PHP, you will have to install PHP from source.

Installing from source means downloading the source *.tgz* file from *http://www.php.net/*. Follow the installation instructions contained on the PHP site. You already have Linux running, so this should be a breeze.

> I recommend installing PHP 5, as it's the most current version and it has language features that support writing more robust applications.

With PHP installed, you should be able to navigate to the *index.php* page that you built earlier in this process and see output like Figure 1-7.

Checking Your ISP Installation

To check the specifics of your ISP's PHP installation, you need to create a test page on your ISP server and surf your browser over to it. The contents of the test page should be:

```
<?php
phpinfo( );
?>
```

With this file up on your server, you should be able to surf to it in your browser and see something like Figure 1-7. This will give you a complete listing of how the PHP interpreter was compiled, as well as what modules are installed.

Two of the most common problems are lack of a database interface and lack of graphics tools. You should make sure that your ISP account has these installed. If you don't have these libraries installed, file a service ticket with your ISP to add these features (you shouldn't get much resistance; these are standard PHP libraries, useful to all PHP programmers).

If you do not already have an ISP, make sure that any prospective ISPs have what you need installed before signing up. A small survey of hosting sites taken during the writing of this book indicated that most sites support both PHP 4 and PHP 5, but that many of them support PHP 5 as a CGI extension, which is slower than having it installed directly into the Apache Web Server. If PHP 5 is important to you, ensure that the site supports PHP 5 directly as an Apache plug-in, and not via CGI.

Installing MySQL

PHP is just one part of what is called the LAMP architecture. *LAMP* stands for Linux, Apache, PHP (Python, Perl, or Ruby), and MySQL. The LAMP architecture is extremely popular because it's easy to install, easy to learn, very stable, and, best of all, free. Each piece of the LAMP puzzle contributes a major portion to the whole. Linux is the operating system upon which all the pieces run. Apache is the super-stable web server. PHP is the easy-to-use scripting language. And MySQL is where all of the data is stored. Because any reasonably complex web application will have some structured data storage requirements, most Unix ISPs offer Apache, PHP, and MySQL, which means that your code will not only be easy to develop, but also will run almost anywhere.

Installing MySQL is very easy. Binary installers are available for Windows, Mac OS X, and some flavors of Linux; these are the easiest ways to get MySQL running quickly.

Additionally, the source code compiles easily on all the Unix platforms. To build MySQL from source, first download the latest source code *.tgz* file from the official MySQL site (*http://www.mysql.com/*). Unpack that file and follow the instructions in the documentation on building the source and installing it. This will require super-user access, and access to the command line.

Managing the Databases

Once MySQL is installed, you will want to create a database to hold the tables for your web application. To create a new database, use the following command:

```
% mysqladmin --user=root --password=password create dbname
```

You will have to change the username and password to whatever is appropriate for your installation. *dbname* needs to change to whatever name you want for your database.

Most of the hacks in this book create a database for use in the hack. These databases are given different names so that they don't overlap each other. Ideally, each PHP application should be using a different MySQL database.

Removing a database is just as easy:

```
% mysqladmin --user=root --password=password drop foo
Dropping the database is potentially a very bad thing to do.
Any data stored in the database will be destroyed.

Do you really want to drop the 'foo' database [y/N] y
Database "foo" dropped
%
```

In this case, I'm dropping the database named *foo*. By default, MySQL prompts to see whether you really want to drop the table. You can disable the prompt by adding the -f directive:

```
% mysqladmin --user=root --password=password drop -f foo
Database "foo" dropped
```

 This directive is particularly handy when automating database updates.

After creating a database, the next step is to add tables and data to it. The easiest way to do that is simply to redirect the SQL file that has the database schema into the mysql client application. Here is an example:

```
% mysqladmin --user=root --password=password create btest
% mysql --user=root --password=passworddbtest < books.sql
```

The first command creates a database named *btest*, and the second loads it up with the table definitions and data in *books.sql*.

> You can accomplish this schema and data loading in several ways, but I find this process to be the most convenient.

If you don't like to use command lines, you can always manage the database through the phpMyAdmin (*http://www.phpmyadmin.net*) web application. This user-friendly application allows you to add and remove databases, create and alter tables, query data, and even insert and update data through the web interface.

See Also

- "Install PEAR Modules" [Hack #2]

 HACK **Install PEAR Modules**
#2   Access the vast PEAR source code repository to find cool functionality to add to your PHP applications.

The PEAR library is a set of user-contributed PHP modules that are structured in a common way so that they can be downloaded, installed, and versioned consistently. PEAR is so fundamental to PHP that it now comes as a standard part of the PHP installation.

To find out what is available in the PEAR library, surf on over to the PEAR site (*http://pear.php.net/*). There you can find the list of modules or search by module name. When you find a module you want to install, simply run the pear program on your command line.

On Windows, the invocation looks like this:

```
C:\> pear install DB
downloading DB-1.7.6.tgz ...
Starting to download DB-1.7.6.tgz (124,807 bytes)
.........................done: 124,807 bytes
install ok: DB 1.7.6
```

In this case, I am installing the PEAR module named DB [Hack #35], an object-oriented database wrapper that is used extensively in this book.

On Windows, you might need to make sure that the *pear.bat* batch file, located in the *bin* directory of your PHP installation directory, is on the path. In addition, the directory where the PEAR modules are installed is often not created by default. In that case, you need to use Windows Explorer or the command line to create the PEAR directory. If you installed PHP in *c:\php5*, the PEAR directory is *c:\php5\pear*. You might also need to add this directory to the modules path in the *c:\windows\php.ini* file.

On Unix systems, including Mac OS X, running the pear program is just as easy:

```
% sudo pear install HTTP_Client
downloading HTTP_Client-1.0.0.tgz ...
Starting to download HTTP_Client-1.0.0.tgz (6,396 bytes)
.....done: 6,396 bytes
install ok: HTTP_Client 1.0.0
%
```

Here I am installing the HTTP_Client PEAR module [Hack #84]. You'll have to use the sudo command because the PEAR module will be installed system-wide.

To get a list of available PEAR modules, run the list-all command:

```
% pear list-all
All packages:
=============
Package          Latest     Local
APC              3.0.3
Cache            1.5.4      1.5.4
Cache_Lite       1.4.1
apd              1.0.1
memcache         1.4
parsekit         1.0
...
```

 Because this is not making any changes to system-wide files, super-user access is not required.

Some PEAR modules are listed as *unstable*. This means that they are currently in development. Asking PEAR to install them will result in an error message:

```
% sudo pear install Services_Amazon
No release with state equal to: 'stable' found for 'Services_Amazon'
```

Here, the Amazon Web Services module is so new—and possibly unstable—that it's marked as alpha or beta. So you need to force PEAR to install the module using the -f directive:

```
% sudo pear install -f Services_Amazon
Warning: Services_Amazon is state 'beta' which is less stable than state
    'stable'
downloading Services_Amazon-0.2.0.tgz ...
Starting to download Services_Amazon-0.2.0.tgz (8,086 bytes)
.....done: 8,086 bytes
install ok: Services_Amazon 0.2.0
```

Another option is to request a specific version of the module:

```
% sudo pear install Services_Amazon-0.2.0
downloading Services_Amazon-0.2.0.tgz ...
Starting to download Services_Amazon-0.2.0.tgz (8,086 bytes)
.....done: 8,086 bytes
install ok: Services_Amazon 0.2.0
```

This will bypass any stability check and is handy when you want to revert to an earlier version of a module when a later version fails to work.

You can find out which PEAR modules are already installed on your system by using the list command:

```
% pear list
Installed packages:
===================
Package                 Version State
Archive_Tar             1.1     stable
Benchmark               1.2.3   stable
Cache                   1.5.4   stable
Console_Getopt          1.2     stable
DB                      1.7.6   stable
HTML_Template_IT        1.1     stable
HTTP                    1.3.6   stable
HTTP_Client             1.0.0   stable
HTTP_Request            1.2.4   stable
Image_Barcode           1.0.4   stable
Log                     1.8.7   stable
Net_Curl                0.2     stable
Net_SmartIRC            1.0.0   stable
Net_Socket              1.0.6   stable
Net_URL                 1.0.14  stable
Net_UserAgent_Detect    2.0.1   stable
PEAR                    1.3.5   stable
PHPUnit                 1.2.3   stable
PHPUnit2                2.2.1   stable
SOAP                    0.9.1   beta
```

```
Services_Amazon      0.2.0    beta
Services_Google      0.1.1    alpha
Services_Weather     1.3.1    stable
Services_Yahoo       0.1.0    alpha
XML_Parser           1.2.6    stable
XML_RPC              1.2.2    stable
XML_RSS              0.9.2    stable
XML_Serializer       0.16.0   beta
XML_Tree             1.1      stable
XML_Util             1.1.1    stable
```

Don't confuse list with list-all; the first lists installed modules, and the second lists available modules.

Becoming fluent with PEAR is critical to making the best use of PHP. The libraries built into PHP are fine, but the additional PEAR modules make PHP a true rapid application development environment.

Installing PEAR Modules on Your ISP

Because you don't have super-user access on an ISP machine, you will need to be a little cleverer about how you install PEAR modules. The first step is to establish a library directory where the PEAR modules will go. You do this by creating the directory on your ISP machine. Then you use the ini_set command to add the directory onto the include path, as shown in the following code fragment:

```php
<?php
  ini_set( 'include_path',
  ini_get( 'include_path' ).PATH_SEPARATOR."/users/jherr/mylibs" );
?>
```

This code should go into your PHP page or into a common PHP header that is included on every page.

This adds the directory */users/jherr/mylibs* to the list of paths that the include and require directives will search. You must do this before attempting to require or include any installed PEAR modules.

After creating the library directory and tweaking the include path, you can download the PEAR module you want to install from the PEAR site (*http://pear.php.net/*). Unpack it and place the source files in the library directory you just specified (*/users/jherr/mylibs* in this example).

CHAPTER TWO

Web Design

Hacks 3–10

This chapter provides user interface hacks that you can perform with HTML using PHP. The hacks cover building tabs and boxes to clean up your web interface, building interface elements like breadcrumb trails, and building lightweight HTML graphs. The chapter even includes a hack that shows you how to send HTML email to your customers.

HACK #3 Create a Skinnable Interface

Use CSS to allow your user to select how your web application should look.

Have you ever run across a user who just *has* to have every blog he reads appear in his own personal color scheme? Are *you* that kind of user? Thankfully, supporting these users is far easier with CSS support in modern browsers.

CSS defines the fonts, colors, sizes, and even positions of elements of a page independent of the HTML code for that page. You can change the look of a single HTML page drastically simply by redefining its CSS stylesheet. This hack shows how to provide user-selectable CSS and offers some advice on creating customizable interfaces.

The Code

Start out by saving the code in Example 2-1 as *index.php*.

Example 2-1. Simple index page that sets the stage for customizable CSS

```
<html>
<head>
<?php
$style = "default";
```

Example 2-1. Simple index page that sets the stage for customizable CSS (continued)

```php
if ( $_GET["style"] )
        $style = $_GET["style"];

$files = array( );
$dh = opendir( "styles" );
while( $file = @readdir( $dh ) )
{
        if( preg_match( "/[.]css$/", $file ) )
        {
                $file = preg_replace( "/[.]css$/", "", $file );
                $files []= $file;
        }
}
?>
<style type="text/css" media="all">@import url(styles/<?php echo($style); ?>.
css);</style>
</head>
<body>
<table width="800">
<tr>
<td width="200" class="menu" valign="top">
<div class="menu-active"><a href="home.php">Home</a></div>
<div class="menu-inactive"><a href="faq.php">FAQ</a></div>
<div class="menu-inactive"><a href="contact.php">Contact</a></div>
</td>
<td width="600" valign="top">

        <table class="box">
        <tr>
        <td class="box-title">
                Important information
        </td>
        </tr>
        <tr>
        <td class="box-content">
                Lots of information about important events and
                stuff.
        </td>
        </tr>
        </table>

</td>
</tr>
</table>
<form>
Style: <select name="style">
<?php foreach( $files as $file ) { ?>
<option value="<?php echo($file); ?>"
<?php echo( $file == $style ? "selected" : "" ); ?>
><?php echo($file); ?></option>
<?php } ?>
```

Example 2-1. Simple index page that sets the stage for customizable CSS (continued)

```
</select>
<input type="submit" value="Select" />
</form>
</body>
</html>
```

Next, save Example 2-2 (a CSS stylesheet) as *styles/default.css*.

Example 2-2. A CSS stylesheet that uses a simple red-and-white scheme

```
body { font-family: arial, verdana; font-size: small; margin: 0px; }
.box { background: red; }
.box-title { text-align: center; color: white; font-weight: bold; }
.box-content { background: white; font-size: xx-small; padding:10px;}
.menu { margin: 5px; }
.menu-active { margin: 2px; padding:5px; background: black; }
.menu-active a { text-decoration: none; color: white; font-weight: bold; }
.menu-inactive { margin: 2px; padding:5px; background: #ccc; }
.menu-inactive a { text-decoration: none; }
```

To provide another option for the user, save the CSS in Example 2-3 as *styles/black_and_white.css*.

Example 2-3. A CSS stylesheet for the same HTML, but with a black-and-white scheme

```
body { font-family: arial, verdana; font-size: small; margin: 0px; }
.box { background: #eee; border: 1px solid black; }
.box-title { background: white; text-align: center; font-weight: bold; }
.box-content { background: white; font-size: xx-small; padding:10px;}
.menu { margin: 5px; }
.menu-active { margin: 2px; padding:5px; background: black; }
.menu-active a { text-decoration: none; color: white; font-weight: bold; }
.menu-inactive { margin: 2px; padding:5px; background: #ccc; }
.menu-inactive a { text-decoration: none; }
```

Running the Hack

Upload the files to your PHP server and navigate to the *index.php* page. The code in the page will automatically pick the default skin if one has not been selected. This skin—the red-and-white scheme with a different border and heading color on the information table—is shown in Figure 2-1.

Now select the black-and-white skin from the select box and click the Select button. The page should reload with a slightly altered scheme, as shown in Figure 2-2.

This simple starting point won't satisfy every user's taste for color (or for a *lack* of color). However, by adding additional stylesheets, or even letting

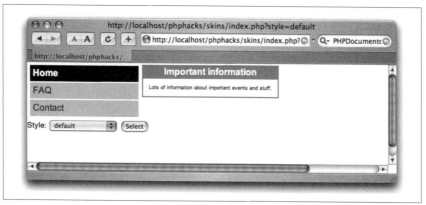

Figure 2-1. The default skin

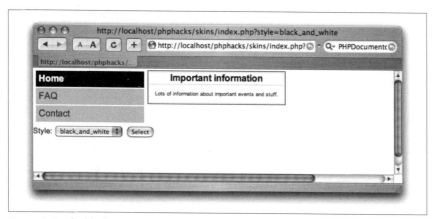

Figure 2-2. The black-and-white skin

users upload their own CSS stylesheets, you can create a completely custom environment for each individual user.

The real magic here is not in the page code, though. The page code just manages the selection of the CSS file and then sets the appropriate @import directive in the style tag. The magic happens when CSS alters the display to change the colors, fonts, and even layout of the page.

Here are some tips for putting together a web design that works well for skinning:

Use CSS layout

CSS allows you to specify the location of div layout items on the page using absolute positioning, relative positioning, or floating elements.

Control your fonts with CSS
Only use CSS to control the fonts, sizes, and text styles on the page. That means avoiding the <font> tag and going with tags like <p>, <div>, and <span> instead, using class attributes that define which CSS class should be applied.

Document your CSS
Have a well-documented default skin that people can use as a template for their own skins. CSS supports comments, and you should use those comments to define which classes are applied to which elements on the page.

ID your layout elements
Use id attributes on <div> tags to break up your layout into sections. Skin authors can then use these to focus their modifications on certain portions of the screen. For example, you might decide that anchor tags in the navigation section should have ID tags, as opposed to all the anchor tags on the page.

Learn from others
Blog software—in particular, Six Apart's Movable Type (*http://sixapart. com/movabletype*)—has been designed for skinning from the start. Install it and have a look at how the folks at Six Apart design their page templates and CSS to make it easy for nontechnical types to alter the look of their blog.

If you are serious about skinning, you should also host a skin exchange on your site, as either a bulletin board or a file exchange. That will encourage people to contribute designs and experiment with the skinning feature. A starting point for this feature is a media upload/download center **[Hack #97]**.

See Also

- "Create a Media Upload/Download Center" **[Hack #97]**
- "Give Your Customers Formatting Control with XSL" **[Hack #7]**

HACK Build a Breadcrumb Trail
#4   Use a breadcrumb trail to tell your users where they are on your site.

A *breadcrumb trail* is a list of links at the top of a page that indicates where a person is in the site's organizational hierarchy.

A breadcrumb trail is not, as the term might suggest, the set of pages that a person navigated through to get to his destination. The user already has the Back button for retracing his steps.

A breadcrumb trail allows a user to navigate back up the hierarchy a little to where he would find more relevant information. For example, the trail might be: *Home | Platforms | Portables | PSP*. The user could easily navigate back to the Portables page, which lists all of the portable game consoles, the Platforms page, which lists the different gaming platforms, or the home page, all with a single click.

Figure 2-3 shows the breadcrumb trail that Yahoo! uses in its directory to show where you are. In this case, I'm in the Buddy section of the Comedy category, within the Titles area of Movies and Films. As a user, I can go back to any level of organization that suits my interests.

Figure 2-3. The Yahoo! directory breadcrumb trail

By convention, the last item on the list is the current page and is not given a link. The first item on the list is the home page of the site.

The Code

To add breadcrumbs to your own site, save the code shown in Example 2-4 as *showpage.php*.

Example 2-4. Creating a breadcrumb trail

```php
<?php
$id = $_GET['id'];
if ( strlen( $id ) < 1 )
  $id = "home";

$pages = array(
  home => array( id=>"home", parent=>"", title=>"Home",
         url=>"showpage.php?id=home" ),
  users => array( id=>"users", parent=>"home", title=>"Users",
          url=>"showpage.php?id=users" ),
  jack => array( id=>"jack", parent=>"users", title=>"Jack",
         url=>"showpage.php?id=jack" )
);

function breadcrumbs( $id, $pages )
{
  $bcl = array( );
  $pageid = $id;
  while( strlen( $pageid ) > 0 )
  {
    $bcl[] = $pageid;
    $pageid = $pages[ $pageid ]['parent'];
  }
  for( $i = count( $bcl ) - 1; $i >= 0; $i-- )
  {
    $page = $pages[$bcl[$i]];
    if ( $i > 0 )
    {
      echo( "<a href=\"" );
      echo( $page['url'] );
      echo( "\">" );
    }
    echo( $page['title'] );
    if ( $i > 0 )
    {
      echo( "</a> | " );
    }
  }
}
?>
<html>
<head>
<title>Page - <?php echo( $id ); ?></title>
</head>
<body>
```

Example 2-4. Creating a breadcrumb trail (continued)

```
Breadcrumbs: <?php breadcrumbs( $id, $pages ); ?><br/>
Page name: <?php echo( $id ); ?>
</body>
</html>
```

The code is fairly straightforward. It starts by defining the list of pages. The list of pages is constructed as a hash table, with the key as the ID of the page. Then the breadcrumbs function takes the ID of the current page and the overall list of pages and constructs the breadcrumb trail by searching back through the list from the current page. The HTML code then prints both the current page and the output of the breadcrumbs function for the current page.

Running the Hack

Upload this code to your server and navigate to *showpage.php*. By default, this will give you the home page (see Figure 2-4).

Figure 2-4. The home page

This isn't very impressive, because on the home page the breadcrumb trail is blank and lists just the home page without any links. Request a different page by adding *?id=jack* to the URL, though; the result should look something like Figure 2-5.

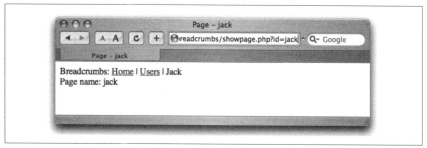

Figure 2-5. The jack page with a breadcrumb trail

As you can see in Figure 2-5, now there's a breadcrumb trail, with the home page and the Users page as links, along with the static text (Jack) for the current page.

Hacking the Hack

It would be a little easier to maintain the page list if it were represented as XML. Here is an example of what that XML would look like:

```
<pages>
    <page id="home" parent="" title="Home" url="showpage.php?id=home" />
    <page id="users" parent="home" title="Users" url="showpage.php?id=users"
/>
    <page id="jack" parent="users" title="Jack" url="showpage.php?id=jack" />
</pages>
```

To parse this, you could use the XML parser functions built into PHP, or you could use some regular expressions [Hack #38].

See Also

- "Create Dynamic Navigation Menus" [Hack #17]
- "Create Pop-Up Hints" [Hack #12]

HACK #5   Create HTML Boxes

Use HTML and simple graphics to create attractive boxes for your web pages.

Sometimes it's useful to put your page content into boxes to make it easier for users to navigate your site. You can draw attention to a particular piece of content, create newspaper-like interfaces, or just go with a little cubism to impress your artsy friends. The scripts in this hack make it easy to draw boxes around any content you like.

The Code

Save the code in Example 2-5 as *box1test.php*.

Example 2-5. A test page for boxing up content

```
<html>
<head>
<? include( "box1.php" );
add_box_styles( );
?>
</head>
<body>
<div style="width:200px;">
<? start_box( "News" ); ?>
```

Example 2-5. A test page for boxing up content (continued)

```
Today's news is that there is no news. Which is probably a good thing since
the news can be fairly distressing at times.<br/><br/>
<a href="morenews.html">more...</a>
<? end_box(); ?>
</div>
</body>
</html>
```

For the PHP portion of the mini-application, save the code in *Example 2-6* as *box1.php*.

Example 2-6. Adding a little PHP and CSS

```
<?
function add_box_styles() { ?>
<style type="text/css">
.box {
    font-family: arial, verdana, sans-serif;
    font-size: x-small;
    background: #ccc;
}
.box-title {
    font-size: small;
    font-weight: bold;
    color: white;
    background: #777;
    padding: 5px;
    text-align: center;
}
.box-content {
    background: white;
    padding: 5px;
}
</style>
<? }

function start_box( $name ) { ?>
<table class="box" cellspacing="2" cellpadding="0">
<tr><td class="box-title"><? print( $name ) ?></td></tr>
<tr><td class="box-content">
<? }

function end_box() { ?>
</td></tr></table>
<? } ?>
```

More important than this particular set of CSS tags is the fact that you can easily customize the box to your liking, highlighting any portion of the box's content that you want. You can even combine this with user-selectable CSS [Hack #3], and let the user decide on his own box styles!

Running the Hack

Navigate your browser to the *box1test.php* script. You will see something like Figure 2-6.

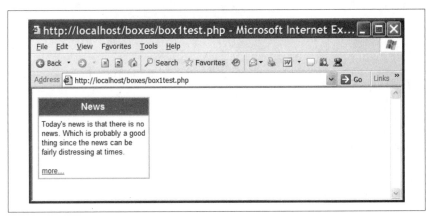

Figure 2-6. The resulting HTML box

The news blurb is boxed up in a black-and-white box because that code is bracketed with the start_box and end_box calls. The title of the box is a parameter to the start_box function.

> If you want several different colors of boxes, you can create different CSS classes for the colors. Or you can put style attributes on the table and td tags to override the color on a per-box basis.

Hacking the Hack

If you want something a little more attractive, you can create rounded boxes using a set of *gif* or *png* files. Start by saving the code in Example 2-7 as *box2test.php*.

Example 2-7. Sample HTML file providing a test bed for rounded rectangles

```
<html>
<head>
<? include( "box2.php" );
add_box_styles();
?>
</head>
<body>
<div style="width:200px;">
<? start_box( "News" ); ?>
```

Example 2-7. Sample HTML file providing a test bed for rounded rectangles (continued)

```
Today's news is that there is no news. Which is probably a good thing since
the news can be fairly distressing at times.<br/><br/>
<a href="morenews.html">more...</a>
<? end_box( ); ?>
</div>
</body>
</html>
```

Then save the code in Example 2-8 as *box2.php*.

Example 2-8. Using images in addition to CSS to create fancier boxes

```
<?
function add_box_styles( ) { ?>
<style type="text/css">
.box {
   font-family: arial, verdana, sans-serif;
}
.box-title {
   font-size: small;
   font-weight: bold;
   color: white;
   background: #000063;
   text-align: center;
}
.box-content-container {
   background: #000063;
}
.box-content {
   background: white;
   font-size: x-small;
   padding: 5px;
}
</style>
<? }

function start_box( $name ) { ?>
<table cellspacing="0" cellpadding="0" class="box">
<tr><td>

<table cellspacing="0" cellpadding="0" width="100%" class="box-title">
<tr><td width="20" height="20"><img src="blue_ul.png" /></td>
<td><? print( $name ) ?></td>
<td width="20" height="20"><img src="blue_ur.png"></td></tr></table>

</td></tr>
<tr><td>

<table width="100%" cellspacing="2" cellpadding="0"
   class="box-content-container">
```

Example 2-8. Using images in addition to CSS to create fancier boxes (continued)

```
<tr><td class="box-content">
<? }

function end_box( ) { ?>
</td></tr></table>
<tr><td>

<table cellspacing="0" cellpadding="0" width="100%" class="box-title">
<tr><td width="20" height="20"><img src="blue_ll.png" /></td>
<td> </td>
<td width="20" height="20"><img src="blue_lr.png"></td></tr></table>

</td></tr></table>
<? } ?>
```

With this new version of code on the server, navigate to the *box2test.php* script, and you should see something like Figure 2-7.

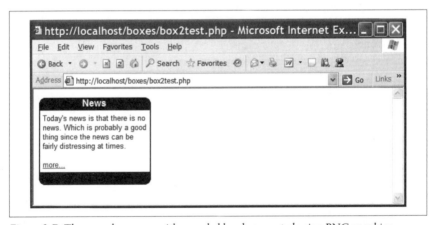

Figure 2-7. The same box, now with rounded borders created using PNG graphics

Now the *png* files sit in the corners of the box. The box is created using start_box and end_box, just as it was before. But the HTML code that creates the box is more complex; a set of three tables is nested within a main table. The first table creates the titlebar, the second holds the content, and the third is the border along the bottom.

The background colors of the borders should match the colors of the graphics exactly. If you want different colors, you will need a different CSS and another set of graphics files.

The graphic files are available on the O'Reilly book site (*http://www.oreilly.com/catalog/phphks*) along with the code. The graphics were created with Macromedia Fireworks. Adobe Photoshop would work as well, of course.

See Also

- "Add Tabs to Your Web Interface" [Hack #6]

HACK #6 Add Tabs to Your Web Interface

Use HTML and CSS to create a tabbed interface for your web application.

Sometimes there is just too much data to put onto one web page. An easy way to break up a site (or even a content-heavy page) is to display it using tabs, where the data is broken up into subelements, each correlating to a named tab. Lucky for us, tabs are a piece of cake with PHP.

The Code

Save the code in Example 2-9 as *index.php*.

Example 2-9. Using the tabs library to show a tabbed interface

```
<?php
require_once("tabs.php");
?>
<html>
<head>
<?php tabs_header( ); ?>
</head>
<body>
<div style="width:600px;">
<?php tabs_start( ); ?>
<?php tab( "Tab one" ); ?>
This is the first tab.
<?php tab( "Tab two" ); ?>
This is the second tab.
<?php tabs_end( ); ?>
</div>
</body>
</html>
```

Next, code up a nice PHP and CSS library. Save the code in Example 2-10 as *tabs.php*.

Example 2-10. Using PHP and some CSS to create user-friendly tabs

```php
<?php
$tabs = array( );

function tabs_header( )
{
?>
<style type="text/css">
.tab {
    border-bottom: 1px solid black;
    text-align: center;
    font-family: arial, verdana;
}
.tab-active {
    border-left: 1px solid black;
    border-top: 1px solid black;
    border-right: 1px solid black;
    text-align: center;
    font-family: arial, verdana;
    font-weight: bold;
}
.tab-content {
    padding: 5px;
    border-left: 1px solid black;
    border-right: 1px solid black;
    border-bottom: 1px solid black;
}
</style>
<?php
}

function tabs_start( )
{
  ob_start( );
}

function endtab( )
{
  global $tabs;

  $text = ob_get_clean( );
  $tabs[ count( $tabs ) - 1 ][ 'text' ] = $text;

  ob_start( );
}

function tab( $title )
{
  global $tabs;

  if ( count( $tabs ) > 0 )
    endtab( );
```

Example 2-10. Using PHP and some CSS to create user-friendly tabs (continued)

```php
$tabs []= array(
  title => $title,
  text => ""
  );
}

function tabs_end( )
{
  global $tabs;

  endtab( );
  ob_end_clean( );

  $index = 0;
  if ( $_GET['tabindex'] )
    $index = $_GET['tabindex'];

?>
<table width="100%" cellspacing="0" cellpadding="0">
<tr>
<?php
  $baseuri = $_SERVER['REQUEST_URI'];
  $baseuri = preg_replace( "/\?.*$/", "", $baseuri );

  $curindex = 0;
  foreach( $tabs as $tab )
  {
    $class = "tab";
    if ( $index == $curindex )
      $class ="tab-active";
?>
<td class="<?php echo($class); ?>">
<a href="<?php echo( $baseuri."?tabindex=".$curindex ); ?>">
<?php echo( $tab['title'] ); ?>
</a>
</td>
<?php
    $curindex += 1;
  }
?>
</tr>
<tr><td class="tab-content" colspan="<?php echo( count( $tabs ) + 1 ); ?>">
<?php echo( $tabs[$index ]['text'] ); ?>
</td></tr>
</table>
<?php
}
?>
```

I designed the API on this tabs system to make it easy to create tabs in your document. It starts with invoking `tabs_header` in the header section of the document. This will set up the CSS for the tabs. Then, within the body, the call to `tabs_start` sets up the tab system. Each new tab starts with a call to `tab` with the name of the tab. The call to `tabs_end` then ends the construction of the tabs.

Internally, the tabs system uses output buffering to hold onto the contents of each tab, and to display whichever tab is selected "on top."

Running the Hack

Upload the files to your PHP server and point your browser at *index.php*. You should see something close to Figure 2-8.

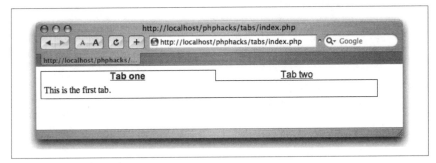

Figure 2-8. The first tab

Click on the second tab (labeled "Tab two"), and you will see the second tab selected and the contents of the second tab (as shown in Figure 2-9).

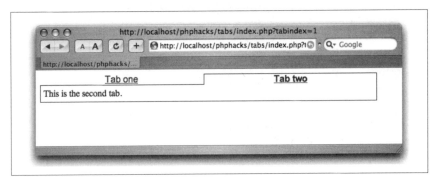

Figure 2-9. The second tab

Each time the user switches tabs, the page is reloaded. Using CSS and Dynamic HTML (DHTML) to create div tags with the content of each tab, and by manually controlling the visibility of the tabs, you can allow users to change tabs without a page refresh.

See Also

- "Build a Breadcrumb Trail" [Hack #4]
- "Create Dynamic Navigation Menus" [Hack #17]

Give Your Customers Formatting Control with XSL

Use PHP's XSL support to enable your customers to design their own pages.

Amazon provides an interesting service to its corporate customers. The customer can skin an Amazon page by providing an XSL stylesheet that formats the XML data about the products, prices, and related data. This means that if you're a corporate customer, you can add your own links and graphics, and even customize the look and feel of Amazon.com to give purchasing pages an integrated look.

This hack does the same with PHP's XSL engine (and no corporate membership is required!). Figure 2-10 shows the flow of XSL processing in this hack (and with XSL in general). The processor takes two inputs. In this case, the *input.xml* file contains the data for the page, and the *format.xsl* file contains the formatting for the page, along with specifications for where the data is to be placed. The XSL processor then takes these two inputs and emits XML, HTML, or text.

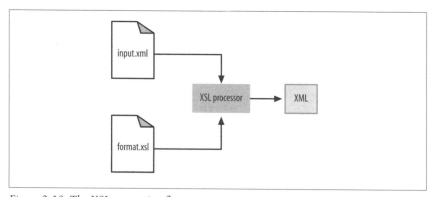

Figure 2-10. The XSL processing flow

The Code

Save the code in Example 2-11 as *conv.php*.

Example 2-11. Generating output from XML and XSL

```php
<?php
$xml = new DOMDocument( );
$xml->Load( "input.xml" );

$xsl = new DOMDocument( );
$xsl->Load( "format.xsl" );

$xslproc = new XSLTProcessor( );
$xslproc->importStylesheet( $xsl );
print( $xslproc->transformToXML( $xml ) );
?>
```

As a sample XML file, save Example 2-12 as *input.xml*.

Example 2-12. A sample XML file

```xml
<books>
        <book name="Code Generation in Action" />
        <book name="MDA Explained" />
        <book name="PHP in a Nutshell" />
</books>
```

Save Example 2-13 and name it *format.xsl*.

Example 2-13. Some sample XSL to handle formatting

```xml
<?xml version="1.0" encoding="UTF-8"?>
<xsl:stylesheet xmlns:xsl="http://www.w3.org/1999/XSL/Transform" version="1.0">
  <xsl:output method="html" />
  <xsl:template match="/">
    <html>
      <body>
        <xsl:for-each select="/books/book">
          <xsl:value-of select="@name" /><br/>
        </xsl:for-each>
      </body>
    </html>
  </xsl:template>
</xsl:stylesheet>
```

Running the Hack

This hack runs using the command-line PHP interpreter. Execute *conv.php* using this command line:

```
% php conv.php
```

You should get the result shown in Figure 2-11.

Figure 2-11. Running the XSL interpreter on the command line

This shows the data provided in the *books.xml* file, formatted into HTML. You could just as easily pipe this output to an HTML file, or set up the script to emit HTML when XML is requested. Whatever your approach, it's easy to take XML and XSL and get HTML (or any other structured markup, such as WML) as a response.

You can provide your own data dynamically from an SQL data source by creating a DOMDocument XML object on the fly that holds the data, allowing even more flexibility. You also might want to allow the XML and XSL to be supplied on the command line—instead of hardcoding them into the PHP—making *conv.php* a useful utility for dynamic web sites.

You can use this code in your own web pages and allow customers to upload XSL stylesheets. "Create a Media Upload/Download Center" [Hack #97] has code for allowing uploads of files and storing them in a local directory. XSLT is a very powerful, if a little cryptic, XML manipulation language. If you get into it, I strongly recommend Michael Kay's excellent book, *XSLT 2.0 Programmer's Reference* (Wiley).

See Also

- "Create a Skinnable Interface" [Hack #3]

HACK #8 Build Lightweight HTML Graphs

Use HTML to create simple graphs for your data.

It seems as though every site you go to these days requires QuickTime or Flash so that you can see fancy images and graphs. For simple bar graphs, though, you don't need fancy image rendering or Flash movies. You can use this hack to create bar graphs with just a few HTML tables and some PHP. The result looks just as cool as those other Flash-heavy sites but doesn't require any extra plug-ins or downloads.

The Code

Save the code in Example 2-14 as *htmlgraph.php*.

Example 2-14. Drawing some simple bar graphs

```
<html>
<?
$data = array(
        array( "movies", 20 ),
        array( "food", 30 ),
        array( "workout", 10 ),
        array( "work", 40 )
);
$max = 0;
foreach ( $data as $d ) { $max += $d[1]; }
?>
<body>
<table width="400" cellspacing="0" cellpadding="2">
<? foreach( $data as $d ) {
$percent = ( $d[1] / $max ) * 100;
?>
<tr>
<td width="20%"><? echo( $d[0] ) ?></td>
<td width="10%"><? echo( $d[1] ) ?>%</td>
<td>
<table width="<? echo($percent) ?>%" bgcolor="#aaa">
        <tr><td> </td></tr>
</table>
</td>
</tr>
<? } ?>
</table>
</body>
</html>
```

You can use several techniques to create HTML graphs. I chose to use two tables; the first contains the textual data, and the second contains a set of nested tables, each with a width value based on the graph value in that row.

I calculate the width by first finding the maximum value of the combined data, and storing that in $max. I then derive the percentage by dividing $max by the current value, and multiplying the result by 100 (to set the scale between 0 and 100). That number is stored in $percent, which is then used in the width attribute of the table.

Running the Hack

Use your browser to surf to the *htmlgraph.php* page. You should see something similar to Figure 2-12.

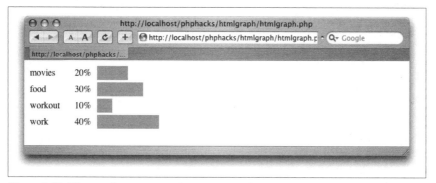

Figure 2-12. The simple HTML graph as seen in Safari

> I know that Figure 2-12 is not going to win any design awards, but it gets the point across! Besides, by now, it shouldn't take much work to add some killer CSS and turn this bland graph into something special.

Hacking the Hack

I admit that gray is not the prettiest color for a graph, so Example 2-15 is a slightly altered version of the script, which adds a little color to the data.

Example 2-15. Adding a splash of color

```
<html>
<?
$data = array(
        array( "movies", 20, "red" ),
        array( "food", 30, "green" ),
        array( "workout", 10, "blue" ),
        array( "work", 40, "black" )
);
$max = 0;
foreach ( $data as $d ) { $max += $d[1]; }
?>
<body>
<table width="400" cellspacing="0" cellpadding="2">
<? foreach( $data as $d ) {
$percent = ( $d[1] / $max ) * 100;
?>
<tr>
```

Example 2-15. Adding a splash of color (continued)

```
<td width="20%"><? echo( $d[0] ) ?></td>
<td width="10%"><? echo( $d[1] ) ?>%</td>
<td>
<table width="<? echo($percent) ?>%" bgcolor="<? echo($d[2]) ?>">
      <tr><td> </td></tr>
</table>
</td>
</tr>
<? } ?>
</table>
</body>
</html>
```

The new third value is used to set the background color of the bar graph table. This gives the output a rainbow look that is a little nicer on the eyes than the gray version.

See Also

- "Build Dynamic HTML Graphs" [Hack #14]
- "Add Vector Graphics with PHP" [Hack #22]
- "Create Beautiful Graphics with SVG" [Hack #28]

 HACK
#9 Properly Size Image Tags

Use PHP image support to set the height and width attributes of your images properly.

All of the modern browsers start showing web pages as quickly as possible so that web surfers feel they are getting fast(er) response times. This means browsers will start showing a page well before any images or other accompanying resources are downloaded. Because the browser hasn't downloaded the image before rendering the page, it doesn't know how big the image should be, unless you specify height and width attributes on the img tag.

If you don't specify the width and height of images, though, the page will jerk around as it's being downloaded. The browser will guess at the size of the image (usually picking 10 pixels by 10 pixels), but then find out after the image is downloaded that the actual size is much larger. Thus, the browser will need to lay out the page again to adjust for the new size.

This hack builds img tags with the proper width and height attributes by using the getimagesize function to retrieve the actual width and height of the image.

The Code

Save the code in Example 2-16 as *imagesize.php*.

Example 2-16. A little image magic

```
<html>
<?php
function placegraphic( $file )
{
  list( $width, $height ) = getimagesize("rss.png");
  echo( "<img src=\"$file\" width=\"$width\" height=\"$height\" />" );
}
?>
<body>
<?php placegraphic( "rss.png" ); ?>
</body>
</html>
```

Running the Hack

Create an image file named *rss.png* in the same directory as this PHP file, and then browse to the *imagesize.php* page. You should see the image displayed properly, without any stretching. Use the View Source command in the browser to view the HTML source code to make sure that the width and height attributes were set properly.

You can use the placegraphic function anywhere you would have put an img tag previously. But I don't recommend using this function in static headers or footers where the size of the images will never change. A performance overhead is associated with figuring out the size of an image. So you should use this function only when you don't know the size of the image until the graphic is requested.

In addition, if you are using a database to store a library of images, I recommend storing the width and height of the image along with the pathname. It is much faster to retrieve the width and height along with the pathname from the database than it is to use the getimagesize function on the fly each time you display the image.

Hacking the Hack

In addition to setting the width and height fields of the tag, you should also set the alt attribute. The alt attribute describes the image in text so that people who are browsing without image downloads enabled, or people with disabilities, can use page readers to navigate your site.

To support the alt attribute, just add another argument to the placegraphic function, and then output the value of the argument in the echo statement.

See Also

- "Split One Image into Multiple Images" [Hack #30]
- "Simplify Your Graphics with Objects" [Hack #29]
- "Create Thumbnail Images" [Hack #27]

Send HTML Email

Use multipart email messages to send email content in both plain text and HTML format.

Email is another interface to your web application. Ideally, you want that interface (and any other, be it a phone or a handheld device) to be as full-featured as the one you provide through a web server. While this isn't always possible, it's a good goal to keep in mind, and it will help push you to create better user interfaces.

This hack describes how to send email using a multipart construction, where one part contains a plain-text version of the email and the other part is HTML. If your customers have HTML email turned off, they will still get a nice email, even if they don't get all of the HTML markup.

Figure 2-13 shows some different forms of mail messages. On the lefthand side is the simplest form of mail, the text message. At the top of the email is the header, which defines the subject, whom the mail is from, whom the mail is going to, and so on. These are followed by a carriage return, and finally, the message text.

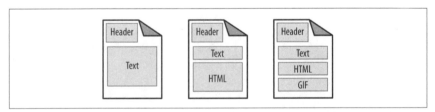

Figure 2-13. Different mail forms

The emails in the middle and on the right in Figure 2-13 are multipart messages. The header remains much the same as with the text message, with the exception that some information about the multiple parts is included. The text is then placed within a part, and the HTML is placed in another part.

This way, mailers can decide which part of the message they want to display. Email with HTML that contains graphics can include the referenced graphics as additional parts of the message, as shown in the righthand image.

The Code

Save the code in Example 2-17 as *htmlemail.php*.

Example 2-17. Sending multipart emails in HTML and text formats

```php
<?php
$to = "to@email.com";
$to_full = "Sally Cool";
$from = "from@email.com";
$from_full = "Joe Schmoe";
$subject = "HTML Mail Test";

$random_hash = "zzz582x";

ob_start( );
?>
To: <?php echo($to_full); ?> <<?php echo($to); ?>>
From: <?php echo($from_full); ?> <<?php echo($from); ?>>
MIME-Version: 1.0
Content-Type: multipart/alternative;
                        boundary="==Multipart_Boundary_<?php echo($random_hash);
?>"
<?php
$headers = ob_get_clean( );
ob_start( );
?>

This is a multi-part message in MIME format.

--==Multipart_Boundary_<?php echo( $random_hash ); ?>
Content-Type: text/plain; charset="iso-8859-1"
Content-Transfer-Encoding: 7bit

This is the text of the message in a simple text format.

--==Multipart_Boundary_<?php echo( $random_hash ); ?>
Content-Type: text/html; charset="iso-8859-1"
Content-Transfer-Encoding: 7bit

<html>
<body>
<p>Here is something with <b>HTML</b> formatting. That can include all of the
usual:</p>
<ul>
```

Example 2-17. Sending multipart emails in HTML and text formats (continued)

```
<li>Bulleted lists</li>
<li>Tables</li>
<li>Images (if you include them as attachments or external links)</li>
<li>Character formatting</li>
<li>...and more!</li>
</ul>
</body>
</html>


---==Multipart_Boundary_<?php echo( $random_hash ); ?>--


<?php
$message = ob_get_clean( );

$ok = @mail( $to, $subject, $message, $headers );

echo( $ok ? "Mail sent\n" : "Mail failed\n" );
?>
```

Running the Hack

Change the email addresses and names in the script. Then use the command-line PHP interpreter to run the script:

```
% php htmlmail.php
Mail sent
%
```

On my OS X machine, the email comes up rapidly in the Mail application, as shown in Figure 2-14.

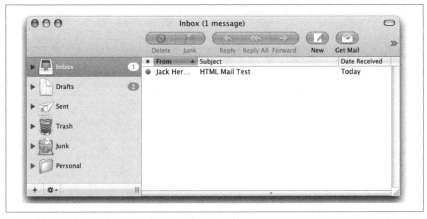

Figure 2-14. The Mail.app application showing the message

Double-clicking on the message shows the content of the message. You can see the HTML formatting with the bulleted list in Figure 2-15.

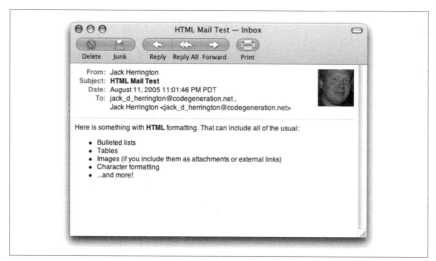

Figure 2-15. The formatted HTML message

All of the standard markup works as long as it's supported by the browser embedded in the mail application.

The only hitch comes from images or other file-based resources. You have two alternatives with images. The first is to reference an image on a remote web server. There are a couple of problems with that approach, though. First, it doesn't work for offline mail reading. Second, many mailers have remote image grabbing turned off because spammers use this mechanism to see whether you have opened their mail, confirming that they've reached a valid address (expect lots more spam to follow).

The second approach is to embed the image as an attachment in another part of the multipart message. This will work, but the email messages themselves will be larger because of the base-64-encoded images.

I've found it's best to just stick with standard text formatting and what can be done with CSS when mailing with HTML. Obviously it's not possible to do that if the image is critical to the content of the email. As you have seen in this chapter, though, you can do a lot with just HTML alone [Hack #8].

See Also

- "Create a Message Queue" [Hack #50]

DHTML

Hacks 11–26

This chapter covers using Dynamic HTML (DHTML) in your web applications. *DHTML* is a term used to define the powerful combination of HTML, CSS, and JavaScript. The hacks in this chapter use DHTML to create all types of interactive interfaces for your web applications, from spreadsheets to dynamic graphs, pop ups, slideshows, vector graphics, and more.

HACK #11 Put an Interactive Spreadsheet on Your Page

Use the ActiveWidgets spreadsheet library to put an interactive JavaScript data control on your page.

Let's face it: some data—particularly financial and statistical data—just looks better when it's presented as a spreadsheet. Unfortunately, HTML does a poor job of giving you an interactive spreadsheet-style feel, especially when it comes to scrolling around, sorting, or any of the truly interactive user experience elements of a spreadsheet.

This hack uses the ActiveWidgets (*http://activewidgets.com/*) grid control to create a spreadsheet-style interface on a web page.

The Code

Save the code in Example 3-1 as *index.php*.

Example 3-1. A script that provides state-specific data in a spreadsheet format

```
<?php $states = array(
    array( "Alabama",4447100,1963711,52419.02,1675.01,50744,87.6,38.7 ),
    array( "Alaska",626932,260978,663267.26,91316,571951.26,1.1,0.5 ),
    array( "Arizona",5130632,2189189,113998.3,363.73,113634.57,45.2,19.3 ),
    array( "Arkansas",2673400,1173043,53178.62,1110.45,52068.17,51.3,22.5 ),
    array( "California",33871648,12214549,163695.57,7736.23,155959.34,217.2,78.3 ),
```

Example 3-1. A script that provides state-specific data in a spreadsheet format (continued)

```
    array( "Colorado",4301261,1808037,104093.57,376.04,103717.53,41.5,17.4 ),
    array( "South Dakota",754844,323208,77116.49,1231.85,75884.64,9.9,4.3 ),
    ...
    array( "Tennessee",5689283,2439443,42143.27,926.15,41217.12,138,59.2 ),
    array( "Texas",20851820,8157575,268580.82,6783.7,261797.12,79.6,31.2 ),
    array( "Utah",2233169,768594,84898.83,2755.18,82143.65,27.2,9.4 ),
    array( "Vermont",608827,294382,9614.26,364.7,9249.56,65.8,31.8 ),
    array( "Virginia",7078515,2904192,42774.2,3180.13,39594.07,178.8,73.3 ),
    array( "Washington",5894121,2451075,71299.64,4755.58,66544.06,88.6,36.8 ),
    array( "West Virginia",1808344,844623,24229.76,152.03,24077.73,75.1,35.1 ),
    array( "Wisconsin",5363675,2321144,65497.82,11187.72,54310.1,98.8,42.7 ),
    array( "Wyoming",493782,223854,97813.56,713.16,97100.4,5.1,2.3 ),
    array( "Puerto Rico",3808610,1418476,5324.5,1899.94,3424.56,1112.1,414.2 )
);
?>
<html>
<head>
<link href="runtime/styles/xp/grid.css" rel="stylesheet" type="text/css" ></link>
<script src="runtime/lib/grid.js"></script>
</head>
<body>
<div style="width:500px;height:300px;">
<script>
var data = [
<?php $first = true; foreach( $states as $state ) { if ( !$first ) echo( "," );
?>
[ "<?php echo($state[0]); ?>", <?php echo($state[1]); ?>,
  <?php echo($state[2]); ?>, <?php echo($state[3]); ?>,
  <?php echo($state[4]); ?>, <?php echo($state[5]); ?>,
  <?php echo($state[6]); ?>, <?php echo($state[7]); ?> ]
<?php $first = false; } ?>
];

var columns = [ "State", "Population", "Housing Units", "Total Area",
 "Total Water", "Total Land", "Population Density", "Housing Density" ];

function dataLookup( row, col )
{
  return data[row][col];
}

function headerLookup( col )
{
  return columns[ col ];
}

var grid = new Active.Controls.Grid;
grid.setRowCount( data.length );
grid.setColumnCount( columns.length );
grid.setDataText( dataLookup );
```

```
grid.setColumnText( headerLookup );
document.write( grid );
</script>
</div>
</body>
</html>
```

Running the Hack

Download the ActiveWidgets grid library and unpack it. Move that directory to your server and place the *index.php* file in the same directory as the ActiveWidgets files. Then point your browser to *index.php*; you should see something like Figure 3-1.

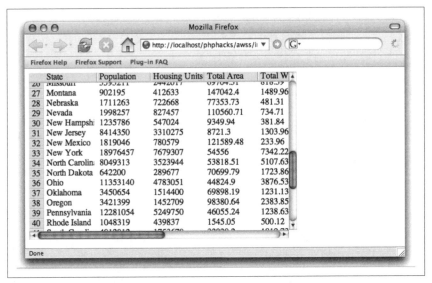

Figure 3-1. An ActiveWidgets grid control with U.S. census data

This simple page does a JavaScript source include on the ActiveWidgets grid control library. Then it loads the data into a JavaScript array and creates the grid control. The script then sets the data lookup to a local function called dataLookup( ), which just returns the data at that row and column. The column headers work the same way.

> At the time of this writing, the grid library is not compatible with Apple's Safari browser.

This library is licensed under the GNU Public License (GPL). If you want to use it in a commercial product, you'll have to buy it from the developers. But if you're looking for a spreadsheet-style HTML control, it's probably well worth the cost.

See Also

- "Create an Interactive Calendar" [Hack #25]
- "Create Link Graphs" [Hack #24]
- "Create Drag-and-Drop Lists" [Hack #13]

HACK #12 Create Pop-Up Hints

Use the overLIB library to pop up hints for words on your web page using JavaScript and PHP.

With the overLIB JavaScript library (*http://www.bosrup.com/web/overlib/*), you can have handy pop-up labels that appear above text on your page. This hack makes it a little easier to create these links by providing a PHP wrapper function to invoke the library.

The Code

Save the code shown in Example 3-2 as *index.php*.

Example 3-2. A wrapper function that simplifies overLIB use, courtesy of PHP

```
<?php
function popup( $text, $popup )
{
?>
<a href="javascript:void(0);" onmouseover="return overlib('<?php echo($popup); ?>
');" onmouseout="return nd();"><?php echo($text); ?></a>
<?php
}
?>
<html>
<head>
<script type="text/javascript" src="overlib.js"><!-- overLIB (c) Erik Bosrup -->
</script>
</head>
<body>
<div id="overDiv" style="position:absolute; visibility:hidden; z-index:1000;">
</div>
So this is just a test of popups. Not something interesting about <?php popup(
    'rabbits', 'Small furry woodland creatures.<br/>Rabbits also make good pets.'
    ); ?>. Because that would just be silly.
</body>
</html>
```

You could also put the wrapper function into a PHP library, include that library in your PHP pages, and turn this into a nice, reusable utility function.

Running the Hack

Download and unpack the overLIB library into your web server's documents directory. Then add in the *index.php* file and surf to it on your browser. You should see something similar to Figure 3-2.

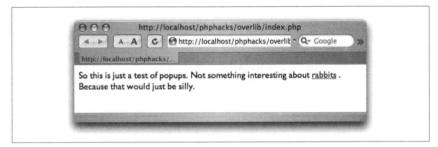

Figure 3-2. The page with the pop-up link

Next, move the mouse over the word *rabbits*, and you will see the pop up appear, which gives you a little more information about rabbits (as seen in Figure 3-3).

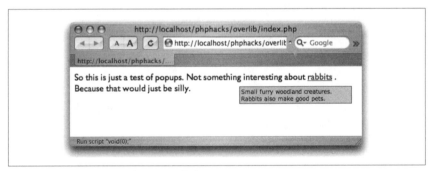

Figure 3-3. Mousing over the pop-up link

This pop up can be as elaborate as you like, with images, tables, different fonts, styles, and whatever else you please.

See Also

- "Create Drop-Down Stickies" **[Hack #16]**

HACK #13 Create Drag-and-Drop Lists

Use JavaScript, DHTML, and PHP to create and use drag-and-drop lists.

Creating an interface that allows the user to prioritize a list has always been a problem when working with HTML. With PHP, though, this is no longer the case. This hack uses an open source drag-and-drop library from Tool-Man (*http://tool-man.org/*) to create drag-and-drop lists.

The Code

Enter the code shown in Example 3-3 and save it as *index.html*.

Example 3-3. Building a drag-and-drop list with HTML and CSS

```html
<html>
<head>

<style>
#states li { margin: 0px; }

ul.boxy li { margin: 3px; }

ul.sortable li {
      position: relative;
}

ul.boxy {
      list-style-type: none;
      padding: 0px;
      margin: 2px;
      width: 20em;
      font-size: 13px;
      font-family: Arial, sans-serif;
}
ul.boxy li {
      cursor:move;
      padding: 2px 2px;
      border: 1px solid #ccc;
      background-color: #eee;
}
.clickable a {
      display: block;
      text-decoration: none;
      cursor: pointer;
      cursor: hand;
}
.clickable li:hover {
      background-color: #f6f6f6;
}

</style>
```

Example 3-3. Building a drag-and-drop list with HTML and CSS (continued)

```
<script language="JavaScript" type="text/javascript"
        src="source/org/tool-man/core.js"></script>
<script language="JavaScript" type="text/javascript"
        src="source/org/tool-man/events.js"></script>
<script language="JavaScript" type="text/javascript"
        src="source/org/tool-man/css.js"></script>
<script language="JavaScript" type="text/javascript"
        src="source/org/tool-man/coordinates.js"></script>
<script language="JavaScript" type="text/javascript"
        src="source/org/tool-man/drag.js"></script>
<script language="JavaScript" type="text/javascript"
        src="source/org/tool-man/dragsort.js"></script>
<script language="JavaScript" type="text/javascript"
        src="source/org/tool-man/cookies.js"></script>

<script language="JavaScript" type="text/javascript">
<!--
var dragsort = ToolMan.dragsort()
var junkdrawer = ToolMan.junkdrawer()

window.onload = function()
{
        dragsort.makeListSortable(document.getElementById("states"),
                verticalOnly, saveOrder)
}

function verticalOnly(item) { item.toolManDragGroup.verticalOnly() }

function saveOrder(item) { }

function prepFields()
{
        document.getElementById( "states_text" ).value = junkdrawer.
serializeList( document.getElementById( "states" ) );
        return true;
}
//-->
</script>
</head>
<body>

<ul id="states" class="boxy">
<li>California</li>
<li>Texas</li>
<li>Alaska</li>
</ul>
```

Example 3-3. Building a drag-and-drop list with HTML and CSS (continued)

```
<form method="post" action="tellme.php">
<input type="hidden" name="states" value="" id="states_text" />
<input type="submit" onclick="return prepFields();">
</form>

</body>

</html>
```

The simple code in Example 3-4—saved as *tellme.php*—prints out values in an array.

Example 3-4. PHP used to print out some values from the list

```
<body>
<html>
You chose: <?php echo( $_POST['states'] ); ?>
</html>
</body>
```

Running the Hack

Download and unpack the drag-and-drop libraries onto your web server. Then upload the files and navigate to the *index.html* page. You should see something that looks like Figure 3-4.

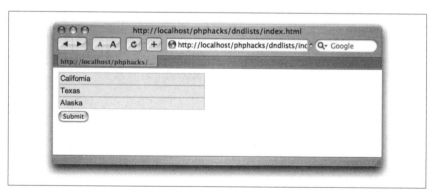

Figure 3-4. The drag-and-drop list

Now drag and drop the lines to rearrange the items however you like; then click the Submit button. At that point, the contents of the list will be transferred into a hidden form variable called states, and uploaded to the server. The *tellme.php* script then prints the values from that variable in the order you specified (as shown in Figure 3-5).

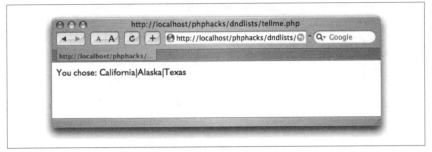

Figure 3-5. After clicking on the Submit button

Dynamic, little interface widgets such as this one can differentiate between your web application and others in terms of ease of use. And sometimes it's good having one just for a little perk during demos! With the results of a drag stored in a form variable, your PHP can easily retrieve the data and do anything you want it to do.

See Also

- "Create Drop-Down Stickies" [Hack #16]
- "Create Pop-Up Hints" [Hack #12]
- "Build a Color Selector" [Hack #23]
- "Create an Interactive Calendar" [Hack #25]

HACK #14 Build Dynamic HTML Graphs

Using DHTML, you can build graphs that change without requiring even a page refresh. The result? Your users can play with data in real time.

Something is fundamentally unsatisfying about the way the Web works. You click on a link, the page disappears, and that lovely spinning ball or ticking clock grinds by as a new page appears section by section, (hopefully) with the information you want. This certainly is not the interactivity we're all used to from our client-side applications.

But, thank goodness, you can make an application that works without a page refresh. This hack shows you how to make an interactive scatter plot using a few graphics, some PHP, and a whole slew of JavaScript.

The Code

The index file, *index.php*, is shown in Example 3-5.

Example 3-5. JavaScript, the real workhorse in this hack

```php
<?php $states = array(
    array( "Alabama",4447100,1963711,52419.02,1675.01,50744,87.6,38.7 ),
    array( "Alaska",626932,260978,663267.26,91316,571951.26,1.1,0.5 ),
    array( "Arizona",5130632,2189189,113998.3,363.73,113634.57,45.2,19.3 ),
    array( "Arkansas",2673400,1173043,53178.62,1110.45,52068.17,51.3,22.5 ),
    array( "California",33871648,12214549,163695.57,7736.23,155959.34,217.2,78.3 ),
    array( "Colorado",4301261,1808037,104093.57,376.04,103717.53,41.5,17.4 ),
    ...
    array( "Washington",5894121,2451075,71299.64,4755.58,66544.06,88.6,36.8 ),
    array( "West Virginia",1808344,844623,24229.76,152.03,24077.73,75.1,35.1 ),
    array( "Wisconsin",5363675,2321144,65497.82,11187.72,54310.1,98.8,42.7 ),
    array( "Wyoming",493782,223854,97813.56,713.16,97100.4,5.1,2.3 ),
    array( "Puerto Rico",3808610,1418476,5324.5,1899.94,3424.56,1112.1,414.2 )
);
?>
<html>
<head>
<script language="Javascript">
var width = 300;
var height = 300;

var axes = [ "population", "housing_units", "total_area", "total_water", "total_
land", "people_density", "housing_density" ];

var data = [
<?php $first = true; foreach( $states as $state ) { if ( !$first ) echo( "," );
?>
{ state: "<?php echo($state[0]); ?>", population: <?php echo($state[1]); ?>,
  housing_units: <?php echo($state[2]); ?>, total_area: <?php echo($state[3]); ?>,
  total_water: <?php echo($state[4]); ?>, total_land: <?php echo($state[5]); ?>,
  people_density: <?php echo($state[6]); ?>, housing_density: <?php
echo($state[7]); ?> }
<?php $first = false; } ?>
];

var axmin = {};
var axmax = {};

for( axind in axes )
{
    axmin[ axes[axind] ] = 100000000;
    axmax[ axes[axind] ] = -100000000;
}
for( ind in data )
{
  row = data[ind];
  for( axind in axes )
  {
    axis = axes[axind];
    if ( row[axis] < axmin[axis] )
      axmin[axis] = row[axis];
```

Example 3-5. JavaScript, the real workhorse in this hack (continued)

```
    if ( row[axis] > axmax[axis] )
      axmax[axis] = row[axis];
  }
}

function cleargraph( )
{
    graph = document.getElementById( "graph" );
    graph.innerHTML = "";
}

function adddot( value, size, x, y, text )
{
    var left = x - ( size / 2 );
    var top = width - ( y + ( size / 2 ) );

    var cleft = "auto";
    var ctop = "auto";
    var cright = "auto";
    var cbottom = "auto";

    if ( left < 0 ) { cright = ( left * -1 ) + "px"; }
    if ( left + size > width ) { cleft = ( width - left ) + "px"; }
    if ( top < 0 ) { ctop = ( top * -1 ) + "px"; }
    if ( top + size > height ) { cbottom = ( height - top ) + "px"; }

    if ( value <= 0.25 )
      img = "ltgray.gif";
    else if ( value <= 0.50 )
      img = "gray.gif";
    else if ( value <= 0.75 )
      img = "dkgray.gif";
    else
      img = "black.gif";

    html = "<img src=\""+img+"\" width=\""+size+"\" height=\""+size+"\" ";
    html += "style=\"position:absolute;left:"+left+"px;top:"+top+"px;";
    html += "clip:rect( "+ctop+" "+cleft+" "+cbottom+" "+cright+" );";
    html += "\" onclick=\"alert(\'"+text+"\')\"/>";

    graph = document.getElementById( "graph" );
    graph.innerHTML += html;
}

function calculate_value( row, field, min, max )
{
    var val = row[ field ] - axmin[ field ];
    var scale = ( max - min ) / ( axmax[ field ] - axmin[ field ] );
    return min + ( scale * val );
}
```

Example 3-5. JavaScript, the real workhorse in this hack (continued)

```
function drawgraph( )
{
    cleargraph( );

    var xvar = document.getElementById( "bottom" ).value;
    var yvar = document.getElementById( "side" ).value;
    var sizevar = document.getElementById( "size" ).value;
    var valuevar = document.getElementById( "color" ).value;

    for( rowind in data )
    {
        var row = data[rowind];
        var x = calculate_value( row, xvar, 5, width - 5 );
        var y = calculate_value( row, yvar, 5, height - 5 );
        var size = calculate_value( row, sizevar, 5, 30 );
        var value = calculate_value( row, valuevar, 0, 1 );
        adddot( value, size, x, y, row.state );
    }
}

function buildselect( axis, current )
{
    var html = "<select id=\""+axis+"\" onchange=\"drawgraph( )\">";
    for( axind in axes )
    {
        var selected = "";
        if ( axes[axind] == current )
            selected = " selected=\"true\"";
        html += "<option value=\""+axes[axind]+"\""+selected+">"+axes[axind]+"
            </option>";
    }
    html += "</select>";
    document.write( html );
}
</script>
</head>
<body onload="drawgraph( );">
Side: <script language="Javascript">buildselect( "side", "population" );</script>
Bottom: <script language="Javascript">buildselect( "bottom", "housing_units" );</
script>
Size: <script language="Javascript">buildselect( "size", "total_area" );</script>
Color: <script language="Javascript">buildselect( "color", "total_water" );</
script>
<div style="position:relative;border:1px solid #eee; clip:rect(0px 0px 300px
300px); width:300px; height:300px;" id="graph">
</div>
</body>
</html>
```

The script starts by creating the data array, first in PHP and then in JavaScript. The data needs to be available to JavaScript so that the graph can be dynamically built on the fly using DHTML. Once the data is loaded into the page, the rest is left up to the browser.

The first thing the browser does is create the drop downs using the buildselect( ) function. Then, the onload( ) event fires on the body tag, which calls the drawgraph( ) function. This function in turn creates a new HTML string that's made up of lots of img tags, one for each state. The size of the image, as well as the position of the image on the graph, depends on which data attributes are assigned to what graph attributes via the drop down. Once the graph is created, the drawgraph( ) function sets the inner HTML of the graph <div> tag to the new HTML, rendering all of the images.

If the user selects a different attribute with one of the drop downs, the drawgraph( ) function is called again, and the graph is updated.

Running the Hack

Upload the PHP page and the images to the server, and then navigate to the page in your web browser. You should see something along the lines of Figure 3-6. Now use the combo boxes to assign different variables to the different portions of the graph. The Side drop down changes the Y axis. The Bottom drop down changes the X axis. The Size drop down sets which of the attributes will alter the size of the ball, and the Color drop down assigns a data attribute to the color of the ball.

The Y axis represents housing units, and land area increases along the X axis. While most of the plot appears closely packed, there are a few outliers. Click on one of these to see which data point is represented; for instance, clicking on the black ball in the lower righthand corner results in the pop up shown in Figure 3-7.

This tells me that, not surprisingly, Alaska has the largest total size but has very few housing units. The size of the ball tells me that Alaska has a large amount of land mass as well. I'm not surprised by the size of the land mass, but the very low housing units number is somewhat interesting. There are also two other outliers: the medium gray ball in the middle of the graph (Texas), and the ball at the very top of the graph (California).

The data for this graph comes from the U.S. Census Bureau (*http://www.census.gov/*). When you are in a pinch for some fun data to play with, this web site is always a good source. The site vends data in text, comma-separated value (CSV), and Excel (XLS) formats.

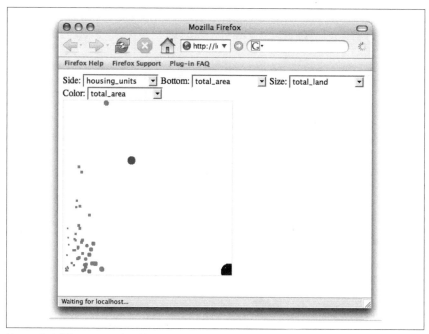

Figure 3-6. The scatter plot after some experimentation

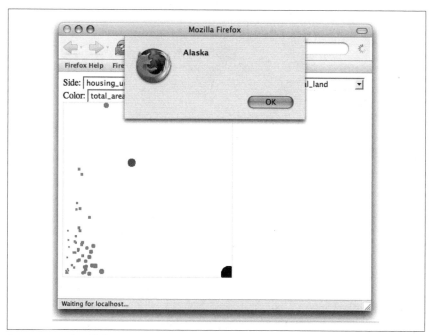

Figure 3-7. After clicking on the ball in the lower-right corner

See Also

- "Build Lightweight HTML Graphs" [Hack #8]

Section Your Content with Spinners

#15

Use spinners to divide your page content into sections, each of which you can show or hide individually.

Sometimes there is just too much great content to have visible on a single page at one time. One approach is to use tabs [Hack #6], and another is to section the content with spinners that allow the user to open up specific sections of content. This hack shows how to create sections on your page with spinners that open and show sections of the content interactively.

The Code

The code for *index.php* is shown in Example 3-6.

Example 3-6. PHP allowing for user selection of a specific spinner

```php
<?php
function start_section( $id, $title )
{
?>
<table cellspacing="0" cellpadding="0">
<tr>
<td width="30" valign="top">
<a href="javascript: void twist('<?php echo($id); ?>');">
<img src="up.gif" border="0" id="img_<?php echo($id); ?>"/>
</a>
</td>
<td width="90%">
<h1><?php echo( $title ); ?></h1>
<div style="visibility:hidden;position:absolute;"
  id="<?php echo($id); ?>" class="spin-content">
<?php
}
function end_section()
{
?>
</div>
</td>
</tr>
</table>
<?php
}
function spinner_header()
{
?>
<style type="text/css">
```

Example 3-6. PHP allowing for user selection of a specific spinner (continued)

```
body { font-family: arial, verdana; }
h1 { font-size: medium; border-bottom: 1px solid black; }
.spin-content { font-size: small; margin-left: 10px; padding: 10px; }
</style>
<script language="Javascript">
function twist( sid )
{
  imgobj = document.getElementById( "img_"+sid );
  divobj = document.getElementById( sid );
  if ( imgobj.src.match( "up.gif" ) )
  {
    imgobj.src = "down.gif";
    divobj.style.position = "relative";
    divobj.style.visibility = "visible";
  }
  else
  {
    imgobj.src = "up.gif";
    divobj.style.visibility = "hidden";
    divobj.style.position = "absolute";
  }
}
</script>
<?php
}
?>
<html>
<head>
<?php spinner_header( ) ?>
</head>
<body>
<?php start_section( "one", "Report part one" ) ?>
This report will tell you a lot of stuff you didn't know before.
And that's good. Because that's what a report should do.<br/><br/>
But it will tell you so much that it needs to be rolled up into sections
so that you don't have to gasp as you see it all at once.
<?php end_section( ) ?>
<?php start_section( "two", "Report part two" ) ?>
This is a table of numbers and such:<br/>
<table>
<tr><th>State</th><th>Total</th></tr>
<tr><td>CA</td><td>$35M</td></tr>
<tr><td>PA</td><td>$22M</td></tr>
<tr><td>NC</td><td>$5M</td></tr>
<tr><td>FL</td><td>$15M</td></tr>
</table>
<?php end_section( ) ?>
</body>
</html>
```

The script starts by defining the start_section and end_section functions, which bracket the blocks of content on the page that will be shown (or hidden) interactively. The top section also defines a spinner_header function that will define the CSS and JavaScript used by the DHTML portion of the system.

> You can move all of this code to another PHP file if you want to modularize the code.

The start_section function creates a table where the first column has the spinner graphic, and the second has the title of the section and a div element that will hold the content. The div element is initially set to be invisible, and its position attribute is set initially to "absolute" (a div element that is positioned as "relative" will still be accounted for in the layout). To make the div element and its content disappear, the position attribute's value is set to "absolute"; it can then be set back to "relative" for a reappearance.

Running the Hack

Upload the code and images to the server, and point your browser at *index.php*. You should see something that looks like Figure 3-8.

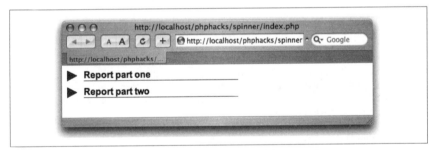

Figure 3-8. The sections closed up

Click on the arrow next to the first part of the report, and watch it spin to expose the report section (as shown in Figure 3-9).

> *up.gif* and *down.gif* are two graphics that were created with Macromedia Fireworks. They could just as easily have been created with Adobe's Photoshop or the open source GIMP graphics editor. If you don't want to create your own graphics, I suggest using Google's image search to look for arrow graphics.

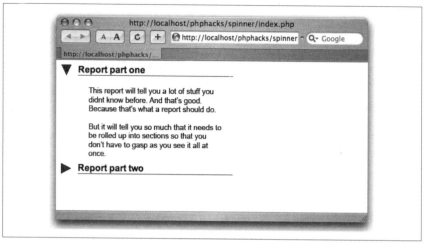

Figure 3-9. The first section opened up

When writing code that does dynamic repositioning, as with this hack, it's very important to test it on every browser you intend to support. Positioning visible and invisible elements is one of those "gotcha" areas in DHTML.

See Also

* "Add Tabs to Your Web Interface" [Hack #6]

HACK #16 Create Drop-Down Stickies

Use DHTML to position sticky drop-down windows relative to keywords in your HTML.

Attaching a drop-down sticky to a word or phrase in your document is an easy way to add valuable information close to the word, without obscuring it. That way, the user can click on the word and get more contextual information, all without scrolling or lots of mouse movement.

The Code

Save the code in Example 3-7 as *index.php*.

Example 3-7. PHP and JavaScript cooperate to make drop-down stickies work

```
<?php
$nextid = 1;
function start_link( $text )
{
  global $nextid;
  $idtext = "a"+$nextid;
```

Example 3-7. PHP and JavaScript cooperate to make drop-down stickies work (continued)

```php
?><a href="javascript: void drop( '<?php echo($idtext); ?>' );">
    <span id="a_<?php echo($idtext); ?>"><?php echo($text); ?></span></a>
    <div id="<?php echo($idtext); ?>" class="drop" style="visibility:hidden;">
<table cellspacing="0" cellpadding="0" width="170"><tr>
<td valign="top" width="20">
<a href="javascript: void close(<?php echo($idtext); ?>)"><img src="close.gif"
border="0"></a>
</td>
<td valign="top" width="150">
<?php
}

function end_link()
{
?>
</td>
</tr></table>
</div><?php
}

function link_header()
{
?>
<style type="text/css">
body { font-family: arial, verdana; }
.drop {
  padding: 5px;
  font-size: small;
  background: #eee;
  border: 1px solid black;
  position: absolute;
}
</style>
<script language="Javascript">
function drop( sid )
{
  aobj = document.getElementById( "a_"+sid );
  divobj = document.getElementById( sid );
  divobj.style.top = aobj.offsetBottom+10;
  divobj.style.left = aobj.offsetLeft+10;
  divobj.style.visibility = "visible";
}
function close( sid )
{
  divobj = document.getElementById( sid );
  divobj.style.visibility = "hidden";
}
</script>
<?php
}
?>
```

Example 3-7. PHP and JavaScript cooperate to make drop-down stickies work (continued)

```
<html>
<head>
<?php link_header( ); ?>
</head>
<body>
Hey <?php start_link( "this is interesting" ); ?>
That really<br/>
Is interesting <?php end_link( ); ?>. How about that.
<br/>
The popup will go over text and all that.<br/>
And it will stay up until it's dismissed with the close
button.
</body>
</html>
```

The script defines three functions at the top of the file: start_link, end_link, and link_header. The call to start_link takes the text of the link as an argument. The contents of the drop-down box are then supplied, and the end_link call is made.

> To get the CSS classes and JavaScript into the header, you need to call the link_header function within the head tag.

Running the Hack

Copy the code and the images to the server. Point your browser to the *index. php* script and you will see something similar to Figure 3-10.

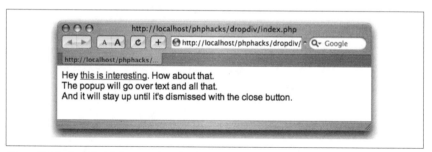

Figure 3-10. A clickable keyword in the document

Now click on the link and you will get the drop-down box with a close icon, as shown in Figure 3-11.

See Also

- "Create Pop-Up Hints" [Hack #12]

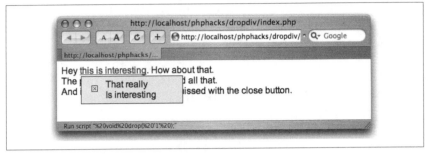

Figure 3-11. The drop down positioned under the link

Create Dynamic Navigation Menus

Use PHP to build a navigation menu widget that works consistently across your site.

Writing the navigation menu for your site can be a pain. You don't want to write the same code over and over on every page. Ideally, you would have a PHP menu function that would render the menu with the current page highlighted. This hack gives you that simple menu function (for the low cost of this book, no less!).

The Code

Save the code in Example 3-8, which demonstrates the use of *menu.php* as *index.php*.

Example 3-8. Using the menu library

```php
<?php
require_once( "menu.php" );

$page = "home";
if ( $_GET['page'] )
        $page = $_GET['page'];
?>
<html>
<head>
<title>Page - <?php echo($page); ?></title>
<?php echo menu_css(); ?>
</head>
<body>
<table cellspaceing="0" cellpadding="5">
<tr>
<td width="200" valign="top">
<?php page_menu( $page ); ?>
</td>
<td width="600" valign="top">
Page: <?php echo( $page ); ?>
```

Example 3-8. Using the menu library (continued)

```
</td>
</tr>
</table>
</body>
</html>
```

Example 3-9 shows the library, which is surprisingly simple.

Example 3-9. Making everything work with the PHP library, menu.php

```php
<?php
function menu_css( ) {
?>
<style type="text/css">
.menu-inactive, .menu-active {
        padding: 2px;
        padding-left: 20px;
        font-family: arial, verdana;
}
.menu-inactive { background: #ddd; }
.menu-active { background: #000; font-weight: bold; }
.menu-inactive a { text-decoration: none; }
.menu-active a { color: white; text-decoration: none; }
</style>
<?php
}

function menu_item( $id, $title, $current ) {
$class = "menu-inactive";
if ( $current == $id )
        $class = "menu-active";
?>
<tr><td class="<?php echo($class); ?>">
<a href="index.php?page=<?php echo( $id ); ?>">
<?php echo( $title ); ?>
</a>
</td></tr>
<?php
}

function page_menu( $page ) {
?>
<table width="100%">
<?php menu_item( 'home', 'Home', $page ); ?>
<?php menu_item( 'faq', 'FAQ', $page ); ?>
<?php menu_item( 'download', 'Download', $page ); ?>
<?php menu_item( 'links', 'Links', $page ); ?>
<?php menu_item( 'credits', 'Credits', $page ); ?>
</table>
<?php
}
?>
```

index.php creates the menu by calling the page_menu function and specifying the page ID. The ID of the page is used to decide which menu item is selected. The *index.php* script also calls the menu_css function to set up the CSS styles for the menu.

You can change the makeup of the menu by altering the bottom portion of the *menu.php* file to add or remove menu items. You can also change the look and feel of the menu by altering the CSS class definitions in the menu_css function.

> You'll obviously need to change the menu titles and pages in this script to match your own site layout.

Running the Hack

Upload the code to the server and point your browser at *index.php*. Your display should look like Figure 3-12.

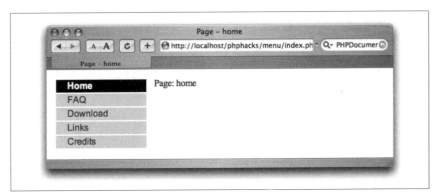

Figure 3-12. The home page

Now click on the FAQ link; you should see something like Figure 3-13.

See Also

- "Build a Breadcrumb Trail" **[Hack #4]**

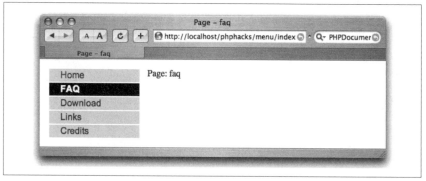

Figure 3-13. The FAQ page

 HACK #18 **Obscure JavaScript Dynamically**

Use PHP to obscure the names of your JavaScript functions, hiding all of your clever code.

Sometimes it's useful to obscure some of your JavaScript code to hide intellectual property. It is impossible to twist the code so completely that users cannot unravel it, but it is possible to do some obfuscation to fend off the casual observer. This hack starts you down the road of JavaScript obfuscation by automatically renaming JavaScript function calls. With this code, you can write JavaScript in the clear on the server, and then have it obfuscated on the way out to the browser.

The Code

Save the sample in Example 3-10 as *index.php*.

Example 3-10. The script using the obscure.php library

```php
<?php
require_once( "obscure.php" );
obscurejs_start() ?>
<html>
<head>
<script language="JavaScript">
function dowrite()
{
        document.write( "This is a test" );
}
</script>
</head>
<body>
<script language="JavaScript">dowrite();</script>
</body>
</html>
<?php obscurejs_end() ?>
```

The library code, *obscure.php*, does all the heavy lifting (see Example 3-11).

Example 3-11. Handling obfuscation of method names

```php
<?php
function obscurejs_start( )
{
    ob_start( );
}

$funcs = array( );

function decreplace( $matches )
{
    global $funcs;

    $newname = "af".count($funcs);

    $funcs[ $matches[1] ] = $newname;

    return "function ".$newname."(";
}

function objscurejs( $matches )
{
    global $funcs;

    $js = $matches[2];
    $js = preg_replace_callback( "/function\s+(.*?)\s*\(/", "decreplace", $js );
    foreach( $funcs as $oldfunc => $newfunc )
    {
      $js = preg_replace( "/".$oldfunc."/", $newfunc, $js );
    }
    return "<script".$matches[1].">".$js."</script>";
}

function obscurejs_end( )
{
    $doc = ob_get_clean( );
    $doc = preg_replace_callback( "/\<script(.*?)\>(.*?)\<\/script\>/s",
"objscurejs", $doc );
    print( $doc );
}
?>
```

Running the Hack

Copy the code onto your PHP server and navigate to *index.php*. Instead of the JavaScript in the original document, you should see this (note the bolded method name, changed from the original name):

```
<html>
<head>
<script language="JavaScript">
function af0( )
{
    document.write( "This is a test" );
}
</script>
</head>
<body>
<script language="JavaScript">af0( );</script>
</body>
</html>
```

The dowrite JavaScript function has been renamed to af0, as have all of the references to it in the HTML.

The code that renames the functions is in the *obscure.php*script. It is invoked with the obscurejs_start and obscurejs_end calls. These calls trap all of the PHP output, and then find the JavaScript blocks and rewrite them. Of course, there are limitations: JavaScript that is sourced in from another file will not be altered, and functions that are used before they are defined will not be renamed appropriately.

> It should be clear that this is hardly an industrial-strength solution, but it is a good starting point. The best solution is usually to put all your JavaScript in external libraries, and then protect those external libraries from prying eyes. But, to create a little chaos, this script is a nice tool.

HACK #19 Build a DHTML Binary Clock

Use a combination of PHP and DHTML to build the bit clock that you can buy on ThinkGeek.com.

A coworker of mine recently bought one of the "bit clocks" from Think-Geek (*http://www.thinkgeek.com/*). The clock has three sections, each with eight lights. The sections represent seconds, minutes, and hours, and the individual lights represent the bits in each value. Though neither he nor I could actually read the clock (!!), we both agreed that it was *very* cool. Along the same lines, here's a hard-to-read clock in PHP, also super-cool to show off.

The Code

clock.php does the work; it's shown in Example 3-12.

Example 3-12. Setting up an array of bit masks, and beyond

```php
<?php
$bit_names = array( 1, 2, 4, 8, 10, 20 );
$bit_masks = array(
  array( '0', '0x1', '1' ),
  array( '1', '0x2', '2' ),
  array( '2', '0x4', '4' ),
  array( '3', '0x8', '8' ),
  array( '4', '0x10', '16' ),
  array( '5', '0x20', '32' )
);

$size = 40;

function bit_table( $name )
{
  global $size;
?>
<table width="<?php echo($size*2); ?>" cellspacing="2" cellpadding="0">
<tr>
<td id="<?php echo( $name ); ?>_1" width="<?php echo($size); ?>" height="<?php
    echo($size); ?>" /></td>
<td id="<?php echo( $name ); ?>_2" width="<?php echo($size); ?>" height="<?php
    echo($size); ?>" /></td>
</tr>
<tr>
<td id="<?php echo( $name ); ?>_4" width="<?php echo($size); ?>" height="<?php
    echo($size); ?>" /></td>
<td id="<?php echo( $name ); ?>_8" width="<?php echo($size); ?>" height="<?php
    echo($size); ?>" /></td>
</tr>
<tr>
<td id="<?php echo( $name ); ?>_10" width="<?php echo($size); ?>" height="<?php
    echo($size); ?>" /></td>
<td id="<?php echo( $name ); ?>_20" width="<?php echo($size); ?>" height="<?php
    echo($size); ?>" /></td>
</tr>
</table>
<?php
}
?>
<html>
<head>
<script>
var second_bits = [];
var minute_bits = [];
var hour_bits = [];

function startup()
{
<?php foreach( $bit_names as $name ) { ?>
    second_bits.push( document.getElementById( "second_<?php echo( $name ) ?>" ) );
```

Example 3-12. Setting up an array of bit masks, and beyond (continued)

```
  minute_bits.push( document.getElementById( "minute_<?php echo( $name ) ?>" ) );
  hour_bits.push( document.getElementById( "hour_<?php echo( $name ) ?>" ) );
<?php } ?>

  set_clock( );

  window.setInterval( "set_clock( )", 200 );
}

function set_state( obj, val, on_color )
{
  obj.style.background = val ? on_color : "white";
}

function set_clock( )
{
  var now = new Date( );
  var seconds = now.getSeconds( );
  var minutes = now.getMinutes( );
  var hours = now.getHours( );

<?php foreach( $bit_masks as $mask ) { ?>
  set_state( second_bits[<?php echo($mask[0] ); ?>], ( ( seconds & <?php
    echo($mask[1] ); ?> ) == <?php echo($mask[2] ); ?> ), "red" );
  set_state( minute_bits[<?php echo($mask[0] ); ?>], ( ( minutes & <?php
    echo($mask[1] ); ?> ) == <?php echo($mask[2] ); ?> ), "green" );
  set_state( hour_bits[<?php echo($mask[0] ); ?>], ( ( hours & <?php
    echo($mask[1] ); ?> ) == <?php echo($mask[2] ); ?> ), "blue" );
<?php } ?>
}
</script>
</head>
<body onload="startup( );">
<table cellpadding="5" cellspacing="0">
<tr><td>
<?php bit_table( "second" ); ?>
</td><td>
<?php bit_table( "minute" ); ?>
</td><td>
<?php bit_table( "hour" ); ?>
</td></tr></table>
</body>
</html>
```

This script starts by setting up the bit table that will be used in the generation of the page and in the JavaScript that updates the clock. The bit_names array is used to name each bit in a clock element, starting at the top left and going down to the bottom right. The bit_masks array stores the bit number in the first position of the array, the JavaScript bit mask value in the second position, and the value of the bit in the third position.

The bit_table( ) function creates an HTML table with positions for each bit. It's used three times: the first for seconds, the second for minutes, and the third for hours. The PHP portion of the script also defines the set_clock( ) function, which decomposes a time value into its bits, and sets the clock accordingly.

Once the page is rendered, it's shown in the browser. The first thing the browser does after rendering the tables for seconds, minutes, and hours is to call the startup( ) function, which initializes the bits to the current time. The startup( ) function calls set_clock( ), which gets the current hour, minute, and second, and calls set_state( ) for each. The set_state( ) function simply sets the background color of the table element using CSS. If the bit is on, it sets the value to a color; otherwise, the element is set to white.

The startup( ) function also creates a timer that calls the set_clock( ) function every 500 ms, giving you a clock that continuously updates on the page.

Running the Hack

Upload *clock.php* to your server and navigate to the it in your web browser. The result should look like Figure 3-14.

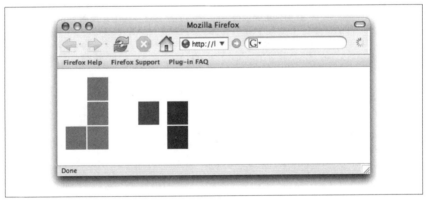

Figure 3-14. The bit clock showing the current time

The bit clock shows the current time in three sections of six bits each, where each section is a different color (shown here in black and white). The red blocks indicate the seconds, the green block indicates minutes, and the blue blocks indicate hours. The hours are, of course, on military time (0–23). If I remember correctly, I took this picture around 8 p.m. But as I said, this is more about the cool factor than about conveying time information any more effectively (or even discernibly) than a regular clock.

See Also

- "Make a DHTML Slideshow" [Hack #21]
- "Create an Interactive Calendar" [Hack #25]
- "Create the Google Maps Scrolling Effect" [Hack #26]

Tame Ajax with JSON #20
Use JSON to make Ajax easier to implement.

The combination of DHTML, CSS, and XML SOAP or REST requests from the browser is known as *Ajax*. Ajax is a great way to create dynamic web interfaces without ever requiring a page fetch. Largely centered on the Java-Script in a page requesting HTTP transfers, Ajax-enabled applications often use DHTML to change the HTML of a page, creating dynamic applications that feel like client-side apps. Typically, JavaScript contacts a PHP or Perl script on a server and then interprets the returned text, which is most often XML.

Parsing the XML isn't rocket science, but it isn't a walk in the park, either. That's why developers created the JSON (*http://json.org/*) library, which makes it easy for JavaScript to interpret the response from the server. This hack uses the JSON PEAR module to format data coming out of the server, and shows how that JSON code is consumed in the browser.

The Code

Save the code shown in Example 3-13 as *getdata.php*.

Example 3-13. PHP responding to an Ajax request

```php
<?php
require( 'JSON.php' );

$records = array();
$records []= array( 'id' => 1, 'last' => 'Herrington', 'first' => 'Jack' );
$records []= array( 'id' => 2, 'last' => 'Herrington', 'first' => 'Megan' );
$records []= array( 'id' => 3, 'last' => 'Herrington', 'first' => 'Lori' );

$json = new JSON();
echo( $json->encode( $records ) );
?>
```

Now create a test page; I've named mine *index.php* (see Example 3-14).

Example 3-14. A simple example of Ajax making a request and updating the page with the returned data

```
<html>
<head>
<title>JSON Test</title>
<script>
var req;

function processReqChange( )
{
  if ( req.readyState == 4 && req.status == 200 )
  {
    var rows = eval( req.responseText );

    var html = "<table>";
    for( r in rows )
    {
        html += "<tr>";
        html += "<td>"+rows[r].id+"</td>";
        html += "<td>"+rows[r].first+"</td>";
        html += "<td>"+rows[r].last+"</td>";
        html += "</tr>";
    }
    html += "</table>";

    document.getElementById( "data" ).innerHTML = html;
  }
}

function getNames( )
{
  if (typeof window.ActiveXObject != 'undefined' )
  {
    req = new ActiveXObject("Microsoft.XMLHTTP");
    req.onreadystatechange = processReqChange;
  }
  else
  {
    req = new XMLHttpRequest( );
    req.onload = processReqChange;
  }
  try {
    req.open( 'GET', 'http://localhost:1222/json/getdata.php', true );
  } catch( e ) {
    alert( e );
  }
  req.send("");
}
</script>
</head>
<body>
<div id="data">
```

Example 3-14. A simple example of Ajax making a request and updating the page with the returned data (continued)

```
</div>
<script>
getNames( );
</script>
</body>
</html>
```

The *index.php* page calls getNames( ), a JavaScript method that creates an HttpRequest object and points it at the *getdata.php* page. That script packs up some data and returns it using the JSON module. The script (back in *index.php*) then unpacks this data using the eval function. With the data unraveled, it's just a matter of putting some HTML together and setting the innerHTML of the data <div> tag.

Figure 3-15 shows the Ajax session between *index.php* and *getdata.php* in this hack. The browser, symbolized here by the computer, requests the *index.php* page. The *index.php* page then makes an HTTP request to *getdata. php*, which in turn returns the JSON-encoded data (avoiding the need for *index.php* to do any XML parsing).

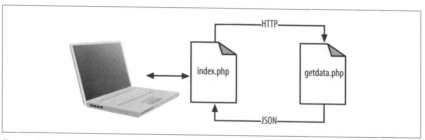

Figure 3-15. A JSON-based Ajax session

Running the Hack

Upload the *index.php* and *getpage.php* pages to the server. Then surf over to the *index.php* page in your browser. You should see something like Figure 3-16.

JSON does make it easier to program Ajax with JavaScript, but that ease comes at a price. Because the web server now returns JSON code instead of XML, your PHP scripts will be harder for other languages to use. Ideally, the *getdata.php* page should vend the data in *either* XML or JSON, depending on what the client wants to see.

Figure 3-16. The JSON test page

Make a DHTML Slideshow
#21

Use the PHP graphics library and DHTML to make a slideshow in your browser.

Family pictures are the classic icebreaker among parents. Who doesn't like to look at pictures of their own kids? (And who isn't bored silly looking at pictures of someone else's kids?) But isn't a set of wallet photos just passé in this modern wired world? How about an online slideshow?

This hack shows how to use a combination of PHP 5, the PHP image library, and some DHTML using JavaScript to create in your browser a slideshow of your favorite images (kids or otherwise).

The Code

Save the code in Example 3-15 as *index.php*.

Example 3-15. PHP script handling image display

```
<?php
$dh = new DirectoryIterator( "pics" );

$files = array( );
foreach( $dh as $file )
{
  if ( preg_match( "/[.]jpg$/", $file ) ) $files []= "$file";
}
?>
<html>
<head>
<title>Slideshow</title>
<style>
```

Example 3-15. PHP script handling image display (continued)

```
body { background: black; }
#thumbnails { height: 140px; width: 100%; overflow: auto; }
#pic { text-align: center; height: 400px; padding: 20px; }
</style>
<script>
var image_list = [
<?php $first = true; foreach( $files as $image ) { ?>
<?php echo( $first ? "" : ", " ); ?>"<?php echo( $image ); ?>"
<?php $first = false; } ?>
];

var curimage = 0;

function switchimg( ind )
{
  var image = image_list[ind];
  var obj = document.getElementById( "selimg" );
  obj.src = "scale.php?image="+image+"&y=400";
  curimage = ind;
}

function nextimage( )
{
  curimage++;
  if ( curimage >= image_list.length ) curimage = 0;
  switchimg( curimage );
}

window.setInterval( "nextimage( )", 2000 );
</script>
</head>
<body>
<div id="thumbnails">
<table width="100%">
<tr>
<?php $ind = 0; foreach( $files as $image ) { ?>
<td width="160" nowrap align="center">
<a href="javascript:switchimg( <?php echo($ind); ?> )">
<img height="100" src="scale.php?image=<?php echo($image); ?>&y=100" border="0" /
>
</a>
</td>
<?php $ind++; } ?>
</tr>
</table>
</div>
<div id="pic">
<img id="selimg" height="400" src="scale.php?image=<?php echo($files[0]); ?>&y=400" />
</div>
</body>
```

Now create *scale.php*, shown in Example 3-16, for handling image resizing.

Example 3-16. Script using PHP's image-handling libraries for image scaling

```php
<?php
$image = $_GET["image"];
$maxy = $_GET["y"];

$im = @imagecreatefromjpeg( "pics/".$image );
$curx = imagesx( $im );
$cury = imagesy( $im );
$ratio = $maxy / $cury;
$newx = $curx * $ratio;
$newy = $cury * $ratio;

$oim = imagecreatetruecolor( $newx, $newy );
imageantialias( $oim, true );
imagecopyresized( $oim, $im, 0, 0, 0, 0,
        $newx, $newy, $curx, $cury );

header( "content-type: image/jpeg" );
imagejpeg( $oim );
?>
```

The JavaScript here is doing the real work. The switchimg( ) function changes the image by setting the src attribute of the <img> tag with the ID of selimg. And the nextimage( ) function is called whenever a two-second timer elapses (that timer is set with the window.setInterval( ) method).

The *scale.php* page is a handy little image-scaler page that you can use in a multitude of applications. If efficiency is your thing, you will probably want to have the *scale.php* page cache the scaled image so that it doesn't have to recompute the scaled image with every image hit. Alternately, you can use a command-line version of the *scale.php* script to create two scaled versions of each image, and upload the static images to the server. That way, you will never be scaling images on the fly.

Running the Hack

Upload the two PHP scripts into a directory on your web server, create a subdirectory called *pics*, and upload some of your favorite JPEG images. Then surf to the *index.php* page with your web browser. You should see something like Figure 3-17.

Every two seconds the image will change on its own, moving to the next image; or you can click on one of the images at the top of the page to go to that particular image.

Figure 3-17. A slideshow of my daughter at the pool

 OK, I admit that part of the reason I wrote this hack was to have some pictures of my kid in the book. Can you blame me? She's cute!

See Also

- "Create an Interactive Calendar" [Hack #25]
- "Section Your Content with Spinners" [Hack #15]
- "Create the Google Maps Scrolling Effect" [Hack #26]

HACK
#22

Add Vector Graphics with PHP

Use JavaScript to render line graphics without plug-ins.

You would think that with its inception as a language for writing scientific papers, HTML would support vector graphics for charting. But alas, it doesn't, and several plug-ins have been developed to enhance the graphics capabilities of HTML browsers. Notable among these are Flash and Scalable Vector Graphics (SVG). Both of these seem like heavyweight solutions for simple graphs, though, so what is a poor DHTML programmer to do?

One option is to use Walter Zorn's JavaScript Vectorgraphics Library (*http://www.walterzorn.com/*). This single JavaScript file can help you put vector graphics anywhere you want on your page, and even allows you to alter those graphics in real time in the browser. The script creates thousands of small <div> tags, one for each pixel of a graph. It's not a subtle approach, but it does the job, and for small graphs it's fast enough to be usable.

The Code

Save the code in Example 3-17 as *index.php*.

Example 3-17. Using PHP and the Zorn JavaScript library for graphs

```php
<?php
$width = 400;
$height = 400;

$point_count = 10;

$points = array( );

for( $point = 0; $point < $point_count; $point++ )
{
    $d = ( 360 / $point_count ) * $point;
    $x = ( $width / 2 ) - ( ( $width / 2 ) * sin( deg2rad( $d ) ) );
    $y = ( $height / 2 ) - ( ( $height / 2 ) * cos( deg2rad( $d ) ) );
    $points []= array( 'x' => $x, 'y' => $y );
}
?>
<html>
<head>
<script src="wz_jsgraphics.js"></script>
</head>
<body>
<div id="graph" style="width:<?php echo($width); ?>px;height:<?php echo($height);
    ?>px;position:relative;">
</div>
<script>
var jg = new jsGraphics( "graph" );
<?php
for( $start = 0; $start < count( $points ); $start++ ) {
    $sx = $points[$start]['x'];
    $sy = $points[$start]['y'];
for( $end = 0; $end < count( $points ); $end++ ) {
    $ex = $points[$end]['x'];
    $ey = $points[$end]['y'];
?>
jg.drawLine( <?php echo($sx); ?>, <?php echo($sy); ?>,
    <?php echo($ex); ?>, <?php echo($ey); ?> );
```

Example 3-17. Using PHP and the Zorn JavaScript library for graphs (continued)

```
<?php
} }
?>
jg.paint( );
</script>
</body>
</html>
```

The code is straightforward. At the start of the script, the PHP uses some simple algebra to figure out the position of 10 points on the 400×400-pixel canvas. The HTML then creates a page with the appropriately sized div canvas. The library doesn't require a div canvas—it can draw directly onto the body of the page—but I find it more convenient this way.

The JavaScript section creates the drawing object. Then some PHP code creates a set of drawLine( ) calls. Finally the paint( ) method is called, which renders the graphics to the canvas.

Running the Hack

Copy the *index.php* file and the *wz_graphics.js* script to the server, and open *index.php* in your web browser. The result is shown in Figure 3-18.

On my Macintosh G4 PowerBook, it takes about four seconds to open the page. That's not the time it took to parse the code, but rather the time it took primarily to render the graphics. Obviously this is not acceptable for gaming applications, but for small graphs this is a real alternative.

See Also

- "Create Beautiful Graphics with SVG" [Hack #28]
- "Simplify Your Graphics with Objects" [Hack #29]
- "Split One Image into Multiple Images" [Hack #30]
- "Create Graphs with PHP" [Hack #31]

H A C K   #23   Build a Color Selector
Use HSB and DHTML to create a PHP color picker.

People like to be able to pick the colors of their site, or the colors that are applied to their data in a web application. This hack demonstrates a DHTML color picker that allows people to select a color from a grid of HSB color values.

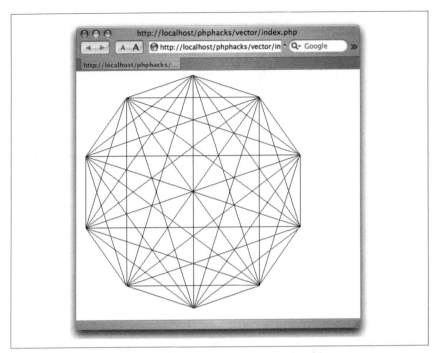

Figure 3-18. A simple geometric shape created with the graphics library

The Code

Example 3-18 is the code for *index.php*.

Example 3-18. Handling conversion between HSB and RGB values

```php
<?php
function hsb( $h, $s, $v )
{
  $r = $g = $b = 0;
  if ( $s == 0 )
  {
    $r = $g = $b = $v;
  }
  else
  {
    $h = $h / 60;
    $i = floor( $h );
    $f = $h - $i;
    $p = $v * ( 1 - $s );
    $q = $v * ( 1 - $s * $f );
    $t = $v * ( 1 - $s * ( 1 - $f ) );
    switch( $i ) {
      case 0: $r = $v; $g = $t; $b = $p; break;
```

Example 3-18. Handling conversion between HSB and RGB values (continued)

```
        case 1: $r = $q; $g = $v; $b = $p; break;
        case 2: $r = $p; $g = $v; $b = $t; break;
        case 3: $r = $p; $g = $q; $b = $v; break;
        case 4: $r = $t; $g = $p; $b = $v; break;
        default: $r = $v; $g = $p; $b = $q; break;
    }
  }
  return array( $r, $g, $b );
}

function hsb2hex( $h, $s, $b )
{
   list( $r, $g, $b ) = hsb( $h, $s, $b );
   return sprintf( "#%02x%02x%02x", $r, $g, $b );
}
?>
<html>
<head>
<script language="Javascript">
function mover( id )
{
  var obj = document.getElementById( id );
  obj.style.borderColor = "black";
}
function mout( id )
{
  var obj = document.getElementById( id );
  obj.style.borderColor = "white";
}
function selectColor( color )
{
  document.getElementById( "color" ).value = color;
}
function hover( color )
{
  document.getElementById( "hoverColor" ).innerHTML = color;
}
</script>
<style type="text/css">
body { font-family: arial, verdana, sans-serif; }
#color { font-family: courier; }
#hoverColor { font-family: courier; }
</style>
</head>
<body>
Color: <input id="color" type="text" size="8" />
<table cellspacing="10" cellpadding="0"><tr><td>
<table cellspacing="0" cellpadding="0">
<?php
$id = 1;
```

Example 3-18. Handling conversion between HSB and RGB values (continued)

```
for( $h = 0; $h < 360; $h += 18 ) { ?>
<tr>
<?php for( $b = 255; $b >= 0; $b -= 10 ) {
$color = hsb2hex( $h, $b / 255, $b );
 ?>
<td>
<div id="cp<?php echo( $id ); ?>" style="height:10px; width:10px; border:1px
solid white; background:<?php echo( $color ); ?>;" onmouseover="mover('cp<?php
echo( $id ); ?>');hover('<?php echo( $color ); ?>');" onmouseout="mout('cp<?php
echo( $id ); ?>')" onclick="selectColor('<?php echo( $color ); ?>');"></div>
</td>
<?php
$id += 1;
} ?>
</tr>
<?php } ?>
</table>
</td><td valign="top">
<div id="hoverColor"></div>
</td></tr></table>
</body>
</html>
```

The big trick here is the HSB( ) function, which converts into RGB a color value that is specified in the hue, saturation, and brightness (HSB) color space. I found this recipe on the Web and did the trivial conversion to PHP from C. The hsb2hex( ) call just wraps the HSB conversion and formats the output RGB value in the #RRGGBB format.

Running the Hack

Upload the *index.php* file to the site and navigate to it in your web browser. The web browser should look like Figure 3-19.

Just roll around the grid with your mouse, and the value on the right will show the RGB value of the color under the mouse. Clicking on a grid item will put the RGB value of the color into the Color text box at the top of the page.

> You can integrate this into your web application by wrapping the color <input> tag in a web form.

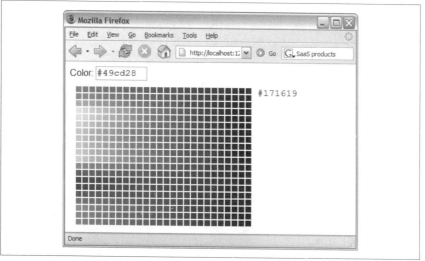

Figure 3-19. The DHTML color picker

Create Link Graphs

Use the font size of links to express the importance of certain terms.

Flikr (*http://flikr.com/*) is a site that allows users to upload images, and then tag those images with single-word terms. You can come back later and search the Flikr database using those terms, and you can see a link graph [Hack #91] that shows the most-used terms in a font larger than that used for the less frequently used terms.

In this hack, I show you how to create a link graph by analyzing an article from the Cable News Network web site (*http://cnn.com/*) for keywords. The words are counted, and the font size of each word is scaled relative to the number of counts.

The Code

Save the code in Example 3-19 as *linkgraph.php*.

Example 3-19. Link graph code

```php
<?php
$wordcounts = array();
```

Example 3-19. Link graph code (continued)

```
$words = split( " ", "CNN number Americans disapproving President Bush job
perance risen highest level presidency according CNN USA Today Gallup poll
released Monday According poll  percent respondents disapproved Bush performance
compared  percent approved margerror plus minus  percentage points  percent
figure highest disapproval rating recorded CNN USA Today Gallup poll Bush
president January approval percentage  percent matches low point late March
point gap between those disapproved approved largest recorded during Bush tenure
As Bush prepares address nation Tuesday defend Iraq policy just  percent those
responding poll approved handling war  percent disapproved Full story approval
rating Iraq unchanged poll late May disapproval figure marked increase
percentage points But poll found issues other Iraq war dragging down Bush numbers
Respondents expressed stronger disapproval handling economy energy policy health
care Social Security lone bright spot president poll handling terrorism which
scored  percent approval rating compared just  percent disapproved presidents
worst numbers latest poll came issue Social Security respondents disapproving
performance margmore percent  percent Bush made changing Social Security system
signature issue second term He  proposed creating voluntary government sponsored
personal retirement accounts workers  younger Under proposal workers could invest
portion their Social Security taxes range government selected funds exchange
guaranteed benefits retirement plan run instiff opposition Democrats accounts are
too risky undermine Social Security system Some Republicans are wary taking such
politically risky economy only  percent poll respondents approved Bush
performance compared  percent disapproved On energy policy percent approved
percent disapproved health care percent approved percent disapproved poll results
based interviews Friday Sunday American adults" );
foreach( $words as $word )
{
  $word = strtolower( $word );
  if ( strlen( $word ) > 0 )
  {
    if ( ! array_key_exists( $word, $wordcounts ) )
      $wordcounts[ $word ] = 0;
    $wordcounts[ $word ] += 1;
  }
}


$min = 1000000;
$max = -1000000;
foreach( array_keys( $wordcounts ) as $word )
{
  if ( $wordcounts[ $word ] > $max )
    $max = $wordcounts[ $word ];
  if ( $wordcounts[ $word ] < $min )
    $min = $wordcounts[ $word ];
}
$ratio = 18.0 / ( $max - $min );
?>
<html>
<head>
```

Example 3-19. Link graph code (continued)

```
<style type="text/css">
body { font-family: arial, verdana, sans-serif; }
.link { line-height: 20pt; }
</style>
</head>
<body>
<div style="width:600px;">
<?php
$wc = array_keys( $wordcounts );
sort( $wc );
foreach( $wc as $word )
{
$fs = (int)( 9 + ( $wordcounts[ $word ] * $ratio ) );
?>
<a class="link" href="http://en.wikipedia.org/wiki/<?php echo($word);
    ?>" style="font-size:<?php echo( $fs ); ?>pt;">
<?php echo( $word ); ?></a>  
<?php } ?>
</div>
</body>
</html>
```

I've hardcoded in the keywords of an article; you could just as easily fetch an article from the Web programmatically.

Running the Hack

Upload the file to your web server and navigate your browser to *linkgraph. php*. You should see something like Figure 3-20.

As you can see, terms like *percent, bush, approved, disapproved, security,* and *social* stand out from the rest because they were used more often. It's interesting that from these clues, it's clear that this CNN article was about recent polling numbers and Bush's second-term efforts on Social Security. The word *disapproved* is slightly larger, which could indicate something negative, or just a writing style in the article. Regardless, even on this simple data set, it's clear that some interesting features in the data appear clearly contrasted in a link graph.

See Also

• "Search Google by Link Graph" [Hack #91]

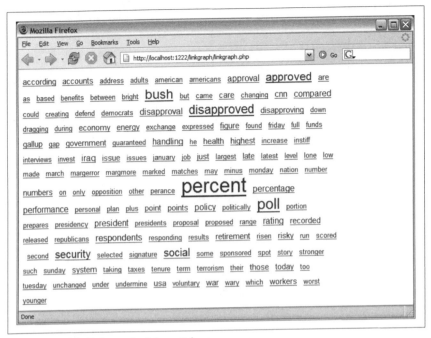

Figure 3-20. The link graph of the article

HACK #25   Create an Interactive Calendar

Use PHP's date functions to create an interactive HTML calendar.

A calendar is often the best way to represent event data. It's something that your users are familiar with, and it is a great way to show lots of information in a small space. Pop-up calendar controls are available on the Web, and open source event calendar systems that include all the event management functionality you need are also available, but, at least when I looked, no simple calendar display controls that could show events in a calendar format were available. This hack creates a simple HTML calendar with controls for navigating back and forth through the months of the year.

The Code

Save the code in Example 3-20 as *cal.php*.

Example 3-20. Making calendaring work using PHP

```
<html>
<head>
<style type="text/css">
.calendar {
  font-family: arial, verdana, sans serif;
}
```

Example 3-20. Making calendaring work using PHP (continued)

```css
.calendar td {
  border: 1px solid #eee;
}
.calendar-title {
  text-align: center;
  font-style: italic;
}
.calendar-day-title {
  text-align: center;
  font-size: small;
  background: #ccc;
  font-weight: bold;
}
.calendar-day, .calendar-outmonth-day {
  height: 60px;
  vertical-align: top;
  text-align: center;
  font-size: small;
  padding: 0px;
}
.calendar-day-number {
  text-align: right;
  background: #ddd;
}
.calendar-content {
  padding: 2px;
  font-size: x-small;
}
.calendar-outmonth-day {
  color: #666;
  font-style: italic;
  background: #ddd;
}
</style>
</head>
<body>
<?php
class Day
{
  function Day( $inmonth, $month, $day, $year )
  {
    $this->{'month'} = $month;
    $this->{'day'} = $day;
    $this->{'year'} = $year;
    $this->{'inmonth'} = $inmonth;
    $this->{'number'} = $number;
    $this->{'text'} = "";
  }
  function get_day( ) { return $this->{'day'}; }
  function get_month( ) { return $this->{'month'}; }
  function get_year( ) { return $this->{'year'}; }
```

Example 3-20. Making calendaring work using PHP (continued)

```php
    function get_inmonth() { return $this->{'inmonth'}; }
    function get_number() { return $this->{'number'}; }
    function get_text() { return $this->{'text'}; }
    function set_text( $text ) { $this->{'text'} = $text; }
}

function setCalendarText( $days, $m, $d, $y, $text )
{
  foreach( $days as $day )
  {
    if ( $day->get_day() == $d &&
         $day->get_month() == $m &&
       $day->get_year() == $y )
       $day->set_text( $text );
  }
}

function get_last_month( $month, $year )
{
  $lastmonth = $month - 1;
  $lastyear = $year;
  if ( $lastmonth < 0 ) { $lastmonth = 11; $lastyear -= 1; }
  return array( $lastmonth, $lastyear );
}

function get_next_month( $month, $year )
{
  $nextmonth = $month + 1;
  $nextyear = $year;
  if ( $nextmonth > 11 ) { $nextmonth = 0; $nextyear += 1; }
  return array( $nextmonth, $nextyear );
}

function makeCalendarDays( $month, $year )
{
  list( $nextmonth, $nextyear ) = get_next_month( $month, $year );
  list( $lastmonth, $lastyear ) = get_last_month( $month, $year );

  $dimlm = cal_days_in_month( CAL_GREGORIAN, $lastmonth, $lastyear );

  $jd = cal_to_jd( CAL_GREGORIAN, $month + 1, 1, $year );
  $day = jddayofweek( $jd );
  $dim = cal_days_in_month( CAL_GREGORIAN, $month + 1, $year );

  $days = array( );

  for( $d = 0; $d < $day; $d++ )
    $days []= new Day( 0, $lastmonth + 1, $dimlm - ( $day - $d ), $lastyear );

  for( $d = 1; $d <= $dim; $d++ )
    $days []= new Day( 1, $month + 1, $d, $year );
```

Example 3-20. Making calendaring work using PHP (continued)

```php
$left = ( ( floor( ( $day + $dim ) / 7 ) + 1 ) * 7 ) - ( $day + $dim );
for( $d = 0; $d < $left; $d++ )
  $days []= new Day( 0, $nextmonth + 1, $d+1, $nextyear );

  return $days;
}


$today = getdate( );

$year = $today['year'];
$month = $today['mon'] - 1;

if ( $_GET['year'] ) $year = $_GET['year'];
if ( $_GET['month'] ) $month = $_GET['month'];

$days = makeCalendarDays( $month, $year );

setCalendarText( &$days, $month + 1, 5, $year, "Meet<br/>Jim" );
setCalendarText( &$days, $month + 1, 10, $year, "Meet<br/>Sue" );

$months = array(
  "January", "February", "March", "April",
  "May", "June", "July", "August",
  "September", "October", "November", "December" );
$day_names = array( "Sun", "Mon", "Tue", "Wed", "Thu", "Fri", "Sat" );
?>
<div style="width:600px;">
<table class="calendar" width="100%" cellspacing="0" cellpadding="1">
<tr><td colspan="7" class="calendar-title" width="13%">
<?php
list( $nextmonth, $nextyear ) = get_next_month( $month, $year );
list( $lastmonth, $lastyear ) = get_last_month( $month, $year );
?>
<a href="cal.php?year=<?php echo($lastyear); ?>&month=<?php echo( $lastmonth );
?>">&lt;&lt;</a>
<?php echo( $months[$month] ); ?> <?php echo( $year ); ?>
<a href="cal.php?year=<?php echo($nextyear); ?>&month=<?php echo( $nextmonth );
?>">&gt;&gt;</a>
</td></tr>
<tr>
<?php foreach( $day_names as $day ) { ?>
<td class="calendar-day-title"><?php echo( $day ); ?></td>
<?php } ?>
</tr>
<?php
$p = 0;
foreach( $days as $d ) {
if ( $p == 0 ) echo ( "<tr>" );
$day_style = $d->get_inmonth( ) ? "calendar-day" : "calendar-outmonth-day";
?>
<td class="<?php echo( $day_style ); ?>" width="13%">
```

Example 3-20. Making calendaring work using PHP (continued)

```
<div class="calendar-day-number">
<?php echo( $d->get_day( ) ); ?>
</div>
<div class="calendar-content">
<?php echo( $d->get_text( ) ); ?>
</div>
</td>
<?php
$p += 1;
if ( $p == 7 ) $p = 0;
}
?>
</tr>
</table>
</div>
<body>
</html>
```

Figure 3-21 shows the members and methods of the Day class central to this hack. Each calendar box is actually a Day object that contains its date, the day number, the inmonth value that specifies whether this box is in or out of the current month, and the text of the item at that date.

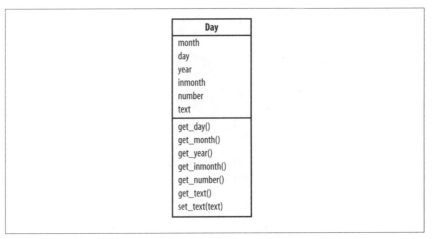

Figure 3-21. The Day class members and methods

It's the script's job to first create the array of Day objects using the makeCalendarDays( ) function, and then to display each object using the PHP and HTML logic at the end of the page.

Running the Hack

Upload the *cal.php* file to your web server and navigate to it in your web browser. You should see something like Figure 3-22.

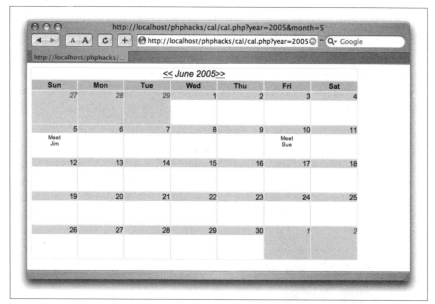

Figure 3-22. The calendar control as seen in Safari

 You can change the events that are shown in the calendar by tweaking the calls to setCalendarText( ), which will change the text that is displayed on any given day.

See Also

- "Build Dynamic HTML Graphs" [Hack #14]
- "Add Vector Graphics with PHP" [Hack #22]

 HACK #26 Create the Google Maps Scrolling Effect

Use a combination of small images, PHP, and JavaScript to allow users to use their mouse to scroll around an image that is much larger than their screen.

When Google Maps (*http://maps.google.com/*) was first introduced, the interactivity of the map blew people's socks off. On older mapping sites, you were presented with a map that had eight arrows positioned around it. When you clicked on an arrow, the page would be refreshed, and the map scrolled by one map unit in the direction you requested. Because of that page refresh, though, you had to reorient yourself to the new location.

Google Maps changed all that. With Google Maps [Hack #95], you simply click on the map and then drag it in whichever direction you want to go. The page never refreshes (although it occasionally redraws), and you never lose track of where you were.

I was so impressed with these maps that I decided to make my own version of the Google Maps code using PHP, some JavaScript, and the very large image created in "Split One Image into Multiple Images" [Hack #30].

Figure 3-23 shows the system's conceptual design. On the lefthand side of the illustration is the page, and on the righthand side is a set of images that contain the sliced-up larger image. The map *moves* within a view rectangle by repositioning the images within the view area. These images are drawn from the bank of images on the righthand side (all of the images are available instantly, without requiring a refresh).

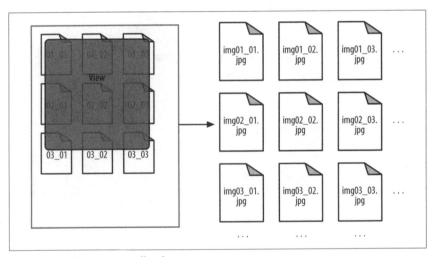

Figure 3-23. The image scroller design

The Code

The code you want is shown in Example 3-21; save it as *index.php*.

Example 3-21. Mimicking Google with a little PHP wizardry

```php
<?php
$rows = 5;
$cols = 5;
```

Example 3-21. Mimicking Google with a little PHP wizardry (continued)

```php
$maxrows = 40;
$maxcols = 40;
$width = 100;
$height = 100;
?>
<html>
<head>
<script language="Javascript">
var origimgs = [];
<?php
for( $col = 0; $col < $maxcols; $col++ ) {
?>
origimgs[ <?php echo($col); ?> ] = [];
<?php
for( $row = 0; $row < $maxrows; $row++ ) {
  $id = sprintf( "img%02d_%02d", $row, $col );
?>
origimgs[ <?php echo($col); ?> ][ <?php echo($row); ?> ] = "<?php echo( $id )
    ?>.jpg";
<?php
} }
?>

var imgs = [];

function startup( )
{
<?php
for( $col = 0; $col < $cols + 2; $col++ ) {
?>
imgs[<?php echo($col) ?>] = [];
<?php
for( $row = 0; $row < $rows + 2; $row++ ) {
  $id = sprintf( "img%02d_%02d", $row, $col );
?>
imgs[<?php echo($col) ?>][<?php echo($row) ?>] = document.getElementById( "<?php
echo( $id ); ?>" );
<?php
} }
?>
  position(0,0);
}

var scrollrows = <?php echo( $rows ); ?>;
var scrollcols = <?php echo( $cols ); ?>;
var width = <?php echo( $width ); ?>;
var height = <?php echo( $height ); ?>;
var maxrows = <?php echo( $maxrows ); ?>;
var maxcols = <?php echo( $maxcols ); ?>;
var xpos = 0;
var ypos = 0;
```

Example 3-21. Mimicking Google with a little PHP wizardry (continued)

```
document.onmousemove = function(e)
{
  if ( dragging )
  {

    xpos += e.pageX - dragx;
    ypos += e.pageY - dragy;

    if ( xpos < 0 )
      xpos = 0;
    if ( ypos < 0 )
      ypos = 0;

    position( xpos, ypos );

    dragx = e.pageX;
    dragy = e.pageY;
  }
}

document.onmousedown = function(e)
{
  dragging = true;
  dragx = e.pageX;
  dragy = e.pageY;
}

document.onmouseup = function(e)
{
  dragging = false;
}


function position( x, y )
{
  if ( x < 0 ) x = 0;
  if ( y < 0 ) y = 0;

  startcol = Math.floor( x / width );
  startrow = Math.floor( y / height );

  offsetx = Math.abs( x - ( startcol * width ) ) * -1;
  offsety = Math.abs( y - ( startrow * height ) ) * -1;

  viewheight = ( scrollrows + 1 ) * height;
  viewwidth = ( scrollcols + 1 ) * width;

  for( var row = 0; row < scrollrows + 2; row++)
  {
    for( var col = 0; col < scrollcols + 2; col++)
    {
```

Example 3-21. Mimicking Google with a little PHP wizardry (continued)

```
        var left = offsetx + ( col * width );
        var top = offsety + ( row * height );
        imgs[row][col].style.left = left;
        imgs[row][col].style.top = top;
        imgs[row][col].src = origimgs[startrow+row][startcol+col];

        remainderx = viewwidth - ( left + width );
        remaindery = viewheight - ( top + height );

        if ( remainderx > width )
          remainderx = width;
        if ( remainderx < 0 )
          remainderx = 0;
        if ( remaindery > height )
          remaindery = height;
        if ( remaindery < 0 )
          remaindery = 0;

        imgs[row][col].style.clip = "rect( 0px 0px "+remaindery+"px
"+remainderx+"px )";
      }
    }
}

var dragging = false;
var dragx = 0;
var dragy = 0;

</script>
</head>
<body onload="startup( );">
<?php
for( $row = 0; $row < $rows + 2; $row++ ) {
for( $col = 0; $col < $cols + 2; $col++ ) {
  $id = sprintf( "img%02d_%02d", $row, $col );
?>
<img src="" style="position:absolute;left:0;top:0;" id="<?php echo($id) ?>" />
<?php
} }
?>
</body>
</html>
```

In the first portion of this script, a two-dimensional JavaScript array of images is set up. The system will use this array when scrolling around the landscape.

Each image in the grid needs to be the same size; their width and height are defined by the width and height values at the start of the script. The rows and cols values define how big the viewport is, and the maxrows and maxcols values define how big the entire map is.

The last thing the PHP code does is to set up the viewport images in the body section of the page. These all start out absolutely positioned in the upper-lefthand corner of the page. Once the page is rendered, the rest of the magic is left to the browser.

The browser calls the startup( ) function in the onload event on the body tag. startup( ) also sets up the image array and calls the position( ) JavaScript function to update the map.

The position( ) function is where the fun really takes place. It calculates which images are required to draw the map, sets the src attribute of the image tags to the correct files, positions the images on the page, and sets the clipping values on each image so that you always get a square.

The onmousedown, onmousemove, and onmouseup functions are used to track the mouse as it's dragging across the page. These functions in turn call position( ) to redraw the map as the mouse moves.

Running the Hack

Upload the code and the source images to your PHP server, and browse to the *index.php* page. You should see something like Figure 3-24.

From here, click on the image and drag down and to the right. The image should scroll seamlessly—without a page refresh—to a point roughly similar to what you see in Figure 3-25.

Keep in mind that this isn't a single image that's being scrolled; it's a set of 1,600 smaller 100 × 100 images that are being swapped in and out of the document seamlessly. This is done using a 7 × 7 grid of image tags. These tags are positioned absolutely on the page with CSS. As the user scrolls around, the images are moved, and their clipping is adjusted. When the user exceeds the extent of the current images on the page, the image sources are updated with the required images.

This is a complex DHTML application, so there will be problems between browsers and even between different versions of the same browser. If you check out the Google Maps code, you will see that *a lot* of code does nothing but handle different browser capabilities. You should be under no illusion that the code provided here will work on all browsers; it was, however, tested on the Firefox browser. If you plan to roll something based on this code into production, you will need to test it on a variety of different popular browsers.

Figure 3-24. The starting position of the scroll plane

With an application like this, doing the work on the browser without a page refresh can be very cool and can result in a much better end-user experience. When pages refresh, the screen turns white, and then (slowly) updates with new content. This can be a very jarring experience, often causing a user to lose his frame of reference. If the page refresh can be avoided, the user will not experience this discontinuity of reference (and happy users make happy programmers, right?).

See Also

- "Build a DHTML Binary Clock" [Hack #19]
- "Build Dynamic HTML Graphs" [Hack #14]

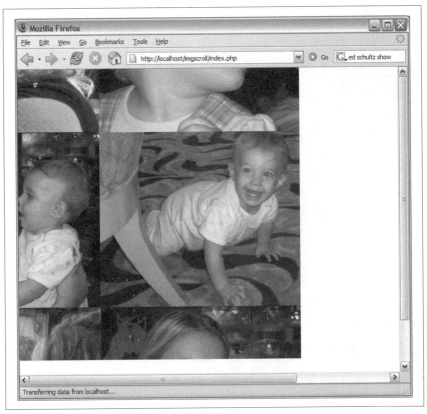

Figure 3-25. The image after having scrolled by dragging with the mouse

Graphics
Hacks 27–33

It's easy to think of PHP as nothing more than a scripting language for HTML. But PHP is far more than that, with support for databases, graphing, image manipulation, and a lot more. This chapter details hacks for building beautiful graphics with bitmaps, vector graphics, and even Dynamic HTML (DHTML). You'll even see how you can take photos from your iPhoto library and export them into HTML—all with that "HTML scripting language," PHP.

HACK #27 Create Thumbnail Images

Use the GD graphics API in PHP to create thumbnails of your images.

This simple hack takes a set of JPEG images in a directory named *pics* and creates thumbnails of them in a directory named *thumbs*. It also creates a file in the same directory as the script called *index.html*, which contains all of the thumbnails, as well as links to the original images.

The Code

Save the code in Example 4-1 as *mkthumbs.php*.

Example 4-1. A script for handling thumbnail creation

```
<?php
$dir = opendir( "pics" );
$pics = array();
while( $fname = readdir( $dir ) )
{
  if ( preg_match( "/[.]jpg$/", $fname ) )
    $pics []= $fname;
}
closedir( $dir );
```

Example 4-1. A script for handling thumbnail creation (continued)

```
foreach( $pics as $fname )
{
  $im = imagecreatefromjpeg( "pics/$fname" );
  $ox = imagesx( $im );
  $oy = imagesy( $im );

  $nx = 100;
  $ny = floor( $oy * ( 100 / $ox ) );

  $nm = imagecreatetruecolor( $nx, $ny );

  imagecopyresized( $nm, $im, 0, 0, 0, 0, $nx, $ny, $ox, $oy );

  print "Creating thumb for $fname\n";

  imagejpeg( $nm, "thumbs/$fname" );
}

print "Creating index.html\n";

ob_start( );
?>
<html>
<head><title>Thumbnails</title></head>
<body>
<table cellspacing="0" cellpadding="2" width="500">
<tr>
<?php
$index = 0;
foreach( $pics as $fname ) {
?>
<td valign="middle" align="center">
<a href="pics/<?php echo( $fname ); ?>"><img src="thumbs/<?php echo( $fname );
    ?>" border="0" /></a>
</td>
<?php
$index += 1;
if ( $index % 5 == 0 ) { echo( "</tr><tr>" ); }
}
?>
</tr>
</table>
</body>
</html>
<?php
$html = ob_get_clean( );
$fh = fopen( "index.html", "w" );
fwrite( $fh, $html );
fclose( $fh );
?>
```

Create Thumbnail Images

HACK
#27

The script starts by iterating through the pictures in the *pics* directory. It then creates a thumbnail for each image in the *thumbs* directory using the GD imagint functions.

To create a thumbnail, the file first has to be read in and handled by the `imagecreatefromjpeg( )` function. After that, the new (thumbnail) size is calculated, and a new image is created (using `imagecreatetruecolor( )`). The original file is then copied in and resized using the `imagecopyresized( )` function. Finally, the thumbnail is saved with `imagejpeg( )`.

The rest of the script creates an HTML index for the thumbnails by using the output buffering functions `ob_start( )` and `ob_get_clean( )`; both are used to store the HTML into a string. That string is then written into a file using `fopen( )`, `fwrite( )`, and `fclose( )`.

Running the Hack

Place the *mkthumbs.php* script into a directory, and then create two subdirectories: *pics* and *thumbs*. In the *pics* directory, place a bunch of JPEG images. Run the script with the PHP command-line interpreter:

```
% php mkthumbs.php
```

This creates all of the thumbnail images and the *index.html* file in Figure 4-1.

Figure 4-1. The HTML file showing the thumbnails

This type of script can be really handy for creating family photo albums. I wish more people would use some sort of thumbnail script. Far too often, I get a message from my friends or relatives pointing me to an Apache directory listing of images from their recent trip—all full size and with none of the blurry or bad shots removed! Lucky for all of us, PHP can turn those reels into a manageable set of thumbnails, and still preserve the originals.

See Also

- "Split One Image into Multiple Images" [Hack #30]
- "Properly Size Image Tags" [Hack #9]

  # Create Beautiful Graphics with SVG
#28 Use the SVG XML standard to create scalable graphics that render beautifully.

Adobe's Scalable Vector Graphics (SVG) XML standard provides a whole new level of graphics functionality to PHP web applications. In this hack, I'll use a web page and a simple PHP script to create a scalable vector graphic.

> It's important to note that before you can view an SVG image you must have an SVG viewer plug-in installed in your browser. Adobe hosts plug-in viewers on its web site, *http:// www.adobe.com/svg/main.html*. SVG is an open standard, which Adobe strongly supports. The SVG.org site (*http://svg. org/*) is an open community supporting the standard across multiple browsers and now even cell phones.

Figure 4-2 demonstrates how the SVG plug-in interacts with the *circle_svg. php* script, which generates the SVG. The SVG object embedded on the page requests the XML from the script, and the script then returns the XML with the SVG plug-in plots.

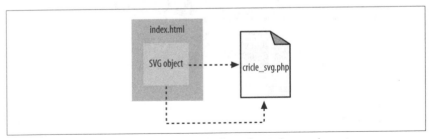

Figure 4-2. The SVG plug-in requesting SVG from the circle_svg.php script

The Code

Save the code in Example 4-2 as *index.html*.

Example 4-2. HTML for demonstration purposes

```
<html>
<body>
<embed width="400" height="400" src="circle_svg.php" name="printable"
    type="image/svg+xml" />
</body>
</html>
```

The work is done in *circle_svg.php*, shown in Example 4-3.

Example 4-3. Where the real SVG work occurs

```php
<?php
header( "content-type: text/xml" );

$points_count = 20;

$points = array( );
for( $p=0; $p<$points_count; $p++ )
{
        $d = ( 360 / $points_count ) * $p;
        $x = 50 + ( cos( deg2rad( $d ) ) * 50 );
        $y = 50 + ( sin( deg2rad( $d ) ) * 50 );
        $points []= array( 'x' => $x, 'y' => $y );
}

echo ("<?xml version=\"1.0\" standalone=\"no\"?>\n" );
?>
<!DOCTYPE svg PUBLIC "-//W3C//DTD SVG 1.0//EN"
  "http://www.w3.org/TR/SVG/DTD/svg10.dtd">
<svg style="shape-rendering:geometricPrecision;" viewBox="0 0 100 100" xml
    space="preserve" xmlns:xlink="http://www.w3.org/1999/xlink" xmlns="http://
    www.w3.org/2000/svg" preserveAspectRatio="xMidYMid meet">
<?php
foreach( $points as $start ) {
        $sx = $start['x'];
        $sy = $start['y'];
foreach( $points as $end ) {
        $ex = $end['x'];
        $ey = $end['y'];
?>
    <path fill-rule="nonzero" style="fill:#000000;stroke:#FF0000;stroke-width:0.2"
        d="M<?php echo( $sx." ".$sy ); ?> L<?php echo( $ex." ".$ey ); ?> Z"/>
<?php
} }
?>
</svg>
```

Running the Hack

Install both files on your server and browse to them in your SVG-enabled browser. In this case, I used Internet Explorer; the result is shown in Figure 4-3.

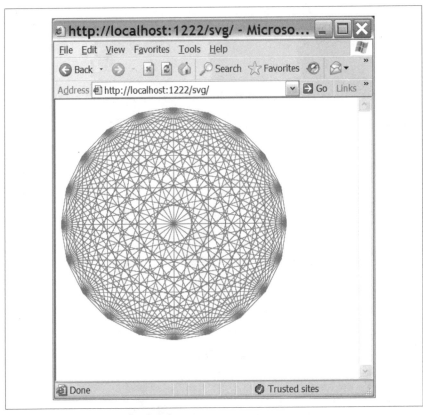

Figure 4-3. The circle rendered with SVG

The HTML page embedded an SVG object, which triggered a call to the *circle_svg.php* script to get the XML code for the SVG file. That PHP page creates an *SVG image*, which is simply a bunch of vectors connecting the various points on a circle, much like a Spirograph. Users can even click and zoom around the image if they want, and the image will scale appropriately since it's based on vector graphics.

SVG supports a huge range of graphics and effects features. It also supports animation and has JavaScript scriptability (I have used none of that here for the sake of simplicity). In fact, when you think about SVG in terms of functionality, you should probably consider it to be on the same level as Flash 8, with the notable exception that SVG uses XML files rather than compiled SWF files. The big downside with SVG, of course, is the install base, which at the time of this writing was far smaller than that of Flash.

If you are interested in using XML to build Flash movies, check out Laszlo (*http://www.laszlosystems.com/*), an open source XML compiler that builds SWF movies.

See Also

- "Simplify Your Graphics with Objects" [Hack #29]

HACK #29 Simplify Your Graphics with Objects

Use the object-oriented features of PHP to simplify your graphics using layering, object-oriented drawing, and viewport scaling.

PHP's support for graphics is great. But when you try to build a complex visualization, PHP becomes difficult to use for several reasons. First, the drawing order is really important. Things that you draw first will be covered by the stuff that you draw later (and there's no good way to get around that limitation). This means that you have to sequence your code based on the drawing order, even when it's difficult to do so programmatically.

Another problem is scaling. To draw into an image, you have to know how big the image is and how to scale your drawing. That means passing around a lot of information about the drawing context. Add that to the layering issues, and PHP image code becomes a real mess.

Lucky for all of us hackers who *aren't* graphics pros, all of these problems have been solved via graphics libraries like PHP's GD library. In this hack, I build a simple object API for graphics that manages drawing order through z buffering, and handles scaling by creating a viewport.

The Code

Save the code in Example 4-4 as *layers.php*.

Example 4-4. Defining several classes used to layer graphics

```php
<?php
class GraphicSpace
{
    var $image;
    var $colors;

    var $xoffset;
    var $yoffset;
```

Example 4-4. Defining several classes used to layer graphics (continued)

```
var $xscale;
var $yscale;

function GraphicSpace( )
{
  $this->colors = array( );
}

function get_image( ) { return $this->image; }
function set_image( $im )
{
  $this->image = $im;
}

function get_color( $id ) { return $this->colors[ $id ]; }
function set_color( $id, $color ) { $this->colors[ $id ] = $color; }

function set_viewport( $left, $top, $right, $bottom )
{
  $this->xoffset = $left;
  $this->yoffset = $top;

  $this->xscale = imagesx( $this->image ) / ( $right - $left );
  $this->yscale = imagesy( $this->image ) / ( $bottom - $top );
}

function transform_x( $x ) { return ( $x - $this->xoffset ) * $this->xscale; }
function transform_y( $y ) { return ( $y - $this->yoffset ) * $this->yscale; }
function scale_x( $x ) { return $x * $this->xscale; }
function scale_y( $y ) { return $y * $this->yscale; }
}

class RenderItem
{
  var $left;
  var $right;
  var $top;
  var $bottom;
  var $color;
  var $z;

  function RenderItem( $left, $top, $right, $bottom, $color, $z )
  {
    $this->left = $left;
    $this->right = $right;
    $this->top = $top;
    $this->bottom = $bottom;
    $this->color = $color;
    $this->z = $z;
  }
```

Example 4-4. Defining several classes used to layer graphics (continued)

```php
  function get_left( ) { return $this->left; }
  function get_right( ) { return $this->right; }
  function get_top( ) { return $this->top; }
  function get_bottom( ) { return $this->bottom; }
  function get_z( ) { return $this->z; }

  function render( $gs ) { }
  function transform( $x, $y ) { }
}

class Line extends RenderItem
{
  var $sx;
  var $sy;
  var $ex;
  var $ey;
  var $thickness;

  function Line( $sx, $sy, $ex, $ey, $color, $z, $thickness )
  {
    $this->RenderItem( min( $sx, $ex ), min( $sy, $ey ),
          max( $sx, $ex ), max( $sy, $ey ),
          $color, $z );
    $this->sx = $sx;
    $this->sy = $sy;
    $this->ex = $ex;
    $this->ey = $ey;
    $this->thickness = $thickness;
  }
  function render( $gs )
  {
    if ( $this->thickness > 1 )
      imagesetthickness( $gs->get_image( ), $this->thickness );
    $this->drawline( $gs->get_image( ),
      $gs->transform_x( $this->sx ),
      $gs->transform_y( $this->sy ),
      $gs->transform_x( $this->ex ),
      $gs->transform_y( $this->ey ),
      $gs->get_color( $this->color ) );
    if ( $this->thickness > 1 )
      imagesetthickness( $gs->get_image( ), 1 );
  }
  function drawline( $im, $sx, $sy, $ex, $ey, $color )
  {
    imageline( $im, $sx, $sy, $ex, $ey, $color );
  }
}

class DashedLine extends Line
{
```

Example 4-4. Defining several classes used to layer graphics (continued)

```
  function drawline( $im, $sx, $sy, $ex, $ey, $color )
  {
    imagedashedline( $im, $sx, $sy, $ex, $ey, $color );
  }
}

class Ball extends RenderItem
{
  var $text;

  function Ball( $x, $y, $size, $color, $text, $z )
  {
    $width = $size / 2;
    if ( $text )
      $width += 20;
    $this->RenderItem( $x, $y,
          $x + $width, $y + ( $size / 2 ),
          $color, $z );
    $this->text = $text;
    $this->size = $size;
  }

  function render( $gs )
  {
    imagefilledellipse( $gs->get_image( ),
      $gs->transform_x( $this->left ),
      $gs->transform_y( $this->top ),
      $gs->scale_x( $this->size ),
      $gs->scale_x( $this->size ),
      $gs->get_color( $this->color ) );
    if ( strlen( $this->text ) )
      imagestring($gs->get_image( ), 0,
        $gs->transform_x( $this->left ) + 7,
        $gs->transform_y( $this->top )-5, $this->text,
        $gs->get_color( $this->color ) );
  }
}

function zsort( $a, $b )
{
  if ( $a->get_z( ) == $b->get_z( ) )
    return 0;
  return ( $a->get_z( ) > $b->get_z( ) ) ? 1 : -1;
}

class RenderQueue
{
  var $items;

  function RenderQueue( ) { $this->items = array( ); }
  function add( $item ) { $this->items [] = $item; }
```

Example 4-4. Defining several classes used to layer graphics (continued)

```
function render( $gs )
{
  usort( &$this->items, "zsort" );
  foreach( $this->items as $item ) { $item->render( $gs ); }
}
function get_size()
{
  $minx = 1000; $maxx = -1000;
  $miny = 1000; $maxy = -1000;
  foreach( $this->items as $item )
  {
    if ( $item->get_left() < $minx )
      $minx = $item->get_left();
    if ( $item->get_right() > $maxx )
      $maxx = $item->get_right();
    if ( $item->get_top() < $miny )
      $miny = $item->get_top();
    if ( $item->get_bottom() > $maxy )
      $maxy = $item->get_bottom();
  }
  return array( left => $minx, top => $miny, right => $maxx, bottom => $maxy );
}
}

$width = 400;
$height = 400;

function calcpoint( $d, $r )
{
  $x = cos( deg2rad( $d ) ) * $r;
  $y = sin( deg2rad( $d ) ) * $r;
  return array( $x, $y );
}

$render_queue = new RenderQueue();

$ox = null;
$oy = null;

for( $d = 0; $d < 380; $d += 10 )
{
  list( $x, $y ) = calcpoint( $d, 10 );

  $render_queue->add( new Ball( $x, $y, 1, "line", "", 10 ) );
  $render_queue->add( new Line( 0, 0, $x, $y, "red", 1, 1 ) );

  if ( $ox != null && $oy != null )
  {
    $render_queue->add( new Line( $ox, $oy, $x, $y, "red", 1, 1 ) );
  }
  $ox = $x;
```

Example 4-4. Defining several classes used to layer graphics (continued)

```
  $oy = $y;
}

$gsize = $render_queue->get_size( );

$fudgex = ( $gsize['right'] - $gsize['left'] ) * 0.1;
$gsize['left'] -= $fudgex;
$gsize['right'] += $fudgex;
$fudgey = ( $gsize['bottom'] - $gsize['top'] ) * 0.1;
$gsize['top'] -= $fudgey;
$gsize['bottom'] += $fudgey;

print_r( $gsize );

$im = imagecreatetruecolor( $width, $height );
imageantialias( $im, true );
$bg = imagecolorallocate($im, 255, 255, 255);
imagefilledrectangle( $im, 0, 0, $width, $height, $bg );

$gs = new graphicspace( );
$gs->set_image( $im );
$gs->set_color( 'back', $bg );
$gs->set_color( 'line', imagecolorallocate($im, 96, 96, 96) );
$gs->set_color( 'red', imagecolorallocate($im, 255, 0, 0) );
$gs->set_viewport( $gsize['left'], $gsize['top'], $gsize['right'],
$gsize['bottom'] );

$render_queue->render( $gs );

imagepng( $im, "test.png" );
imagedestroy( $im );
?>
```

Figure 4-4 shows the layout of the classes in this script. RenderQueue refers to two objects: an array of RenderItems, and a GraphicSpace that holds the image and the transformation information. The derived classes of RenderItem create the different types of shapes: lines, balls, and dashed lines. To add more items, just add more child classes of RenderItem.

Each RenderItem has a z level associated with it. Items that have a lower z level (or z value) will be rendered behind items that have a larger z value. This allows you to create objects in any order you like, assign them z values, and know that they will be sorted and rendered in the proper order.

For the coordinate system, I used a mechanism called a *viewport*. The viewport is a virtual graphics space. The coordinates can be anything you like, ranging from 0 to 1 or from 0 to 1 billion. The system automatically scales the graphics to the size of the image.

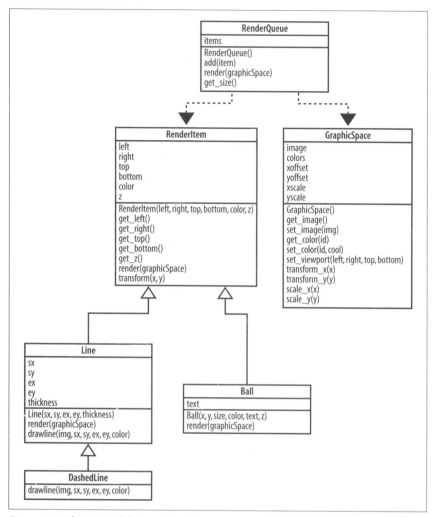

Figure 4-4. The UML of the graphics objects

Starting with this simple object API, you can create much more complex graphics far more easily than if you used the PHP graphics API directly. The object code is also far easier to understand and maintain.

Running the Hack

Use the PHP command-line interpreter to run the *layers.php* script:

```
% php layers.php
Array
(
```

```
        [left] => -12.05
        [top] => -12.05
        [right] => 12.55
        [bottom] => 12.55
    )
```

Then use your browser to look at the resulting *test.png* file, shown in Figure 4-5.

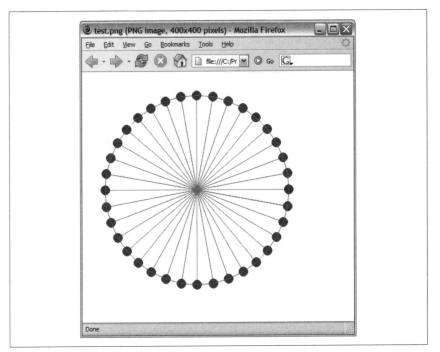

Figure 4-5. A circle built with graphics objects

There are three sets of objects in this graph: the lines that go from the center to the balls, the gray balls, and the lines that go between the balls along the perimeter. The lines radiating out from the center are at a z level of 1. The balls are at a z level of 10. And the lines that run along the perimeter are at a z level of 20.

To change the z order of the perimeter lines, you can just change the z value from, for example, 20 to 1:

```
if ( $ox != null && $oy != null )
{
    $render_queue->add( new Line( $ox, $oy, $x, $y, "red", 1, 1 ) );
}
```

Now if you rerun the script and look at the results in the browser, you'll see that the balls are on top of the lines (see Figure 4-6), whereas before they were underneath them.

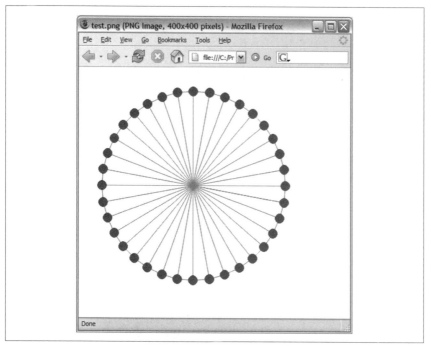

Figure 4-6. Dropping the connectors behind the gray balls

Now the perimeter lines have dropped behind the gray balls because of the lower z order.

See Also

- "Create Beautiful Graphics with SVG" **[Hack #28]**
- "Create Modular Interfaces" **[Hack #51]**

Split One Image into Multiple Images

Use PHP's graphics engine to break a single large image into multiple small images.

Sometimes it's handy to have a group of smaller images that make up a single image rather than the one small image. An example is "Create the Google Maps Scrolling Effect" **[Hack #26]**, which scrolls many smaller images around the screen seamlessly, creating the effect of moving around one large image. To accomplish that trick, though, you might have to break up a large image first; this hack does just that.

The Code

Save the code in Example 4-5 as *imgsplit.php*.

Example 4-5. Breaking up images

```php
<?php
$width = 100;
$height = 100;

$source = @imagecreatefromjpeg( "source.jpg" );
$source_width = imagesx( $source );
$source_height = imagesy( $source );

for( $col = 0; $col < $source_width / $width; $col++)
{
        for( $row = 0; $row < $source_height / $height; $row++)
        {
                $fn = sprintf( "img%02d_%02d.jpg", $col, $row );

                echo( "$fn\n" );

                $im = @imagecreatetruecolor( $width, $height );
                imagecopyresized( $im, $source, 0, 0,
                        $col * $width, $row * $height, $width, $height,
                        $width, $height );
                imagejpeg( $im, $fn );
                imagedestroy( $im );
        }
}
?>
```

This is the inverse of the code in Example 4-6 in the upcoming "Hacking the Hack" section of this hack. It creates—from a single big image—lots of smaller images and puts them in a grid. It's a useful match for the Google Maps scrolling effect hack in "Create the Google Maps Scrolling Effect" [Hack #26].

The constants at the top of the file define how big the output images should be. The script reads in the source image and figures out how big it is; then it uses a set of nested for loops to iterate around all of the grid items, creating an image, copying the section from the original image, and then saving the image.

Running the Hack

This code is run on the command line using PHP's command-line interpreter:

```
% php imgsplit.php
img00_00.jpg
img01_00.jpg
...
```

The script looks for a file called *source.jpg* and breaks it up into a set of files named *img<col>_<row>.jpg*, where the col and row items are padded with zeroes. So the image in column zero, row zero would be named *img00_00.jpg*. Each created image is 100×100 pixels. Those values are set with the $width and $height values at the top of the script.

Hacking the Hack

Instead of splitting images, how about merging images? The next script creates a single large image from a collage of smaller images. You can use this code as the foundation of a scrolling panorama, as shown in "Create the Google Maps Scrolling Effect" **[Hack #26]**, or simply as a collage of multiple images suitable for a background or desktop image.

Save the code shown in Example 4-6 as *imgmerge.php*.

Example 4-6. Merging images, yet another task PHP can handle easily

```php
<?php
$targetsize_x = 4000;
$targetsize_y = 4000;
$outfile = "merged.jpg";
$quality = 100;

$im = @imagecreatetruecolor( $targetsize_x, $targetsize_y );

$sources = array();
$dh = opendir( "." );
while (($file = readdir($dh)) !== false)
{
        if ( preg_match( "/[.]jpg$/", $file ) &&
            $file != $outfile )
        {
                $sources []= imagecreatefromjpeg( $file );
        }
}

$x = 0;
$y = 0;
$index = 0;
```

Example 4-6. Merging images, yet another task PHP can handle easily (continued)

```
while( true )
{
        $width = imagesx( $sources[ $index ] );
        $height = imagesy( $sources[ $index ] );

        imagecopy( $im, $sources[ $index ],
                $x, $y, 0, 0, $width, $height );

        $x += $width;
        if ( $x >= $targetsize_x )
        {
                $x = 0;
                $y += $height;
                if ( $y >= $targetsize_y )
                        break;
        }

        $index += 1;
        if ( $index >= count( $sources ) )
                $index = 0;
}

imagejpeg( $im, $outfile, $quality );

imagedestroy( $im );
?>
```

This is a fairly simple script that takes image files from a directory and stores them into an array of sources. Then the script creates a huge image, into which it copies the original source images. The while loop wraps around the large image, creating rows of smaller images, until it gets to the bottom of the output image. At the end of the script, the large composite image is saved as a JPEG using imagejpeg( ).

This code is run from the command line in a directory full of JPEG images.

The input files must end with the *.jpg* extension, and all of the input images must be the same size. Otherwise, the composite will have lots of "empty" spaces in it (if it doesn't crash altogether).

An example image is shown in Figure 4-7.

The command is run in this way:

```
% php imgmerge.php
```

Figure 4-7. One of the sample source images

The output file is created in the same directory as the source images, and it is named *merged.jpg*. With some sample images of my wife (Lori) and my daughter (Megan), I created the composite shown in Figure 4-8.

Figure 4-8. The completed graphic, shown scaled down in Firefox

Even better—and nothing more than a happy accident—Firefox does something pretty cool here. It scales the image down to fit it within the browser. If you hold the mouse over the image, the cursor will turn into a magnifying glass, and you can zoom in on the composite to see it at 100% magnification.

You can adjust the quality of the merged image by tweaking the $quality value. This value goes from 0 to 100, with 100 being the best quality. $targetsize_x and $targetsize_y define the desired width and height of the merged image, and the $outfile variable specifies the filename of the merged image.

See Also

- "Create the Google Maps Scrolling Effect" [Hack #26]

HACK #31   Create Graphs with PHP

Use PHP's image toolkit to create dynamic graphs from your data.

PHP has excellent dynamic imaging capabilities. You can use these to overlay images [Hack #32], or to create whole new images on the fly. This hack uses the image toolkit to do some simple scientific graphing of sine waves (proving that PHP is great for math as well as for imaging).

The Code

Save the code in Example 4-7 as *graph.php*.

Example 4-7. Graphing a mathematical function

```
<?
$width = 400;
$height = 300;

$data = array( );
for( $i = 0; $i < 500; $i++ )
{
        $data []= sin( deg2rad( ( $i / 500 ) * 360 ) );
}

$xstart = $width/10;
$ystart = $height - ($height/10);

$image = imagecreate($width, $height);
$back = imagecolorallocate($image, 255, 255, 255);
$border = imagecolorallocate($image, 64, 64, 64);

imageline( $image, $xstart, 0, $xstart, $ystart, $border );
```

Example 4-7. Graphing a mathematical function (continued)

```
imageline( $image, $xstart, $ystart, $width, $ystart, $border );

imagestring( $image, 2, $xstart-20, $ystart-10, "1", $border );
imagestring( $image, 2, $xstart-20, 0, "-1", $border );
imagestring( $image, 2, $xstart, $ystart+5, "0", $border );
imagestring( $image, 2, $width-20, $ystart+5, "360", $border );

$datatop = 1;
$databottom = -1;

$oldx = 0;
$oldy = 0;
$datacount = count( $data );
$xscale = ( $width - $xstart ) / $datacount;
$yscale = $ystart / ( $datatop - $databottom );
$midline = $ystart / 2;
for( $i = 0; $i < $datacount; $i++ )
{
        $x = $xstart + ( $i * $xscale );
        $y = $midline - ( $data[$i] * $yscale );
        if ( $i > 0 )
        {
                imageline( $image, $oldx, $oldy, $x, $y, $border );
        }
        $oldx = $x;
        $oldy = $y;
}

header("Content-type: image/png");
imagepng($image);
imagedestroy($image);
?>
```

The script starts with some constants that define the size of the output image. Then the new image is created, and colors are allocated. Next, the border of the graph is drawn, along with the axis values using imagestring( ). With the axis values in place, the script draws the mathematical data using a for loop to iterate over each data point and uses the imageline( ) function to draw a line between the current position and the previous position.

Because this script is intended for use on the Web, the content type of the output needs to be set properly to image/png, which tells browsers to expect a PNG graphic. Many browsers will automatically detect image content, but it's best to set the content type properly. With that done, the image is output using the imagepng( ) function.

It's best to leave the content-type header for the end of the script; that way, if the script fails, you will see the error results in the browser. If you set the header too early, the browser will get the content type and attempt to interpret the PHP error message as a PNG image.

Running the Hack

Put the files up on the PHP server and navigate to the *graph.php* page. You should see something like Figure 4-9.

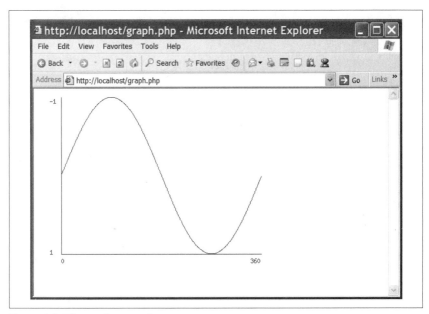

Figure 4-9. The resulting graph

If you don't see the graph in Figure 4-9, it's likely that there is a server configuration problem. PHP is very flexible about how it's installed, and the image library doesn't need to be installed for PHP (in general) to run properly; but without the graphing libraries (obviously), you won't get a graphical PNG (you should see an error message).

See Also

- "Create Beautiful Graphics with SVG" [Hack #28]
- "Build Dynamic HTML Graphs" [Hack #14]
- "Build Lightweight HTML Graphs" [Hack #8]

Create Image Overlays

Using PHP's graphics capabilities to build a single image from several source images.

One common graphics scenario is to put some overlay images at specific data-driven locations, stacking those overlays on top of another base graphic. This hack starts with the map in Figure 4-10 as the base image.

Figure 4-10. The map graphic

Then it places the star graphic in Figure 4-11 onto the map, over the city of San Francisco, as it might appear if you were looking up a location by city or Zip code.

Figure 4-11. The star graphic

The Code

Save the (rather simple) code in Example 4-8 as *graphic.php*.

Example 4-8. PHP making overlaying graphics almost trivial

```php
<?php
$map = imagecreatefrompng("map.png");
$star = imagecreatefromgif("star.gif");
imagecopy( $map, $star, 5, 180, 0, 0, imagesx( $star ), imagesy( $star ) );
header("Content-type: image/png");
imagepng($map);
?>
```

The code starts by reading in the map and star graphics. Then it creates a new image, superimposing the star onto the map using the imagecopy( ) function. The new version of the map—which at this point exists only in memory—is then output to the browser using the imagepng( ) function.

Running the Hack

After uploading the PHP script and the images to your server, navigate your browser to *graphic.php*. There you will see an image like that shown in Figure 4-12.

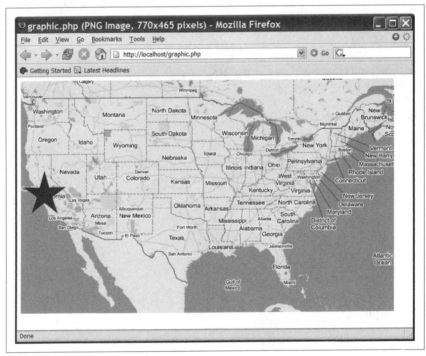

Figure 4-12. The star graphic overlaid on the map graphic

Hacking the Hack

The star on the map is cool, but it's a bit big. Instead of sitting on top of San Francisco, it ends up sitting on top of most of California. Let's scale it down a little. Save the code in Example 4-9 as *graphic2.php*.

Example 4-9. A little bit of scaling

```
<?
$map = imagecreatefrompng("map.png");
$star = imagecreatefromgif("star.gif");
imagecopyresized( $map, $star, 25, 205, 0, 0,
    imagesx( $star )/5, imagesy( $star )/5,
    imagesx( $star ), imagesy( $star ) );
header("Content-type: image/png");
imagepng($map);
?>
```

Then navigate to the new script in your web browser; you should see the graphic shown in Figure 4-13.

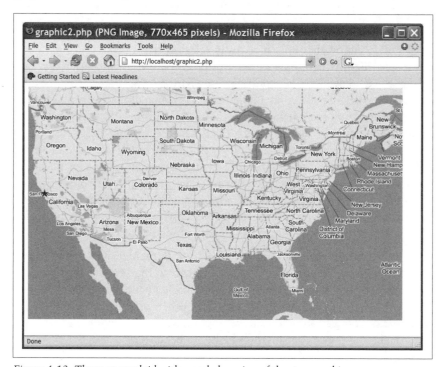

Figure 4-13. The map overlaid with a scaled version of the star graphic

This new version of the script uses the `imagecopyresized()` function to change the size of the star image as it's copied onto the map. The script divides the star's width and height by 5, scaling the image to 20% of its original size.

> Because the star is a pixilated graphic, if you make the image larger than the original, you'll start to see some jagged edges.

See Also

- "Create Thumbnail Images" [Hack #27]
- "Access Your iPhoto Pictures with PHP" [Hack #33]
- "Split One Image into Multiple Images" [Hack #30]

HACK
#33   Access Your iPhoto Pictures with PHP
Use PHP's XML capabilities to parse through iPhoto's picture database.

Apple is a company known for producing innovative and easy-to-use products. Following on that line, it recently released the iLife suite (*http://www. apple.com/ilife/*), which makes it easy to produce and organize rich media. I was a bit dismayed by my options for sharing my photos from iPhoto, though. In particular, after having imported my digital photos from my camera and organizing them using iPhoto, I wanted to show off these pictures to family and friends. I didn't want to sign up for hosting, open an account with a photo printing service, wait for hundreds of files to upload somewhere, export photos to a smaller size, or reorganize all of my images in some other program after having already done the work in iPhoto. I wanted them available to everybody—right now—and I didn't want to have to lift a finger to make it so. I'd already done plenty of work by taking the actual photos, not to mention organizing and captioning them!

This is what got me working on myPhoto (*http://agent0068.dyndns.org/ ~mike/projects/myPhoto*). One Mac OS X feature that most users often do not notice is the built-in web server; Mac OS X includes both Apache and PHP, and both are itching to be enabled. When you combine this and a broadband connection with all of the information readily available in iPhoto, sharing photos becomes (as it should be) a snap.

If your PHP project requires a photo gallery component, it might be tempting to place the burden on users to upload, caption, and organize all of their photos into your system. However, if users have already done the work in iPhoto, do the rest for them! Armed with a simple XML parser, it's possible to extract all of the meaningful data from iPhoto and reformat it into a simpler format that's more appropriate and convenient for use with PHP.

A Look Behind the Scenes: iPhoto Data

The first logical step is to get up close and personal with iPhoto so that you know what data is easily available.

I am basing this discussion on iPhoto Version 5.x, the most current version of iPhoto available as of this writing. With a few small tweaks here or there, though, it's trivial to apply these same concepts to other versions of iPhoto—something I've been doing since iPhoto 2.0.

Figure 4-14 shows a small selection from my iPhoto album.

Figure 4-14. iPhoto showing pictures from my wedding

A quick look in ~/*Pictures/iPhoto Library/* shows almost everything we could ever need from iPhoto:

Directories broken down by date

For instance, ~/*Pictures/iPhoto Library/2005/07/02/* contains photos from July 2, 2005. The image files in this directory are the actual full-size photos, but they contain all of the edits the user made from within iPhoto (i.e., rotations, color corrections, etc.). It also contains two other subdirectories: *Thumbs*, which contains 240×180 thumbnails corresponding to each image, and *Originals*, which contains the original, unmodified versions of the images (only if the user has performed any edits in iPhoto). Furthermore, in nearly all cases, these photos are in JPEG format, which is perfect for the Web.

> One notable exception: if the user takes photos in RAW format (available on higher-end cameras), the *Originals* directory contains the RAW files and all other images are JPEG representations.

AlbumData.xml

This XML document contains all of the really interesting (and uninteresting) data surrounding these photos: file paths for a given photo, captions, ratings, modification dates, etc. This file also contains information about groups of photos—also called *albums*—as well as user-defined keywords. Some version information and meta-information is included as well, but that's not terribly helpful.

So now we need to make some sense of that *AlbumData.xml* file. First off, it's not just any XML file; it's an Apple Property List. This means that a limited set of XML tags is being used to represent common programmatic data structures like strings, integers, arrays, and dictionaries (also known as *associative arrays* in some languages). Therefore, for the interesting structures within this file, we should look at some sample content, since the XML tags themselves aren't terribly descriptive. Rather, the tagged content is where the meaty structure is. I've cut some pieces out for the sake of brevity, but the more important parts of the file are here.

The beginning of the file looks something like this—not terribly interesting:

```
<?xml version="1.0" encoding="UTF-8"?>
<plist version="1.0">
<dict>
  <key>Application Version</key>
  <string>5.0.4 (263)</string>
  <key>Archive Path</key>
    <string>/Users/mike/Sites/myPhoto/iPhoto Library</string>
```

But further down is a listing of all the photos in the dictionary keyed by unique identifiers for each photo. In the following example, you can see that we're looking at an individual photo with a unique ID of 5. Furthermore, it's an image (rather than, say, a video) which has a caption of "No more pictures, please" as well as an optional keyword associated with it (the keyword's unique keyword ID is 2):

```
<key>Master Image List</key>
<dict>
<key>5</key>
<dict>
  <key>MediaType</key>
  <string>Image</string>
  <key>Caption</key>
  <string>No more pictures, please</string>
  <key>Aspect Ratio</key>
  <real>0.750000</real>
  <key>Rating</key>
  <integer>0</integer>
  <key>DateAsTimerInterval</key>
  <real>62050875.000000</real>
  <key>ImagePath</key>
  <string>/Users/mike/Sites/myPhoto/iPhoto Library/2002/12/19/DSC00107.JPG</string>
  <key>OriginalPath</key>
  <string>/Users/mike/Sites/myPhoto/iPhoto Library/2002/12/19/Originals/DSC00107.JPG</string>
  <key>ThumbPath</key>
  <string>/Users/mike/Sites/myPhoto/iPhoto Library/2002/12/19/Thumbs/5.jpg</string>
  <key>Keywords</key>
  <array>
    <string>2</string>
  </array>
</dict>
<key>6</key>
...and so on...
</dict>
```

Another section of this file (shown in the next fragment of XML) lists all user-defined groups of photos, known in iPhoto as *albums*. These are stored in a user-defined order in an array (unlike the Master Image List, which is unordered and stored by keys). This includes all kinds of albums—normal albums, smart albums, folders, slideshow albums, book albums, etc. Various album attributes are described—a unique ID, a name, an ordered list of photo IDs for photos contained in the album, an indicator if the album is the "master" album (each photo library should have only one master album), the parent album ID if this album is in a "folder album," etc.:

```
<key>List of Albums</key>
<array>
<dict>
  <key>AlbumId</key>
  <integer>2</integer>
  <key>AlbumName</key>
  <string>Vacation to somewhere</string>
  <key>KeyList</key>
  <array>
    <string>4425</string>
    <string>4423</string>
    <string>4421</string>
    <string>4419</string>
  </array>
  <key>Master</key>
  <true/>
  <key>PhotoCount</key>
  <integer>2868</integer>
  <key>Parent</key>
  <integer>2196</integer>
</dict>
<dict>
...and so on...
</dict>
</array>
```

Also worth noting is that there is a structure whose key is "List of Rolls," which is structurally identical to "List of Albums." This automatically-generated list groups photos together each time they are imported into iPhoto, treating the group as if it were one "roll" of film.

Finally, the last major section of the file is the list of keywords, a dictionary keyed by IDs. These are user-defined keywords that you can use to tag multiple photos, instead of manually captioning each photo with the same word. This consists of ID/keyword pairs; in this example, the ID is 1 and the keyword is _Favorite_:

```
<key>List of Keywords</key>
<dict>
<key>1</key>
<string>_Favorite_</string>
<key>2</key>
<string>...and so on...
</dict>
```

Keep in mind that in older versions of iPhoto, the file format is slightly different; be sure you know and understand this file for the versions of iPhoto you plan on being compatible with. Minor details do change periodically, and they can cripple your parsing code if you don't anticipate or account for them.

The Code

Save the code in Example 4-10 as *iphoto_parse.php*.

Example 4-10. Handling iPhoto XML parsing

```php
<?php
//$curTag denotes the current tag that we're looking at in string-stack form
//$curKey denotes the current tagged attribute so that we have some recollection
//of what the last seen attribute was.
//   i.e. $curKey="AlbumName" for <key>AlbumName</key>
//$data denotes the element between tags.
//   i.e. $data="Library" for <string>Library</string>
//When reading code, note that $curKey is not necessarily equal to $data.

$curTag="";
$curKey="";
$readingAlbums=false;
$firstTimeAlbum=true;
$firstTimeAlbumEntry=true;

$readingImages=false;
$firstTimeImage=true;
$firstTimeImageEntry=true;
$curID=0;


$masterImageList=array( );

class Photo
{
  var $Caption;
  var $Date;
  var $ImagePath;
  var $ThumbPath;
}

function newPhoto($capt, $dat, $imgPath, $thumb) {
  $aPhoto=new Photo( );
  $aPhoto->Caption=$capt;
  $aPhoto->Date=$dat;
  $aPhoto->ImagePath=$imgPath;
  $aPhoto->ThumbPath=$thumb;
  return $aPhoto;
}
```

Example 4-10. Handling iPhoto XML parsing (continued)

```php
//this function is called on opening tags
function startElement($parser, $name, $attrs)
{
  global $curTag;
  $curTag .= "^$name";
}


//this function is called on closing tags
function endElement($parser, $name)
{
  global $curTag;
  $caret_pos = strrpos($curTag,'^');
  $curTag = substr($curTag,0,$caret_pos);
}


//this function has all of the real logic to look at what's between the tags
function characterData($parser, $data)
{
  global $curTag, $curKey, $outputAlbums, $outputImages,
       $readingAlbums, $firstTimeAlbum, $firstTimeAlbumEntry,
       $readingImages, $masterImageList, $firstTimeImage,
       $firstTimeImageEntry, $curID;

  //do some simple cleaning to prevent garbage
  $data = str_replace('!$-a-O*', '&', $data);
  if(!ereg("(\t)+(\n)?$", $data) && !ereg("^\n$", $data))
                   //if $data=non-whitespace
  {
    //some common place-signatures...really just a list of unclosed tags
    $albumName = "^PLIST^DICT^ARRAY^DICT^KEY"; //album attributes, i.e
      "AlbumName"
    $integerData = "^PLIST^DICT^ARRAY^DICT^INTEGER";//album ID
    $stringData = "^PLIST^DICT^ARRAY^DICT^STRING";  //the actual album name
    $albumContents = "^PLIST^DICT^ARRAY^DICT^ARRAY^STRING"; //photo ID number
    $majorList = "^PLIST^DICT^KEY";        //"List of Albums", "Master Image
      List"
    $photoID = "^PLIST^DICT^DICT^KEY";      //the unique ID of an individual
      photo
    $photoAttr="^PLIST^DICT^DICT^DICT^KEY"; //"Caption", "Date", "ImagePath", etc
    $photoValStr="^PLIST^DICT^DICT^DICT^STRING"; //caption, file paths, etc
    $photoValReal="^PLIST^DICT^DICT^DICT^REAL"; // date, aspect ratio, etc

    if($curTag == $majorList)
    {
      if($data=="List of Albums")
      {
        //flag so that there's no ambiguity, i.e. for <key>List of Rolls</key>
        $readingAlbums=true;
        $readingImages=false;
      }
      else if($data=="Master Image List")
      {
```

Example 4-10. Handling iPhoto XML parsing (continued)

```php
    $readingAlbums=false;
    $readingImages=true;
  }
  else
    $readingAlbums=false;
}

if($readingAlbums)
{
  if ($curTag==$integerData)
  {
    if($data == "AlbumId")
    {
      $curKey = $data;
    }
  }
  else if ($curTag==$albumName) //we're looking at an attribute, i.e
      AlbumName
  {                             //so the next thing we'll see is the album name
                          //or the listing of all photos contained in the album
    if($data == "AlbumName" || $data="KeyList")
    {
      $curKey = $data;        //$curKey will be that reminder for us next time
    }
  }
  else if($curTag == $stringData || $curTag == $integerData)
                          //now we are looking at interesting data....
  {
    if($curKey == "AlbumName") //so the last attribute we saw was AlbumName..

    {
      $curAlbum = $data;       //say the album name was "Library"...
                              //then now $data="Library"
      $curAlbum = str_replace("&amp;", '&', $data);

      $serializedObj = "";
      if(!$firstTimeAlbum)
        $serializedObj.="\n\t\t)\n\t,\n";
      $serializedObj .= "\t\"".addslashes($curAlbum)."\" =>\n\t\tarray(\n";
      $firstTimeAlbum=false;
      fileWrite($outputAlbums,$serializedObj,'a');
      $firstTimeAlbumEntry=true;
    }
  }
  else if($curTag == $albumContents)  // looking at a listing of photos {
    if($curKey == "KeyList")
    {
      //$data==the photo ID number of a photo in $curAlbum
      $serializedObj = "";
      if(!$firstTimeAlbumEntry)
```

Example 4-10. Handling iPhoto XML parsing (continued)

```php
            $serializedObj.=",\n";
            $serializedObj .= "\t\t\t$data";
            fileWrite($outputAlbums,$serializedObj,'a');
            $firstTimeAlbumEntry=false;
        }
    }
    //fill in all your other album cases of interest...
}
else if($readingImages)
{
    if($curTag==$photoID)       //we've encountered a new photo, store the ID...
    {
        $curID="";
        if(!$firstTimeImage)
            $curID=")},\n";
        $curID.="\t\"$data\"=>array(";
        $firstTimeImageEntry=true;
        $firstTimeImage=false;
    }
    else if($curTag==$photoAttr)
    {
        if($data=="Caption" || $data=="DateAsTimerInterval" ||
            $data=="ImagePath" || $data=="ThumbPath")
            $curKey=$data;
        else
            $curKey="";
    }
    else if($curTag==$photoValStr || $curTag==$photoValReal)
    {
        if($curKey == "Caption" || $curKey == "DateAsTimerInterval" ||
            $curKey=="ImagePath" || $curKey=="ThumbPath")
        {
            if(!$firstTimeImageEntry)
                $curID.=", ";

            if($curKey=="Caption")
                $curID .= "\"caption\"=>\"".addslashes($data)."\"";
            else if($curKey=="DateAsTimerInterval") //timeinterval based dates
                                                    //are measured in seconds from 1/1/2001
                $curID .= "\"date\"=>\"".
                        date("F j, Y, g:i a", mktime(0,0,$data,1,1,2001)).
                        "\"";
            else
                $curID .= "\"$curKey\"=>\"$data\"";
            $firstTimeImageEntry=false;
        }
        if($curKey=="ThumbPath")        //the last attribute we see for a photo...
            fileWrite($outputImages,$curID,'a');
        //...and any other image data worth extracting...
    }
}
```

Example 4-10. Handling iPhoto XML parsing (continued)

```
  }
}

//this function is what you call to actually parse the XML
function parseAlbumXML($albumFile)
{
  global $outputAlbums, $outputImages;
  $xml_parser = xml_parser_create( );
  xml_parser_set_option($xml_parser, XML_OPTION_CASE_FOLDING, true);
  //hook the parser up with our helper functions
  xml_set_element_handler($xml_parser, "startElement", "endElement");
  xml_set_character_data_handler($xml_parser, "characterData");
  if (!($fp = fopen($albumFile, "r")))
    die("Can't open file: $albumFile");
  fileWrite($outputAlbums,"<?php\n\$albumList = array (\n",'w');
  fileWrite($outputImages,"<?php\n//key=photo ID, value={",'w');
  fileWrite($outputImages," [0]caption, [1]date, [2]image ",'w');
  fileWrite($outputImages,"path, [3]thumb path}\n\$masterList = array (\n",'w');
  while ($data = fread($fp, 4096))
  {
    $data = str_replace('&', '!$-a-0*', $data);
    if (!xml_parse($xml_parser, $data, feof($fp)))
    {
      die(sprintf("$albumFile : ".$lang["errXMLParse"].": %s at line %d",
          xml_error_string(xml_get_error_code($xml_parser)),
          xml_get_current_line_number($xml_parser)));
    }
  }
  fileWrite($outputAlbums,"\n\t\t)\n\t\n\n);\n?>",'a');
  fileWrite($outputImages,")\n);\n?>",'a');
  //we're done, throw out the parser
  xml_parser_free($xml_parser);
  echo "Done parsing.";
}

function fileWrite($dest, $dataToWrite, $writeMode)
{
    global $err;
    if (is_writable($dest))
    {
        if (!$fp = fopen($dest, $writeMode))
            $err .= "Can't open file: ($dest) <br>";
        else
        {
            if (!fwrite($fp, $dataToWrite))
                $err .= "Can't write file: ($dest) <br>";
            fclose($fp);
        }
    }
    else
        $err .= "Bad file permissions: ($dest) <br>";
}
```

Example 4-10. Handling iPhoto XML parsing (continued)

```
set_time_limit(0);    //if you have an enormous AlbumData.xml,
//PHP's default 30-second execution time-out is the enemy

$outputImages="out_images.php";
$outputAlbums="out_albums.php";
parseAlbumXML("myPhoto/iPhoto Library/AlbumData.xml");
?>
```

Also, to use the output from the preceding parser, save the code in Example 4-11 as *iphoto_display.php*; this file will handle displaying the photos on the Web.

Example 4-11. The script displaying the photos

```
<?php
include "out_images.php";
$photoIDs=array_keys($masterList);
$thumbsPerPage=6;
$thumbsPerRow=3;
if(!isset($_GET["tStart"]))
  $thumbStart=0;
else
  $thumbStart=$_GET["tStart"];
if($thumbStart+$thumbsPerPage>count($photoIDs))
  $thumbLimit=count($photoIDs);
else
  $thumbLimit=$thumbStart+$thumbsPerPage;
echo "<table border=\"0\" width=\"100%\">\n";
for($x=$thumbStart; $x<$thumbLimit; $x++)
{
  $aPhoto=$masterList[$photoIDs[$x]];
  $thumb="<table>";
  $thumb.="<tr><td align=\"center\"><img ";
  $thumb.="src=\"".$aPhoto["ThumbPath"]."\"></td></tr>";
  $thumb.="<tr><td align=\"center\"><small>";
  $thumb.=$aPhoto["date"]."<br>".$aPhoto["caption"]."</small></td></tr>";
  $thumb.="</table>";
  if($x % $thumbsPerRow == 0)
    echo "\n<!--New row-->\n<tr><td>\n".$thumb."\n</td>\n";
  else if($x % $thumbsPerRow == ($thumbsPerRow-1))
    echo "\n<td>\n".$thumb."\n</td></tr>\n<!--End row-->\n";
  else
    echo "\n<td>\n".$thumb."\n</td>\n";
}
echo "\n</table>\n";
?>
```

Running the Hack

The last few lines of *iphoto_parse.php* contain hardcoded paths to the *AlbumData.xml* file, as well as to the output files (as does *iphoto_display. php*), so be sure that you enter the correct paths. Then, simply load up *iphoto_parse.php* in your web browser. Also, note that PHP will need to have permission to write to the output files; otherwise, you'll get no output.

Your web browser will indicate when the script has finished executing with a page that says, "Done parsing." Open the output files, and you should see an array in each, similar to the following samples.

out_albums.php will look something like this:

```php
<?php
$albumList = array (
    "Library" =>
        array(
            4425,
            4423,
...
            3796,
            3794,
            3792
        )
);
?>
```

And *out_images.php* will look something like this:

```php
<?php
//key=photo ID, value={[0]caption, [1]date, [2]image path, [3]thumb path}
$masterList = array (
"13"=>array(
"caption"=>"The wreath, out of focus again",
"date"=>"December 23, 2002, 2:59 am",
"ImagePath"=>"/~mike/myPhoto/iPhoto Library/2002/12/22/DSC00151.JPG",
"ThumbPath"=>"/~mike/myPhoto/iPhoto Library/2002/12/22/Thumbs/13.jpg"),
...
);
?>
```

You can also examine some of the resulting output visually by loading up *iphoto_display.php* in your web browser, as shown in Figure 4-15.

While XML is a versatile format, considering how verbose the *AlbumData. xml* file is and how large it can get for photo libraries of even moderate size, it needs to be massaged. After all, I have only 2,868 photos in my library, but my *AlbumData.xml* file is 2.4 MB. I thus chose to employ the XML

Figure 4-15. iPhoto wedding photos in my browser

parser included with PHP 4 (*expat*) to parse *AlbumData.xml* into meaningful components, which I then output using a much simpler format. Specifically, the output is piped into two separate files containing the data of interest represented as PHP arrays.

The core idea for the parser is to use a string representing the hierarchy of tags so that we have some context as we walk through the file's content. It's sort of like a stack that is represented as a string rather than as the more common array or linked list. Note that this parser parses only some of the elements of the albums section, as well as the images section of *AlbumData. xml*. I've also included a demonstration as to how you can work with the resulting output of this parser.

Before writing any code, it's probably a good idea to decide how to serve your photos. For instance, by default, Mac OS X will not allow Apache (and therefore, PHP) access to *~/Pictures/* where iPhoto data is stored, so you need to get your permissions straight. You can approach this in a number of ways:

- Modify your /etc/httpd/httpd.conf file.
- Use a symbolic link.
- Quit iPhoto, move your iPhoto *Library* folder into your ~/*Sites/* folder, relaunch iPhoto, and when it panics that all the photos are gone, point it to the new location of the *Library* folder.
- Upload your iPhoto *Library* folder to some other machine using FTP, rsync, or any other file-transfer program that floats your boat.

Hacking the Hack

You have a lot of room to work with this hack:

- Add further cases to the XML parser so that it extracts all of the data that you're interested in, rather than just the albums and the images that they contain.
- Instead of outputting the processed *AlbumData.xml* file into a flat text file, store the information in an SQL database or some other, more versatile format.
- If you're going to be this user friendly by getting all of the information out of iPhoto, why not go the extra mile and make this entire process automatic? Automating this process is actually very simple. At this point, we have a means for parsing the XML file as well as a means for caching what we discover from parsing the XML file. The final step calls for knowing when we should be using the cache and when we should be rebuilding the cache. The answer to this question depends on your application, but here are some possibilities worth considering:
  - Run a cron job that invokes your cache rebuild function hourly/daily/whenever.
  - Keep track of the modification date of *AlbumData.xml*. If that date is newer than the last time you parsed it, reparse.

So, for example, using the latter approach, add a function that looks something like this:

```
//returns a boolean value indicating whether or not
//a cache rebuild (reparse) is necessary
function needToUpdateCache( )
{
  global $cacheTime, $albumFile, $err;

  $cacheTimeFile="lastCacheTime.txt";   //text file where
                    //a string indicates
                    //last cache rebuild time.
                    //i.e. "January 28 2005 16:31:26."
```

```php
$compareFile="iPhoto Library/AlbumData.xml";
if (file_exists($cacheTimeFile))
{
  //first, check the file where the last known cached time was stored
  if($fp = fopen($cacheTimeFile, "r"))
  {
    $lastTime = fread($fp, filesize($cacheTimeFile));
    fclose($fp);
  }
  else
  {
    $err.= "Can't read last cache time";
    return true;
  }

  //now, determine the last time the iPhoto data has changed
  //if we need to reparse, it will write the
  //current time into $cacheTimeFile
  //(since we will therefore reparse now)
  if($lastTime!=date ("F d Y H:i:s.", filemtime($compareFile)))
  {
    if (!$fp = fopen($cacheTimeFile, 'w'))
    {
      $err.= "Can't open file: $cacheTimeFile";
    }
    else
    {
      if (!fwrite($fp, date ("F d Y H:i:s.", filemtime($compareFile)) ))
        $err.= "Can't open file: $cacheTimeFile";
      fclose($fp);
    }
    return true;
  }
  else
    return false;
}
else
{
  $err.= "Can't find file: $cacheTimeFile";
  return true;
}
}

//and at the beginning of every page load, call this to ensure
//viewers are getting the latest photos
if(needToUpdateCache())
 parseAlbumXML($pathToYourAlbumXMLFile);
```

This will ensure that you parse the file only when changes have been made in iPhoto that will require a reparse.

—Michael Mulligan

See Also

- "Create Thumbnail Images" [Hack #27]
- "Create Image Overlays" [Hack #32]

CHAPTER FIVE

Databases and XML

Hacks 34–50

At the core of most PHP applications is the database, and in most cases that database is MySQL. This chapter has a variety of hacks to help you develop code for database access and for your work with XML. In particular, you should check out the dynamic database object hack, which provides a single class that will talk to any database. Add to that the code generation hacks, which will help automate your database access code from an XML representation of the database schema, and PHP and databases are going to be a piece of cake!

HACK #34 Design Better SQL Schemas

Most PHP applications use an SQL database. Here are some hints to help you avoid common problems.

PHP applications usually use MySQL databases for the back end. I've worked on a bunch of my own applications, as well as with open source application databases and some commercial ones. In my travels, I have seen a few common problems appear repeatedly; here are a few of those problems, along with easy solutions.

Bad Primary Keys

To find a unique record in a database table, you need a primary key. This is usually a unique, nonrepeating integer that starts at 1. All databases have the ability to handle this for you, but it seems that some engineers aren't aware of it.

Take the simple schema in Example 5-1. You have an author table with an id and a name.

Example 5-1. SQL without a primary key

```
DROP TABLE IF EXISTS author;
CREATE TABLE author (
      id INT,
      name TEXT
      );
```

But who ensures that the ID is unique? Often the PHP code that uses a table like this will first do a SELECT to find the maximum value of the ID field, and then create a new record with that value plus 1. But that takes an extra SQL statement and assumes the PHP developer remembers to take this step. It's much better to let the database handle this (rather routine) task.

A much better version of the schema from Example 5-1 is shown in Example 5-2.

Example 5-2. Adding an auto-incrementing ID field

```
DROP TABLE IF EXISTS author;
CREATE TABLE author (
      id INT NOT NULL AUTO_INCREMENT,
      name TEXT,
      PRIMARY KEY( id )
      );
```

Now the ID field is specified as an auto-incrementing integer that cannot be null. It's also identified as the primary key.

To insert a record into this type of table, follow this recipe:

```
INSERT INTO author VALUES ( 0, "Brad Phillips" );
```

MySQL replaces the 0 value for the ID with an auto-incrementing value. To find out the value of the ID from the most recent insert, use this SELECT statement:

```
SELECT LAST_INSERT_ID( );
```

This version of the table is also faster than the first version because the primary key specification creates an index that speeds up the look-up process.

If you find that the code that inserts records into the database is first doing a SELECT to find the largest ID value, and then running INSERT with that value plus 1, you know the code is not auto-incrementing primary keys. This is not only a performance hit, but it's also a problem on high-traffic sites where records could easily be added with duplicate primary keys because of the separation in time between the SELECT that finds the largest primary key value and the INSERT that creates a new record.

Misunderstanding Relational Databases

Relational databases, such as Oracle and MySQL, are different from in-memory data structures that you would develop in structured programming languages (e.g., PHP, C, and Java) or object-oriented languages. In particular, programming languages can have a data structure that includes an array. Data structures like this don't translate directly over to relational databases.

The sample SQL in Example 5-3 shows a schema where a text field is used as an array of IDs.

Example 5-3. Approximating an array in a programming language

```
DROP TABLE IF EXISTS author;
CREATE TABLE author (
        id INT,
        name TEXT
        );

DROP TABLE IF EXISTS book;
CREATE TABLE book (
        id INT,
        name TEXT,
        authors TEXT
        );
```

Figure 5-1 shows the relationship between these two tables (that is, the *lack* of a real relationship).

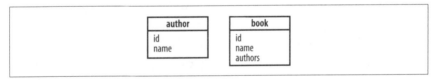

Figure 5-1. The name and book tables

Here is an example of how you might use these tables:

```
INSERT INTO author VALUES ( 1, "Brad Phillips" );
INSERT INTO author VALUES ( 2, "Don Charles" );
INSERT INTO author VALUES ( 3, "Brad silver" );
INSERT INTO book VALUES ( 1, "MySQL in a bucket", "1,2" );
INSERT INTO book VALUES ( 2, "Databases for Delinquents", "3" );
```

The books are added with comma-delimited lists of author IDs. Hardly takes advantage of the database's structure, does it.

To find out which authors belong to which books, the script first queries the book record, then splits the authors text field using preg_split( ), and finally does another set of queries against those IDs (hopefully this makes you cringe as much as it does me).

Now let's talk about how this *should* be done. Example 5-4 shows a corrected schema with three tables. One is for authors, another is for books, and a third table relates the first two.

Example 5-4. Using a join table to couple two tables together

```
DROP TABLE IF EXISTS author;
CREATE TABLE author (
        id INT NOT NULL AUTO_INCREMENT,
        name TEXT,
        PRIMARY KEY( id )
        );

DROP TABLE IF EXISTS book;
CREATE TABLE book (
        id INT NOT NULL AUTO_INCREMENT,
        name TEXT,
        PRIMARY KEY( id )
        );

DROP TABLE IF EXISTS book_author;
CREATE TABLE book_author (
        book_id INT,
        author_id INT
        );
```

The third table in this schema is critical. It relates the two tables, author and book, by the id field in each. For each author of a book, there will be a record in the book_author table. Figure 5-2 shows the relationship among these three tables.

Figure 5-2. The author and book tables now properly related

Here is how the initial data is loaded:

```
INSERT INTO author VALUES ( 0, "Brad Phillips" );
INSERT INTO author VALUES ( 0, "Don Charles" );
INSERT INTO author VALUES ( 0, "Brad silver" );
INSERT INTO book VALUES ( 0, "MySQL in a bucket" );
INSERT INTO book VALUES ( 0, "Databases for Delinquents" );
INSERT INTO book_author VALUES ( 1, 1 );
INSERT INTO book_author VALUES ( 1, 2 );
INSERT INTO book_author VALUES ( 2, 3 );
```

The last set of INSERT statements assigns the first two authors to the first book and the third author to the last book.

Here is a query that returns a table with one line for every book and author combination:

```
SELECT
        a.name AS author,
        b.name AS book,
        a.id AS author_id,
        b.name AS book_id
FROM
        author AS a,
        book AS b,
        book_author AS ba
WHERE
        a.id = ba.author_id AND
        b.id = ba.book_id;
```

And here is a similar query (augmented with another conditional to specify a single book):

```
SELECT
        a.name AS author,
        b.name AS book,
        a.id AS author_id,
        b.name AS book_id
FROM
        author AS a,
        book AS b,
        book_author AS ba
WHERE
        a.id = ba.author_id AND
        b.id = ba.book_id AND
        ba.book_id = 1;
```

This query will return all of the authors of a single book without subqueries or string parsing. The results are a faster query and a database schema that takes advantage of a database's strengths (relationships) rather than its weaknesses (text parsing).

Use Not Null Fields

Databases can provide a lot of validation on the data stored in them. But even rudimentary validations go unused by programmers who don't know that the validations exist. Take the table in Example 5-5, for instance.

Example 5-5. A table that omits some implied requirements of the data it stores

```
DROP TABLE IF EXISTS user;
CREATE TABLE user (
        id INT,
```

Example 5-5. A table that omits some implied requirements of the data it stores (continued)

```
first TEXT,
last TEXT,
username TEXT,
password TEXT,
description TEXT
);
```

What do we know about this table? Well, we know that the `first`, `last`, `username`, and `password` fields must never be empty. Wouldn't it be great if the database could help us to ensure that? Of course, it actually can—check out Example 5-6.

Example 5-6. Small changes that make for dramatic results

```
DROP TABLE IF EXISTS user;
CREATE TABLE user (
        id INT NOT NULL AUTO_INCREMENT,
        first TEXT NOT NULL,
        last TEXT NOT NULL,
        username TEXT NOT NULL,
        password TEXT NOT NULL,
        description TEXT,
        PRIMARY KEY ( id )
        );
```

Here, I have not only upgraded the primary key so that it's automatically generated, but also added NOT NULL specifications to the fields that must not be empty. This will ensure that inserts will fail if the data is invalid. Why rely on good programming when your database can enforce these rules on its own?

See Also

- "Create Bulletproof Database Access" **[Hack #35]**
- "Export Database Schema as XML" **[Hack #39]**
- "Generate Database SQL" **[Hack #41]**

Create Bulletproof Database Access

HACK #35

Learn how to use PEAR's DB module to create bulletproof database access for your web applications.

I've read a number of books on PHP over the years, and almost all of them make the same mistakes when it comes to database access. Applications that use SQL improperly are susceptible to SQL injection attacks, which can literally hand your entire database (and its contents) over to hackers. What's even worse is that the proper way to do database access is actually *easier* than the improper way.

To illustrate, Example 5-7 shows proper SQL command construction.

Example 5-7. Proper SQL command construction

```php
<?php
require_once("DB.php");

$dsn = 'mysql://root:password@localhost/books';
$db =& DB::Connect( $dsn, array( ) );
if (PEAR::isError($db)) { die($db->getMessage( )); }

$sth = $db->prepare( "INSERT INTO author VALUES ( null, ? )" );
$db->execute( $sth, array( $_POST['name'] ) );
?>
```

I use the PEAR DB module to prepare a statement, with the ? placed where arguments are to go. Then I execute the statement against the database and provide an array of arguments that will fill in the ? fields. The driver performs all of the quoting and escaping required to ensure that the command runs properly regardless of the input.

Along the same lines, Example 5-8 is an example of a query performed against the database in the proper manner.

Example 5-8. An SQL SELECT statement that isn't going to cause any problems

```php
<?php
require_once("DB.php");

$dsn = 'mysql://root:password@localhost/books';
$db =& DB::Connect( $dsn, array( ) );
if (PEAR::isError($db)) { die($db->getMessage( )); }

$res = $db->query( "SELECT * FROM author WHERE id = ?", array( $id ) );
while( $res->fetchInto( $row ) )
{
    ...
}
?>
```

In this case, the query method is called with an SQL string where the arguments are indicated with the ? character. The arguments are supplied using the second argument, which is always an array (regardless of the number of arguments supplied).

You might be saying to yourself, "If this is right, what is wrong?" I'm not going to put the wrong version in the book because readers might use that sample without first reading that the code is incorrect!

Some in the PHP community suggest that PEAR DB is slower. I haven't experienced that; and even if that were the case, I would still use PEAR DB because it provides portability and security features that the direct database access functions do not.

A new alternative to PEAR DB is on the horizon, as well; it's the PHP Data Objects (PDO) library. It's currently experimental, but it's worth monitoring in the long term as an alternative to PEAR DB. It's interesting to note that if you use the code generators provided in this chapter, you will be able to migrate between PEAR DB and PDO without modifying the application that sits on top of your database access layer.

See Also

* "Design Better SQL Schemas" [Hack #34]

HACK #36   Create Dynamic Database Access Objects

Use the new object-oriented features of PHP 5 to create classes that wrap access to any database table.

PHP 5 represents a substantial upgrade in terms of object-oriented support in the PHP language. Along with a number of upgrades in performance, PHP 5 has a major upgrade in the ability to create *dynamic classes*. These are classes where the methods and attributes change from object to object. This can be very handy in building database applications.

Usually, there is one PHP class for each table in the database. For example, if you have tables named books, authors, and publishers, you would have PHP classes named Book, Author, and Publisher. Each PHP class has methods to get and set the values in a record in the corresponding table.

On the one hand, this is a very clean and easy-to-understand model. On the other hand, it's a lot of work to maintain these classes (and that's just for three tables!). Is it possible to write a single class that will wrap any table in the database? Yes. With PHP 5's support for __call, __get, and __set methods, it is.

To understand why __call, __get, and __set are important you need to understand how methods on objects get called. When you invoke a method on an object, the interpreter first looks at the class to see whether the method exists. If the method does exist, it's called; if it doesn't, the base class of the class is inspected; if that fails, the base class of the base class is examined, and so on, up the chain of classes.

In PHP 5, when the method lookup fails, the __call method is invoked, if it exists. This method has two arguments: the name of the method and the array of arguments for that method. If you implement the __call method and return a real value, PHP 5 is satisfied that it has found a method and that the method invocation worked.

The __get and __set methods correspond to the getting and setting of instance variables on the object. The __get method has a single parameter, the name of the instance variable. The __set method has two parameters, the name of the instance variable and the new value.

That means that you can effectively create new methods and instance variables on your objects on the fly. And that means that you can have a class that loads a record from a database table and has dynamic methods and instance variables that make it look like an object built just for that record.

Figure 5-3 shows how these dynamic methods and fields work. The code calls the class for either a method or a field. Then the object indicates that there is no such field. PHP calls to get the field value or method value, and then—if given a valid response—returns that value to the calling code as though the field or method were there.

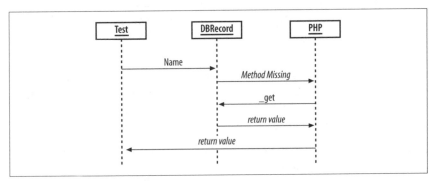

Figure 5-3. The control flow with dynamic fields

If all of this seems a little confusing, don't worry. This is a powerful new paradigm for object-oriented programming that takes a little while to understand, and even longer to implement successfully and safely. Think of this hack as just a taste of what is possible.

The Code

Save the code in Example 5-9 as *dbrecord.php*.

Example 5-9. Some simple PHP that makes for a surprisingly robust script

```php
<?php
require_once( "DB.php" );
$dsn = 'mysql://root:password@localhost/books';
$db =& DB::Connect( $dsn, array() );
if (PEAR::isError($db)) { die($db->getMessage( )); }

class DBRecord
{
  var $h;

  public function DBRecord( $table, $id )
  {
     global $db;
     $res = $db->query( "SELECT * from $table WHERE id=?", array( $id ) );
     $res->fetchInto( $row, DB_FETCHMODE_ASSOC );
    $this->{'h'} = $row;
  }
  public function __call( $method, $args )
  {
    return $this->{'h'}[strtolower($method)];
  }
  public function __get( $id )
  {
    return $this->{'h'}[strtolower($id)];
  }
}
?>
```

To test the code, enter Example 5-10 and save it as *test.php*.

Example 5-10. A simple script that tests the database access script

```php
<?php
require_once( "DBrecord.php" );

$rec = new DBRecord( "author", 2 );
print $rec->Name( )."\n";
?>
```

books.sql, shown in Example 5-11, handles database setup for the example.

Example 5-11. An SQL script that sets up a simple test database

```sql
DROP TABLE IF EXISTS author;
CREATE TABLE author (
  id MEDIUMINT NOT NULL AUTO_INCREMENT,
  name TEXT,
```

Example 5-11. An SQL script that sets up a simple test database (continued)

```
 PRIMARY KEY( id )
);

INSERT INTO author VALUES ( 0, "jack" );
INSERT INTO author VALUES ( 0, "bob" );
```

Running the Hack

This hack is run with PHP on the command line:

```
% mysql --user=root --password=password books < books.sql
% php test.php
bob
```

It doesn't look like much; but what's interesting is that we have an object that *looks* like the row in the author table. However, this same object could just as easily represent a record in the book, or the publisher table; it's not hardwired to any particular database schema or table.

The code simply creates a new DBRecord object with the name of the table and the ID of the record in the table. Then the Name( ) method is called; but there is no Name( ) method on the DBRecord object, so the __call method is invoked. The __call method then converts the method name to lowercase (part of the process PHP always follows). Then the __call method on the DBRecord object checks the hash of information read from the database—and stored in the $h instance variable—and returns the value of the requested field.

Hacking the Hack

Reading data from the database is one thing. But can we update the code so that it can read and write from a record? Sure. Save the code in Example 5-12 as *dbrecord2.php*.

Example 5-12. Code addition for handling database updates as well as reads

```php
<?php
require_once( "DB.php" );
$dsn = 'mysql://root:password@localhost/books';
$db =& DB::Connect( $dsn, array( ) );
if (PEAR::isError($db)) { die($db->getMessage()); }

class DBRecord
{
  var $h;
  var $table;
  var $id;
```

Example 5-12. Code addition for handling database updates as well as reads (continued)

```php
public function DBRecord( $table, $id )
{
    global $db;
    $res = $db->query( "SELECT * from $table WHERE id=?", array( $id ) );
    $res->fetchInto( $row, DB_FETCHMODE_ASSOC );
    $this->{'h'} = $row;
    $this->{'table'} = $table;
    $this->{'id'} = $id;
}

public function __call( $method, $args )
{
    return $this->{'h'}[strtolower($method)];
}

public function __get( $id )
{
    print "Getting $id\n";
    return $this->{'h'}[strtolower($id)];
}

public function __set( $id, $value )
{
    $this->{'h'}[strtolower($id)] = $value;
}

public function Update( )
{
    global $db;

    $fields = array( );
    $values = array( );

    foreach( array_keys( $this->{'h'} ) as $key )
    {
        if ( $key != "id" )
        {
            $fields []= $key." = ?";
            $values []= $this->{'h'}[$key];
        }
    }
    $fields = join( ",", $fields );
    $values []= $this->{'id'};

    $sql = "UPDATE {$this->{'table'}} SET $fields WHERE id = ?";
    $sth = $db->prepare( $sql );
    $db->execute( $sth, $values );
}
}
?>
```

Create Dynamic Database Access Objects

To test this new code, enter Example 5-13 and save it as *test2.php*.

Example 5-13. A script that tests dynamic database updates

```php
<?php
require_once( "DBrecord2.php" );

$rec = new DBRecord( "author", 2 );
print $rec->Name( )."\n";
$rec->Name = "New Name";
$rec->Update( );
?>
```

Now let's run *test2.php*:

```
% php test2.php
bob
% php test2.php
New Name
%
```

First, the script prints the current value of the record in the database. Then it sets the value to ?New Name?and updates the database record. I've run the script again to verify that the value is updated.

The trick here is that the __set method is called with the value ?New Name?, so the hash of fields from the record is updated with the new value. Then the Update( ) method is called, which executes an UPDATE command in the SQL database.

The Rails framework (*http://www.rubyonrails.org/*) for Ruby (*http://ruby-lang.org/*) uses a technique similar to this to allow web applications to quickly adapt to any database schema. It looks like Cake (*http://cakephp.org*) might do something similar for PHP.

See Also

- "Turn Any Object into an Array" [Hack #53]
- "Generate Database Select Code" [Hack #42]
- "Generate CRUD Database Code" [Hack #37]

Generate CRUD Database Code

Automatically generate the code to create, read, update, and delete (CRUD) records from your database tables.

This book presents several hacks that will help you speed up your database development by generating the required PHP and SQL code. In this hack, I show you how to build a generator that will create PHP 4 (or 5) classes that wrap database records. With these classes, you will be able to create, read, update, and delete individual records on any table, without spending lots of time writing the database code yourself.

Figure 5-4 shows the flow from the schema file into the generator, which in turn creates the output PHP code. I've rendered the output code as dashes because it's temporary and should never be altered manually.

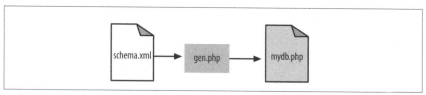

Figure 5-4. The flow through the generator

The Code

Save the XML representing a database schema (shown in Example 5-14) as *schema.xml*.

Example 5-14. An XML document that maps to the database schema

```xml
<schema>
  <table name="book">
    <field name="id" type="int" primary-key="true" />
    <field name="title" type="text" />
    <field name="publisher_id" type="int" />
    <field name="author_id" type="int" />
  </table>
  <table name="publisher">
    <field name="id" type="int" primary-key="true" />
    <field name="name" type="text" />
  </table>
  <table name="author">
    <field name="id" type="int" primary-key="true" />
    <field name="name" type="text" />
  </table>
</schema>
```

Example 5-15 shows the generation code; I saved this script as *gen.php*.

Example 5-15. PHP that handles database code generation

```php
<?php
$tables = array( );

function start_element( $parser, $name, $attribs )
{
  global $tables;
  if ( $name == "TABLE" )
  {
    $table = array( );
    $fields = array( );

    $table['name'] = $attribs['NAME'];
    $table['fields'] = array( );

    $tables []= $table;
  }
  if ( $name == "FIELD" )
  {
    $field = array( );
    $field['name'] = $attribs['NAME'];
    $field['type'] = $attribs['TYPE'];
    $field['pk'] = ( $attribs['PRIMARY-KEY'] ==  "true" ) ? 1 : 0;
    $tables[count($tables)-1]['fields'] []= $field;
  }
}
function end_element( $parser, $name ) { }

$parser = xml_parser_create( );
xml_set_element_handler($parser, "start_element", "end_element" );
while( !feof( STDIN ) ) {
  $text = fgets( STDIN );
  xml_parse( $parser, $text );
}
xml_parser_free( $parser );

ob_start( );

echo( "<?php\n" );
?>
require_once( "dbwrap.php" );

<?php

foreach( $tables as $table ) {
  $pk = null;
  $updsets = array( );
  $updfields = array( );
  $insfields = array( );
```

Example 5-15. PHP that handles database code generation (continued)

```php
$insvalues = array( );
$insvars = array( );

foreach( $table['fields'] as $field ) {
    $insfields []= $field['name'];
    if ( $field['pk'] )
        {
    $pk = $field['name'];
        $insvalues []= 0;
        }
        else
        {
            $updsets []= $field['name']."=?";
            $updfields []= '$this->'.$field['name'];

            $insvalues []= '?';
            $insvars []= '$this->'.$field['name'];
        }
}

$insvars = join( $insvars, ", " );
$insvalues = join( $insvalues, ", " );
$insfields = join( $insfields, ", " );
$updfields []= '$this->'.$pk;
$updfields = join( $updfields, ", " );
$updsets = join( $updsets, ", " );
?>
class <?php echo( ucfirst( $table['name'] ) ) ?>
{
<?php
    foreach( $table['fields'] as $field ) {
?>
    var $<?php echo( $field['name'] ); ?>;
<?php
}
?>

    function <?php echo( ucfirst( $table['name'] ) ) ?>()
    {
        $this->id = null;
    }

    function load($id)
    {
        $data = selectOne( "SELECT * FROM <?php echo( $table['name'] ) ?> WHERE <?php
echo( $pk ); ?> = ?", array( $id ) );
<?php
    foreach( $table['fields'] as $field ) {
?>
        $this-><?php echo( $field['name'] ); ?> = $data['<?php echo( $field['name'] ]
); ?>'];
```

Example 5-15. PHP that handles database code generation (continued)

```php
<?php
}
?>
  }

<?php
  foreach( $table['fields'] as $field ) {
?>
  function get_<?php echo( $field['name'] ) ?>() { return $this-><?php echo(
    $field['name'] ) ?>; }

  function set_<?php echo( $field['name'] ) ?>( $val ) { $this-><?php echo(
    $field['name'] ) ?> = $val; }

<?php
}
?>
  function update()
  {
    if ( $this->id != null ) { $this->updateRecord(); }
    else { $this->insertRecord(); }
  }

  function insertRecord()
  {
    return executeCommand( "INSERT INTO <?php echo( $table['name'] ) ?> ( <?php
      echo($insfields); ?> ) VALUES ( <?php echo($insvalues); ?> )",
      array( <?php echo( $insvars ); ?> ) );
  }

  function updateRecord()
  {
    return executeCommand( "UPDATE <?php echo( $table['name'] ) ?> SET <?php
      echo($updsets); ?> WHERE <?php echo( $pk ); ?>=?",
      array( <?php echo( $updfields ); ?> ) );
  }

  function deleteRecord( $id )
  {
    return executeCommand( "DELETE FROM <?php echo( $table['name'] ) ?> WHERE
      <?php echo( $pk ); ?>=?", array( $id ) );
  }
}

<?php }
echo( "?>" );

$php = ob_get_clean();
```

Example 5-15. PHP that handles database code generation (continued)

```
$fh = fopen( "mydb.php", "w" );
fwrite( $fh, $php );
fclose( $fh );
?>
```

Believe it or not, though, there's more code to write; *dbwrap.php* (shown in Example 5-16) handles connecting to a specific database. You'll want to have one of these scripts for each database you connect to.

Example 5-16. A script that handles database-specific details

```
<?php
require_once( "DB.php" );
$dsn = 'mysql://root:password@localhost/books';
$db =& DB::Connect( $dsn, array() );
if (PEAR::isError($db)) { die($db->getMessage()); }

function selectOne( $sql, $args )
{
  global $db;
  $res = $db->query( $sql, $args );
  $res->fetchInto($row, DB_FETCHMODE_ASSOC);
  return $row;
}

function selectBlock( $sql, $args )
{
  global $db;
  $res = $db->query( $sql, $args );
  $rows = array();
  while( $res->fetchInto($row, DB_FETCHMODE_ASSOC) ) { $rows []= $row; }
  return $rows;
}

function executeCommand( $sql, $args )
{
  global $db;
  $sth = $db->prepare( $sql );
  return $db->execute( $sth, $args );
}
?>
```

Save the code in Example 5-17 as *insert.php*. It handles the process of testing database inserts.

Example 5-17. A script that tests database inserts

```
<?php
require_once( "mydb.php" );

$auth = new Author( );
$auth->set_name( "Jack" );
$auth->update( );
?>
```

Example 5-18 tests the process of loading data; save the script as *load.php*.

Example 5-18. A script that tests loading data from the database

```
<?php
require_once( "mydb.php" );

$auth = new Author( );
$auth->load( 1 );
?>
Name: <?php echo( $auth->get_name( ) ); ?>
```

Save the code in Example 5-19 as *delete.php*. It tests deletion using generated classes.

Example 5-19. A script that handles deletion testing

```
<?php
require_once( "mydb.php" );

$auth = new Author( );
$auth->deleteRecord( 1 );
?>
```

The largest portion of code for this hack is in the *gen.php* script. That code is
the generator that builds the code. The code built relies on the *dbwrap.php*
code and is tested by the *insert.php*, *load.php*, and *delete.php* scripts.

The *gen.php* script starts by reading in the XML document that maps to your
database schema. In fact, a lot of the script is dedicated to reading the XML
into an in-memory data structure. This is the section of code from the beginning to the xml_parse( ) line, which reads in the XML and calls the XML
event handlers to parse up the tags.

After the XML is read in, code creation can begin. This kicks off with an ini-
tialization of the output buffering using ob_start( ). Then the generator
loops through the tables and fields, creating classes one by one. Once the
classes are created, the output buffering is closed and the generated database access code—now stored in a string—is written out to the file.

Generate CRUD Database Code

Running the Hack

To generate the code for your database, first you must create a schema for
the database in an XML file. I've provided an example file called *schema.xml*
that defines a simple schema for a book database. To generate the code for
this database, I use the command-line PHP interpreter:

```
% php gen.php < schema.xml
```

The code generator then creates a file called *mydb.php*, which contains the
PHP classes that will wrap the database records. With the example schema,
the output looks like this:

```php
<?php
require_once( "dbwrap.php" );

class Book
{
  var $id;
  var $title;
  var $publisher_id;
  var $author_id;

  function Book( )
  {
    $this->id = null;
  }

  function load($id)
  {
    $data = selectOne( "SELECT * FROM book WHERE id = ?", array( $id ) );
    $this->id = $data['id'];
    $this->title = $data['title'];
    $this->publisher_id = $data['publisher_id'];
    $this->author_id = $data['author_id'];
  }

  function get_id( ) { return $this->id; }

  function set_id( $val ) { $this->id = $val; }

  function get_title( ) { return $this->title; }

  function set_title( $val ) { $this->title = $val; }

  function get_publisher_id( ) { return $this->publisher_id; }

  function set_publisher_id( $val ) { $this->publisher_id = $val; }

  function get_author_id( ) { return $this->author_id; }

  function set_author_id( $val ) { $this->author_id = $val; }
```

```
function update( )
{
  if ( $this->id != null ) { $this->updateRecord( ); }
  else { $this->insertRecord( ); }
}

function insertRecord( )
{
  return executeCommand( "INSERT INTO book ( id, title, publisher_id,
      author_id ) VALUES ( 0, ?, ?, ? )",
    array( $this->title, $this->publisher_id, $this->author_id ) );
}

function updateRecord( )
{
  return executeCommand( "UPDATE book SET title=?, publisher_id=?, author
      id=? WHERE id=?",
    array( $this->title, $this->publisher_id, $this->author_id, $this->
      id ) );
}

function deleteRecord( $id )
{
  return executeCommand( "DELETE FROM book WHERE id=?", array( $id ) );
}
}

class Publisher
{
  var $id;
  var $name;

  function Publisher( )
  {
    $this->id = null;
  }

  function load($id)
  {
    $data = selectOne( "SELECT * FROM publisher WHERE id = ?", array
      ( $id ) );
    $this->id = $data['id'];
    $this->name = $data['name'];
  }

  function get_id( ) { return $this->id; }

  function set_id( $val ) { $this->id = $val; }

  function get_name( ) { return $this->name; }

  function set_name( $val ) { $this->name = $val; }
```

```
function update( )
{
  if ( $this->id != null ) { $this->updateRecord( ); }
  else { $this->insertRecord( ); }
}

function insertRecord( )
{
  return executeCommand( "INSERT INTO publisher ( id, name ) VALUES
    ( 0, ? )",
    array( $this->name ) );
}

function updateRecord( )
{
  return executeCommand( "UPDATE publisher SET name=? WHERE id=?",
    array( $this->name, $this->id ) );
}

function deleteRecord( $id )
{
  return executeCommand( "DELETE FROM publisher WHERE id=?", array
    ( $id ) );
}
}

class Author
{
  var $id;
  var $name;

  function Author( )
  {
    $this->id = null;
  }

  function load($id)
  {
    $data = selectOne( "SELECT * FROM author WHERE id = ?", array( $id ) );
    $this->id = $data['id'];
    $this->name = $data['name'];
  }

  function get_id( ) { return $this->id; }

  function set_id( $val ) { $this->id = $val; }

  function get_name( ) { return $this->name; }

  function set_name( $val ) { $this->name = $val; }

  function update( )
  {
```

```
    if ( $this->id != null ) { $this->updateRecord( ); }
    else { $this->insertRecord( ); }
}

function insertRecord( )
{
  return executeCommand( "INSERT INTO author ( id, name ) VALUES
    ( 0, ? )",
    array( $this->name ) );
}

function updateRecord( )
{
  return executeCommand( "UPDATE author SET name=? WHERE id=?",
    array( $this->name, $this->id ) );
}

function deleteRecord( $id )
{
  return executeCommand( "DELETE FROM author WHERE id=?", array( $id ) );
}
}

?>
```

There are three classes here, one for each table in the database. Each has member variables for all of the fields in the XML, a constructor that sets the ID to null, a set of get and set accessor methods, and functions to update or delete records.

To test these classes, run the *insert.php* file from the command line:

```
% php insert.php
```

This adds a new author to the database. Now you can run the *load.php* script:

```
% php load.php
Name: Jack
```

That confirms that the new record went in as expected. Finally, delete the record with the *delete.php* script:

```
% php delete.php
```

This generator, in combination with the other generators presented in this book, will allow you to generate redundant database access code much more quickly and accurately than you can by hand.

See Also

- "Generate Database SQL" [Hack #41]
- "Generate Database Select Code" [Hack #42]
- "Create Bulletproof Database Access" [Hack #35]
- "Design Better SQL Schemas" [Hack #34]

HACK #38 Read XML on the Cheap with Regular Expressions

Use regular-expression hacks to read XML without paying the expense of firing up the XML parser functions.

You can read XML with PHP using very few PHP libraries. For example, XML support is actually an extension that might or might not be installed on the server your code is running on. To avoid reliance on an optional extension, it's sometimes easier and more portable to extract data from XML with a few regular expressions than it is to fire up the XML parser.

The Code

Save the XML in Example 5-20 as *books.xml*.

Example 5-20. Some simple XML code, serving as a demonstration

```
<books>
        <book name="Pragmatic Programmer" />
        <book
                name="Code Generation in Action" />
        <book id="8951234" name="Podcasting Hacks" />
</books>
```

Now save the code in Example 5-21 as *bookread.php*.

Example 5-21. A simple script that uses regular expressions to read XML

```php
<?php
$xml = "";
while( !feof(STDIN) ) { $xml .= fgets( STDIN ); }

preg_match_all( "/\<book\s+.*?name=[\"|\']('.*?)[\"|\'].*?\/\>/is", $xml,
    $found );

foreach( $found[1] as $name ) { print( "$name\n" ); }
?>
```

This script uses preg_match_all( ) to find all the occurrences of the book tag in the XML. Then it groups the content in the name field and pulls that out. The s modifier flag is critical because it tells the regular-expression engine to match across multiple lines. All of the variants of the book tag in *books.xml* are valid, so this regular expression needs to be flexible enough to handle them.

Running the Hack

Run the *bookread.php* file from the command line using the php command:

```
% php bookread.php < books.xml
Pragmatic Programmer
Code Generation in Action
Podcasting Hacks
```

Hacking the Hack

Another common XML situation is to have a complex nested structure that you need to parse as units. Take a list of people such as this one:

```
<people>
        <person>
                <first>Jack</first>
                <last>Herrington</last>
        </person>
        <person>
                <last>Katzen</last>
                <first>Molly</first>
        </person>
</people>
```

Ideally, you probably want an array of each person, complete with first and last names. Example 5-22 is a script that uses successive regular expression calls to first find the person tags and then search within the tags to find the first and last names.

Example 5-22. Regular expressions dealing with complex XML

```
<?php
$text = "";
while( !feof( STDIN ) ) { $text .= fgets( STDIN ); }

preg_match_all( "/\<person\>(.*?)\<\/person\>/si", $text, $people );

$list = array( );
```

Example 5-22. Regular expressions dealing with complex XML (continued)

```
foreach( $people[1] as $person )
{
        preg_match( "/\<first\>(.*?)\<\/first\>/is", $person, $res );
        $first = $res[1];
        preg_match( "/\<last\>(.*?)\<\/last\>/is", $person, $res );
        $last = $res[1];
        $list []= array(
                'first' => $first,
                'last' => $last
        );
}
print_r( $list );
?>
```

Because the first and last tags can appear in any order, this script is more
robust than the one shown in Example 5-21, which uses a single regular
expression to try to get first and last simultaneously.

Using the command-line version of PHP, run the command like this:

```
% php peopleread.php < people.xml
Array
(
    [0] => Array
        (
            [first] => Jack
            [last] => Herrington
        )

    [1] => Array
        (
            [first] => Molly
            [last] => Katzen
        )
)
```

The print_r( ) function shows the contents of the array in an "easy for a
programmer to read" manner. At this point, you can use this information
however you want—without having to rely on PHP's XML extension libraries.

See Also

- "Create a Simple XML Query Handler for Database Access" [Hack #40]
- "Create XML the Right Way" [Hack #54]

HACK #39   Export Database Schema as XML

Use PHP to read the schema from your database and export it as XML for documentation or code generation.

It can be handy to have a dump of the current database schema for several reasons. First, you can use it to generate PHP for database access [Hack #37]. You can also use it to compare two versions of a schema to build a migration script for software upgrades.

The Code

schema.php is shown in Example 5-23.

Example 5-23. Script that extracts XML for a database schema representation

```php
<?php
$dbuser = "root";
$dbpassword = "password";
$dbserver = "localhost";
$dbname = "wordpress";

$db = mysql_connect( $dbserver, $dbuser, $dbpassword );

mysql_select_db( $dbname );

$tables_res = mysql_query( "SHOW TABLES FROM ".$dbname, $db );
$tables = array();
while( $tableinfo = mysql_fetch_row($tables_res) ) {
  $tables[] = $tableinfo[ 0 ];
}
mysql_free_result( $tables_res );

header( "content-type: text/xml" );
?>
<schema>
<?php foreach( $tables as $table ) { ?>
<table name="<?php echo( $table ); ?>">
<?php
$fields_res = mysql_query( "SHOW FIELDS FROM ".$table, $db );
while( $fieldinfo = mysql_fetch_row($fields_res) ) {
?>
<field
  name="<?php echo( $fieldinfo[0]); ?>"
  type="<?php echo( $fieldinfo[1]); ?>"
  />
<?php }
mysql_free_result( $fields_res );
?>
</table>
<?php } ?>
</schema>
```

This small script reads the schema from a MySQL database and outputs XML that describes the schema to the console (of course, you can pipe this output to a file). The script starts by defining the connection to the database through a set of constants. Then the script connects to the database and finds out what tables are available using SHOW TABLES. Next, the script iterates over each table and uses SHOW FIELDS to find the fields for each table. All of the returned information is dropped into XML, formatted on the fly by the script.

Running the Hack

Use the command-line version of PHP to run this script, like so:

```
% php schema.php
<schema>
<table name="wp_categories">
<field
    name="cat_ID"
    type="bigint(20)"
/>
<field
    name="cat_name"
    type="varchar(55)"
/>
<field
    name="category_nicename"
    type="varchar(200)"
/>
<field
    name="category_description"
    type="longtext"
/>
<field
    name="category_parent"
    type="int(4)"
/>
...
```

In this example, I pointed the script at my WordPress database, which is fairly complex. The XML result has a base schema tag that contains a table tag for each table. Within each table tag, the fields are listed with individual field tags that specify a name and a type.

This script is specific to MySQL. Reflection queries such as SHOW TABLES and SHOW FIELDS are available for other databases but are specified slightly differently; you should be able to make a few changes to get this running on your database of choice.

See Also

- "Generate Database SQL" [Hack #41]
- "Generate Database Select Code" [Hack #42]
- "Generate CRUD Database Code" [Hack #37]

 ## HACK #40 Create a Simple XML Query Handler for Database Access

XSLT can read XML data from URLs directly. This hack is a quick script that exposes your entire database to XSLT from a URL.

XSLT is a great language for reporting or data conversion. It can even read data directly from URLs. However, without extensions, it can't natively access a database. This hack opens up your entire database through your web server (a cool, albeit questionable, idea). It exports queries that are specified on the URL as XML.

The Code

Save the script in Example 5-24 as *query.php*.

Example 5-24. An insecure script

```php
<?php
$dbuser = "root";
$dbpassword = "password";
$dbserver = "localhost";
$dbname = "test";

$db = mysql_connect( $dbserver, $dbuser, $dbpassword );
mysql_select_db( $dbname );

$query = "SELECT * FROM user";
if ( $_GET["query"] )
  $query = $_GET["query"];

$res = mysql_query( $query, $db );

header( "content-type: text/xml" );
?>
<result>
<?php while( $row = mysql_fetch_assoc($res) ) { ?>
  <row>
  <?php foreach( $row as $key => $value ) { ?>
    <data field="<?php echo( $key ); ?>"><?php echo( htmlentities( $value ) ); ?>
    </data>
```

Example 5-24. An insecure script (continued)

```
<?php } ?>
</row>
<?php } ?>
</result>
```

This simple—and incredibly insecure—script starts by defining the connection parameters to the database. Then the script creates an SQL query and executes it against the database.

> You can augment the SQL query by adding a query parameter to the URL.

Once the query is run, the script generates XML as output with the returned fields from each row as elements in the output XML.

Running the Hack

Copy the file to your PHP server and test it by navigating your browser to the URL.

> Before running this hack, make sure that your client and server are within your firewall and are not accessible to the Internet. Otherwise, you are opening your entire database to the outside world!

To specify a query, add a query argument to the URL: *http://localhost/phphacks/xmlquery/query.php?query=SELECT%20*%20FROM%20user*.

This query selects the entire user table from my test database. The XML that's returned looks like this:

```
<result>
  <row>
    <data field="id">1</data>
    <data field="name">jack</data>
  </row>
  <row>
    <data field="id">2</data>
    <data field="name">lori</data>
  </row>
  <row>
    <data field="id">3</data>
    <data field="name">megan</data>
  </row>
</result>
```

On Internet Explorer, you will see a formatted XML display. On other browsers, you might have to view the returned source to see the result. Now you can point your XSLT stylesheet to this URL and have XML access to all the data you want.

See Also

- "Give Your Customers Formatting Control with XSL" **[Hack #7]**

HACK

#41   ## Generate Database SQL

Use PHP to create SQL scripts automatically from a database schema represented as XML.

One of the most common problems with writing database code is the PHP code getting out of sync with the database's structure, or vice versa. Generally we use a *.sql* script to preload the database with the tables and data required to run the application. But this SQL script can be a pain to maintain, especially when you need to update the PHP that references the SQL tables at the same time.

This hack presents some simple scripts to build SQL and PHP automatically from an XML description of the database. This will ensure that the SQL and the PHP are kept in sync. It also means that if you change database servers or versions of PHP, you can still use the same *schema.xml* file. All you need to do is change the generator to emit code for a different type of server or PHP version.

Figure 5-5 shows the program flow with the *schema.xml* file being used as input to the generator code—written in PHP—that creates the MySQL file, which will in turn create the database.

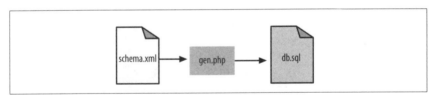

Figure 5-5. The generator creating SQL from a schema XML file

The Code

Save the sample XML document representing a database schema in Example 5-25 as *schema.xml*.

Example 5-25. XML representing the database structure

```
<schema>
  <table name="book">
    <field name="id" type="int" primary-key="true" />
    <field name="title" type="text" />
    <field name="publisher_id" type="int" />
    <field name="author_id" type="int" />
  </table>
  <table name="publisher">
    <field name="id" type="int" primary-key="true" />
    <field name="name" type="text" />
  </table>
  <table name="author">
    <field name="id" type="int" primary-key="true" />
    <field name="name" type="text" />
  </table>
</schema>
```

Save the generation code shown in Example 5-26 as *gen.php*.

Example 5-26. A script that handles database and code generation

```
<?php
$tables = array();

function start_element( $parser, $name, $attribs )
{
  global $tables;
  if ( $name == "TABLE" )
  {
    $table = array();
    $fields = array();

    $table['name'] = $attribs['NAME'];
    $table['fields'] = array();

    $tables []= $table;
  }
  if ( $name == "FIELD" )
  {
    $field = array();
    $field['name'] = $attribs['NAME'];
    $field['type'] = $attribs['TYPE'];
    $field['pk'] = ( $attribs['PRIMARY-KEY'] == "true" ) ? 1 : 0;
    $tables[count($tables)-1]['fields'] []= $field;
  }
}
function end_element( $parser, $name ) { }

$parser = xml_parser_create();
xml_set_element_handler($parser, "start_element", "end_element" );
while( !feof( STDIN ) ) {
```

Example 5-26. A script that handles database and code generation (continued)

```php
$text = fgets( STDIN );
xml_parse( $parser, $text );
}
xml_parser_free( $parser );

ob_start();

foreach( $tables as $table ) {
$pk = null;
?>
DROP TABLE IF EXISTS <?php echo( $table['name'] ) ?>;
CREATE TABLE <?php echo( $table['name'] ) ?> (
<?php
$first = 1;
foreach( $table['fields'] as $field ) {
?>
  <?php echo( $first ? "" : "," ) ?>
<?php echo( $field['name'] ) ?> <?php echo( $field['type'] ) ?>
<?php if ( $field['pk'] ) {
$pk = $field['name'];
?> NOT NULL AUTO_INCREMENT<?php } ?>

<?php
$first = 0;
} ?>
<?php if ( $pk ) { ?>
  ,primary key( <?php echo( $pk ) ?> )
<?php } ?>
);
<?php }

$sql = ob_get_clean();

$fh = fopen( "db.sql", "w" );
fwrite( $fh, $sql );
fclose( $fh );
?>
```

Running the Hack

Use the command-line PHP interpreter to run the code:

```
php gen.php < schema.xml
```

This will create a *db.sql* file that contains code like this (obviously, your results will vary with different databases and tables):

```
DROP TABLE IF EXISTS book;
CREATE TABLE book (
        id int NOT NULL AUTO_INCREMENT
        ,title text
        ,publisher_id int
```

```
        ,author_id int
        ,primary key( id )
);
DROP TABLE IF EXISTS publisher;
CREATE TABLE publisher (
        id int NOT NULL AUTO_INCREMENT
        ,name text
        ,primary key( id )
);
DROP TABLE IF EXISTS author;
CREATE TABLE author (
        id int NOT NULL AUTO_INCREMENT
        ,name text
        ,primary key( id )
);
```

This SQL code creates the table to match the schema described in the *schema.xml* file. The XML contains all of the tables and their fields in an XML format and can be used to generate both SQL **[Hack #42]** and the PHP that uses it **[Hack #37]**. That way, the SQL and PHP never go out of sync.

> Never update the *db.sql* file manually. Always make revisions to the schema XML file and then rerun the generator to create the new SQL.

See Also

- "Generate Database Select Code" **[Hack #42]**
- "Generate CRUD Database Code" **[Hack #37]**

HACK #42 Generate Database Select Code

Use PHP to build code for database access directly from an XML description of the schema.

Building database access classes for SQL tables can require a lot of annoying, error-prone grunt work. In this hack, I use an XML file that describes a database schema and a code generator written in PHP to create the PHP classes automatically.

> I used the same *schema.xml* file that I use in this hack, to generate the corresponding SQL **[Hack #41]**.

Figure 5-6 illustrates how the abstract schema XML is taken as input by the generator. The generator in turn creates the PHP classes in the *mydb.php* file.

This output file is temporary and you should never edit it directly.

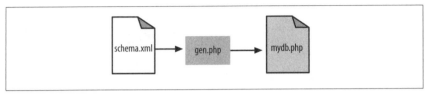

Figure 5-6. The flow of the PHP SQL Select generator

The Code

schema.xml, representing the database, is shown in Example 5-27.

Example 5-27. XML representing a database schema

```
<schema>
   <table name="book">
     <field name="id" type="int" primary-key="true" />
     <field name="title" type="text" />
     <field name="publisher_id" type="int" />
     <field name="author_id" type="int" />
   </table>
   <table name="publisher">
     <field name="id" type="int" primary-key="true" />
     <field name="name" type="text" />
   </table>
   <table name="author">
     <field name="id" type="int" primary-key="true" />
     <field name="name" type="text" />
   </table>
</schema>
```

As when generating CRUD code [Hack #37], you'll need a database wrapper; save Example 5-28 as *dbwrap.php*.

Example 5-28. A wrapper providing database-specific access information

```
<?php
require_once( "DB.php" );
$dsn = 'mysql://root:password@localhost/books';
$db =& DB::Connect( $dsn, array() );
if (PEAR::isError($db)) { die($db->getMessage()); }

function selectOne( $sql, $args )
{
  global $db;
  $res = $db->query( $sql, $args );
```

Example 5-28. A wrapper providing database-specific access information (continued)

```php
  $res->fetchInto($row, DB_FETCHMODE_ASSOC);
  return $row;
}

function selectBlock( $sql, $args )
{
  global $db;
  $res = $db->query( $sql, $args );
  $rows = array();
  while( $res->fetchInto($row, DB_FETCHMODE_ASSOC) ) { $rows []= $row; }
  return $rows;
}
?>
```

Next, save the code in Example 5-29 as *gen.php*. Here is where the actual code generation takes place.

Example 5-29. The script that does the actual code generation

```php
<?php
$tables = array();

function start_element( $parser, $name, $attribs )
{
  global $tables;
  if ( $name == "TABLE" )
  {
    $table = array();
    $fields = array();

    $table['name'] = $attribs['NAME'];
    $table['fields'] = array();

    $tables []= $table;
  }
  if ( $name == "FIELD" )
  {
    $field = array();
    $field['name'] = $attribs['NAME'];
    $field['type'] = $attribs['TYPE'];
    $field['pk'] = ( $attribs['PRIMARY-KEY'] ==  "true" ) ? 1 : 0;
    $tables[count($tables)-1]['fields'] []= $field;
  }
}
function end_element( $parser, $name ) { }

$parser = xml_parser_create();
xml_set_element_handler($parser, "start_element", "end_element" );
while( !feof( STDIN ) ) {
  $text = fgets( STDIN );
  xml_parse( $parser, $text );
}
```

Example 5-29. The script that does the actual code generation (continued)

```php
xml_parser_free( $parser );

ob_start( );

echo( "<?php\n" );
?>
require_once( "dbwrap.php" );

<?php

foreach( $tables as $table ) {
  $pk = null;
  foreach( $table['fields'] as $field ) {
    if ( $field['pk'] )
      $pk = $field['name'];
  }
?>
class <?php echo( ucfirst( $table['name'] ) ) ?>
{
  function getOne( $id )
  {
    return selectOne( "SELECT * FROM <?php echo( $table['name'] ) ?> WHERE
        <?php echo( $pk ); ?> = ?", array( $id ) );
  }
  function getAll( )
  {
    return selectBlock( "SELECT * FROM <?php echo( $table['name'] ) ?>", array( )
);
  }
}

<?php }
echo( "?>" );

$php = ob_get_clean( );

$fh = fopen( "mydb.php", "w" );
fwrite( $fh, $php );
fclose( $fh );

?>
```

This generator code starts by reading the XML into an in-memory data structure. Then it starts buffering the output into a string and creates a class for each table using standard PHP templating techniques. Once all of the class code for the tables is created, the output buffering is turned off and the buffered output is stored into a string, which is then saved into a file using fopen( ), fwrite( ), and fclose( ).

Running the Hack

Use the command-line version of PHP to run the generator against the XML schema file:

```
php gen.php < schema.xml
```

This will create a file called *mydb.php* in the same directory, much like this:

```php
<?php
require_once( "dbwrap.php" );

class Book
{
  function getOne( $id )
  {
    return selectOne( "SELECT * FROM book WHERE id = ?", array( $id ) );
  }
  function getAll()
  {
    return selectBlock( "SELECT * FROM book", array() );
  }
}

class Publisher
{
  function getOne( $id )
  {
    return selectOne( "SELECT * FROM publisher WHERE id = ?", array( $id )
);
  }
  function getAll()
  {
    return selectBlock( "SELECT * FROM publisher", array() );
  }
}

class Author
{
  function getOne( $id )
  {
    return selectOne( "SELECT * FROM author WHERE id = ?", array( $id ) );
  }
  function getAll()
  {
    return selectBlock( "SELECT * FROM author", array() );
  }
}

?>
```

How cool is that! PHP that creates PHP!

The script starts by parsing through the schema file and then uses simple PHP to create the code that uses the functions in *dbwrap.php* to query the data from the database. Each class has two functions: one gets all of the items in the table, and the other gets just a single record.

To test this, create *index.php* (shown in Example 5-30) and use it to create a Publisher object to query the publisher table.

Example 5-30. A script that tests the database code

```
<?php
require_once( "mydb.php" );
$pub = new Publisher( );
?>
<html>
<body>
<table>
<?php
$rows = $pub->getAll( );
foreach( $rows as $row ) {
?>
<tr><td><?php echo( $row['id'] ); ?></td>
<td><?php echo( $row['name'] ); ?></td></tr>
<?php } ?>
</table>
</body>
</html>
```

Use your browser to navigate to the page to see the contents of the publisher table. Figure 5-7 shows the publisher table in the browser.

See Also

- "Generate Database SQL" **[Hack #41]**
- "Generate CRUD Database Code" **[Hack #37]**

HACK #43   Convert CSV to PHP

Use PHP to create PHP data arrays from comma-separated value (CSV) datafiles.

Every once in a while, I have a static list of values that I don't want to put into a database, but that I do want to use in my PHP application. That static data can come from a variety of sources, but often it's in a spreadsheet. This handy hack converts any CSV data (one of the easiest formats to pull from a spreadsheet) to PHP code that I can then copy and paste into my PHP page.

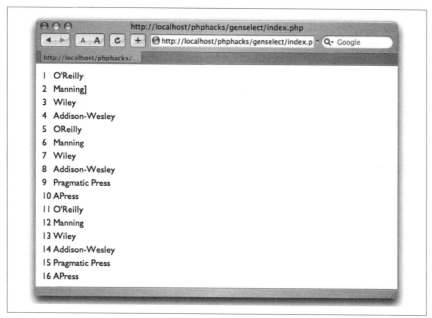

Figure 5-7. The publisher table as shown in the browser

The Code

Save the code in Example 5-31 as *index.php*.

Example 5-31. Page that sets up some comma-separated values to convert

```
<html>
<body>
<form method="post" action="commaconv.php" />
<table>
<tr><td>CSV Data:</td>
<td><textarea name="data" cols="40" rows="10">
"Alabama",4530182
"Alaska",655435
"Arizona",5743834
"Arkansas",2752629
"California",35893799
"Colorado",4601403
"Connecticut",3503604
"Delaware",830364
"District of Columbia",553523
"Florida",17397161
"Georgia",8829383
"Hawaii",1262840
"Idaho",1393262
"Illinois",12713634
"Indiana",6237569
```

Example 5-31. Page that sets up some comma-separated values to convert (continued)

```
"Iowa",2954451
"Kansas",2735502
"Kentucky",4145922
"Louisiana",4515770
"Maine",1317253
"Maryland",5558058
"Massachusetts",6416505
"Michigan",10112620
"Minnesota",5100958
"Mississippi",2902966
"Missouri",5754618
"Montana",926865
"Nebraska",1747214
"Nevada",2334771
"New Hampshire",1299500
"New Jersey",8698879
"New Mexico",1903289
"New York",19227088
"North Carolina",8541221
"North Dakota",634366
"Ohio",11459011
"Oklahoma",3523553
"Oregon",3594586
"Pennsylvania",12406292
"Rhode Island",1080632
"South Carolina",4198068
"South Dakota",770883
"Tennessee",5900962
"Texas",22490022
"Utah",2389039
"Vermont",621394
"Virginia",7459827
"Washington",6203788
"West Virginia",1815354
"Wisconsin",5509026
"Wyoming",506529</textarea></td></tr>
<tr><td> Field Name 1:</td><td><input name="field0" value="state" /></td></tr>
<tr><td> Field Name 2:</td><td><input name="field1" value="population" /></td>
    </tr>
<tr><td> Field Name 3:</td><td><input name="field2" value="" /></td></tr>
<tr><td> Field Name 4:</td><td><input name="field3" value="" /></td></tr>
<tr><td> Field Name 5:</td><td><input name="field4" value="" /></td></tr>
</table>
<input type="submit" />
</form>
</body>
</html>
```

The code in Example 5-32—*commaconv.php*—handles the data conversion.

Example 5-32. PHP that converts data from CSV just as easily as from XML or SQL

```
<html><body>
<div style="font-family:courier; font-size:small;">
$data = array(<br/>
<?
$fieldnames = array(
  $_POST['field0' ],
  $_POST['field1' ],
  $_POST['field2' ],
  $_POST['field3' ],
  $_POST['field4' ] );
$rows = split( "\n", $_POST['data'] );
$index = 0;
foreach( $rows as $row )
{
  if ( $index != 0 )
    print( ",<br/>" );
  $index++;

  print( "  array(" );
  $fields = split( ",", $row );
  for( $f = 0; $f < count( $fields ); $f++ )
  {
    $data = $fields[ $f ];
    $data = preg_replace( "/\\\\"/", "\"", $data );

    if ( $f > 0 )
      print( ", " );
    print( $fieldnames[ $f ] );
    print( " => " );
    print( $data );
  }
  print( "  )" );
}
?><br/>
);
</div>
</body></html>
```

Running the Hack

First navigate to the *index.php* page on the server. There you will see the form shown in Figure 5-8. Paste the CSV data you have into the CSV Data field (or you can use the state data provided by default). Then type the names of the fields from the CSV data into the Field Name fields that follow.

> The page currently hardwires in five fields, but it would be trivial to change the HTML to allow for more field names.

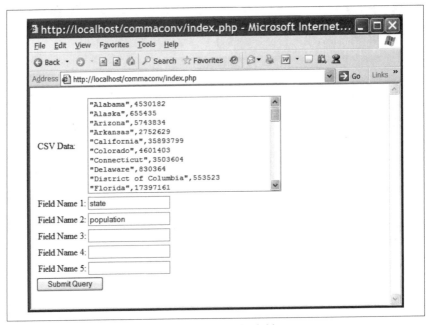

Figure 5-8. The entry form for the CSV data and the field names

Once you are done entering data and column names, click the Submit Query button and the form will submit the data to the *commaconv.php* script. The output of the script looks like Figure 5-9.

Select all of the text on this page and use the Copy command in the browser to put the text into the clipboard. You can then use the Paste command in your favorite text editor to put this code into your page.

H A C K

#44   Scrape Web Pages for Data

Use regular expressions to scrape data from sources like Metacritic.

What do you do when you want the data from a site, but the site won't let you export that data in a predictable format (like XML **[Hack #38]** or CSV **[Hack #43]**)? One popular option is to perform what's called a *screen scrape* on the HTML to extract the data. Screen scraping starts with downloading the contents of the page containing the data into either a string in memory or a file. Regular expressions are then used to extract the relevant data from the string or file.

You can scrape almost any web site for data; for the example in this hack, I chose the Metacritic DVD review page (*http://www.metacritic.com/video/*).

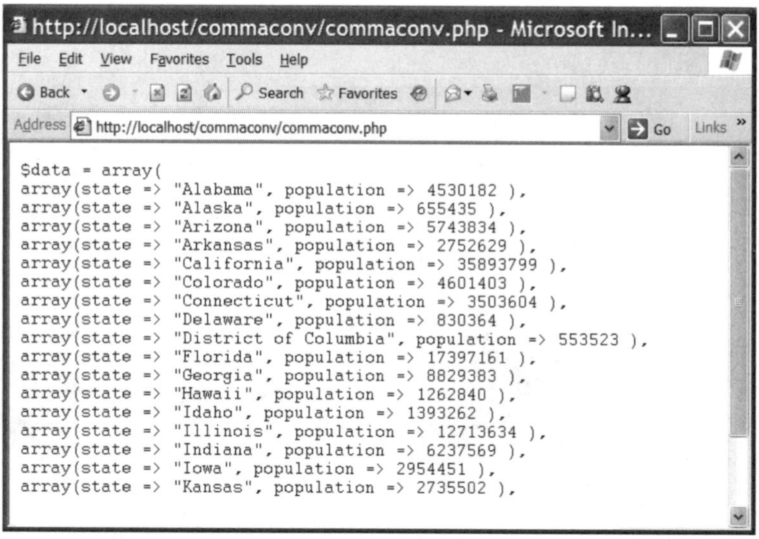

Figure 5-9. The resulting generated PHP

Metacritic is a site where movies, music, and video games are given a review score based on a selection of reviews. Figure 5-10 shows the Metacritic page that I scraped for this hack. On the lefthand side of the window is a list of movies ordered by name, along with their review scores.

I can tell from the size of the page that I want only a small portion of the HTML. I use View Source to see what the code looks like, and indeed there is a section for these scores well defined by a div tag that contains what I'm looking for:

```
</TR>
</TABLE>
  <DIV ID="sortbyname1">
  <P CLASS="listing">
  <SPAN CLASS="yellow">51</SPAN>
      <A HREF="/video/titles/800bullets">800 Bullets</A><BR>
  <SPAN CLASS="yellow">58</SPAN>
      <A HREF="/video/titles/actsofworship">Acts of Worship</A><BR>
  <SPAN CLASS="green">81</SPAN>
      <A HREF="/video/titles/badeducation"><B>Bad Education</B></A><IMG
SRC="/_images/scores/star.gif" WIDTH="11" HEIGHT="11" ALIGN="absmiddle"><BR>
  ...
```

The first step will be to extract just this div tag. Then we need to use another regular expression to pick out each movie entry from text within the div tag. Notice that each movie listing starts with a span tag and ends with a

Figure 5-10. The Metacritic DVD and Video Review page

br tag; that's good enough to delineate each movie. The third listing has some extra stuff around the movie title that I strip out with another set of regular expressions.

I strongly recommend using a divide-and-conquer technique when writing screen-scraping code. Don't try to do all of the work with a single regular expression, or you'll end up with indecipherable code that even you can't maintain.

The Code

Save the code in Example 5-33 as *scrapecritic.php*.

Example 5-33. PHP for loading a URL and scraping content from it

```
<html>
<?
// Set up the CURL object
$ch = curl_init( "http://www.metacritic.com/video/" );

// Fake out the User Agent
curl_setopt( $ch, CURLOPT_USERAGENT, "Internet Explorer" );
```

Example 5-33. PHP for loading a URL and scraping content from it (continued)

```php
// Start the output buffering
ob_start( );

// Get the HTML from MetaCritic
curl_exec( $ch );
curl_close( $ch );

// Get the contents of the output buffer
$str = ob_get_contents( );
ob_end_clean( );

// Get just the list sorted by name
preg_match( "/\<DIV ID=\"sortbyname1\"\>(.*?)\<\/DIV\>/is",
        $str, $byname );

// Get each of the movie entries
preg_match_all( "/\<SPAN.*?>(.*?)\<\/SPAN\>.*?\<A.*?\>(.*?)\<BR\>/is",
        $byname[0], $moviedata );

// Work through the raw movie data
$movies = array( );
for( $i = 0; $i < count( $moviedata[1] ); $i++ )
{
        // The score is ok already
        $score = $moviedata[1][$i];

        // We need to remove tags from the title and decode
        // the HTML entities
        $title = $moviedata[2][$i];
        $title = preg_replace( "/<.*?>/", "", $title );
        $title = html_entity_decode( $title );

        // Then add the movie to the array
        $movies []= array( $score, $title );
}
?>
<body>
<table>
<tr>
<th>Name</th><th>Score</th>
</tr>
<? foreach( $movies as $movie ) { ?>
<tr>
<td><? echo( $movie[1] ) ?></td>
<td><? echo( $movie[0] ) ?></td>
</tr>
<? } ?>
</table>
</body>
</html>
```

The *scrapecritic.php* script starts by downloading the current contents of the Metacritic DVD page into a string. It does this by using the ob_start( ), ob_get_contents( ), and ob_end_clean( ) functions to grab the text that curl_exec( ) would have put into the page, and instead copies it into a string.

The next step is to grab just the div tag that corresponds to the list sorted by name, using a preg_match( ) with a regular expression customized to this particular page. This is a clear demonstration of the primary technical problem with screen scraping: if the site being scraped changes its formatting in even the slightest way, it can (and probably will) break the scraping code. It's always better to get an XML feed for the data if that's possible. XML is far more resilient to changes in format.

With the name-sorted list in hand, the script then uses preg_match_all( ) to extract all of the movie names and scores into an array. The final step is to take this array of movies and strip the movie name of any extraneous tags or formatting.

At this point, the data is cleaned and ready to be presented. The script uses a simple foreach loop to create a table that shows the name of the movie and the aggregated review score.

Running the Hack

To run the hack, copy the file onto your PHP server and surf to it in your web browser. The result should look like Figure 5-11.

> Another use for screen scraping is content type conversion. You can take what was an HTML page and turn it into a WML page for web-enabled phones, or an RSS feed for news aggregators.

Problems with Screen Scraping

There are two major problems with screen scraping. The first is technical and the second is legal. On the technical side, screen scraping is inclined to break when the site being scraped changes its format. In addition, the scraping code for one site will likely not work on other sites because of formatting issues. Finally, screen scraping can be slow or even break when the target site is not responding to web requests in a timely manner.

Judiciously choosing which pages you can scrape is also important. Look for pages that were generated by a web application, as opposed to written by

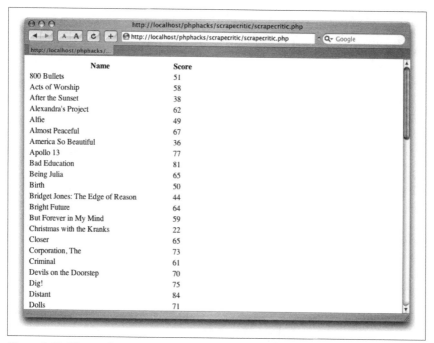

Figure 5-11. The resulting screen-scraped page

hand. Handwritten pages will have almost random markup; application-generated pages usually have a predictable format that will make writing regular expressions to match the format a lot easier.

> Web application pages normally end with extensions such as
> *.php*, *.jsp*, *.asp*, or some similar variant. Handwritten pages
> usually have the *.htm* or *.html* extension.

On the legal side, you must always make sure that you have permission to use the data in this way before adding this functionality to your site. There's nothing worse than writing lots of screen-scraping code only to find out that the content you've scraped was obtained illegally and cannot be used.

See Also

- "Spider Your Site" **[Hack #84]**
- "Test Your Application with Robots" **[Hack #83]**

HACK #45 Suck Data from Excel Uploads

Using the XML from Excel 2003, you can read data directly from spreadsheets that customers upload to your site.

Your customers' data can come from many different sources. Making it easy for them to get their data into your system can mean the difference between getting their business and having them go somewhere else for their data needs (and taking their money with them). Supporting data import from common data sources such as Excel can be a very compelling feature for customers.

This hack shows you how to save Excel spreadsheets in the new XML format supported by Excel and Microsoft Office 2003 and how to read that format and display the data back to the user. Figure 5-12 illustrates the flow between the browser (shown here as the computer) and the import system. The first page is *index.php*, which presents the Browse button. The user then selects an Excel XML file, which is submitted to the *import.php* page; that page returns an HTML rendering of the data in the file.

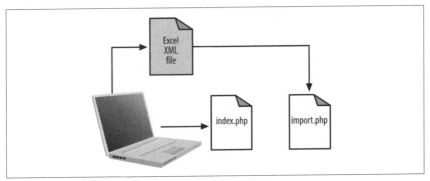

Figure 5-12. The flow of the Excel XML import

The Code

index.php (shown in Example 5-34) is responsible for getting the Excel data into your PHP scripts.

Example 5-34. The PHP for getting Excel data into your scripts

```
<html>
<body>
  <form enctype="multipart/form-data" action="import.php" method="post">
  Excel XML file:
      <input type="hidden" name="MAX_FILE_SIZE" value="2000000" />
```

Example 5-34. The PHP for getting Excel data into your scripts (continued)

```
    <input type="file" name="file" /><br/>
    <input type="submit" value="Upload" />
  </form>
</body>
</html>
```

Save the code in Example 5-35 as *import.php*. It handles the data import.

Example 5-35. PHP that handles Excel data import

```php
<html>
<body>
<?php
$data = array();
if ( $_FILES['file']['tmp_name'] )
{
  $dom = DOMDocument::load( $_FILES['file']['tmp_name'] );
  $rows = $dom->getElementsByTagName( 'Row' );
  foreach ($rows as $row)
  {
      $cells = $row->getElementsByTagName( 'Cell' );
      $datarow = array();
      foreach ($cells as $cell)
      {
          $datarow []= $cell->nodeValue;
      }
      $data []= $datarow;
  }
}
?>
<table>
<?php foreach( $data as $row ) { ?>
<tr>
<?php foreach( $row as $item ) { ?>
<td><?php echo( $item ); ?></td>
<?php } ?>
</tr>
<?php } ?>
</table>
</body>
</html>
```

The *import.php* page, which is at the heart of this hack, starts by opening up
the uploaded file using the XML DOM reader. Then it iterates through each
Row element, and within each, it works through the Cell elements. In each
Cell, the script finds the actual data, which is stored into an array called
$datarow. That stored data is then output as HTML using standard PHP text
templating techniques (at the end of the script).

Running the Hack

Running this hack begins with creating an Excel spreadsheet. As is my practice, I went to the U.S. Census Bureau (*http://www.census.gov*) to score some data. In this case, I've used median family income in various brackets in the 50 states. (By the way, for a two-person family, the state with the highest median income was Alaska; go figure!) Anyway, the data looks like Figure 5-13.

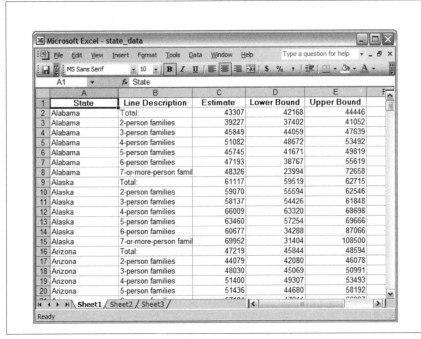

Figure 5-13. The original Excel spreadsheet

Now I have to convert it to the XML spreadsheet format using Save As, as shown in Figure 5-14.

It's interesting to note here that I can keep the spreadsheet in XML format indefinitely; there is no loss of fidelity or precision between the binary version and the XML version. If you have a customer with Office 2003 and you are giving him a spreadsheet to start with, just give him the XML version! That way he can keep working in it and never know the difference.

Now, with XML in hand, we can upload the pages to the site; using the browser, surf to *index.php*. The page is shown in Figure 5-15.

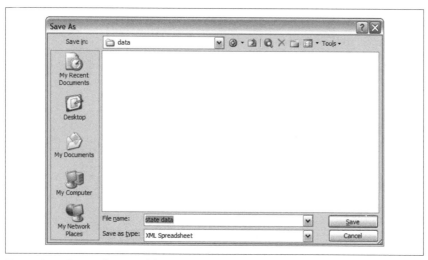

Figure 5-14. Saving the spreadsheet in XML format

Figure 5-15. Uploading the spreadsheet to the server

Now click on the Browse button and find the XML spreadsheet. Then click on the Upload button, and that will submit the XML data to the *import.php* page. This page uses the XML DOM and XPath support in PHP to parse up the XML and extract the table data. Then it uses some simple PHP to format the data as an HTML table. The result for the example census data I showed in Figure 5-13 is shown in Figure 5-16.

> Obviously, if you want to input the data into the database, you should change the code from formatting HTML to running SQL INSERT statements.

State	Line Description	Estimate	Lower Bound	Upper Bound
Alabama	Total	43307	42168	44446
Alabama	2-person families	39227	37402	41052
Alabama	3-person families	45849	44059	47639
Alabama	4-person families	51082	48672	53492
Alabama	5-person families	45745	41671	49819
Alabama	6-person families	47193	38767	55619
Alabama	7-or-more-person families	48326	23994	72658
Alaska	Total	61117	59519	62715
Alaska	2-person families	59070	55594	62546
Alaska	3-person families	58137	54426	61848
Alaska	4-person families	66009	63320	68698

Figure 5-16. The spreadsheet data in HTML format

These types of user convenience features can be extremely compelling. Instead of spending hours typing their data into HTML forms and working with a clunky web interface, your customers can simply use tools they are familiar with, such as Excel.

See Also

- "Load Your Database from Excel" [Hack #46]

HACK #46 Load Your Database from Excel

Use Excel 2003's XML capability to load your SQL database from an Excel spreadsheet.

More than a few times, I have had an Excel spreadsheet full of data that I needed to load into my database. Before Office 2003, I had to export each sheet as a CSV, and then use a custom loader to insert the records into the database. With Excel 2003's ability to save spreadsheets, macros, and even formatting as XML, that custom loader can go the way of eight-track tapes. The script in this hack turns Excel XML data into SQL that you can feed to your database. Figure 5-17 shows how the Excel-generated XML, taken as input to the *gen.php* script, is converted to SQL, which is then fed into the database.

Figure 5-17. The flow between the Excel XML and the database

The Code

Save the code in Example 5-36 as *gen.php*.

Example 5-36. The code to generate SQL from an Excel XML file

```php
<?php
$tables = array( );
$indata = 0;

function encode( $text )
{
  $text = preg_replace( "/'/", "''", $text );
  return "'".$text."'";
}

function start_element( $parser, $name, $attribs )
{
  global $tables, $indata;
  if ( $name == "WORKSHEET" )
  {
        $tables []= array(
                'name' => $attribs['SS:NAME'],
                'data' => array( )
        );
  }
  if ( $name == "ROW" )
  {
        $tables[count($tables)-1]['data'] []= array( );
  }
  if ( $name == "DATA" )
  {
        $indata = 1;
  }
}
function text( $parser, $text )
{
  global $tables, $indata;
  if ( $indata )
  {
```

Example 5-36. The code to generate SQL from an Excel XML file (continued)

```
        $data =& $tables[count($tables)-1]['data'];
        $data[count($data)-1] []= $text;
  }
}
function end_element( $parser, $name )
{
  global $indata;
  if ( $name == "DATA" )
        $indata = 0;
}

$parser = xml_parser_create( );
xml_set_element_handler( $parser, "start_element", "end_element" );
xml_set_character_data_handler( $parser, "text" );
while( !feof( STDIN ) ) {
  $text = fgets( STDIN );
  xml_parse( $parser, $text );
}
xml_parser_free( $parser );

foreach( $tables as $table ) {
  $name = $table['name'];
  $data =& $table['data'];
  $cols = implode( ", ", $data[0] );
  for( $in = 1; $in < count( $data ); $in++ ) {
        $sqldata = implode( ", ", array_map( "encode", $data[$in] ) );
?>
INSERT INTO <?php echo( $name )?> ( <?php echo( $cols ) ?> ) VALUES ( <?php echo(
    $sqldata ); ?> );

<?php } } ?>
```

This script is primarily an XML parser. Most of the code is in the XML parsing where the script looks for <Data> tags, which hold the spreadsheet's data. When the data is found, it's stored in an in-memory list of data tables. Then, for each table, there is a set of <Data> rows. These <Data> rows contain the data for each cell in the spreadsheet.

The second half of the script formats the fields and data within the $tables array into INSERT INTO commands (for simplicity, these are just output to the console). You can easily redirect that output into the mysql command, loading the data directly into the database, or you can store the output in a file for later (or repeated) use.

Running the Hack

First create a spreadsheet in Excel 2003. I created the simple sheet shown in Figure 5-18 to preload the publisher table of my database.

Figure 5-18. A sample Excel spreadsheet with data for the database

I removed the worksheets that I didn't need—empty sheets just bloat the XML—and then renamed the first worksheet publisher.

> The script in Example 5-36 uses the name of the sheet containing the data as the name of the table into which to load the data.

The first row of the worksheet contains the names of the fields. All subsequent rows contain the data to load into the table.

Next, save the file as XML using the Save As command in Excel's File menu. Here is a portion of the XML data from that file:

```xml
<?xml version="1.0"?>
<Workbook xmlns="urn:schemas-microsoft-com:office:spreadsheet"
 xmlns:o="urn:schemas-microsoft-com:office:office"
 xmlns:x="urn:schemas-microsoft-com:office:excel"
 xmlns:html="http://www.w3.org/TR/REC-html40"
 xmlns:ss="urn:schemas-microsoft-com:office:spreadsheet">
<DocumentProperties xmlns="urn:schemas-microsoft-com:office:office">
 <Author>Jack Herrington</Author>
 <LastAuthor>Jack Herrington</LastAuthor>
 <Created>2005-05-23T03:36:24Z</Created>
 <Company>MM</Company>
 <Version>11.257</Version>
</DocumentProperties>
```

```
<OfficeDocumentSettings xmlns="urn:schemas-microsoft-com:office:office">
<AllowPNG/>
</OfficeDocumentSettings>
<ExcelWorkbook xmlns="urn:schemas-microsoft-com:office:excel">
<WindowHeight>15080</WindowHeight>
<WindowWidth>24840</WindowWidth>
<WindowTopX>80</WindowTopX>
<WindowTopY>-20</WindowTopY>
<Date1904/>
<AcceptLabelsInFormulas/>
<ProtectStructure>False</ProtectStructure>
<ProtectWindows>False</ProtectWindows>
</ExcelWorkbook>
<Styles>
<Style ss:ID="Default" ss:Name="Normal">
<Alignment ss:Vertical="Bottom"/>
<Borders/>
<Font ss:FontName="Verdana"/>
<Interior/>
<NumberFormat/>
<Protection/>
</Style>
</Styles>
<Worksheet ss:Name="Publisher">
<Table ss:ExpandedColumnCount="2" ss:ExpandedRowCount="7" x:
FullColumns="1"
 x:FullRows="1">
 <Row>
 <Cell><Data ss:Type="String">ID</Data></Cell>
 <Cell><Data ss:Type="String">Name</Data></Cell>
 </Row>
 <Row>
 <Cell ss:Formula="=&quot;0&quot;"><Data ss:Type="String">0</Data></Cell>
 <Cell><Data ss:Type="String">O'Reilly</Data></Cell>
 </Row>
 <Row>
 <Cell ss:Formula="=&quot;0&quot;"><Data ss:Type="String">0</Data></Cell>
 <Cell><Data ss:Type="String">Manning</Data></Cell>
 </Row>
 ...
```

From this XML, I want the name of the worksheet, as well as the rows of data.

Use the command-line version of PHP to run the SQL generator script on the Excel XML data:

```
% php gen.php < data.xml
INSERT INTO Publisher ( ID, Name ) VALUES ( '0', 'O''Reilly' );
INSERT INTO Publisher ( ID, Name ) VALUES ( '0', 'Manning' );
INSERT INTO Publisher ( ID, Name ) VALUES ( '0', 'Wiley' );
INSERT INTO Publisher ( ID, Name ) VALUES ( '0', 'Addison-Wesley' );
INSERT INTO Publisher ( ID, Name ) VALUES ( '0', 'Pragmatic Press' );
INSERT INTO Publisher ( ID, Name ) VALUES ( '0', 'APress' );
```

You can also pipe this right into a file, for example:

```
% php gen.php < data.xml > publishers.sql
```

See Also

- "Suck Data from Excel Uploads" [Hack #45]
- "Create Excel Spreadsheets Dynamically" [Hack #49]

HACK #47 Search Microsoft Word Documents

Search the text in Microsoft Word documents by parsing WordML files.

A lot of valuable data is locked up in Microsoft Word documents. In particular, documents such as resumes are particularly tempting for data-mining applications. Job boards need code that parses Word documents and finds keywords or phrases to categorize the job candidates. This hack demonstrates how to search Word documents saved as WordML for text strings.

The Code

Save the code shown in Example 5-37 as *index.php*.

Example 5-37. HTML that handles data uploads

```
<html>
<body>
  <form enctype="multipart/form-data" action="search.php" method="post">
    WordML file: <input type="hidden" name="MAX_FILE_SIZE" value="2000000" />
    <input type="file" name="file" /><br/>
    <input type="submit" value="Upload" />
  </form>
</body>
</html>
```

Save the code in Example 5-38 as *search.php*. This script looks through the uploaded WordML for specific features.

Example 5-38. Script that handles searching

```
<html>
<body>
<?php
$wordlist = array();

$dom = new DOMDocument();
if ( $_FILES['file']['tmp_name'] )
{
  $dom->load( $_FILES['file']['tmp_name'] );
  $found = $dom->getElementsByTagName( "t" );
```

Example 5-38. Script that handles searching (continued)

```
foreach( $found as $element )
{
  $words = split( ' ', $element->nodeValue );
  foreach( $words as $word )
  {
    $word = preg_replace( '/[,]|[.]/', '', $word );
    $word = preg_replace( '/^\s+/', '', $word );
    $word = preg_replace( '/\s+$/', '', $word );
    if ( strlen( $word ) > 0 )
    {
      $word = strtolower( $word );
      $wordlist[ $word ] = 0;
    }
  }
}

$words = array_keys( $wordlist );
sort( $words );

foreach( $words as $word ) {
?>
<?php echo( $word ); ?><br/>
<?php } ?>
</body>
</html>
```

The *search.php* script starts by taking the uploaded WordML file and opening it using the XML DOM objects. Then it finds all of the t nodes. t nodes are where the text of the document is stored. From there, it removes any punctuation. It then chops up the remaining text into words and stores those words into a hash table called $wordlist. That word list is then written out at the end of the script.

Running the Hack

Write a simple Microsoft Word 2003 document and save it as a WordML file somewhere on your disk. Then upload these files to your web server and navigate your browser to *index.php*. It should look like Figure 5-19.

Click on the Browse button and select the WordML file. Then click on the Upload button. That will send the file to the *search.php* script. That script uses the XML DOM to read the file. The data in the WordML file is sorted and reported on the HTML page, as shown in Figure 5-20.

From here, you can look for specific words, or count the occurrence of certain words [Hack #24].

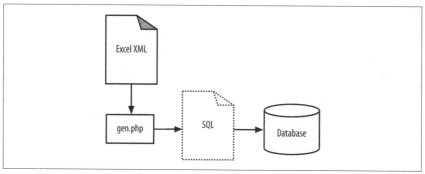

Figure 5-19. The upload page

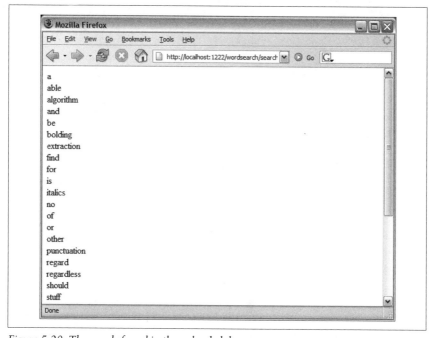

Figure 5-20. The words found in the uploaded document

 WordML is only supported by Microsoft Word 2003 and later versions. It's not currently supported on the Macintosh, though I expect it will be in later versions. To support older versions of Microsoft Word, you might want to rewrite the hack code to parse RTF instead of WordML. Every recent version of Microsoft Word supports RTF.

See Also

- "Create RTF Documents Dynamically" **[Hack #48]**

Create RTF Documents Dynamically

HACK
#48   Use PHP to generate Rich Text Format (RTF) documents dynamically.

Rich Text Format (RTF) is a text format used by word processors, notably Microsoft Word, and some text editors and viewers to store highly styled documents. If you want to generate documents dynamically with all of the features of a word processor, RTF gives you an opportunity to do that.

Start with a word processing document in an editor such as Microsoft Word. Figure 5-21 shows the document used in this hack.

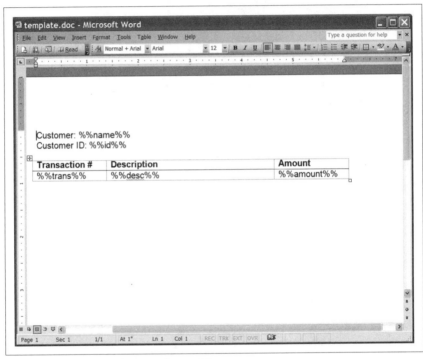

Figure 5-21. The original Microsoft Word document

The sections of the document with the %% markers around them are where I want the dynamic data to go. I could have picked any special characters, but %% has the advantage of being pretty distinct and unusual; further, the percent signs aren't encoded in RTF.

With the document in hand, use the Save As command to save the file as RTF. Then, using that RTF file as a template, you can start writing the PHP code that will generate the RTF.

The Code

Save the file shown in Example 5-39 as *rtf.php*.

Example 5-39. Using escape sequences to represent RTF

```
<? header( "content-type: application/msword" );
$customerName = "First customer";
$customerID = "cust_0001";
$data = array(
  array( trans => "123", desc => "Books", amount => '$123.25' ),
  array( trans => "345", desc => "Stamps", amount => '$22.93' ),
  array( trans => "1531", desc => "Candles", amount => '$56.27' )
);
?>
{\rtf1\ansi\ansicpg1252\uc1\deff0\stshfdbch0\stshfloch0\stshfhich0\stshfbi0\
deflang1033\deflangfe1033
{\fonttbl{\f0\froman\fcharset0\fprq2{\*\panose 02020603050405020304}
Times New Roman;}{\f1\fswiss\fcharset0\fprq2{\*\panose
020b0604020202020204}Arial;}
{\f180\froman\fcharset238\fprq2 Times New Roman CE;}{\f181\froman\fcharset204\
fprq2 Times New Roman Cyr;}
{\f183\froman\fcharset161\fprq2 Times New Roman Greek;}{\f184\froman\fcharset162\
fprq2 Times New Roman Tur;}
{\f185\froman\fcharset177\fprq2 Times New Roman (Hebrew);}
{\f186\froman\fcharset178\fprq2 Times New Roman (Arabic);}
{\f187\froman\fcharset186\fprq2 Times New Roman Baltic;}
{\f188\froman\fcharset163\fprq2 Times New Roman (Vietnamese);}
{\f190\fswiss\fcharset238\fprq2 Arial CE;}{\f191\fswiss\fcharset204\fprq2 Arial
Cyr;}
{\f193\fswiss\fcharset161\fprq2 Arial Greek;}{\f194\fswiss\fcharset162\fprq2
Arial Tur;}
{\f195\fswiss\fcharset177\fprq2 Arial (Hebrew);}
{\f196\fswiss\fcharset178\fprq2 Arial (Arabic);}
{\f197\fswiss\fcharset186\fprq2 Arial Baltic;}{\f198\fswiss\fcharset163\fprq2
Arial (Vietnamese);}
}{\colortbl;\red0\green0\blue0;\red0\green0\blue255;\red0\green255\blue255;\red0\
green255\blue0;
\red255\green0\blue255;\red255\green0\blue0;\red255\green255\blue0;\red255\
green255\blue255;
\red0\green0\blue128;\red0\green128\blue128;\red0\green128\blue0;\red128\green0\
blue128;
\red128\green0\blue0;\red128\green128\blue0;\red128\green128\blue128;
\red192\green192\blue192;}{\stylesheet{\ql
\li0\ri0\widctlpar\aspalpha\aspnum\faauto\adjustright\rin0\lin0\itap0
\fs24\lang1033\langfe1033\cgrid\langnp1033\langfenp1033 \snext0 Normal;}
{\*\cs10 \additive \ssemihidden Default Paragraph Font;}{\*
\ts11\tsrowd\trftsWidthB3\trpaddl108\trpaddr108\trpaddfl3\trpaddft3\trpaddfb3\
trpaddfr3\tscellwidthfts0\tsvertalt\tsbrdrt\tsbrdrl\tsbrdrb\tsbrdrr\tsbrdrdgl\
tsbrdrdgr\tsbrdrh\tsbrdrv
\ql \li0\ri0\widctlpar\aspalpha\aspnum\faauto\adjustright\rin0\lin0\itap0
\fs20\lang1024\langfe1024\cgrid\langnp1024\langfenp1024 \snext11
\ssemihidden Normal Table;}{\*\ts15\tsrowd\trbrdrt\brdrs\brdrw10
```

Example 5-39. Using escape sequences to represent RTF (continued)

```
\trbrdrl\brdrs\brdrw10 \trbrdrb\brdrs\brdrw10
\trbrdrr\brdrs\brdrw10 \trbrdrh\brdrs\brdrw10 \trbrdrv\brdrs\brdrw10
\trftsWidthB3\trpaddl108\trpaddr108\trpaddfl3\trpaddft3\trpaddfb3\trpaddfr3\
tscellwidthfts0\tsvertalt\tsbrdrt\tsbrdrl\tsbrdrb\tsbrdrr\tsbrdrdgl\tsbrdrdgr\
tsbrdrh\tsbrdrv
\ql \li0\ri0\widctlpar\aspalpha\aspnum\faauto\adjustright\rin0\lin0\itap0
\fs20\lang1024\langfe1024\cgrid\langnp1024\langfenp1024 \sbasedon11 \snext15
\styrsid6312866 Table Grid;}}{\*\latentstyles\lsdstimax156\lsdlockeddef0}{\*\
rsidtbl \rsid6312866}
{\*\generator Microsoft Word 11.0.6359;}{\info{\title Customer <? print(
$customerName ) ?> }
{\author jherring}{\operator jherring}{\creatim\yr2005\mo4\dy30\hr21\min46}
{\revtim\yr2005\mo4\dy30\hr21\min46}{\version2}{\edmins0}{\nofpages1}{\
nofwords15}{\nofchars91}
{\*\company Macromedia Inc.}{\nofcharsws105}{\vern24703}}
\widowctrl\ftnbj\aenddoc\noxlattoyen\expshrtn\noultrlspc\dntblnsbdb\nospaceforul\
formshade\horzdoc\dgmargin\dghspace180\dgvspace180\dghorigin1800\dgvorigin1440\
dghshow1\dgvshow1
\jexpand\viewkind1\viewscale125\pgbrdrhead\pgbrdrfoot\splytwnine\ftnlytwnine\
htmautsp\nolnhtadjtbl\useltbaln\alntblind\lytcalctblwd\lyttblrtgr\lnbrkrule\
nobrkwrptbl\snaptogridincell\allowfieldendsel\wrppunct\asianbrkrule\nojkernpunct\
rsidroot6312866 \feto
\sectd \linex0\endnhere\sectlinegrid360\sectdefaultcl\sftnbj
{\*\pnseclvl1\pnucrm\pnstart1\pnindent720\pnhang {\pntxta .}}
{\*\pnseclvl2\pnucltr\pnstart1\pnindent720\pnhang {\pntxta .}}
{\*\pnseclvl3\pndec\pnstart1\pnindent720\pnhang {\pntxta .}}
{\*\pnseclvl4\pnlcltr\pnstart1\pnindent720\pnhang {\pntxta )}}
{\*\pnseclvl5\pndec\pnstart1\pnindent720\pnhang {\pntxtb (}{\pntxta )}}
{\*\pnseclvl6\pnlcltr\pnstart1\pnindent720\pnhang {\pntxtb (}{\pntxta )}}
{\*\pnseclvl7\pnlcrm\pnstart1\pnindent720\pnhang
{\pntxtb (}{\pntxta )}}{\*\pnseclvl8\pnlcltr\pnstart1\pnindent720\pnhang {\pntxtb
(}
{\pntxta )}}{\*\pnseclvl9\pnlcrm\pnstart1\pnindent720\pnhang {\pntxtb (}{\pntxta
)}}
\pard\plain \ql \li0\ri0\widctlpar\aspalpha\aspnum\faauto\adjustright\rin0\lin0\
itap0
\fs24\lang1033\langfe1033\cgrid\langnp1033\langfenp1033
{\f1\insrsid6312866\charrsid6312866 Customer: <? print( $customerName) ?>
\par Customer ID: <? print( $customerID ) ?>
\par
\par }\trowd \irow0\irowband0\ts15\trgaph108\trleft-108\trftsWidth1\trftsWidthB3\
trftsWidthA3\trautofit1\trpaddl108\trpaddr108\trpaddfl3\trpaddft3\trpaddfb3\
trpaddfr3\tbllkhdrrows\tbllklastrow\tbllkhdrcols\tbllklastcol \clvertalt\clbrdrt\
brdrtbl \clbrdrl
\brdrtbl \clbrdrb\brdrs\brdrw10 \clbrdrr\brdrtbl \cltxlrtb\clftsWidth3\
clwWidth2088\clshdrawnil
\cellx1980\clvertalt\clbrdrt\brdrtbl \clbrdrl\brdrtbl \clbrdrb\brdrs\brdrw10 \
clbrdrr\brdrtbl
\cltxlrtb\clftsWidth3\clwWidth4680\clshdrawnil \cellx6660
\clvertalt\clbrdrt\brdrtbl \clbrdrl\brdrtbl \clbrdrb\brdrs\brdrw10
```

Example 5-39. Using escape sequences to represent RTF (continued)

```
\clbrdrr\brdrtbl \cltxlrtb\clftsWidth3\clwWidth2088\clshdrawnil \cellx8748\pard \
ql
\li0\ri0\widctlpar\intbl\aspalpha\aspnum\faauto\adjustright\rin0\lin0 {
\b\f1\insrsid6312866\charrsid6312866 Transaction #\cell Description\cell Amount\
cell }\pard
\ql \li0\ri0\widctlpar\intbl\aspalpha\aspnum\faauto\adjustright\rin0\lin0
{\b\f1\insrsid6312866\charrsid6312866 \trowd \irow0\irowband0
\ts15\trgaph108\trleft-108\trftsWidth1\trftsWidthB3\trftsWidthA3\trautofit1\
trpaddl108\trpaddr108\trpaddfl3\trpaddft3\trpaddfb3\trpaddfr3\tbllkhdrrows\
tbllklastrow\tbllkhdrcols\tbllklastcol \clvertalt\clbrdrt\brdrtbl \clbrdrl\
brdrtbl \clbrdrb
\brdrs\brdrw10 \clbrdrr\brdrtbl \cltxlrtb\clftsWidth3\clwWidth2088\clshdrawnil
\cellx1980\clvertalt\clbrdrt\brdrtbl \clbrdrl\brdrtbl
\clbrdrb\brdrs\brdrw10 \clbrdrr\brdrtbl \cltxlrtb\clftsWidth3\clwWidth4680\
clshdrawnil
\cellx6660\clvertalt\clbrdrt
\brdrtbl \clbrdrl\brdrtbl \clbrdrb\brdrs\brdrw10 \clbrdrr\brdrtbl
\cltxlrtb\clftsWidth3\clwWidth2088\clshdrawnil \cellx8748\row }\trowd
\irow1\irowband1\lastrow
<? foreach( $data as $row ) { ?>
\ts15\trgaph108\trleft-108\trftsWidth1\trftsWidthB3\trftsWidthA3\trautofit1\
trpaddl108\trpaddr108\trpaddfl3\trpaddft3\trpaddfb3\trpaddfr3\tbllkhdrrows\
tbllklastrow\tbllkhdrcols\tbllklastcol \clvertalt\clbrdrt\brdrs\brdrw10 \clbrdrl\
brdrtbl \clbrdrb
\brdrtbl \clbrdrr\brdrtbl \cltxlrtb\clftsWidth3\clwWidth2088\clshdrawnil
\cellx1980\clvertalt\clbrdrt\brdrs\brdrw10 \clbrdrl\brdrtbl \clbrdrb\brdrtbl
\clbrdrr\brdrtbl \cltxlrtb\clftsWidth3\clwWidth4680\clshdrawnil \cellx6660\
clvertalt\clbrdrt
\brdrs\brdrw10 \clbrdrl\brdrtbl \clbrdrb\brdrtbl \clbrdrr\brdrtbl
\cltxlrtb\clftsWidth3\clwWidth2088\clshdrawnil \cellx8748\pard \ql
\li0\ri0\widctlpar\intbl\aspalpha\aspnum\faauto\adjustright\rin0\lin0
{\f1\insrsid6312866 <? print( $row['trans'] ) ?>\cell <? print( $row['desc'] ) ?>
\cell
<? print( $row['amount'] ) ?>\cell }\pard \ql
\li0\ri0\widctlpar\intbl\aspalpha\aspnum\faauto\adjustright\rin0\lin0 {\f1\
insrsid6312866
\trowd \irow1\irowband1\lastrow
\ts15\trgaph108\trleft-108\trftsWidth1\trftsWidthB3\trftsWidthA3\trautofit1\
trpaddl108\trpaddr108\trpaddfl3\trpaddft3\trpaddfb3\trpaddfr3\tbllkhdrrows\
tbllklastrow\tbllkhdrcols\tbllklastcol \clvertalt\clbrdrt\brdrs\brdrw10 \clbrdrl\
brdrtbl \clbrdrb
\brdrtbl \clbrdrr\brdrtbl \cltxlrtb\clftsWidth3\clwWidth2088\clshdrawnil
\cellx1980\clvertalt\clbrdrt\brdrs\brdrw10 \clbrdrl\brdrtbl \clbrdrb\brdrtbl
\clbrdrr\brdrtbl \cltxlrtb\clftsWidth3\clwWidth4680\clshdrawnil \cellx6660\
clvertalt\clbrdrt
\brdrs\brdrw10 \clbrdrl\brdrtbl \clbrdrb\brdrtbl \clbrdrr\brdrtbl
\cltxlrtb\clftsWidth3\clwWidth2088\clshdrawnil \cellx8748\row }
<? } ?>
\pard \ql \li0\ri0\widctlpar\aspalpha\aspnum\faauto\adjustright\rin0\lin0\itap0
{\f1\insrsid6312866\charrsid6312866
\par }}
```

The code you see is just the output of the Word RTF file with a header function at the top and some PHP segments to add the code where it's required. The header function tells the browser that this is an RTF file and not some seriously malformed HTML or text.

RTF is a complex file format, especially when it comes to rendering documents with heavy formatting. You don't need to understand the RTF format completely to generate documents. You can simply do what I did, which is to use your word processor as you normally would, but put markers in the document that you can use to identify where the dynamic content should go. In other words, this hack is about pure grunt work, rather than some mystical transformation process. Boring, yes, but still pretty useful!

Running the Hack

When I navigate to the PHP script, the first thing I see in Internet Explorer is the dialog in Figure 5-22.

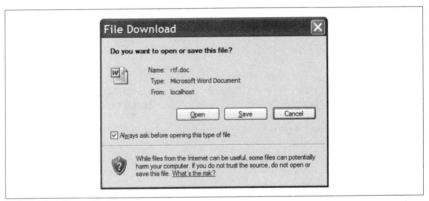

Figure 5-22. The security dialog that pops up as the page is loaded

This security dialog allows the user to decide how RTF files generated by the server should be handled. I choose to open the file, and I see the embedded Word control shown in Figure 5-23.

The sections marked with %% are replaced with live data from the server that could easily have come from a database.

See Also

- "Create Excel Spreadsheets Dynamically" [Hack #49]

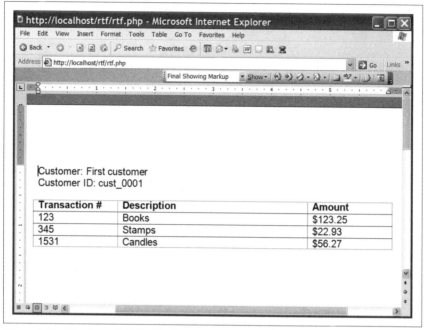

Figure 5-23. The dynamic RTF file shown in Internet Explorer

HACK #49 Create Excel Spreadsheets Dynamically

Use the new XML format supported by Microsoft Office 2004 to generate spreadsheets dynamically.

Word processing documents aren't the only things you might want to generate dynamically [Hack #48]. You also can create spreadsheets dynamically. With the new XML features of Microsoft Office 2004, we can build spreadsheets by simply using XML.

Start by creating a document in Excel, as shown in Figure 5-24.

Use the Save As command to save the spreadsheet in XML format. Then use the XML that's exported by Excel as the basis of your PHP file.

The Code

Save the code in Example 5-40 as *spreadsheet.php*.

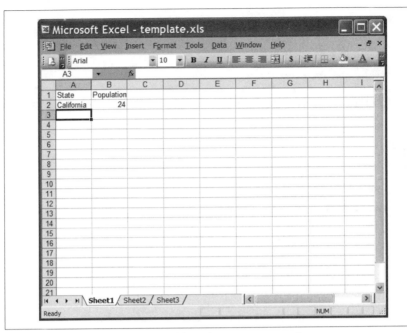

Figure 5-24. The simple Excel spreadsheet that I use as a template

Example 5-40. Using state data to represent a spreadsheet

```
<?
header( "content-type: text/xml" );

$data = array(
array(state => "Alabama", population => 4530182 ),
array(state => "Alaska", population => 655435 ),
array(state => "Arizona", population => 5743834 ),
array(state => "Arkansas", population => 2752629 ),
array(state => "California", population => 35893799 ),
...
array(state => "Washington", population => 6203788 ),
array(state => "West Virginia", population => 1815354 ),
array(state => "Wisconsin", population => 5509026 ),
array(state => "Wyoming", population => 506529 )
);

echo( "<?xml version=\"1.0\"?>\n" );
echo( "<?mso-application progid=\"Excel.Sheet\"?>\n" );
?>
<Workbook xmlns="urn:schemas-microsoft-com:office:spreadsheet"
 xmlns:o="urn:schemas-microsoft-com:office:office"
 xmlns:x="urn:schemas-microsoft-com:office:excel"
 xmlns:ss="urn:schemas-microsoft-com:office:spreadsheet"
 xmlns:html="http://www.w3.org/TR/REC-html40">
```

Example 5-40. Using state data to represent a spreadsheet (continued)

```
<DocumentProperties xmlns="urn:schemas-microsoft-com:office:office">
 <Author>Jack Herrington</Author>
 <LastAuthor>Jack Herrington</LastAuthor>
 <Created>2005-04-30T14:08:07Z</Created>
 <LastSaved>2005-04-30T14:09:14Z</LastSaved>
 <Company>Myself</Company>
 <Version>11.6360</Version>
</DocumentProperties>
<OfficeDocumentSettings xmlns="urn:schemas-microsoft-com:office:office">
 <DownloadComponents/>
 <LocationOfComponents HRef="file:///C:\APPINSTALL\Microsoft\Office_Pro_2003\"/>
</OfficeDocumentSettings>
<ExcelWorkbook xmlns="urn:schemas-microsoft-com:office:excel">
 <WindowHeight>15930</WindowHeight>
 <WindowWidth>20025</WindowWidth>
 <WindowTopX>480</WindowTopX>
 <WindowTopY>105</WindowTopY>
 <ProtectStructure>False</ProtectStructure>
 <ProtectWindows>False</ProtectWindows>
</ExcelWorkbook>
<Styles>
 <Style ss:ID="Default" ss:Name="Normal">
  <Alignment ss:Vertical="Bottom"/>
  <Borders/>
  <Font/>
  <Interior/>
  <NumberFormat/>
  <Protection/>
 </Style>
</Styles>
<Worksheet ss:Name="States">
 <Table ss:ExpandedColumnCount="2"
  ss:ExpandedRowCount="<? print( count( $data ) + 1 ) ?>"
  x:FullColumns="1"
  x:FullRows="1">
  <Row>
   <Cell><Data ss:Type="String">State</Data></Cell>
   <Cell><Data ss:Type="String">Population</Data></Cell>
  </Row>
<? foreach( $data as $row ) { ?>
  <Row>
   <Cell><Data ss:Type="String"><? print( $row["state"] ) ?></Data></Cell>
   <Cell><Data ss:Type="Number"><? print( $row["population"] ) ?></Data></Cell>
  </Row>
<? } ?>
 </Table>
 <WorksheetOptions xmlns="urn:schemas-microsoft-com:office:excel">
  <Selected/>
  <Panes>
   <Pane>
    <Number>3</Number>
```

Example 5-40. Using state data to represent a spreadsheet (continued)

```
        <ActiveRow>2</ActiveRow>
      </Pane>
     </Panes>
     <ProtectObjects>False</ProtectObjects>
     <ProtectScenarios>False</ProtectScenarios>
    </WorksheetOptions>
   </Worksheet>
 </Workbook>
```

I used the original XML spreadsheet as the basis for the script and then added the header( ) function at the beginning to indicate that this is XML data (so that the browser won't mishandle it). The data in the script is the hardcoded data of the state populations of the United States from the 2000 census. I use a foreach loop to create the rows of the table in the spreadsheet.

Getting ss:ExpandedRowCount correct is critical. If these numbers don't match up, Excel will refuse to load the spreadsheet and will give only a cryptic error response. In general, as I have created spreadsheets using this mechanism, I find that Excel is finicky about data integrity. I try to make small adjustments to the XML until I get it where I want it. Making too many changes in one shot is an exercise in frustration, as Excel is likely to refuse the faulty data, with little or no indication as to exactly what went wrong.

Running the Hack

Copy the files to the server and navigate to the PHP script using Internet Explorer. The first thing you'll see is Figure 5-25.

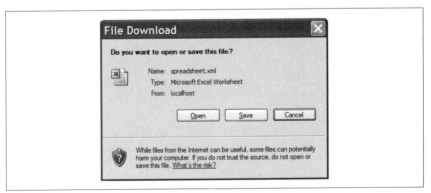

Figure 5-25. The security dialog that pops up when the page is loaded

Internet Explorer brings up this security dialog when it sees non-HTML content. Clicking the Open button launches the Excel control within the Internet Explorer window with the XML spreadsheet data. This is shown in Figure 5-26; just what we wanted!

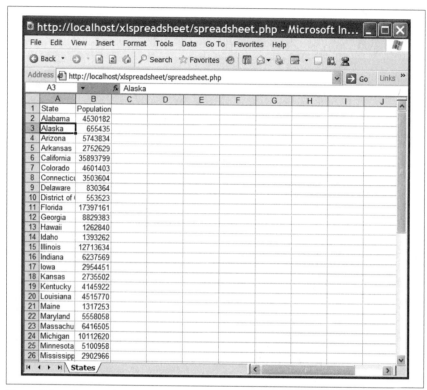

Figure 5-26. The completed spreadsheet with the dynamic data

See Also

- "Create RTF Documents Dynamically" [Hack #48]
- "Suck Data from Excel Uploads" [Hack #45]

HACK #50 Create a Message Queue

Use a MySQL table to create a simple message queue for delayed notifications.

Background processing is always a problem in web applications. Users like to get snappy responses from their web pages, but sometimes processing can take a while. A classic example is a web notification mail-out. The user initiates some process that requires mailing a notice to 100 people, but mailing to 100 people takes a while. Making the server wait for all the mail to go out isn't a good idea. It looks like the application is hung or about to crash. Ideally we could return a page to the user, and then in the background, send out the 100 messages. But how do we do that?

One method is to create a simple database-driven message queue. The web page puts some data into the queue, which is executed by another process later (usually fired off by the cron task-scheduling system). The message queue in this system takes two parameters: the function to be run and the arguments to the function. Therefore, you can delay almost any processing you want.

Figure 5-27 shows the simple schema for the message queue. There are really only two fields: func, which holds the name of the function, and args, which holds the XML version of the arguments.

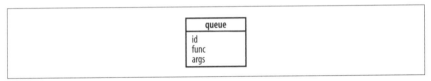

queue
id
func
args

Figure 5-27. The schema for the queue

Figure 5-28 shows the status of the *queue* table. It starts empty, with no messages. Then a couple of messages are added. Messages are removed as they are processed.

Empty message queue

id	func	args

After two message adds

id	func	args
1	mail_notification	<xml>...</xml>
2	mail_notification	<xml>...</xml>

After one message removal

id	func	args
2	mail_notification	<xml>...</xml>

Figure 5-28. The queue after a few operations

One of the great things about a message queue is that since it's in the database, it persists even if the process that is reading or writing the queue table crashes.

The Code

Save the SQL in Example 5-41 as *queue.sql*.

Example 5-41. SQL that sets up the queue in the database

```
DROP TABLE IF EXISTS queue;
CREATE TABLE queue (
  id MEDIUMINT NOT NULL AUTO_INCREMENT,
  func TEXT,
  args TEXT,
  PRIMARY KEY ( id )
);
```

The queue itself is handled by the code in Example 5-42 (saved as *queue. php*).

Example 5-42. Script that handles queue management

```
<?php
require( "DB.php" );
$db =& DB::connect("mysql://root:password@localhost/queue", array() );
if (PEAR::isError($db)) { die($db->getMessage()); }

function add_to_queue( $func, $args )
{
  global $db;

  $dom = new DomDocument();
  $root = $dom->createElement( "arguments" );
  foreach( $args as $argtext )
  {
    $arg = $dom->createElement( "argument" );
    $arg->appendChild( $dom->createTextNode( $argtext ) );
    $root->appendChild( $arg );
  }
  $dom->appendChild( $root );

  $sth = $db->prepare( "INSERT INTO queue VALUES ( 0, ?, ? )" );
  $db->execute( $sth, array( $func, $dom->saveXML() ) );
}

function run_queue()
{
  global $db;

  $delsth = $db->prepare( "DELETE FROM queue WHERE id = ?" );

  $res = $db->query( "SELECT id, func, args FROM queue" );
  while( $res->fetchInto( $row ) )
  {
    $id = $row[0];
    $func = $row[1];
```

Example 5-42. Script that handles queue management (continued)

```
$argxml = $row[2];

$dom = new DomDocument( );
$dom->loadXML( $argxml );
$args = array( );
foreach( $dom->getElementsByTagName( "argument" ) as $node )
{
  $args []= $node->nodeValue;
}

call_user_func_array( $func, $args );

$db->execute( $delsth, array( $id ) );
  }
}
?>
```

add.php, shown in Example 5-43, tests addition of mail to the queue.

Example 5-43. A simple script that fires off a mail notification

```
<?php
require_once( 'queue.php' );

add_to_queue( 'mail_notification',
  array(
    'jack@oreilly.com',
    'You owe us some money. Pay up.'
  ) );
?>
```

run.php (Example 5-44) gives a quick status notice.

Example 5-44. A script that shows what's going on (sort of) to the user

```
<?php
require_once( "queue.php" );

function mail_notification( $user, $text )
{
  print "Mailing $user:\n$text\n\n";
}

run_queue( );
?>
```

The primary code in this example is in the *queue.php* library, used by both the *add.php* script, which adds elements to the queue, and the *run.php* script, which runs the elements currently stored in the queue.

The queue library defines two functions: add_to_queue( ), which inserts a record into the queue, and run_queue( ), which selects all of the rows from the table and runs them one by one. The run_queue( ) function is fun because it never actually knows what it's going to do! It simply reads the function name and the arguments to the function out of the database. Then it invokes the call_user_func_array( ) PHP function, which takes a function name as a parameter, as well as the arguments to that function as a second parameter. That means you can add functionality to the queue without ever changing these basic add and run functions.

Running the Hack

Running the hack starts by setting up the queue table in the database:

```
% mysqladmin --user=root --password=password create queue
% mysql --user=root --password=password queue < queue.sql
```

Running the *add.php* script using the PHP command-line interpreter adds a message to the message queue (this kind of code would run on the web page). In this case, it adds an example email item to the queue. You can run the script several times if you want to create several example email messages:

```
% php add.php
```

Then, running the *run.php* script executes the messages in the event queue:

```
% php run.php
Mailing jack@oreilly.com:
You owe us some money. Pay up.
```

Each message is printed to the console but can be mailed out to someone easily.

See Also

- "Observe Your Objects" [Hack #67]

CHAPTER SIX

Application Design
Hacks 51–66

Sitting on top of the database and below the HTML is application logic. This chapter concentrates on hacks that will add stability and flexibility to your application logic. Topics covered include security and roles, password management, login and session management, and e-commerce.

HACK #51 Create Modular Interfaces

Use dynamic loading to allow users to write snap-in modules for your application.

Most of the really popular PHP open source applications have an extension mechanism that allows for PHP coders to write small fragments of code that are dynamically loaded into the application. This hack demonstrates an XML-based drawing script that you can extend simply by placing new PHP classes into a modules directory; of course, the point is not as much the drawing code as the way you can extend it easily.

The Code

Save the code in Example 6-1 as *modhost.php*.

Example 6-1. The code that handles a modular PHP architecture

```php
<?php
class DrawingEnvironment
{
  private $img = null;
  private $x = null;
  private $y = null;
  private $colors = array( );

  public function __construct( $x, $y )
  {
    $this->img = imagecreatetruecolor( $x, $y );
```

Example 6-1. The code that handles a modular PHP architecture (continued)

```php
    $this->addColor( 'white', 255, 255, 255 );
    $this->addColor( 'black', 0, 0, 0 );
    $this->addColor( 'red', 255, 0, 0 );
    $this->addColor( 'green', 0, 255, 0 );
    $this->addColor( 'blue', 0, 0, 255 );

    imagefilledrectangle( $this->image( ),
      0, 0, $x, $y, $this->color( 'white' ) );
  }

  public function image( ) { return $this->img; }
  public function size_x( ) { return $this->x; }
  public function size_y( ) { return $this->y; }
  public function color( $c ) { return $this->colors[$c]; }

  public function save( $file )
  {
    imagepng( $this->img, $file );
  }

  protected function addColor( $name, $r, $g, $b )
  {
    $col = imagecolorallocate($this->img, $r, $g, $b);
    $this->colors[ $name ] = $col;
  }
}

interface DrawingObject
{
  function drawObject( $env );
  function setParam( $name, $value );
}

function loadModules( $dir )
{
  $classes = array( );

  $dh = new DirectoryIterator( $dir );
  foreach( $dh as $file )
  {
    if( $file->isDir( ) == 0 && preg_match( "/[.]php$/", $file ) )
    {
      include_once( $dir."/".$file );
      $class = preg_replace( "/[.]php$/", "", $file );
      $classes []= $class;
    }
  }

  return $classes;
}
```

Example 6-1. The code that handles a modular PHP architecture (continued)

```php
$classes = loadModules( "mods" );

$dom = new DOMDocument( );
$dom->load( $argv[1] );
$nl = $dom->getElementsByTagName( "image" );
$root = $nl->item( 0 );

$size_x = $root->getAttribute( 'x' );
$size_y = $root->getAttribute( 'y' );
$file = $root->getAttribute( 'file' );

$de = new DrawingEnvironment( $size_x, $size_y );

$obs_spec = array( );

$el = $root->firstChild;
while( $el != null )
{
  if ( $el->tagName != null )
  {
    $params = array( );
    for( $i = 0; $i < $el->attributes->length; $i++ )
    {
      $p = $el->attributes->item( $i )->nodeName;
      $v = $el->attributes->item( $i )->nodeValue;
      $params[ $p ] = $v;
    }

    $obs_spec []= array(
      'type' => $el->tagName,
      'params' => $params
    );
  }
  $el = $el->nextSibling;
}

foreach( $obs_spec as $os )
{
  $ob = null;
  eval( '$ob = new '.$os['type'].'( );' );
  foreach( $os[ 'params' ] as $key => $value )
    $ob->setParam( $key, $value );
  $ob->drawObject( $de );
}

$de->save( $file );
?>
```

Save the code in Example 6-2 as *mods/Circle.php*.

Example 6-2. An example module that draws circles

```php
<?php
class Circle implements DrawingObject
{
  private $radius = null;
  private $color = null;
  private $x = null;
  private $y = null;

  function drawObject( $env )
  {
    $r2 = $this->radius / 2;
    imagefilledellipse( $env->image( ),
      $this->x - $r2, $this->y - $r2,
      $this->radius, $this->radius,
      $env->color( $this->color )
    );
  }

  function setParam( $name, $value )
  {
    if ( $name == "radius" ) $this->radius = $value;
    if ( $name == "color" ) $this->color = $value;
    if ( $name == "x" ) $this->x = $value;
    if ( $name == "y" ) $this->y = $value;
  }
}
?>
```

Running the Hack

This hack is run on the command line. The first thing to do is to create an
XML test file:

```
<image x='100' y='100' file='out.png'>
        <Circle x='20' y='40' color='red' radius='15' />
        <Circle x='60' y='30' color='green' radius='30' />
        <Circle x='70' y='75' color='blue' radius='35' />
</image>
```

This XML file specifies that the image should be 100×100 pixels and named
out.png, and that the image should have three circles, each of varying size
and color.

With the XML in hand, run the script:

```
% php modhost.php test.xml
```

The first argument to the script is the name of the XML file that contains the image specifications. The output image file looks like Figure 6-1.

Figure 6-1. The output image

To explain a little about what happened here, let me start with the *modhost. php* file. At the start of the file, I've defined the `DrawingEnvironment` class, which is just a wrapper around an image with a few accessors. This environment will be passed to any drawing objects so that those objects can paint into the image. The next point of interest is the `DrawingObject` interface, which objects must conform to for drawing.

The real trick comes in the `loadModules( )` function, which loads all of the modules from the specified directory into the PHP environment. Then the script reads the XML file supplied to it, and parses it into the `$obs_spec` object, which is an array version of the XML file. The next step is to create the drawing environment and build the drawing objects based on the `$obs_spec` values; these values are then rendered into the image. Finally, the image is stored to a file.

Figure 6-2 shows the relationships between the `DrawingEnvironment` and the `DrawingObjects`, as well as how the dynamically loaded `Circle` class implements the `DrawingObject` interface.

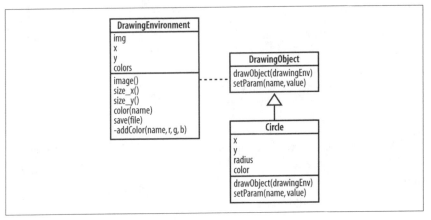

Figure 6-2. The structure of the drawing system

This is a simple illustration of this technique.

The specification of an interface makes this a PHP 5-specific script, but the include_once( ) and eval( ) functions were in PHP 4; it would take a bit of modification, but there is no reason that you can't do something similar to this in PHP 4.

I strongly recommend adding an extension mechanism such as this to any reasonably sized PHP application, especially when you expect deployment in multiple environments that you don't control. This approach gives end users the ability to customize the program to their requirements, without you having to go in and alter code directly for every new feature or object type.

See Also

- "Create Objects with Abstract Factories" [Hack #68]
- "Observe Your Objects" [Hack #67]
- "Abstract Construction Code with a Builder" [Hack #70]

Support Wiki Text

Make it easier for your customers to enter styled text into your application by supporting the Wiki syntax.

A new form of content management system for the Web, *Wikis* are a collection of pages, each titled with a *WikiWord*, which is a set of two or more capitalized words joined together without spaces. The ease with which you can install and update Wikis has made them extremely popular both on intranets and on the Internet. Perhaps the most famous Wiki is Wikipedia (*http://www.wikipedia.org/*). This is an encyclopedia on the Web that anyone can contribute content to by using just their web browser.

Another reason wikis are so popular is that formatting a Wiki page is a lot easier than writing the equivalent HTML code. For example, you specify a paragraph break by just typing two returns—there is no need to add p tags. In fact, most of the time tags aren't used at all. For example, you create a bulleted list by putting an asterisk at the start of each line; this is far easier than using the equivalent ul and li tags. This hack demonstrates using the wiki-formatting PEAR module in a PHP application.

The Code

Save the code in Example 6-3 as *index.php*.

Example 6-3. The page that allows you to edit Wiki text

```
<html>
<body>
<form method="post" action="render.php">
<textarea name="text" cols="80" rows="20">
+ Header Level 1

Here's a paragraph and a link to AnotherPage.

* list item 1
* list item 2

Link to a NewPage like this.
</textarea><br/>
<input type="submit" />
</form>
</body>
</html>
```

Then save the code in Example 6-4 as *render.php*.

Example 6-4. The PHP that renders the Wiki text

```
<html>
<body>
<?php
// Include the Wiki Text Pear library
require_once( "Text/Wiki.php" );

// Create the Wiki object
$wiki = new Text_Wiki();

// Render the text field sent to us in the form
echo( $wiki->transform( $_POST["text"], 'Xhtml' ) );
?>
</body>
</html>
```

Running the Hack

This code requires the Text_Wiki PEAR module [Hack #2]. After installing the module and creating the PHP files, navigate the browser to the *index.php* page shown in Figure 6-3.

Type some Wiki text into the form and click the Submit button. With the text shown in the example, the output looks like Figure 6-4.

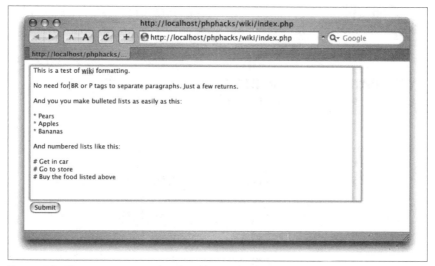

Figure 6-3. The text input page for the Wiki text renderer

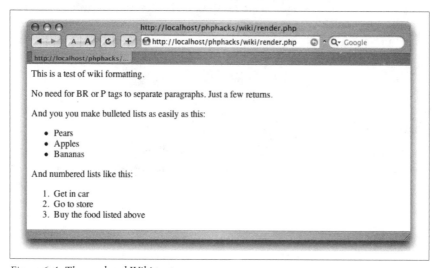

Figure 6-4. The rendered Wiki text

A complete list of the wiki formatting rules is on the Text_
Wiki PEAR component home page at *http://wiki.ciaweb.net/
yawiki/index.php?area=Text_Wiki&page=WikiRules*.

Hacking the Hack

The Text_Wiki module is very well architected and written. New text formatting rules can be added, and the default formatting rules can be enabled and disabled to suit the application. The enableRule( ) and disableRule( ) meth-ods enable and disable the built-in text formatting rules. The addRule( ) method adds new rules to the formatting engine.

HACK #53 Turn Any Object into an Array

Use the Iterator interface in PHP 5 to turn any object into an array.

If you have ever used the DOM interface to read or write XML in PHP, you're already familiar with the DOMNodeList interface. Many methods in the DOM return an array of nodes. That array is implemented by the DOMNodeList object. To read the node list, you have to write code like this:

```
$dl = $doc->getElementsByTagName( "foo" );
for( $i = 0; $i < $dl->length; $i++ )
{
    $n = $dl->item( $i );
    ...
}
```

That's kind of unfortunate, isn't it, since PHP has that beautiful foreach operator that gives access to arrays with almost no potential for messing things up. Wouldn't it be great if the interface to DOM looked more like this?

```
foreach($doc->getElementsByTagName( "foo" ) as $n ) {
    ...
}
```

That is a lot cleaner and far less error prone.

Thanks to the additions in PHP 5, we can now allow foreach to work on any object, simply by having that class implement the Iterator interface. In this hack, I'll show how to implement an Observer pattern [Hack #67] using the Iterator interface.

The Code

Save the code in Example 6-5 as *iterator.php*.

Example 6-5. A class that uses PHP 5's new Iterator interface

```
<?php
interface Listener
{
    public function invoke( $caller, $data );
}

class ListenerList implements Iterator
{
    private $listeners = array( );
```

Example 6-5. A class that uses PHP 5's new Iterator interface (continued)

```php
  public function __construct()
  {
  }

  public function add( $listener )
  {
    $this->listeners []= $listener;
  }

  public function invoke( $caller, $data )
  {
    foreach( $this as $listener )
    {
      $listener->invoke( $caller, $data );
    }
  }

  public function rewind()
  {
    reset($this->listeners);
  }

  public function current()
  {
    return current($this->listeners);
  }

  public function key()
  {
    return key($this->listeners);
  }

  public function next()
  {
    return next($this->listeners);
  }

  public function valid()
  {
    return ( $this->current() !== false );
  }
}

class SimpleListener implements Listener
{
  private $v;
  public function __construct( $v ) { $this->v = $v; }
  public function invoke( $caller, $data )
  {
    echo( $this->v." invoked with with '$data'\n" );
  }
```

Example 6-5. A class that uses PHP 5's new Iterator interface (continued)

```php
    public function __tostring( ) { return "Listener ".$this->v; }
}

$ll = new ListenerList( );

$ll->add( new SimpleListener( "a" ) );
$ll->add( new SimpleListener( "b" ) );
$ll->add( new SimpleListener( "c" ) );

print("Listeners:\n\n");
foreach( $ll as $listener )
{
  print( $listener );
  print( "\n" );
}

print("\nInvoking Listeners:\n\n");
$ll->invoke( null, "Some data" );
?>
```

The first section of the code defines a Listener interface for objects that are to be registered with ListenerList. The second part defines ListenerList, which is just a wrapper around an array with the addition of the add( ) and invoke( ) methods. The other methods all implement the Iterator interface. SimpleListener is just an implementation of the listener that prints when called.

Figure 6-5 shows the model for the code in this hack. ListenerList contains zero or more objects that implement the Listener interface. SimpleListener implements the Listener interface and just prints out a message whenever it's invoked.

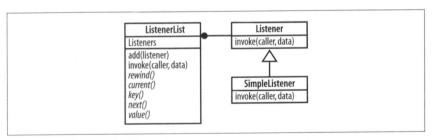

Figure 6-5. The UML for ListenerList

Running the Hack

You run this hack on the command line using the command-line interpreter:

```
% php iterator.php
Listeners:
```

```
Listener a
Listener b
Listener c

Invoking Listeners:

a invoked with with 'Some data'
b invoked with with 'Some data'
c invoked with with 'Some data'
%
```

If you look at the end of the code from Example 6-5, you will see the tests that output here. The first test iterates through the list with a foreach statement. You see the result of this at the top of the run. The second section shows the result of the invoke( ) method being called on the ListenerList object.

The great thing about the Iterator interface is that you can now pass around complex interfaces in any case where you could only previously use arrays. Those array interfaces will still work, but now you can have additional methods as well.

See Also

- "Observe Your Objects" [Hack #67]

HACK   Create XML the Right Way
#54   Use the XML DOM to create XML without errors.

Creating XML from your PHP web application is easy to get wrong. You can screw up the encoding so that special characters are not formatted properly, and you can miss start or end tags. Both of these problems, which are common in even simple PHP applications, will result in invalid XML and will keep the XML from being read properly by other XML consumers. Almost all of the problems result from working with XML as streams of characters instead of using an XML API such as DOM.

This hack will show you how to create XML DOMs in memory and then export them as text. This method of creating XML avoids all of these encoding and formatting issues, so your XML will be well-formed every time.

Figure 6-6 shows the in-memory XML tree that we will create in this hack. Each element is an object. The base of the system is DOMDocument, which points to the root node of the tree. From there, each DOMElement node can contain one or more child nodes and attribute nodes.

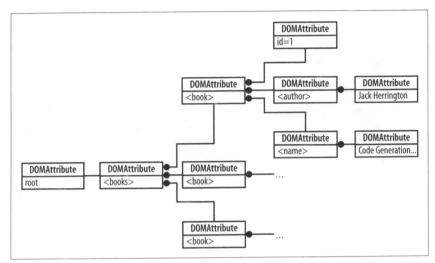

Figure 6-6. The in-memory XML tree

The Code

Save the code in Example 6-6 as *xmldom.php*.

Example 6-6. Sample code that builds XML the right way

```php
<?php
$books = array(
  array (
      id => 1,
      author => "Jack Herrington",
      name => "Code Generation in Action"
  ),
  array (
      id => 2,
      author => "Jack Herrington",
      name => "Podcasting Hacks"
  ),
  array (
      id => 3,
      author => "Jack Herrington",
      name => "PHP Hacks"
```

Example 6-6. Sample code that builds XML the right way (continued)

```
     )
  );

$dom = new DomDocument( );
$dom->formatOutput = true;

$root = $dom->createElement( "books" );
$dom->appendChild( $root );

foreach( $books as $book )
{
  $bn = $dom->createElement( "book" );
  $bn->setAttribute( 'id', $book['id'] );

  $author = $dom->createElement( "author" );
  $author->appendChild( $dom->createTextNode( $book['author'] ) );
  $bn->appendChild( $author );

  $name = $dom->createElement( "name" );
  $name->appendChild( $dom->createTextNode( $book['name'] ) );
  $bn->appendChild( $name );

  $root->appendChild( $bn );
}

header( "Content-type: text/xml" );
echo $dom->saveXML( );
?>
```

Running the Hack

Upload this file to your server and surf to the *xmldom.php* page. You should see something like Figure 6-7.

This is nicely formatted and well-formed XML, and I didn't have to manually output a single tag name or attribute value. Instead, the DOM handles object creation and ties the objects together via the appendChild( ) method. Finally, saveXML( ) is used to export the XML as text. This is the easy and object-oriented way to create XML that is valid every time.

See Also

* "Design Better SQL Schemas" [Hack #34]
* "Create Bulletproof Database Access" [Hack #35]

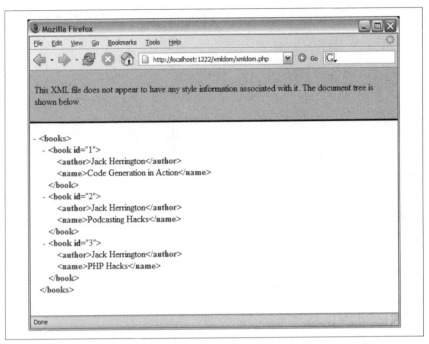

Figure 6-7. The book XML shown in the Firefox browser

HACK #55   Fix the Double Submit Problem

Use a transaction table in your database to fix the classic double submit problem.

I have a couple of pet peeves when it comes to bad web application design. One of the biggest is the wealth of bad code written to fix "double submits." How often have you seen an e-commerce site that implores you, "Do not hit the submit button twice"?

This class problem results when a browser posts the contents of a web form to the server twice. However, if the user hits "submit" twice, this is exactly what the browser *should* do; it's the server that needs to determine whether this is an error.

Figure 6-8 shows the double submit problem graphically. The browser sends two requests because the user clicks twice. The first submit is accepted, and before the HTML is returned, the second submit goes out. Then the first response comes in, followed by the second response.

Figure 6-9 illustrates a fix to the double submit problem; the first request stores a unique ID in the page being processed. That way, when the second request comes in with the same ID, the redundant transaction is denied.

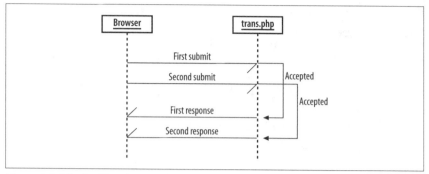

Figure 6-8. The double submit problem sequence diagram

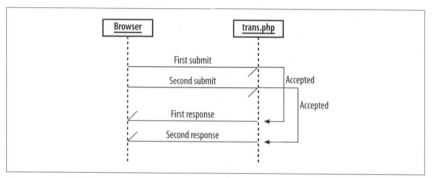

Figure 6-9. The double submit solution requires denying the second request

The Code

Save the code in Example 6-7 as *db.sql*.

Example 6-7. The database code for the transaction checker

```
DROP TABLE IF EXISTS transcheck;
CREATE TABLE transcheck (
        transid TEXT,
        posted TIMESTAMP
        );
```

Save the code in Example 6-8 as *index.php*.

Example 6-8. The HTML form that has the transaction ID

```
<? require_once( "trans.php" ); ?>
<html>
<body>
<form action="handler.php" method="post">
<input type="hidden" name="transid" value="<?php echo( get_transid() ); ?>" />
```

Example 6-8. The HTML form that has the transaction ID (continued)

```
Name: <input type="text" /><br/>
Amount: <input type="text" size="5" /><br/>
<input type="submit" />
</format>
```

Save the code in Example 6-9 as *handler.php*.

Example 6-9. The code that receives the form data and checks the transaction

```
<? require_once( "trans.php" ); ?>
<html>
<body>
<?php if ( check_transid( $_POST["transid"] ) ) { ?>
This form has already been submitted.
<?php } else {
add_transid( $_POST["transid"] );
?>
Ok, you bought our marvelous product. Thanks!
<?php } ?>
</body>
</html>
```

Save the code in Example 6-10 as *trans.php*.

Example 6-10. The transaction checking library

```
<?php
require_once( "DB.php" );
$dsn = 'mysql://root:password@localhost/transtest';
$db =& DB::Connect( $dsn, array() );
if (PEAR::isError($db)) {
   die($db->getMessage());
}

function check_transid( $id )
{
  global $db;
  $res = $db->query( "SELECT COUNT(transid) FROM transcheck WHERE transid=?",
    array($id) );
  $res->fetchInto($row);
  return $row[0];
}

function add_transid( $id )
{
  global $db;
  $sth = $db->prepare( "INSERT INTO transcheck VALUES( ?, now( ) )" );
  $db->execute( $sth, array( $id ) );
}
```

Example 6-10. The transaction checking library (continued)

```
function get_transid( )
{
  $id = mt_rand( );
  while( check_transid( $id ) ) { $id = mt_rand( ); }
  return $id;
}
?>
```

Running the Hack

Upload the files to the server, and then use the mysql command to load the *db.sql* schema into your database:

```
mysql --user=myuser --password=mypassword mydb < db.sql
```

Next, navigate to the *index.php* page with your browser, and you will see the simple e-commerce form shown in Figure 6-10.

Figure 6-10. The e-commerce form

Fill in some bogus data and click Submit. You should see the result shown in Figure 6-11, which shows a successful transaction. This is a good start, as it shows that we can successfully complete a transaction. Now we'll move on to denying redundant transactions.

Figure 6-11. A successful purchase

Click the Back button and click Submit again. You should see the result in
Figure 6-12.

Figure 6-12. The result of a double submit

What happened is that *index.php* has requested a unique ID from the
trans.php script. The *handler.php* script, which receives the form variables,
first checks the ID to see whether it has been used already by calling the
check_transid( ) function. If the ID has been used, the code should return
the result shown in Figure 6-12.

If the ID is not in the database, we use the add_transid( ) function to add
the ID to the database, and tell the user that the processing has been successful, as shown in Figure 6-11.

The astute reader will note the race condition here. If another form submit
comes in between the use of the check_transid( ) function and the call to
the add_transid( ) function, you could get a double submit that *is* appropriate to process. If your database supports stored procedures, you can write a
single transaction that will check to see whether the transaction has completed and then add the transaction to the completed list. This will avoid the
race condition and ensure that you cannot have double submits.

> At the time of this writing, MySQL did not support stored
> procedures, though it is in the feature request line for later
> releases.

HACK #56   Create User-Customizable Reports

Use a PHP reporting engine that takes an XML definition file and creates a
custom report.

Reporting engines allow end users to customize the reports generated in
their applications. This is extremely valuable in enterprise applications
because these systems rarely are exactly what the customer wants. The ability to tweak the reports, notifications, or other front-facing features is critical for a satisfying user experience.

A reporting engine gives the user a declarative method for specifying a report. The host page sets up the query, gets the data, and then runs the report engine to format the data. Some reporting engines, like RLIB (*http:// rlib.sf.net/*), can export not only to HTML, but also to PDF, XML, and other formats. In this hack, I use the PHPReports system (*http://phpreports.sf.net/*) to implement a simple book report.

The Code

Save the code in Example 6-11 as *index.php*.

Example 6-11. The PHP that runs the report generator

```php
<?php
require_once( "PHPReportMaker.php" );
$rep = new PHPReportMaker();
$rep->setUser( "root" );
$rep->setPassword( "" );
$rep->setDatabaseInterface( "mysql" );
$rep->setConnection( "localhost" );
$rep->setDatabase( "books" );
$rep->setSQL( "SELECT NAME,AUTHOR FROM BOOK ORDER BY NAME" );

$rep->setXML( "bookreport.xml" );

$rep->run();
?>
```

Save the code in Example 6-12 as *bookreport.xml*.

Example 6-12. The report's XML specification

```xml
<REPORT MARGINWIDTH="5" MARGINHEIGHT="5">
<TITLE>Book Report</TITLE>
<CSS>report.css</CSS>
<PAGE BORDER="0" SIZE="10" CELLSPACING="0" CELLPADDING="5">
</PAGE>
<GROUPS>
<GROUP NAME="author" EXPRESSION="AUTHOR">
<HEADER>
<ROW>
<COL CELLCLASS="header"><XHTML><i>Name</i></XHTML></COL>
<COL CELLCLASS="header">Author</COL>
</ROW>
</HEADER>
<FIELDS>
<ROW>
<COL TYPE="FIELD">NAME</COL>
<COL TYPE="FIELD">AUTHOR</COL>
```

Example 6-12. The report's XML specification (continued)

```
</ROW>
</FIELDS>
<FOOTER>
</FOOTER>
</GROUP>
</GROUPS>
</REPORT>
```

Save the code in Example 6-13 as *report.css*.

Example 6-13. The CSS for the report

```
.header { font-weight: bold; }
```

Running the Hack

Download and install the PHPReports system per the instructions included with the download. Upload the files to the server and navigate to the *index.php* page in your browser. The result should look like Figure 6-13.

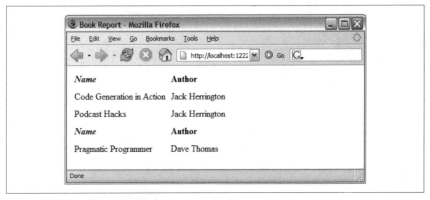

Figure 6-13. The formatted book report

Changing the look of the report is as easy as tweaking the XML in the *bookreport.xml* file. The PHPReports system provides for control over the color, fonts, and layout of the report through both HTML and CSS. It also allows for data grouping through the inclusion of dynamic HTML elements like anchor tags and scripts.

PHPReports also has a flexible back end, allowing you to render to a single page of HTML, text, or even a multipage HTML report (the HTML is broken into multiple pages, and the generated markup has navigation at the bottom of each page). You can also create your own output plug-in, allowing you to create whatever output form you need.

See Also

- "Give Your Customers Formatting Control with XSL" [Hack #7]

 HACK #57 Create a Login System

Sturdy login systems are required for any complex multi-user web application.

With any multi-user web application, you are going to need a user authentication system. You can use Apache's authentication mechanism, which pops up a dialog with a username and password when pages are accessed, but that means integrating your application and database with that authentication mechanism. And, unfortunately, it means that you don't have control over the login dialog; you can't include an "I've forgotten my password" option or a contact link.

Figure 6-14 shows the page flow of the login system. The user starts at *index.php*, the login page. From there, *login.php* verifies the login credentials the user provides.

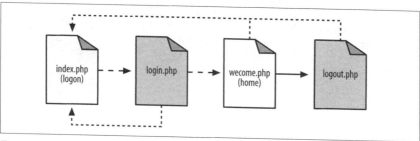

Figure 6-14. The page flow of the login system

If *login.php* approves the credentials, the user receives a session and is sent to *welcome.php*. At *welcome.php*, the user can click on the logout link, which takes him back to the *logout.php* script, removes his session, and then finally sends him to the original *index.php* page. If the user types the *welcome.php* URL directly into his browser's location field without logging in, the *welcome.php* page will detect that and will send the sneaky user back to the *index.php* login page.

The Code

Save the code in Example 6-14 as *users.sql*.

Example 6-14. The database definition for the users

```
DROP TABLE IF EXISTS users;
CREATE TABLE users (
            id MEDIUMINT NOT NULL AUTO_INCREMENT,
            name TEXT,
            password TEXT,
            PRIMARY KEY( id )
);

INSERT INTO users VALUES ( 0, 'jack', MD5( 'toronto' ) );
INSERT INTO users VALUES ( 0, 'megan', MD5( 'seattle' ) );
```

Save the code in Example 6-15 as *index.php*.

Example 6-15. The login page

```
<html>
<head><title>Login</title></head>
<body>
<?php if ( $_GET['bad'] == 1 ) { ?>
<font color="red">Bad login or password, please try again<br/></font>
<?php } ?>
<form action="login.php" method="post">
<table width="300" border="0" cellspacing="0" cellpadding="2">
<tr><td>User name:</td><td><input type="text" name="user" /></td></tr>
<tr><td>Password:</td><td><input type="password" name="password" /></td></tr>
<tr><td colspan="2"><center><input type="submit" value="Login" /></center></td></
tr>
</table>
</form>
</body>
</html>
```

Save the code in Example 6-16 as *login.php*.

Example 6-16. The form handler for the login

```
<?php
require_once( "DB.php" );
$dsn = 'mysql://root:password@localhost/time';
$db =& DB::Connect( $dsn, array() );
if (PEAR::isError($db)) { die($db->getMessage()); }

$res = $db->query( "SELECT id FROM users WHERE name=? AND password=MD5(?)",
        array( $_POST['user'], $_POST['password'] ) );

$row = array( null );
if ( $res != null )
        $res->fetchInto( $row );

if ( $row[0] != null )
{
```

Example 6-16. The form handler for the login (continued)

```
                session_start( );
                $_SESSION['user'] = $row[0];
                header( "Location: welcome.php" );
}
else
{
                header( "Location: index.php?bad=1" );
}
?>
```

Save the code in Example 6-17 as *welcome.php*.

Example 6-17. The home page for the users

```
<?php
session_start( );
if ( $_SESSION['user'] == null || $_SESSION['user'] < 1 )
{
                header( "Location: index.php" );
                exit;
}

require_once( "DB.php" );
$dsn = 'mysql://root:password@localhost/time';
$db =& DB::Connect( $dsn, array() );
if (PEAR::isError($db)) { die($db->getMessage( )); }

$res = $db->query( "SELECT name FROM users WHERE id=?",
        array( $_SESSION['user'] ) );
$res->fetchInto( $row );
?>
<html>
<head><title>Welcome</title></head>
<body>
Welcome <?php echo( $row[0] ); ?><br/><br/>
<a href="logout.php">Logout</a>
</body>
</html>
```

Save the code in Example 6-18 as *logout.php*.

Example 6-18. The logout handler

```
<?php
session_destroy( );
header( "Location: index.php" );
?>
```

This hack starts with the *index.php* page, which presents a login form to the user. From there, the user enters her name and password, and the form is submitted to the *login.php* page, which queries the database to see whether the user is in the system and the password matches. If the credentials match, the script sets the session and forwards her to the *welcome.php* page, which acts as her home page. From there, she can log out by clicking a link to the *logout.php* page. That page removes her session.

Running the Hack

After uploading the files to the server, the first step is to set up the users database:

```
% mysqladmin --user=root --password=password create time
% mysql --user=root --password=password time < users.sql
```

The first command creates the database. The second loads the SQL script into the database, creates the users table, and adds a few accounts.

The next step is to surf over to the *index.php* page. This should look like Figure 6-15.

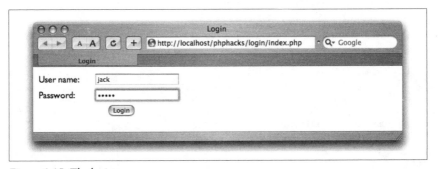

Figure 6-15. The login page

To test the login, first try a bad password. Type "jack" into the "User name" field and "hello" as the password; then click on the Login button. The *login.php* page checks the login, figures out that it's wrong, and forwards you back to the *index.php* page with the 3 value set to 1. This also brings up red error text, as shown in Figure 6-16.

This time, type "jack" as the username and "toronto" as the password, and click the Login button again. Now the *login.php* page verifies that the information is correct, and configures your session with the valid user ID. You're then forwarded to the *welcome.php* page. That page displays your user account and offers you the opportunity to log out, as shown in Figure 6-17.

If you click on the Logout link, the *logout.php* page will end your session and forward you back to the login page.

Figure 6-16. The login page after a bad username or password

Figure 6-17. The home page after a successful login

You can build your multi-user application on this simple authentication framework by using the *welcome.php* page as a template for your other pages. When you use this as a starting point for other pages, each page will check to make sure the user is logged in properly and will forward him back to the *index.php* page if he doesn't have an active session.

See Also

- "Apply Security by Role" [Hack #58]

HACK
#58   Apply Security by Role

Use security roles to provide varying levels of access to your web application.

Not all users who approach a system have the same rights within that system. For example, some users can add and remove users, some can post, some can only read messages, and some can do a combination of all of these.

A proper role-based system not only restricts access to parts of the system, but also reduces the complexity of pages for users with restricted rights. The user should not be able to see links that she cannot use, and she *should* have links to the tasks appropriate for her. This hack demonstrates a fairly straightforward role-based security system.

Figure 6-18 shows the page flow among the different pages in the hack. The user starts on the *index.php* page, which has the login. That page submits to the *login.php* page, which checks the login information. If the login credentials are accepted, the user is logged in and is forwarded on to the *welcome. php* page. If the login credentials aren't accepted, the user is sent back to the *index.php* page. From the *welcome.php* page, the user can do one of two things. She can log out by clicking a link to the *logout.php* page, which dumps her session and sends her back to *index.php*, or she can try to go to the *manage.php* page directly; that page checks her credentials and sends her back to the *welcome.php* page if she doesn't have proper credentials.

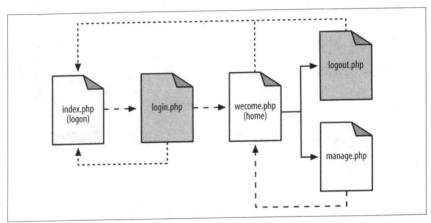

Figure 6-18. The page flow in this hack

The *welcome.php* page also checks to see whether the user's session is valid. If the session is not valid, the user is sent back to the *index.php* page to log in. In other words, people can't bypass the login to get into the site simply by typing in a direct URL.

The Code

Save the code in Example 6-19 as *dblib.php*.

Example 6-19. The database library for the roles system

```php
<?php
require_once( "DB.php" );
$dsn = 'mysql://root:password@localhost/roles';
$db =& DB::Connect( $dsn, array( ) );
if (PEAR::isError($db)) { die($db->getMessage( )); }

function get_db( ) { global $db; return $db; }

function get_role_id( $role )
{
```

Example 6-19. The database library for the roles system (continued)

```
  global $db;
  $res = $db->query( "SELECT id FROM roles WHERE name=?", array( $role ) );
  if ( $res != null )
  {
    $res->fetchInto( $row );
    return $row[0];
  }
  return null;
}

function has_role( $user, $role )
{
  global $db;

  $role_id = get_role_id( $role );

  $res = $db->query( "SELECT user_id FROM user_role WHERE user_id=? AND role_
    id=?",
    array( $user, $role_id ) );

  if ( $res != null )
  {
    $res->fetchInto( $row );
    return ( (int)$row[0] == (int)$user ) ? true : false;
  }
  return false;
}
?>
```

Save the code in Example 6-20 as *index.php*.

Example 6-20. The login page

```
<html>
<head><title>Login</title></head>
<body>
<?php if ( $_GET['bad'] == 1 ) { ?>
<font color="red">Bad login or password, please try again<br/></font>
<?php } ?>
<form action="login.php" method="post">
<table width="300" border="0" cellspacing="0" cellpadding="2">
<tr><td>User name:</td><td><input type="text" name="user" /></td></tr>
<tr><td>Password:</td><td><input type="password" name="password" /></td></tr>
<tr><td colspan="2"><center><input type="submit" value="Login" /></center></td></
tr>
</table>
</form>
</body>
</html>
```

Save the code in Example 6-21 as *login.php*.

Example 6-21. The login processor

```php
<?php
require_once( "dblib.php" );

$db = get_db( );

$res = $db->query( "SELECT id FROM users WHERE name=? AND password=MD5(?)",
  array( $_POST['user'], $_POST['password'] ) );

$row = array( null );
if ( $res != null )
  $res->fetchInto( $row );

if ( $row[0] != null )
{
    session_start( );
    $_SESSION['user'] = $row[0];
    header( "Location: welcome.php" );
}
else
{
    header( "Location: index.php?bad=1" );
}
?>
```

Save the code in Example 6-22 as *logout.php*.

Example 6-22. The logout processor

```php
<?php
session_destroy( );
header( "Location: index.php" );
?>
```

Save the code in Example 6-23 as *manage.php*.

Example 6-23. A page that should be visible only to managers

```php
<?php
require_once( "security.php" );

session_start( );
if ( $_SESSION['user'] == null || $_SESSION['user'] < 1 )
{ header( "Location: index.php" ); exit; }

check_roles( $_SESSION['user'], array( 'manager' ) );
?>
<html>
<body>
From here you manage the users.<br/><br/>
Back to the <a href="welcome.php">home page</a>.
</body>
</html>
```

Save the code in Example 6-24 as *security.php*.

Example 6-24. The security library functions

```php
<?php
require_once( "dblib.php" );

function check_roles( $user, $roles )
{
  foreach( $roles as $role )
  {
    if ( !has_role( $user, $role ) )
    {
?>
You do not have permission to access this page.<br/><br/>
Return to the <a href="welcome.php">home page</a>.
<?php
      exit;
    }
  }
}
?>
```

Save the code in Example 6-25 as *users.sql*.

Example 6-25. The SQL code for this example

```sql
DROP TABLE IF EXISTS roles;
CREATE TABLE roles (
 id MEDIUMINT NOT NULL AUTO_INCREMENT,
 name TEXT,
 PRIMARY KEY( id )
);

DROP TABLE IF EXISTS users;
CREATE TABLE users (
 id MEDIUMINT NOT NULL AUTO_INCREMENT,
 name TEXT,
 password TEXT,
 PRIMARY KEY( id )
);

DROP TABLE IF EXISTS user_role;
CREATE TABLE user_role (
 user_id MEDIUMINT,
 role_id MEDIUMINT
);

INSERT INTO roles VALUES ( 0, 'user' );
INSERT INTO roles VALUES ( 0, 'manager' );

INSERT INTO users VALUES ( 0, 'jack', MD5( 'toronto' ) );
INSERT INTO users VALUES ( 0, 'megan', MD5( 'seattle' ) );
```

Example 6-25. The SQL code for this example (continued)

```
INSERT INTO user_role VALUES ( 1, 1 );
INSERT INTO user_role VALUES ( 2, 1 );
INSERT INTO user_role VALUES ( 2, 2 );
```

Save the code in Example 6-26 as *welcome.php*.

Example 6-26. The home page for when a user has logged in

```php
<?php
require_once( "dblib.php" );

session_start();
if ( $_SESSION['user'] == null || $_SESSION['user'] < 1 )
{ header( "Location: index.php" ); exit; }

$db = get_db();

$res = $db->query( "SELECT name FROM users WHERE id=?", array( $_SESSION['user'] ) );
$res->fetchInto( $row );
?>
<html>
<head><title>Welcome</title></head>
<body>
Welcome <?php echo( $row[0] ); ?><br/><br/>
<?php
if ( has_role( $_SESSION['user'], 'manager' ) ) {
?>
<a href="manage.php">Manage the users</a><br/><br/>
<?php } ?>
<a href="logout.php">Logout</a>
</body>
</html>
```

The system starts with the *index.php* page, which presents the login form to the user. Once the user inputs his login name and password, the form is submitted to the *login.php* page, which processes the login. If the login is valid, the code sets up the session with the user ID. From there, the user is forwarded to the *welcome.php* page, which acts as his home page once he has logged in.

The *welcome.php* page has a link to the *manage.php* page. That page is valid only if you are a manager, so the code for that page checks the permissions. If the user doesn't have the manager role, he is sent back to the home page.

The last thing to handle is logging out. That works through the *logout.php* script, which ends the user's session and sends him back to the login page.

The code at the top of each page in the system needs to check whether the user is logged in. If the user is logged in, the page should render normally. Otherwise, the user needs to be forwarded back to the login page. Obviously the login page doesn't have that code. Otherwise, the user would get into an endless loop just trying to log in.

Running the Hack

Running the hack starts with loading up the database:

```
% mysqladmin --user=root --password=password create roles
% mysql --user=root --password=password roles < users.sql
```

With that done, upload the rest of the code to the web server and point your browser at *index.php*. This should look like Figure 6-19.

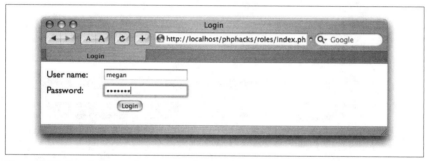

Figure 6-19. Logging in as the manager "megan"

Log in with the username "megan" and the password "seattle,"and you will get the home page shown in Figure 6-20.

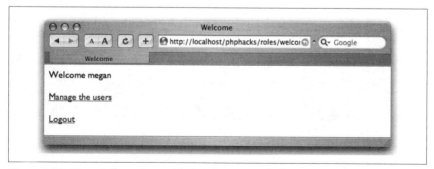

Figure 6-20. Megan's home page with the management link

The link to the user management page (*management.php*) is shown because the "megan" account is linked to the *manager* role, and this page checks for that role using the has_role( ) function.

Click on "Manage the users," and you will get something like Figure 6-21.

Figure 6-21. Clicking on the manage pages is allowed

This page makes sure that anyone who looks at it is a manager. In this case, the person who is logged in, Megan, is a manager, so the page is displayed.

Now let's log out; log back in as "jack," as shown in Figure 6-22. The password for this account is "toronto."

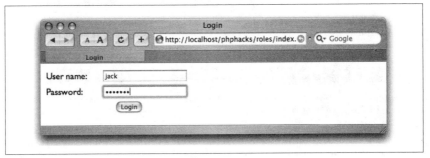

Figure 6-22. Logging in as the nonmanager "jack" account

This time the home page does not have the user management link, as seen in Figure 6-23.

Figure 6-23. The home page without the management link

Even a clever user who goes directly to the *management.php* page by typing in the URL manually will get a page that tells him he doesn't have the correct permissions to look at the page. You can see the error message in Figure 6-24.

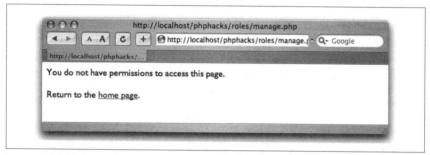

Figure 6-24. Refusing direct access to the management page

This is a very rudimentary form of role-based security. If your application is small, or security is divided into just two or three roles, this type of system might suffice.

The next step up from here is to create a model of the objects within the application inside the roles system. Then you can have different permissions for reading, adding, removing, and updating each object.

Following on from that, add the ability to assign groups of permissions to a named role. For example, the *administrator* role would have the permissions to read, add, remove, and update user accounts. A *manager* role might only have the ability to update user accounts. The business logic would ask the security system whether the current user has a specific permission, and the system would see whether the user's roles contain that permission. The application does *not* look for a particular role, since roles are just named collections of permissions.

See Also

- "Create a Login System" [Hack #57]

Migrate to MD5 Passwords

Use a migration script to turn your plain-text passwords into MD5-encrypted passwords.

From years of consulting work, I can tell you that although people say their web applications have encrypted passwords, they often do not. Realistically, though, encrypting passwords is just not that difficult to do. Even worse, any site that can send you the exact text of your password when you click the "I forgot my password" link stores a copy of your password in clear text somewhere. Needless to say, this isn't a good thing.

So why are encrypted passwords so important? First, because anyone who gets access to the database through a security hole can get access to the entire system. Second, most people talk about using different passwords on different accounts, but end up using the same, or similar, passwords, simply because it's easier. Getting a password on one machine can mean having access to other, possibly more important accounts. This hack describes how to migrate a table of users and passwords from plain text to MD5 encryptions.

The Code

Save the code in Example 6-27 as *schema.sql*.

Example 6-27. The original schema file

```
DROP TABLE IF EXISTS users;
CREATE TABLE users (
  id MEDIUMINT NOT NULL AUTO_INCREMENT,
  name TEXT,
  pass TEXT,
  PRIMARY KEY( id )
);
```

Save the code in Example 6-28 as *users.sql*.

Example 6-28. The original nonencoded passwords

```
INSERT INTO users VALUES ( 0, "jack", "toronto" );
INSERT INTO users VALUES ( 0, "megan", "omaha" );
```

Save the code in Example 6-29 as *migrate.php*.

Example 6-29. The script to migrate from plain-text passwords to MD5-encoded passwords

```php
<?php
require_once( "DB.php" );
$dsn = 'mysql://root:password@localhost/migpass';
$db =& DB::Connect( $dsn, array() );
if (PEAR::isError($db)) { die($db->getMessage()); }

$res = $db->query( "SELECT id, pass FROM users", array() );

$sth = $db->prepare( "UPDATE users SET pass=MD5(?) WHERE id=?" );

while( $res->fetchInto( $row ) )
```

Example 6-29. The script to migrate from plain-text passwords to MD5-encoded passwords (continued)

```
{
    $db->execute( $sth, array( $row[1], $row[0] ) );
}
?>
```

Save the code in Example 6-30 as *list.php*.

Example 6-30. The script to list the users

```php
<?php
require_once( "DB.php" );
$dsn = 'mysql://root:password@localhost/migpass';
$db =& DB::Connect( $dsn, array() );
if (PEAR::isError($db)) { die($db->getMessage()); }

$res = $db->query( "SELECT id, name, pass FROM users", array() );

$sth = $db->prepare( "UPDATE users SET pass=MD5(?) WHERE id=?" );

while( $res->fetchInto( $row ) )
{
    print( $row[0]." - ".$row[1]." - ".$row[2]."\n" );
}
?>
```

Save the code in Example 6-31 as *check.php*.

Example 6-31. The script to check the password encoding

```php
<?php
require_once( "DB.php" );
$dsn = 'mysql://root:password@localhost/migpass';
$db =& DB::Connect( $dsn, array() );
if (PEAR::isError($db)) { die($db->getMessage()); }

$user = "jack";
$pass = "toronto";

$res = $db->query( "SELECT id, name FROM users WHERE name=? AND pass=MD5(?)",
    array( $user, $pass ) );

while( $res->fetchInto( $row ) )
{
    print( $row[0]." - ".$row[1]."\n" );
}
?>
```

There's really not much going on here; the guts of the conversion are handled by PHP in the MDB( ) function used within the *migrate.php* script.

Running the Hack

This hack uses the PHP command-line interpreter, so start on the command line by loading the MySQL database with the schema and some sample user data:

```
% mysqladmin --user=root --password=password create migpass
% mysql --user=root --password=password migpass < schema.sql
% mysql --user=root --password=password migpass < users.sql
```

The first command creates the database. The second creates the users table within the database, and the final line adds the sample user accounts.

The next thing to do is to see whether the data has been loaded properly:

```
% php list.php
1 - jack - toronto
2 - megan - omaha
```

This shows that there are two accounts in the table. The first is for a user named "jack" with a plain-text password of "toronto." The second is for a user named "megan" with a password of "omaha."

The next step is to migrate the passwords using the PHP scripts and then check for success:

```
% php migrate.php
% php list.php
1 - jack - 79cca97018f48e834a46f1b634e9a427
2 - megan - c365303299c8e35dbd443faa065feb5f
```

The first command converts the password text in the tables by running it through the MD5() conversion function in MySQL. The *list.php* script then shows the current contents of the database with the encrypted passwords.

The last step is to check to make sure that we can still authenticate users by using the MD5 function in the SQL query:

```
% php check.php
1 - jack
```

The *check.php* script tries to authenticate the account named "jack" with the incoming text, "toronto," for the password. Instead of using just the plain-text version of "toronto," the modified code needs to run the password through the MD5 function and compare that with the password value in the database. The same text run through MD5 will always produce the same output, so this is a valid way to compare MD5-encrypted passwords.

Because the application and database no longer store plain-text versions of users' passwords, the web application can no longer send out clear-text versions of these passwords if users request them. In addition to this migration script, then, the web application will also need to alter the flow behind the "forgot my password" functionality. Usually, this involves resetting the password to a safe (and random) value and then sending that new password to the email account associated with the account. Emails like this should provide a link that allows the account holder to reset the password to something he can remember (at least for a couple of days) and expiring the password sent in clear text after a few days.

See Also

- "Create a Login System" [Hack #57]
- "Apply Security by Role" [Hack #58]

Make Usable URLs with mod_rewrite

#60

Use Apache's mod_rewrite module to create URLs that are easy to understand and use.

The Apache server's mod_rewrite module gives you the ability to redirect one URL to another transparently, all without the user's knowledge. This opens up all sorts of possibilities, from simply redirecting old URLs to new addresses, to cleaning up the "dirty" URLs (filled with extra parameters and data your application will never use) coming from a poor publishing system—turning them into URLs that are friendlier to both readers and search engines.

An Introduction to Rewriting

Readable URLs are nice. A well-designed web site will have a logical file-system layout with smart folder names and filenames and as many implementation details left out as possible. In the better-designed sites, readers can even guess at filenames with a high level of success.

However, sometimes the best possible design still can't stop your site's URLs from being nigh impossible to use. For instance, you might be using a content management system that serves out URLs that look something like *http://www.site.com/viewcatalog.php?category=hats&prodID=53.*

This is a horrible URL, but it and its brethren are becoming increasingly prevalent in these days of dynamically generated pages. There are a number of problems with a URL of this kind:

- It exposes the underlying technology of the web site (in this case, PHP). This can give potential hackers clues as to what type of data they should send, along with the query string needed, to perform a front-door attack on the site. You shouldn't give away information like this if you can help it.

> Even if you're not overly concerned with the security of your site, the technology you're using is at best irrelevant—and at worst a source of confusion—to your readers, so you should hide it from them if at all possible.
>
> If at some point in the future, you decide to change the language that your site is based on (to ASP, for instance), all of your old URLs will stop working. This is a pretty serious problem, as anyone who has tackled a full-on site rewrite will attest.

- The URL is littered with awkward punctuation, such as the question mark and ampersand. Those & characters, in particular, are problematic; if another webmaster links to this page using that URL, the unescaped ampersands will invalidate his XHTML.

- Some search engines won't index pages that they think are generated dynamically. Because of the danger of finding infinite pages by changing the query string of a URL, many search engine spiders are designed to avoid adding pages like this to their index.

Luckily, using rewriting, it's easy to clean up this URL to something far more manageable. For example, you can map the URL to *http://www.site.com/catalog/hats/53/.*

Much better, isn't it? This URL is more logical, readable, and memorable, and will be picked up by all search engines. The faux directories are short and descriptive. As an added benefit, it looks more permanent.

To use mod_rewrite, you supply it with the URLs you want the server to match (these are the dirty URLs mentioned earlier) and the real URLs that these will be redirected to. The URLs to be matched can be normal file addresses, which will match one file, or they can be regular expressions, which can match many files at the same time.

Basic Rewriting

Some servers will not have mod_rewrite enabled by default. As long as the module is present in an Apache installation, though, you can enable it simply by creating an Apache configuration file. Call this file *.htaccess* (or open one if it already exists), and place it in your site's root directory so that rewriting is enabled throughout your site. Once you have created the file, add this line:

```
RewriteEngine on
```

Basic redirects. We'll start off with a straight redirect; this is as if you had moved a file to a new location and want all links to the old location to be forwarded to the new location. Here's the code for a simple file redirect:

```
RewriteEngine on
RewriteRule ^old\.html$ new.html
```

Though this is the simplest example possible, it might still throw a few people off. The structure of the "old" URL is the only difficult part in RewriteRule. There are three special characters in there:

- The caret, ^, signifies the start of a URL to be matched under the directory the *.htaccess* file is in. If you had omitted the caret, the preceding code would also match a file called *cold.html*. Because of the unintended matches that this can cause, you should start almost all of your matches with the caret.

- The dollar sign, $, signifies the end of the string to be matched. You should add this to stop your rules from matching the first part of longer URLs.

- The period, ., placed before the file extension, is a special character in regular expressions and would mean something special if we didn't escape it with the backslash, telling Apache to treat it as a normal character.

So, this rule will make your server transparently redirect from the *old.html* page to the *new.html* page. Your reader will have no idea that it happened, and it's pretty much instantaneous.

Forcing new requests. Sometimes you *do* want your readers to know a redirect has occurred, and you can do this by forcing a new HTTP request for the new page. This will make the browser load the new page as if it were the page originally requested, and the location bar will change to show the URL of the new page. All you need to do is turn on the [R] flag by appending it to the rule:

```
RewriteRule ^old\.html$ new.html [R]
```

Figure 6-25 shows this redirect in action.

Using Regular Expressions

Now we get on to the *really* useful stuff. The power of mod_rewrite comes at the expense of complexity. If this is your first encounter with regular expressions [Hack #87], you might find them to be a tough nut to crack, but the options they afford you are well worth the work it takes to learn and master them.

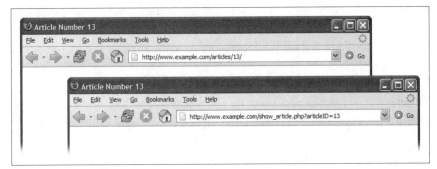

Figure 6-25. old.html redirecting the user to new.html

With regular expressions, you can have your rules match a set of URLs at a time and mass-redirect them to actual pages. This is very useful when building a large site with many pages that are generated from a single PHP file. For example, you might design your site to have the URL structure *http://www.example.com/articles/<article_id>*.

This is a nice, clean structure. However, if all of your articles are generated from one *show_article.php* script, as is often the case, you're going to want to set up redirects from each URL to its real location. Take this rule:

```
RewriteRule ^articles/([0-9][0-9])/$ show_article.php?articleID=$1
```

This will match any URLs that start with *articles/*, followed by any two digits, followed by a forward slash. For example, this rule will match a URL such as *articles/12/* or *articles/99/* and redirect it to the PHP script (see Figure 6-26 for an example).

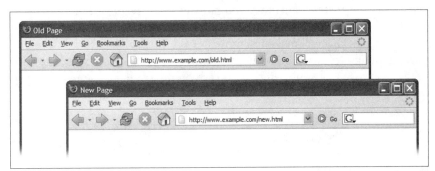

Figure 6-26. A redirect from a clean URL to the article's location in the underlying PHP system

The parts in square brackets are called *ranges*. In this case, we're allowing anything in the range 0–9, which is any digit. Other ranges might be [A-Z], for any uppercase letter, [a-z] for any lowercase letter, and [A-Za-z] for any letter in either case.

We have encased the regular-expression part of the URL in parentheses because we want to store whatever value was found here for later use. In this case, we're sending this value to a PHP script as an argument. Once we have a value in parentheses, we can use it through a *back-reference*. Each part you've placed in parentheses is given an index, starting with 1. So, the first back-reference is $1, the third is $3, etc. Thus, once the redirect is done, the page loaded in the reader's browser will be something like *show_article. php?articleID=12*.

Adding trailing slashes. If your site visitor had entered something like *articles/ 12* into his browser's location bar, the preceding rule won't do a redirect, as the slash at the end of the URL is missing. To promote good URL writing, take care of this by doing a direct redirect to the same URL with the slash appended:

```
RewriteRule ^articles/([0-9][0-9])$ articles/$1/ [R]
```

Multiple redirects in the same *.htaccess* file can be applied in sequence, which is what we're doing here. This rule is added before the one we did earlier, like so:

```
RewriteRule ^articles/([0-9][0-9])$ articles/$1/ [R]
RewriteRule ^articles/([0-9][0-9])/$ show_article.php?articleID=$1
```

Thus, if the user types in the URL *articles/12*, the first rule kicks in, rewriting the URL to include the trailing slash and doing a new request for *articles/ 12/*. Then the second rule has something to match and transparently redirects this URL to *show_article.php?articleID=12*. Pretty slick, huh?

Match modifiers. You can expand your regular-expression patterns by adding some modifier characters, which allow you to match URLs with an indefinite number of characters. In the earlier examples, we were allowing only two numbers for each article's ID number. This isn't the most expandable solution, because if the number of articles published ever grew beyond these initial confines of 99 articles, resulting in a URL such as *show_article. php?articleID=100*, our rules would cease to match this URL.

So, instead of hardcoding a set number of characters to look for, we'll work in some room to grow by allowing any number of digits to be entered. The following rule does just that:

```
RewriteRule ^articles/([0-9]+)$ articles/$1/ [R]
```

Note the plus sign (+) that has sneaked in there. This modifier changes whatever comes directly before it by saying "one or more of the preceding character or range." In this case, it means that the rule will match any URL that starts with *articles/* and ends with at least one digit. So this'll match both *articles/1* and *articles/1000.*

Other match modifiers you can use in the same way are the asterisk, *, which means "zero or more of the preceding character or range," and the question mark, ?, which means "zero or only one of the preceding character or range." Using URL rewriting means less confusing 404 errors for your readers, and a site that seems to run a whole lot smoother all around.

—*Ross Shannon*

HACK #61 Build an Ad Redirector

Add the ability for your site to serve up ads on a random basis between link clicks.

Content sites, like the IGN gaming site (*http://www.ign.com/*) have revenues based on serving ads. If you click on an article link, you might get the article, or you might get an ad page. The ad page has both the ad and a link to the requested article (so that you can manually go to the requested page). The ad page will also automatically forward you to your article if you let it sit for a few seconds.

I have to admit that I thought twice about writing and including this hack, because I don't like this behavior all that much. But I figured I would let you decide for yourself. It's sort of like the *Anarchist's Cookbook*; just because there is a book on how to make a bomb doesn't mean you have to make one for yourself.

The illustration in Figure 6-27 shows the relationship among the pages in the ad redirector system. All of the links on the *index.php* page go to the *redir.php* redirector page. Based on a random value, the *redir.php* page decides whether you will stay there and watch an ad or be sent to the originally requested article.

The Code

Save the code in Example 6-32 as *index.php.*

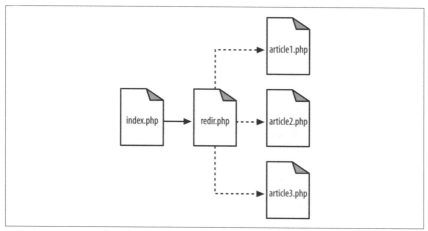

Figure 6-27. The ad redirector page flow

Example 6-32. The home page with article links

```php
<?php
function redir_link( $url, $text )
{
?>
<a href="redir.php?url=<?php echo( $url ); ?>"><?php echo( $text ); ?></a>
<?php
}
?>
<html>
<body>
Here are my articles:<br/><br/>
<?php redir_link( 'article1.html', 'Article one' ); ?><br/>
<?php redir_link( 'article2.html', 'Article two' ); ?><br/>
<?php redir_link( 'article3.html', 'Article three' ); ?><br/>
</body>
</html>
```

Save the code in Example 6-33 as *redir.php*.

Example 6-33. The ad redirector

```php
<?php
srand(time());
if ( mt_rand(0,10) < 7 )
{
  header( "Location: ".$_GET['url'] );
  exit;
}
?>
<html>
<head>
<script language="Javascript">
```

Example 6-33. The ad redirector (continued)

```
function redir( )
{
  window.location='<?php echo( $_GET['url'] ); ?>';
}
function startTimer( )
{
  window.setTimeout( "redir( );", 2000 );
}
</script>
</head>
<body onload="startTimer( )">
Here is my groovy ad. You can continue onto the article
<a href="<?php echo( $_GET['url'] ); ?>">here</a>. Or just
wait for a couple of seconds.
</body>
</html>
```

Save the code in Example 6-34 as *article1.html*.

Example 6-34. The first article

```
<html>
<head><title>Article one</title></head>
<body>
Article one
</body>
</html>
```

Save the code in Example 6-35 as *article2.html*.

Example 6-35. The second article

```
<html>
<head><title>Article two</title></head>
<body>
Article two
</body>
</html>
```

Save the code in Example 6-36 as *article3.html*.

Example 6-36. The third article

```
<html>
<head><title>Article three</title></head>
<body>
Article three
</body>
</html>
```

Running the Hack

Upload the files to the PHP server and navigate your browser to *index.php*.
You should see something like Figure 6-28.

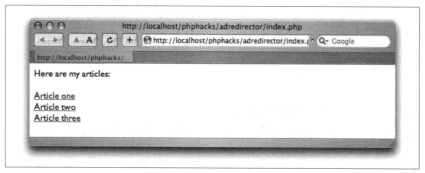

Figure 6-28. The home page with the article links

Click on the link for "Article two," which is actually a link to *redir.php*.
Sometimes *redir.php* will send you to an ad page, as shown in Figure 6-29.

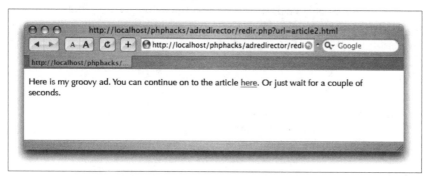

Figure 6-29. The ad page with the timer and the link to the article

There is a direct link to the article if people want to skip through the ad.
Additionally, there's a timer on the page that, once expired, triggers a redirection to the user's target page.

In cases where the random generator doesn't cause an ad to appear, users go
directly to the article, as shown in Figure 6-30.

There are several ways to implement this ad redirector mechanism. With the
implementation shown here, the user can still link directly to articles by referencing the redirection page and supplying the exact URL of the target
page. If you want the ads to appear even on direct links, you can invert this
mechanism by putting a check at the top of *every* page in your application,
randomly redirecting users to an ad instead of displaying requested articles
or pages.

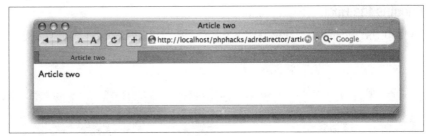

Figure 6-30. The article page

 HACK **#62**

Add a Buy Now Button

Use PayPal to add a Buy Now button to your PHP web application.

PayPal's Buy Now buttons are ideal for e-commerce impulse sales. They are easy for the customer to use, and there's no lengthy checkout procedure. One click and you're on PayPal's secured site.

These buttons are also very easy to install; because of their simplicity, though, web applications often don't put in the extra work required to track and secure sales. This hack shows how to track and secure purchases made using Buy Now buttons. I will take you through the steps of creating a Buy Now button, modifying it to create a database record of the purchase, and I'll show how to secure the purchase using Instant Payment Notification (IPN).

 This hack requires PHP 5 and MySQL Version 4.1.3 or higher, along with the `mysqli` extension.

Creating a Buy Now Button

You don't need to worry about manually creating the HTML form for a Buy Now button. Just go to your PayPal account, choose Merchant Tools, and click on the Buy Now Buttons link. Within seconds, you'll have the HTML form ready to embed into your web site. The Buy Now button looks like Figure 6-31.

Object Oriented PHP - 24.95 [Buy Now]

Figure 6-31. The Buy Now button

As it stands right now, this form has a couple of shortcomings. It's not geared toward tracking purchases in a database, and like any form on the Internet, it is subject to hijacking. A local copy of the form can be made, and values can be changed, all in an effort to sabotage your site (and your customers); even worse, if there is no way of crosschecking the values from this form against a correct set of values, an order might easily be processed at discounted prices.

The *buynow.html* file in Example 6-37 (shown shortly) contains the HTML for the Buy Now button. It differs in one major respect from the code generated by PayPal: the action attribute of the form tag doesn't point to the PayPal site, but to another script, *presubmit.php* (shown in Example 6-39). This intermediary script allows information to be added to a database before submitting purchases to PayPal.

Tracking the Sale

Briefly stated, the code in *presubmit.php* inserts a record into a tblorders table and into a related tblorderitems table. The order ID is then retrieved and added to the query string constructed from the values posted to this page. Finally, this query string is forwarded to the PayPal site, as shown in Figure 6-32.

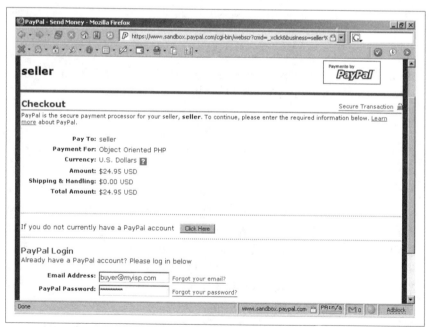

Figure 6-32. The PayPal checkout page

Creating a database entry and passing the order number along to PayPal will assist in tracking and securing the purchase.

Since you're accessing the database using the relatively new object-oriented (OO) interface to the mysqli extension, a few comments are in order. Even if you have no experience in OO programming, it is easy to understand the code that inserts a record into the orders table. Since this table has an auto_ increment field, it's necessary to retrieve the order ID after insertion, so as to identify the order later.

The way you insert a record into the tblorderitems table is not as straightforward. To create a record in this table, the code uses a prepared statement; the mysqli extension supports this MySQL 4.1 capability. Prepared statements are commonly used to insert multiple records into a database and are much more efficient than a series of individual SQL statements. However, the code here uses a prepared statement because data passed to a prepared statement does not have to be escaped first. Prepared statements automatically escape data (a nice convenience feature taken advantage of here).

Verifying the Sale

Securing a payment means ensuring that the payment is made to the correct account in the correct amount and is not a duplicate of an earlier transaction. IPN allows us to do this programmatically by identifying a URL that will receive notification of payment.

When a purchase is made at the site, the sequence of events is as follows:

1. Clicking the Buy Now button invokes the script, creating a database record, and then forwards the buyer to the PayPal site.
2. After PayPal receives payment, a hidden post is made to the IPN URL. This post contains encrypted code and information about the payment.
3. To ensure that this post is not specious and did in fact originate at PayPal, we must return this post to PayPal.
4. PayPal will then respond, verifying that the post originated with them.

verifypurchase.php (in Example 6-40) contains the code that confirms the source of the post and validates the data. It can be summarized as follows:

1. The PayPal post is captured and resubmitted, adding the name/value pair cmd=_notify-validate as required by PayPal.
2. If this resubmitted post is verified as having originated from PayPal, the code confirms the details of the purchase.
3. The price for the specific item is retrieved from the database and is compared to the posted value.

4. The code then makes sure that the transaction ID is not a duplicate of an earlier purchase and, by verifying the receiver's email, ensures that the payment has been made into the correct account.

A few comments on less-obvious features of the code are in order. Using the CURL package is not the only way to handle the resubmission of posted values to PayPal, but it certainly does make it easy. When using IPN, the names of some of the values retrieved are different from the ones originally posted. `receiver_email` is synonymous with the business email posted from the form. `mc_gross` holds the payment amount and, in this example, its value should be equal to the price of the purchased item. On the other hand, `item_number` and `custom` have not changed at all. Again, access to the database is through the OO interface of `mysqli`.

> Depending on server settings, the port and socket settings might or might not be required when creating a connection object. Notice also that you can specify the database when creating the connection. Also, since this code uses (and depends on) PHP 5, objects are automatically passed by reference, and there is no need to adjust syntax when objects are function parameters.

The Code

Save the code in Example 6-37 as *buynow.html*.

Example 6-37. An example Buy Now page

```
<html>
<head>
<title>Buy Now Button</title>
</head>
<body>
<!-- alter action of form-->
<form action="presubmit.php" method="post">
<label>Purchase: Object-Oriented PHP for 24.95</label>
<input type="hidden" name="cmd" value="_xclick" />
<input type="hidden" name="business" value="seller@myisp.com" />
<input type="hidden" name="item_name" value="Object-Oriented PHP" />
<input type="hidden" name="item_number" value="673498" />
<input type="hidden" name="amount" value="24.95" />
<input type="hidden" name="no_note" value="1" />
<input type="hidden" name="currency_code" value="USD" />
<input type="image" src="https://www.paypal.com/en_US/i/btn/x-click-but23.gif"
border="0" name="submit" alt="" />
</form>
</body>
</html>
```

Save the code in Example 6-38 as *connection.php*.

Example 6-38. The connection information

```php
<?php
  $hostname = "localhost";
  $databasename = "books";
  $username = "username";
  $password = "password";
?>
```

Save the code in Example 6-39 as *presubmit.php*.

Example 6-39. The script that stores the order on the way to PayPal

```php
<?php
  include "connection.php";
  //create a connection using mysqli
  $con = new mysqli($hostname, $username, $password, $databasename,
      3306, "/var/lib/mysql/mysql.sock");
  //create an order id
  $strsql = "INSERT INTO tblorders SET orderdate = CURDATE( )";
  $con->query($strsql);
  //retrieve insertid - property not method
  $id = $con->insert_id;
  $item_number = $_POST['item_number'];
  //now add order item to db
  $strsql = "INSERT INTO tblorderitems SET orderid = ?, ".
    "inventorynumber = ?";
  //use statement even though only one insert
  $stmt = $con->stmt_init( );
  $stmt->prepare($strsql);
  //bind integer and string values
  $stmt->bind_param('ii', $id, $item_number);
  $stmt->execute( );
  //resubmit
  $querystring = "?";
  //loop for posted values
  foreach($_POST as $key => $value)
  {
    $value = urlencode(stripslashes($value));
    $querystring .= "$key=$value&";
  }
  //update querystring with order id
  //use "custom" not "on0" for order id value
  $querystring .= "custom=$id";
  header('location:https://www.paypal.com/cgi-bin/webscr'.$querystring);
  exit( );
?>
```

Save the code in Example 6-40 as *verifypurchase.php*.

Example 6-40. The purchase verification script

```php
<?php
include "connection.php";
/////////////////////////////////////////////////////////////
function check_txnid($con, $txnid)
{
  $valid_txnid = false;
  //get result set
  $strsql = "SELECT * FROM tblorders ".
    " WHERE txnid = '$txnid'";
  $rs = $con->query($strsql);
  if($rs->num_rows == 0)
  {
    $valid_txnid = true;
  }
  return $valid_txnid;
}
/////////////////////////////////////////////////////////////
function check_price($con, $price, $inventoryid)
{
  $valid_price = false;
  //get result set
  $strsql = "SELECT listprice FROM tblbooks ".
    " WHERE inventorynumber = '$inventoryid'";
  $rs = $con->query($strsql);
  $row = $rs->fetch_array();
  $num = (float)$row[0];
  if($num == $price)
  {
    $valid_price = true;
  }
  return $valid_price;
}
/////////////////////////////////////////////////////////////
function check_email($email)
{
  $valid_email = false;
  //compare to paypal merchant email
  if($email == "seller@myisp.com" )
  {
    $valid_email = true;
  }
  return $valid_email;
}
/////////////////////////////////////////////////////////////
function do_post($data)
{
  //now send back to paypal
  $c = curl_init('https://www.paypal.com/cgi-bin/webscr');
  curl_setopt($c, CURLOPT_POST,1);
  curl_setopt($c, CURLOPT_POSTFIELDS, $data);
  curl_setopt($c, CURLOPT_SSL_VERIFYPEER,FALSE);
```

Example 6-40. The purchase verification script (continued)

```
curl_setopt($c, CURLOPT_RETURNTRANSFER, 1);
$status = curl_exec($c);
curl_close($c);
return $status;
}
/////////////////////////////////////////////////////////////
//loop for posted values
$data = "";
foreach($_POST as $key => $value)
{
  $value = urlencode(stripslashes($value));
  $data .= "$key=$value&";
}
//must add this before returning to paypal
$data .= "cmd=_notify-validate";
$status = do_post($data);
//strip CR
$status = rtrim($status);
$payment_status = $_POST['payment_status'];
//get transaction id
$txn_id = $_POST['txn_id'];
if ($status == "VERIFIED" && $payment_status == "Completed")
{
  //need these variables
  $price = $_POST['mc_gross'];
  //get order number
  $orderid = $_POST['custom'];
  $inventoryid = $_POST['item_number'];
  //merchant's email i.e. paypal account
  //equals business in paynow.html
  $receiver_email = $_POST['receiver_email'];
  //create a mysqli connection
  $con = new mysqli($hostname, $username, $password, $databasename, 3306,
    "/var/lib/mysql/mysql.sock");
  //check merchant email, price & not recycled txn id
  //no need to change syntax to pass object by reference
  $valid_txnid = check_txnid($con, $txn_id);
  $valid_price = check_price($con, $price, $inventoryid);
  $valid_email = check_email($receiver_email);
  //if all checks write record
  if($valid_price && $valid_email && $valid_txnid)
  {
    //update database with txn id
    $strsql = "UPDATE tblorders SET txnid = '$txn_id' " .
      "WHERE orderid = $orderid";
    $con->query($strsql);
    $message ="Successful, transaction id: $txn_id\n";
  }
  else
  {
```

Example 6-40. The purchase verification script (continued)

```
    //unsuccessful transaction
    $message ="Unsuccessful, transaction id: $txn_id\n";
  }
}
else if($status == "INVALID")
{
  //notify suspicious transaction
  $message ="Suspicious IPN with transaction id: $txn_id";
}
else
{
  //deal with other types
  $message ="Incomplete purchase with transaction id: $txn_id";

}
mail ("notify@myisp.com", "PayPal", $message);
?>
```

Running the Hack

First, you will need a PayPal account. Create one by going to the PayPal home page and signing up for a business account.

Then you need to alter the sample scripts and pages to match your application specifications. Your *buynow.html* file will of course reflect the product you are selling. You will also need to change the email addresses in both the *buynow.html* file and the *verifypurchase.php* script. Replace *seller@myisp.com* with the email address associated with your PayPal account. This is important because it identifies the account that will receive payment. Change *notify@myisp.com* to the appropriate address for receiving confirmation of payment.

> You might not need a payment confirmation at all, or you might want to replace it with code to write a logfile, especially in the case of a failed payment.

Change the *connection.php* script to reflect values appropriate to your MySQL server. No changes are required for the *presubmit.php* script unless you change the database structure.

You will doubtless create a database suited to your specific business needs, but if you want to test this code as is, here are the SQL statements that will create the minimum required database structure:

```
CREATE TABLE `tblbooks` (
  `inventorynumber` int(11) NOT NULL auto_increment,
  `title` varchar(150) NOT NULL default '',
```

```
 `author` varchar(100) NOT NULL default '',
 `cost` float(6,2) NOT NULL default '0.00',
 `listprice` float(7,2) NOT NULL default '0.00',
 `publicationdate` varchar(4) default NULL,
 `publisher` varchar(4) NOT NULL default '',
 PRIMARY KEY  (`inventorynumber`),
 KEY `authidx` (`author`),
 KEY `titleidx` (`title`),
) ENGINE=MyISAM DEFAULT CHARSET=latin1

CREATE TABLE `tblorders` (
 `orderid` int(11) NOT NULL auto_increment,
 `customerid` int(11) default NULL,
 `orderdate` date default NULL,
 `txnid` varchar(17) default NULL,
 PRIMARY KEY  (`orderid`)
) ENGINE=MyISAM DEFAULT CHARSET=latin1

CREATE TABLE `tblorderitems` (
 `orderid` int(11) NOT NULL default '0',
 `inventorynumber` int(11) NOT NULL default '0',
 PRIMARY KEY  (`orderid`,`inventorynumber`)
) ENGINE=MyISAM DEFAULT CHARSET=latin1
```

Next, upload the files to your server, ensuring that the *connection.php*, *buynow.html*, and *presubmit.php* files are in the same directory. You can put the *verifypurchase.php* script in the same directory as well, but it's probably better off in its own directory. If you do put this script in a separate directory, be sure to change the include path for the *connection.php* file.

Go to your PayPal account, turn on IPN, and enter the fully qualified URL for the *verifypurchase.php* script. To make a purchase, point your browser at *buynow.php*. You will know that everything is working when you click on the Buy Now button and are taken to the PayPal site, and when payment is complete you receive an email containing the transaction ID.

Hacking the Hack

One size never fits all. In this particular case, the price of the individual item purchased is identical to the total price. However, in many cases, shipping charges might need to be added and different currencies taken into account. You can easily accommodate such changes by adjusting the check_price( ) function.

Use of mysqli is not a requirement, although it is apparent that prepared statements can be a real advantage, especially when processing a shopping cart rather than a single item.

Signing up for a PayPal developer account makes sense for someone who regularly develops PayPal applications. It certainly is an advantage to use the PayPal sandbox to test applications before going live with them. This is especially important for an application like IPN, where there is only server-to-server interaction and no user input.

Debugging an automated server response also presents challenges, as there's no browser to display errors. One option is to email the variable that holds the data reposted to PayPal. Email this value; you should see something like the following:

```
mc_gross=24.95&address_status=confirmed&payer_id=TYWM55XFZCN8S
&tax=0.00&address_street=36+Main+Street
&payment_date=16%3A00%3A32+Aug+11%2C+2005+PDT
&payment_status=Completed&charset=windows-1252&address_zip=12345
&first_name=Peter&mc_fee=0.82&address_country_code=US
&address_name=Peter+Buyer&notify_version=1.9&custom=20
&payer_status=unverified&business=seller%40isp.com
&address_country=United+States&address_city=Toledo&quantity=1
&verify_sign=ACUe-E7HjxmeeI8FjYAtjnx-yjHAAVhtx75Yq6UdimmRaeJhnewrOugZ
&payer_email=buyer%40myisp.com&txn_id=1E044782YK461110T
&payment_type=instant&last_name=Buyer&address_state=OH
&receiver_email=seller%40isp.com&payment_fee=0.82
&receiver_id=JEFVKNSSDLTBL&txn_type=web_accept
&item_name=Object+Oriented+PHP&mc_currency=USD
&item_number=06734980548&test_ipn=1&payment_gross=24.95
&shipping=0.00&cmd=_notify-validate
```

Do this, and you can confirm all the name/value pairs posted.

—Peter Lavin

See Also

- "Create a Shopping Cart" [Hack #66]

Find Out Where Your Guests Are Coming From

Use the Net-Geo PEAR module to tell you where in the world the people surfing to your site are coming from.

Have you ever wondered where the guests to your site are coming from? It turns out that finding out is not as tough as you might think. First, the IP address of every incoming request is provided to you through the Apache request handler. Second, a simple PEAR library is available that will turn an IP address into a physical location. This hack will show you how it all works.

The Code

Save the code in Example 6-41 as *geo.php*.

Example 6-41. An IP-to-geography converter

```
<html>
<body>
<?php
require_once( "cache/lite.php" );
require_once( "net/geo.php" );

$ip = $_SERVER['REMOTE_ADDR'];
$ip = "64.246.30.37";

$geo = new Net_Geo( );
?>
<table>
<tr><td>IP</td><td><?php echo( $ip ); ?></td></tr>
<tr><td>City</td><td><?php echo( $res['CITY'] ); ?></td></tr>
<tr><td>State</td><td><?php echo( $res['STATE'] ); ?></td></tr>
<tr><td>Country</td><td><?php echo( $res['COUNTRY'] ); ?></td></tr>
<tr><td>Latitude</td><td><?php echo( $res['LAT'] ); ?></td></tr>
<tr><td>Longitude</td><td><?php echo( $res['LONG'] ); ?></td></tr>
</table>
</body>
</html>
```

This is about as simple as it gets. Require the correct PHP and PEAR modules, and all you need is the Net_Geo( ) function. You can break up the returned object into city, state, country, latitude, and longitude, all through simple parameters.

Running the Hack

For starters, you need the Net-Geo PEAR module [Hack #2]. Install that and surf on over to *geo.php*; you should see something like Figure 6-33.

How cool is that? Now I know the city, state, and country of the request. And even the latitude and longitude. With that information, I can plot all the requests on a map and see where everyone is coming from graphically.

See Also

- "Create Custom Google Maps" [Hack #95]

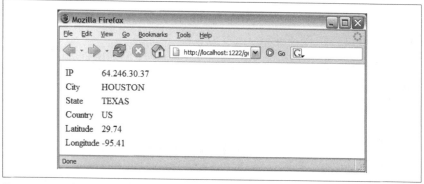

Figure 6-33. The geographical location of the request

Import Information from vCards

Teach your PHP application to read the vCard standard for the storage of
contact information.

All too often, we ask web application users to recode data in files that they
already have, when a flexible application could simply read the user's
(already-existing) files directly. An example of this is the *vCard file*, a univer-
sal mechanism for storing contact information, particularly information like
email and physical addresses. Every reasonable email and address book program can import and export the vCard (*.vcf*) file format.

This hack shows you how to read this format using the Contact_Vcard_
Parse PEAR module [Hack #2].

The Code

Save the code in Example 6-42 as *index.php*.

Example 6-42. A simple file upload page

```
<html>
<body>
  <form enctype="multipart/form-data" action="read.php" method="post">
  VCF file: <input type="hidden" name="MAX_FILE_SIZE" value="2000000" />
  <input type="file" name="file" /><br/>
  <input type="submit" value="Upload" />
  </form>
</body>
</html>
```

Save the code in Example 6-43 as *read.php*.

Example 6-43. The vCard reader

```
<html>
<body>
<?php
require_once( 'Contact_Vcard_Parse.php' );
if ( $_FILES['file']['tmp_name'] )
{
    $parse = new Contact_Vcard_Parse();
    $cardinfo = $parse->fromFile( $_FILES['file']['tmp_name'] );
    foreach( $cardinfo as $card )
    {
      $first = $card['N'][0]['value'][0][0];
      $last = $card['N'][0]['value'][1][0];
      $email = $card['EMAIL'][0]['value'][0][0];
?>
<a href="mailto:<?php echo( $email ); ?>">
<?php echo( $first ); ?> <?php echo( $last ); ?>
</a><br/>
<?php
    }
}
?>
</body>
</html>
```

The real work in this hack is done in the *read.php* script; it reads the temporary downloaded file using the fromFile() method on the Contact_Vcard_
Parse object. The script then dumps each email it finds in the card using
standard PHP text-templating techniques.

Running the Hack

Create a vCard file by exporting a contact from your email program or
address book. Then upload the code to the server and surf to the *index.php*
page. There you should see something similar to Figure 6-34.

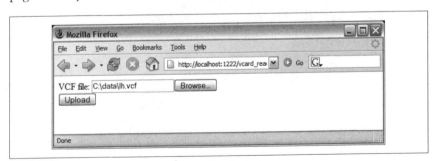

Figure 6-34. The page that accepts vCard files for import

Browse to the VCF file by clicking the Browse... button. Then click on the Upload button to send the file to the server. You should see something similar to Figure 6-35.

Figure 6-35. A simple import page that shows the name from the card with its email

This page shows just the first and last name from the vCard, bracketed in an anchor tag that points to the person's email address. vCards can contain multiple records, and if the file contains many records, the user will see each in a list of individual links.

See Also

- "Create vCard Files from Your Application's Data" [Hack #65]

HACK #65 Create vCard Files from Your Application's Data

Use a simple vCard template to create vCards dynamically from your application's data.

If you have a database of contacts on your web site, it's handy to put up a link to the email address of each contact, but wouldn't it be great to get all the information in one handy format? Well, it turns out that the vCard contact formula (VCF) is perfect for this task. And, you can create vCards automatically with PHP (as well as by reading the VCF format [Hack #64]).

The Code

Save the code in Example 6-44 as *vcard.php*.

Example 6-44. A vCard writer

```php
<?php
header( "Content-type:text/x-vCard" );

$first = "Howard";
$last = "Dean";
$email = "dean@dnc.org";
?>
```

Example 6-44. A vCard writer (continued)

```
BEGIN:VCARD
VERSION:2.1
N:<?php echo($last); ?>;<?php echo($first); ?>
FN:<?php echo($first); ?> <?php echo($last); ?>
EMAIL;PREF;INTERNET:<?php echo($email); ?>
REV:20050626T024452Z
END:VCARD
```

Running the Hack

Upload the code to your server and surf to it in your browser. You should get a download box similar to Figure 6-36.

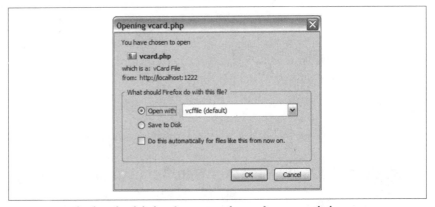

Figure 6-36. The download dialog that opens after surfing to vcard.php

Accept the default action, which turns out (on Windows) to very conveniently launch Outlook and create a new contact file. You can add this person to your contact list by clicking on the "Save and Close" option, as shown in Figure 6-37.

The secret sauce is really the Content-type header item, which tells the downloading client that this is a vCard and not just plain text. Once that's in place, the operating system takes over and sends the vCard to the user's application that is set up to handle vCards.

> In the unlikely event that your machine has no client that can read vCards, you will just get the option to save the file somewhere on your machine.

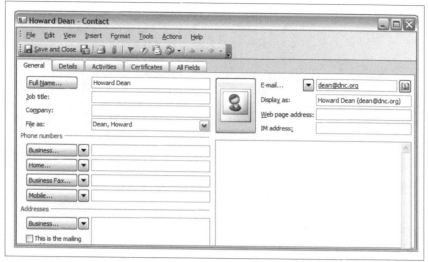

Figure 6-37. Importing the vCard into Outlook auto-magically

See Also

- "Import Information from vCards" **[Hack #64]**

HACK #66 Create a Shopping Cart

Use cookies and sessions to create a simple shopping cart application.

This hack demonstrates a simple shopping cart application using PHP and session variables.

Figure 6-38 shows the relationship among the pages in the shopping cart application. The user starts on the *index.php* page and can traverse freely between there and the *checkout.php* page (which shows his shopping cart). On the *index.php* page, he can add items to the cart by clicking on the Add button, which submits the information to the *add.php* page and sends him back to the *index.php* page. From the *checkout.php* page, he can remove items, a process that follows the same routine as the add logic but uses the *delete.php* page and returns him to the *checkout.php* page.

The Code

Save the code in Example 6-45 as *shopcart.sql*.

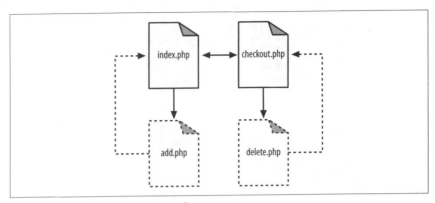

Figure 6-38. The shopping cart page flow

Example 6-45. The shopping cart schema

```
DROP TABLE IF EXISTS product;
CREATE TABLE product (
        id MEDIUMINT NOT NULL AUTO_INCREMENT,
        name TEXT,
        price FLOAT,
        PRIMARY KEY( id )
);

INSERT INTO product VALUES ( 0, "Code Generation in Action", 49.99 );
INSERT INTO product VALUES ( 0, "Podcasting Hacks", 29.99 );
INSERT INTO product VALUES ( 0, "PHP Hacks", 29.99 );
```

Save the code in Example 6-46 as *dblib.php*.

Example 6-46. The database library

```
<?php
require_once( "DB.php" );
$dsn = 'mysql://root:password@localhost/shopcart';
$db =& DB::Connect( $dsn, array( ) );
if (PEAR::isError($db)) { die($db->getMessage( )); }

function get_db( ) { global $db; return $db; }

function get_products( )
{
  global $db;
  $res = $db->query( "SELECT * FROM product", array( ) );
  $out = array( );
  if ( $res != null )
    while( $res->fetchInto( $row, DB_FETCHMODE_ASSOC ) ) { $out []= $row; }
  return $out;
}

function product_info( $id )
```

Example 6-46. The database library (continued)

```
{
  global $db;

  $res = $db->query( "SELECT * FROM product WHERE id=?",
    array( $id ) );

  if ( $res != null )
  {
    $res->fetchInto( $row, DB_FETCHMODE_ASSOC );
    return $row;
  }
  return null;
}
?>
```

Save the code in Example 6-47 as *index.php*.

Example 6-47. The product page

```
<?php
require_once( "dblib.php" );
session_start();
$products = get_products();
?>
<html>
<head>
<title>My Products</title>
</head>
<style type="text/css">
h1 { border-bottom: 1px solid black; font-size: medium; margin-bottom: 10px; }
</style>
<script>
function buy( prod_id )
{
        document.getElementById( 'prod_id' ).value = prod_id;
        document.getElementById( 'buyform' ).submit();
        return null;
}
</script>
<body>
<form id="buyform" action="add.php" method="post">
<input type="hidden" name="prod_id" id="prod_id" value="" />
</form>
<table width="600" border="0" cellspacing="0" cellpadding="5">
<tr>
<td width="70%" valign="top">
<h1>Products</h1>
<table width="100%">
<?php foreach( $products as $product ) { ?>
<tr>
```

Example 6-47. The product page (continued)

```php
<td width="70%"><?php echo( $product['name'] ); ?></td>
<td width="15%" align="right">$<?php echo( $product['price'] ); ?></td>
<td width="15%" align="center"><a href="javascript:buy( <?php echo(
    $product['id'] ); ?> );">buy</a>
</tr>
<?php } ?>
</table>
</td>
<td width="30%" valign="top">
<h1>Shopping cart</h1>
<?php
if( isset( $_SESSION['cart'] ) ) {
?>
<!-- CART : <?php echo( join( ",", array_keys( $_SESSION['cart'] ) ) ); ?> -->
<table width="100%" cellspacing="0" cellpadding="5">
<?php
foreach( array_keys( $_SESSION['cart'] ) as $product ) {
$info = product_info( $product );
?>
<tr><td>
<?php echo( $info['name' ] ); ?>
</td></tr>
<?php } ?>
<tr><td align="center">
<a href="checkout.php">Checkout</a>
</td></tr>
</table>
<?php
}
?>
</td>
</tr>
</table>
</body>
</html>
```

Save the code in Example 6-48 as *add.php*.

Example 6-48. The script to add items to the cart

```php
<?php
session_start();
if ( !isset( $_SESSION['cart'] ) )
        $_SESSION['cart'] = array();
$_SESSION['cart'][$_POST['prod_id']] = 1;
header( "location: index.php" );
?>
```

Save the code in Example 6-49 as *checkout.php*.

Example 6-49. The checkout page

```php
<?php
require_once( "dblib.php" );
session_start();
?>
<html>
<head>
<title>Your Cart</title>
<script language="Javascript">
function submit_delete()
{
        document.getElementById( "delform" ).submit();
        return null;
}
</script>
<style type="text/css">
h1 { border-bottom: 1px solid black; font-size: medium; margin-bottom: 10px; }
</style>
</head>
<body>
<?php
if ( isset( $_SESSION['cart'] ) && count( $_SESSION['cart'] ) > 0 ) {
?>
<!-- CART : <?php echo( join( ",", array_keys( $_SESSION['cart'] ) ) ); ?> -->
<form id="delform" action="delete.php" method="post">
<table width="600">
<tr>
<th width="3%"></th>
<th width="77%">Product</th>
<th width="20%">Price</th>
</tr>
<?php
foreach( array_keys( $_SESSION['cart'] ) as $product )
{
        $prod = product_info( $product );
?>
<tr>
<td><input type="checkbox" name="ids[]" value="<?php echo( $product ); ?>" />
    </td>
<td><?php echo( $prod['name'] ); ?></td>
<td align="right"><?php echo( $prod['price'] ); ?></td>
</tr>
<?php } ?>
<tr>
<td></td>
<td align="center"><a href="javascript:submit_delete()">Delete checked items</a>
       
<a href="index.php">Return to store</a>
       
<a href="buy.php">Buy these items</a>
</tr>
</table>
```

Example 6-49. The checkout page (continued)

```
</form>
<?php } else { ?>
You should go and <a href="index.php">buy some stuff</a>.
<?php } ?>
</body>
</html>
```

Save the code in Example 6-50 as *delete.php*.

Example 6-50. The script to remove items from the cart

```
<?php
session_start();

foreach( $_POST['ids'] as $did )
        unset( $_SESSION['cart'][$did] );

header( "location: checkout.php" );
?>
```

The shopping cart starts with the *index.php* page, which shows the products from the database. Clicking on one of the products will add it to the shopping cart via calls going out to the *add.php* page, which sets up the session and adds the product to it. The *add.php* script then redirects the user back to the product page, which shows both the products and the contents of the shopping cart.

Once the shopping cart has some stuff in it, the user is given a link to the *checkout.php* page. That page shows the contents of the cart and has links to delete items from the cart. Those links go to the *delete.php* script, which deletes items from the cart and sends the user back to the *checkout.php* page.

Running the Hack

This hack starts with creating the database and loading it with the schema:

```
% mysqladmin --user=root --password=password create shopcart
% mysql --user=root --password=password shopcart < shopcart.sql
```

Now upload the PHP scripts to the server and surf over to the *index.php* page. You will see the store's home page, as shown in Figure 6-39.

On the lefthand side of the page is the list of products with links that the user can click to buy the products. Clicking on the link will post the product ID to the *add.php* script, which adds the product to the cart that is stored in the user's session variable.

The *add.php* script forwards the user back to the *index.php* page, which shows the updated cart on the righthand side of the display (as seen in Figure 6-40).

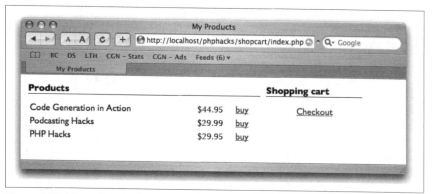

Figure 6-39. The index.php home page for the store

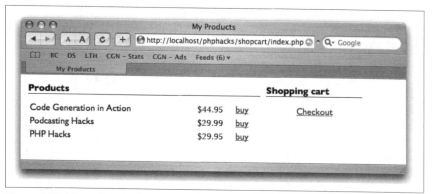

Figure 6-40. After clicking on the "buy" link for Podcasting Hacks

The next thing to do after clicking "buy" on all of the books is to check out. Clicking on the Checkout link will send the user to the *checkout.php* page, as shown in Figure 6-41.

Here the checkout page shows that three books have been put in the cart. The user now has the opportunity to select some items and remove them from the cart, or to continue to buy the items in the cart.

Deleting the books from the cart starts with selecting them, as shown in Figure 6-42.

After selecting the books, the user needs to click on the "Delete checked items" link to remove the items from the cart. The link submits the page to the *delete.php* script, which just removes the values from the cart array. The script then forwards the user back to the checkout page, as shown in Figure 6-43.

To finish off the cart you need to implement the "Buy these items" link. "Add a Buy Now Button" [Hack #62] covers the buy phase of the e-commerce cycle in depth.

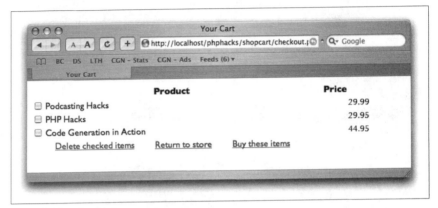

Figure 6-41. The checkout page

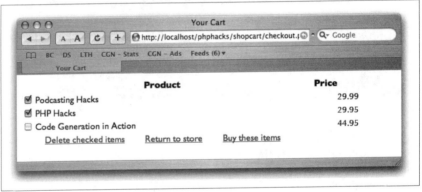

Figure 6-42. Selecting a couple of books to remove from the cart

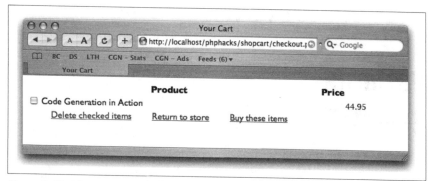

Figure 6-43. After removing the books from the cart

See Also

- "Add a Buy Now Button" [Hack #62]

Patterns
Hacks 67–78

In 1994, Erich Gamma, Richard Helm, Ralph Johnson, and John Vlissides published *Design Patterns* (Addison Wesley). The book quickly became a computer science classic because of its useful material, and it even pioneered a new metalanguage in the engineering and architecture communities. The book's underlying principle, which was to provide a set of patterns of object structure and intra-object structure, was adopted from building architecture and was smoothly applied to programming.

The set of 40 patterns presented in the book were gleaned from years of experience. Each pattern was presented in a language-neutral form, and most could be applied to any development environment.

 A few of the patterns, such as the Iterator pattern, were specifically developed to make up for shortcomings in a language (in the case of Iterator, that language was C++). PHP implements the Iterator pattern inherently through the foreach method.

Patterns have been notoriously underused in PHP. Not until the advent of PHP 5 were the language and environment taken seriously in the enterprise software development community. Now, with a robust object model, solid IDEs, and wide developer adoption, the enterprise community is starting to notice PHP. Several books on PHP have recently covered the use of patterns in the language, and I think it's worth visiting them here.

In this book, I chose to use the original *Design Patterns* book as reference. I chose a subset of patterns from that book to implement here; these patterns and their implementations are solid architectural foundations, as well as sources of inspiration for your own code.

Observe Your Objects

#67

Use the Observer pattern to loosely couple your objects.

Loose coupling is critical to any large-scale project, but few people actually understand what the term really means. Have you ever made a small change in a project, and it seems that as a result, almost everything else has to change as well? This occurs all too often because of tight coupling among the modules in the program. Each module relies on the exact state or function of several other modules. When one fails, they all fail. When one changes, they all must change.

The Observer pattern loosens up the bonds among objects by providing a simpler intra-object contract. An object allows itself to be observed by providing a mechanism where objects can register with it. When the observed object changes, it notifies the observing objects through a notification object. The observed object does not care how or why it is being observed, nor does it even know what types of objects are observing it. Further, the observers usually don't care why or how the object is changing; all they are looking for is a change.

A classic example is the code in a dialog observing the state of a checkbox. The checkbox doesn't care if it's being observed by one object or a thousand objects. It simply sends out a message when its state changes. In the same way, the dialog doesn't care how the checkbox is implemented; it only cares about the box's state and about being notified when that state changes.

In this hack, I'll demonstrate the Observer pattern by setting up an observable customer list. This object represents a database table of customers. The CustomerList object will send out notifications when new customers are added. The object uses a SubscriptionList object to implement its observability. The listeners object is an instance of SubscriptionList that other objects can use to register themselves with CustomerList. Listeners use the add( ) method to add themselves to the list, and CustomerList uses the invoke( ) method to send out a message to the listeners. It doesn't matter if there are no listeners, or if there are thousands of listeners. The beauty here is that listening objects have no direct interaction with or dependence on CustomerList; listeners are insulated from the customers by the SubscriptionList class.

In this example, there will be one listener: a Log object that outputs any messages sent from CustomerList to the console. The relationship between the objects is shown in Figure 7-1.

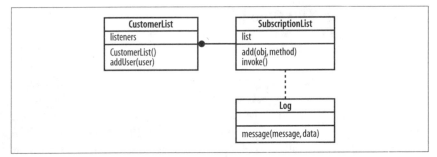

Figure 7-1. CustomerList and its SubscriptionList with attached Log

The Code

Save the code in Example 7-1 as *observer.php*.

Example 7-1. The Observer pattern example

```php
<?php
class Log
{
  public function message( $sender, $messageType, $data )
  {
    print $messageType." - ".$data."\n";
  }
}

class SubscriptionList
{
  var $list = array( );

  public function add( $obj, $method )
  {
    $this->list []= array( $obj, $method );
  }

  public function invoke( )
  {
    $args = func_get_args( );
    foreach( $this->list as $l ) { call_user_func_array( $l, $args ); }
  }
}

class CustomerList
{
  public $listeners;

  public function CustomerList( )
  {
    $this->listeners = new SubscriptionList( );
  }
```

Example 7-1. The Observer pattern example (continued)

```
public function addUser( $user )
{
  $this->listeners->invoke( $this, "add", "$user" );
}
}

$l = new Log( );
$cl = new CustomerList( );
$cl->listeners->add( $l, 'message' );
$cl->addUser( "starbuck" );
?>
```

Running the Hack

You run this code on the command line like this:

```
% php observer.php
add - starbuck
```

The code first creates a log and a customer list. Then the log is subscribed to the customer list using the add( ) method. The final step is to add a user to the customer list. The addition of the customer fires off a message to the listeners—in this case, the log—that puts out the message about the addition of the customer.

It would be easy to extend this code either to do some customer provisioning based on the addition of a customer or to send out a new user email—both without changing the code in CustomerList. This is loose coupling, and it's why the Observer pattern is so important.

There are innumerable uses for the Observer pattern in software development. Windowing systems use Observer patterns and call them *events*. Companies like Tibco run their entire business model via the Observer pattern, connecting large business systems like Human Resources and Payroll. Database systems use an Observer pattern and call code that listens to event *triggers*. These triggers are activated when certain types of records are changed in the database. An Observer-patterned approach is also handy whenever you think a state change is relevant but don't yet understand to whom it will be relevant; you can code the listeners later and not tie them to the object that will be observed.

One potential "gotcha" with the Observer pattern is the *infinite loop*. This can happen when items that observe a system can also alter that system. For example, a drop-down combo alters a value and tells the data structure about it. That data structure then notifies the drop-down combo that the value has changed, whereupon the drop-down combo changes its value to match, only to send out another notification to the data structure, and so on. The easiest way to solve this problem is to code the drop-down combo so that recursion is prevented. It should simply ignore a message from the data structure if it's currently in the middle of notifying the data structure about a new value.

See Also

- "Turn Any Object into an Array" [Hack #53]
- "Create a Message Queue" [Hack #50]

 H A C K **#68** ## Create Objects with Abstract Factories
Use an Abstract Factory pattern to control what type of object is created.

The *Abstract Factory pattern* is the vending machine of design patterns. You ask it for what you want, and it vends you an object based on your criteria. The value is that you can change what types of objects are created throughout the system by altering just the factory.

The super-simple factory in this example creates Record objects, where each record has an ID, a first name, and a last name. The relationship between these classes is shown in Figure 7-2.

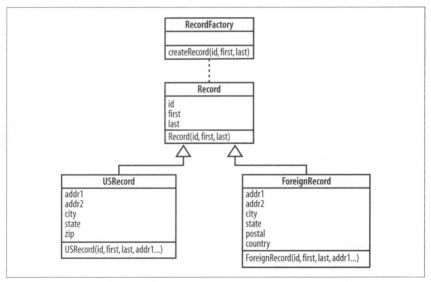

Figure 7-2. The Record and the RecordFactory classes

Factory objects often create more than one type of object. To keep this example simple, though, I've limited the factory to creating only a single object type.

There is no way to strictly enforce that only the factory can create objects of a particular type in PHP. But if you use a factory often enough, engineers copying and pasting your code will end up using the factory; it will quickly become the de facto way of creating the different types of objects.

The Code

Save the code in Example 7-2 as *abs_factory.php*.

Example 7-2. An Abstract Factory pattern example

```php
<?php
class Record
{
  public $id = null;
  public $first = null;
  public $last = null;

  public function __construct( $id, $first, $last )
  {
    $this->id = $id;
    $this->first = $first;
    $this->last = $last;
  }
}

class USRecord extends Record
{
  public $addr1 = null;
  public $addr2 = null;
  public $city = null;
  public $state = null;
  public $zip = null;

  public function __construct( $id, $first, $last,
    $addr1, $addr2, $city, $state, $zip )
  {
    parent::__construct( $id, $first, $last );
    $this->addr1 = $addr1;
    $this->addr2 = $addr2;
    $this->city = $city;
    $this->state = $state;
    $this->zip = $zip;
  }
}
```

Example 7-2. An Abstract Factory pattern example (continued)

```php
class ForeignRecord extends Record
{
  public $addr1 = null;
  public $addr2 = null;
  public $city = null;
  public $state = null;
  public $postal = null;
  public $country = null;

  public function __construct( $id, $first, $last,
    $addr1, $addr2, $city, $state, $postal, $country )
  {
    parent::__construct( $id, $first, $last );
    $this->addr1 = $addr1;
    $this->addr2 = $addr2;
    $this->city = $city;
    $this->state = $state;
    $this->postal = $postal;
    $this->country = $country;
  }
}

class RecordFactory
{
  public static function createRecord( $id, $first, $last,
    $addr1, $addr2, $city, $state, $postal, $country )
  {
  if ( strlen( $country ) > 0 && $country != "USA" )
    return new ForeignRecord( $id, $first, $last,
      $addr1, $addr2, $city, $state, $postal, $country );
  else
    return new USRecord( $id, $first, $last,
      $addr1, $addr2, $city, $state, $postal );
  }
}

function readRecords( )
{
  $records = array( );

  $records []= RecordFactory::createRecord(
  1, "Jack", "Herrington", "4250 San Jaquin Dr.", "",
  "Los Angeles", "CA", "90210", ""
  );
  $records []= RecordFactory::createRecord(
  1, "Megan", "Cunningham", "2220 Toorak Rd.", "",
  "Toorak", "VIC", "3121", "Australia"
  );

  return $records;
}
```

Example 7-2. An Abstract Factory pattern example (continued)

```
$records = readRecords( );
foreach( $records as $r )
{
  $class = new ReflectionClass( $r );
  print $class->getName( )." - ".$r->id." - ".$r->first." - ".$r->last."\n";
}
?>
```

The first section of the code implements the Record base class, as well as the USRecord and ForeignRecord derived classes. These are all fairly simple data structure wrappers. Then the factory class can build either a USRecord or a ForeignRecord depending on the data being passed in. The test code at the end of the script adds a few records, and then prints out their type along with some of their data.

Running the Hack

You run this hack using the PHP command-line interpreter, like this:

```
% php abs_factory.php
USRecord - 1 - Jack - Herrington
ForeignRecord - 1 - Megan - Cunningham
```

You can use the Abstract Factory pattern in a PHP database application in several ways:

Database object creation
    The factory vends any of the object types associated with the different tables in the database.

Portable object creation
    The factory vends a number of different objects depending on either the type of operating system the code is being run on or the different databases that the application is attaching itself to.

Creation by standard
    The application supports various file format standards and uses the factory to create an object appropriate to the given file type. File readers can register themselves with the factory to add file support without having to change any downstream clients.

After using patterns for a while, you will develop a sense for when it makes sense to use a particular pattern. You would use this pattern when you are doing an awful lot of object construction with various types of objects. You will find that if you ever need to change what types of objects are created, or how they are created, you will have a lot of code to change. If you use a factory, you will need to change that object creation in only one place.

See Also

- "Flexible Object Creation with Factory Methods" [Hack #69]

 HACK **Flexible Object Creation with Factory Methods**

#69 Use the Factory Method pattern when creating objects to allow derived classes to alter what types of objects are created.

Closely related to the Abstract Factory pattern is the *Factory Method pattern*. This one is fairly commonsense. If you have a class that is creating a lot of objects, you can use protected methods to encapsulate the object creation. That way, a derived class can just override the protected method(s) in the factory to create a different type of object.

In this case, the RecordReader class, instead of using a Factory class, uses a method called newRecord( ) to create a new Record object. That way, a class that derives from RecordReader can change the type of Record objects created by overriding the newRecord( ) method. This is shown graphically in Figure 7-3.

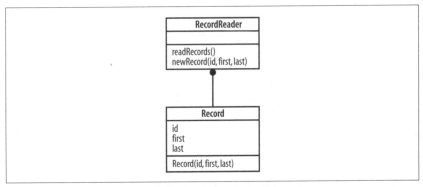

Figure 7-3. The relationship between RecordReader and Record

The Code

Save the code in Example 7-3 as *factory_method.php*.

Example 7-3. An example of factory methods on a class

```php
<?php
class Record
{
    public $id = null;
    public $first = null;
    public $last = null;
```

Example 7-3. An example of factory methods on a class (continued)

```php
  public function Record( $id, $first, $last )
  {
    $this->id = $id;
    $this->first = $first;
    $this->last = $last;
  }
}

class RecordReader
{
  function readRecords( )
  {
    $records = array( );

    $records []= $this->newRecord( 1, "Jack", "Herrington" );
    $records []= $this->newRecord( 2, "Lori", "Herrington" );
    $records []= $this->newRecord( 3, "Megan", "Herrington" );

    return $records;
  }
  protected function newRecord( $id, $first, $last )
  {
    return new Record( $id, $first, $last );
  }
}

$rr = new RecordReader( );
$records = $rr->readRecords( );
foreach( $records as $r )
{
  print $r->id." - ".$r->first." - ".$r->last."\n";
}
?>
```

Running the Hack

You run this hack on the command line using the PHP interpreter:

```
% php factory_method.php
1 - Jack - Herrington
2 - Lori - Herrington
3 - Megan - Herrington
```

In this code, the RecordReader object is instantiated and its readRecords( )
method is called. This method in turn calls the newRecord( ) method to create all of the Record objects. The created objects are then printed to the console using a foreach loop.

The most visible example of the Factory Method pattern is in the W3C's XML DOM API, installed as part of the PHP 5 base installation. The DOMDocument object, which is at the root of any DOM tree, has a set of factory methods: createElement( ), createAttribute( ), createTextNode( ), etc. Any implementation that derived from DOMDocument could override these methods to change what objects were created when XML trees were loaded from disk or strings or created on the fly.

As with the Abstract Factory pattern, the key indicator that you should use the Factory Method pattern is when you are writing an awful lot of code that is doing object creation. Using an Abstract Factory pattern or Factory Method pattern will ensure that if the type of objects you want to create, or how those objects are created, changes, the impact to your code will be minimal.

See Also

- "Create Objects with Abstract Factories" [Hack #68]

 HACK #70   Abstract Construction Code with a Builder

Use the Builder pattern to abstract code that performs a routine construction task, such as composing HTML or text for an email.

I've always found that code that constructs something is some of the most elegant code in a system. I suppose that's just because I spent a year writing a book on code generation, which is all about constructing code.

 By the way, the book is *Code Generation in Action* (Manning). It's still available and makes an excellent holiday gift for friends and family.

An example of construction code is the code that reads an XML document off the disk and constructs an in-memory representation of that structure. Another is a module of code that constructs an email message to tell a customer she is behind on her payments.

It's the late-payment mail that I want to focus on in this hack; but I'm going to do it with a twist. I'm going to use the *Builder pattern* so that the same code that creates a message in HTML can also create a message in XHTML or text format.

I'm going to have the code that writes the past-due notice use a builder instead of just creating the string directly. This builder object will have a set of methods, as shown in Figure 7-4. The startBody( ) and endBody( ) methods wrap the creation of the message. The addText( ) method adds some text, and the addBreak( ) method adds a line break.

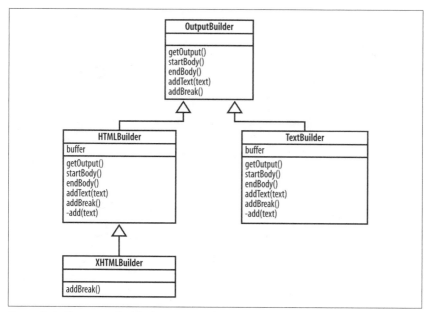

Figure 7-4. The output builder hierarchy

The OutputBuilder abstract class has several concrete instantiations. One is HTMLBuilder, which builds HTML. Deriving from that is XHTMLBuilder, which alters the behavior of its parent just enough to make the output XHTML compliant. And finally there's TextBuilder, which builds a plain-text representation of the message.

The Code

Save the code in Example 7-4 as *builder.php*.

Example 7-4. A set of example builder classes and some test code

```
<?php
abstract class OutputBuilder
{
  abstract function getOutput( );
  abstract function startBody( );
  abstract function endBody( );
  abstract function addText( $text );
  abstract function addBreak( );
}
```

Example 7-4. A set of example builder classes and some test code (continued)

```php
class HTMLBuilder extends OutputBuilder
{
  private $buffer = "";

  public function getOutput()
  {
    return "<html>\n".$this->buffer."\n</html>\n";
  }
  public function startBody() { $this->add( "<body>" ); }
  public function endBody() { $this->add( "</body>" ); }
  public function addText( $text ) { $this->add( $text ); }
  public function addBreak() { $this->add( "<br>\n" ); }

  protected function add( $text ) { $this->buffer .= $text; }
}

class XHTMLBuilder extends HTMLBuilder
{
  public function addBreak() { $this->add( "<br />\n" ); }
}

class TextBuilder extends OutputBuilder
{
  private $buffer = "";

  public function getOutput()
  {
    return $this->buffer."\n";
  }
  public function startBody() { }
  public function endBody() { }
  public function addText( $text ) { $this->add( $text ); }
  public function addBreak() { $this->add( "\n" ); }

  protected function add( $text ) { $this->buffer .= $text; }
}

function buildDocument( $builder )
{
  $builder->startBody();
  $builder->addText( 'Jack,' );
  $builder->addBreak();
  $builder->addText( 'You owe us $10,000. Have a NICE day.' );
  $builder->endBody();
}

print "HTML:\n\n";

$html = new HTMLBuilder();
buildDocument( $html );
echo( $html->getOutput() );
```

Example 7-4. A set of example builder classes and some test code (continued)

```
print "\nXHTML:\n\n";

$xhtml = new XHTMLBuilder( );
buildDocument( $xhtml );
echo( $xhtml->getOutput( ) );

print "\nText:\n\n";

$text = new TextBuilder( );
buildDocument( $text );
echo( $text->getOutput( ) );
?>
```

Running the Hack

You run this hack on the command line using the PHP command-line interpreter:

```
% php builder.php
HTML:

<html>
<body>Jack,<br>
You owe us $10,000. Have a NICE day.</body>
</html>

XHTML:

<html>
<body>Jack,<br />
You owe us $10,000. Have a NICE day.</body>
</html>

Text:

Jack,
You owe us $10,000. Have a NICE day.
```

This shows the output of the three different builders. The first is the HTML version with the correct HTML tags and the <br> tag. The XHTML tag changes the behavior slightly so that the <br> tag has become <br />. The text version is just plain text, with the break turned into a simple carriage return.

Looking at the code, you see the definition of the abstract OutputBuilder class at the start of the file, followed by the concrete instantiations for the different flavors of output. The buildDocument( ) function uses the builder to build the message. The code at the bottom of the file tests the buildDocument( ) function with each of the different flavors of builders.

You can use a Builder pattern in several places in a PHP web application:

File reading
    Any time you are parsing a file, you should use a Builder pattern to abstract the parsing of the file from the creation of the in-memory data structures that hold the data in the file.

File writing
    As I showed in this hack, you can use a Builder pattern to create multiple output formats from a single document-building system.

Generating code
    You can use builders to generate code for any number of languages from a single generation system.

The .NET Framework uses the Builder pattern when creating HTML for the output page to allow the same control to generate multiple flavors of HTML based on the type of web browser requesting the page.

Separate What from How with Strategies

HACK #71

Use the Strategy pattern to abstract the code that traverses structures from the code that operates on those structures.

You use the *Strategy pattern* to abstract the processing of an object, allowing how an object is processed to be separated from where the object is located.

In this hack, I'll use a car chooser as an example. This code will recommend a car based on some search criteria. In this case, I will provide my specs for an ideal car and let the code pick the car that most closely matches my dream specs. The value of the Strategy pattern is that I can alter the car comparison code independently of the car selection code.

The UML for this hack is shown in Figure 7-5. The `CarChooser` object uses a `CarWeighter` object to compare each `Car` to the ideal model. Then the best `Car` match is returned to the client.

The Code

Save the code in Example 7-5 as *strategy.php*.

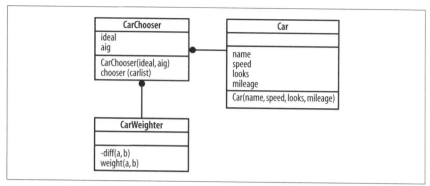

Figure 7-5. The relationship between the CarChooser, CarWeighter, and Car objects

Example 7-5. An example of the Strategy pattern

```php
<?php
class Car
{
  public $name;
  public $speed;
  public $looks;
  public $mileage;
  public function Car( $name, $speed, $looks, $mileage )
  {
    $this->name = $name;
    $this->speed = $speed;
    $this->looks = $looks;
    $this->mileage = $mileage;
  }
}

class CarWeighter
{
  private function diff( $a, $b )
  {
    return abs( $a - $b );
  }

  public function weight( $a, $b )
  {
    $d = 0;
    $d += $this->diff( $a->speed, $b->speed );
    $d += $this->diff( $a->looks, $b->looks );
    $d += $this->diff( $a->mileage, $b->mileage );
    return ( 0 - $d );
  }
}

class CarChooser
{
```

Example 7-5. An example of the Strategy pattern (continued)

```
private $ideal;
private $alg;

function CarChooser( $ideal, $alg )
{
  $this->ideal = $ideal;
  $this->alg = $alg;
}

public function choose( $carlist )
{
  $minrank = null;
  $found = null;
  $alg = $this->alg;

  foreach( $carlist as $car )
  {
    $rank = $alg->weight( $this->ideal, $car );
    if ( !isset( $minrank ) ) $minrank = $rank;
    if ( $rank >= $minrank )
    {
      $minrank = $rank;
      $found = $car;
    }
  }

  return $found;
  }
}

function pickCar( $car )
{
  $carlist = array();
  $carlist []= new Car( "zippy", 90, 30, 10 );
  $carlist []= new Car( "mom'n'pop", 45, 30, 55 );
  $carlist []= new Car( "beauty", 40, 90, 10 );
  $carlist []= new Car( "enviro", 40, 40, 90 );

  $cw = new CarWeighter();
  $cc = new CarChooser( $car, $cw );
  $found = $cc->choose( $carlist );
  echo( $found->name."\n" );
}

pickCar( new Car( "ideal", 80, 40, 10 ) );
pickCar( new Car( "ideal", 40, 90, 10 ) );
?>
```

Starting at the top of the file, I define the Car class, which holds the car name and the metrics for speed, looks, and mileage. Each is rated from 0 to 100 (largely to make the math easy). Then comes the CarWeighter, which compares two cars and returns a comparison metric. Finally, there's the CarChooser, which uses a CarWeighter to select the best car based on some input criteria. The pickCar( ) function creates a set of cars and then uses a CarChooser to choose the car from the list that best fits the criteria (passed in via another Car object).

The test code at the bottom of the file then asks for two cars—one that is heavily weighted in the speed category, and another that is strongly weighted on looks.

Running the Hack

You run this hack on the command line with the PHP interpreter:

```
% php strategy.php
zippy
beauty
```

The output shows that the car recommended to me if I want speed is the "zippy" car: a good approximation. The car recommended to me if I want something a little sexier is the "beauty" car. Excellent!

The code that deduces whether a car is a good match is totally abstracted away from the code that traverses the car list and picks one from that list. You can change the algorithm that weights a certain car independently of the code that picks which is the right car from the weighted list. For example, you can add the cars that have interested you recently or that you have owned in the past into the weighting algorithm. Or you can change the picker code to select the top three and provide a choice among them.

HACK #72   Link Up Two Modules with an Adapter

Use an adapter class to transfer data between two modules when you don't want to change the API of either module.

Sometimes you have to get data from two objects, each of which uses a *different* data format. Changing one or both objects just isn't an option because you'll have to make all sorts of other changes in the rest of your code. One solution to this problem is to use an *adapter* class. An adapter is a class that understands both sides of the data-transfer fence and adapts one object to talk to another.

The adapter demonstrated in this hack adapts data from a mock database object into data usable by a text-graphing engine.

Figure 7-6 shows the RecordGraphAdapter sitting between the TextGraph on the left and the RecordList on the right. The TextGraph object very nicely specifies the format it expects for data using an abstract class called TextGraphDataSource. The RecordList is a container class that has a list of Records, where each Record contains a name, age, and salary.

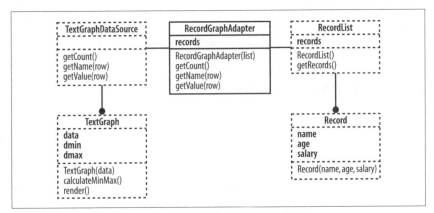

Figure 7-6. The adapter sitting between the graph and the data

For this example, I want a graph of the salaries. The adapter's job is to take data from the RecordList and convert it into a form suitable for the TextGraph by turning the data into a TextGraphDataSource object.

The Code

Save the code in Example 7-6 as *adapter.php*.

Example 7-6. An adapter example using a text graph

```php
<?php
abstract class TextGraphDataSource
{
  abstract function getCount();
  abstract function getName( $row );
  abstract function getValue( $row );
}

class TextGraph
{
  private $data;
  private $dmin;
  private $dmax;
```

Example 7-6. An adapter example using a text graph (continued)

```
  public function TextGraph( $data )
  {
    $this->data = $data;
  }

  protected function calculateMinMax( )
  {
    $this->dmin = 100000;
    $this->dmax = -100000;
    for( $r = 0; $r < $this->data->getCount( ); $r++ )
    {
      $v = $this->data->getValue( $r );
      if ( $v < $this->dmin ) { $this->dmin = $v; }
      if ( $v > $this->dmax ) { $this->dmax = $v; }
    }
  }

  public function render( )
  {
    $this->calculateMinMax( );
    $ratio = 40 / ( $this->dmax - $this->dmin );
    for( $r = 0; $r < $this->data->getCount( ); $r++ )
    {
      $n = $this->data->getName( $r );
      $v = $this->data->getValue( $r );
      $s = ( $v - $this->dmin ) * $ratio;
      echo( sprintf( "%10s : ", $n ) );
      for( $st = 0; $st < $s; $st++ ) { echo("*"); }
      echo( "\n" );
    }
  }
}

class Record
{
  public $name;
  public $age;
  public $salary;
  public function Record( $name, $age, $salary )
  {
    $this->name = $name;
    $this->age = $age;
    $this->salary = $salary;
  }
}

class RecordList
{
  private $records = array( );

  public function RecordList( )
  {
```

Example 7-6. An adapter example using a text graph (continued)

```php
    $this->records []= new Record( "Jimmy", 23, 26000 );
    $this->records []= new Record( "Betty", 24, 29000 );
    $this->records []= new Record( "Sally", 28, 42000 );
    $this->records []= new Record( "Jerry", 28, 120000 );
    $this->records []= new Record( "George", 43, 204000 );
  }

  public function getRecords( )
  {
    return $this->records;
  }
}

class RecordGraphAdapter extends TextGraphDataSource
{
  private $records;

  public function RecordGraphAdapter( $rl )
  {
    $this->records = $rl->getRecords( );
  }
  public function getCount( )
  {
    return count( $this->records );
  }
  public function getName( $row )
  {
    return $this->records[ $row ]->name;
  }
  public function getValue( $row )
  {
    return $this->records[ $row ]->salary;
  }
}

$rl = new RecordList( );

$ga = new RecordGraphAdapter( $rl );

$tg = new TextGraph( $ga );
$tg->render( );
?>
```

The top portion of the file is dedicated to the graph. This portion defines the TextGraphDataSource abstract class as well as the TextGraph class. TextGraph uses a TextGraphDataSource to reference the data. The middle section defines the Record and the RecordList (which holds the data to be graphed). The third section defines the RecordGraphAdapter, which adapts the RecordList to a source usable by the graph.

The text code at the bottom first creates a RecordList and then creates the adapter and the TextGraph, with a reference to the adapter. The graph plots the data by reading the data from the adapter.

Running the Hack

You run this hack on the command line using the PHP command-line interpreter:

```
% php adapter.php
    Jimmy :
    Betty : *
    Sally : ****
    Jerry : *********************
    George : ****************************************
```

The bottom end of the scale is Jimmy, and the top end is George. The graph auto-scales so that Jimmy is shown with no stars (the minimum), and George with 40 stars (the maximum). Good going, George! More importantly, of course, this code handled the data conversion with no problem, and without messing around with the internals of the Record class.

Use an adapter any time you have two APIs that need to work together, and where changing either of those APIs is not an option.

H A C K   #73   Write Portable Code with Bridges

Use a Bridge pattern to hide the implementation on an object, or to change the implementation based on the environment.

In one of my jobs, working for a company that shipped a very large cross-platform C++ application, we used the heck out of the Bridge pattern. The *Bridge pattern* allows you to hide a portion of the implementation of a class in another class, either because you want to hide the code from other implementers or because the implementation of a portion of the code is platform specific.

I've taken the platform-specific approach in this hack to show the benefits of a bridge. Figure 7-7 shows the relationship between two classes, TableCreator and TableCreatorImp. The role of the table creator is to create tables in the target database. The implementation class, TableCreatorImp, is defined in another file, which is included from a database-specific directory.

This flexibility allows for one version of the code specific to Oracle and another for MySQL (or any other database). This is handy, as each database has a different syntax for creating tables.

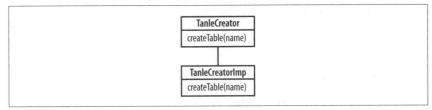

Figure 7-7. The TableCreator class and its implementation class

The Code

Save the code in Example 7-7 as *bridge.php*.

Example 7-7. The base Bridge pattern class

```php
<?php
require( "sql.php" );

class TableCreator
{
  static function createTable( $name )
  {
    TableCreatorImp::createTable( $name );
  }
}

TableCreator::createTable( "customer" );
?>
```

Save the code in Example 7-8 as *mysql/sql.php*.

Example 7-8. An example implementation class for MySQL

```php
<?php
class TableCreatorImp
{
  static public function createTable( $name )
  {
    echo( "MySQL version of createTable for $name\n" );
  }
}
?>
```

Save the code in Example 7-9 as *oracle/sql.php*.

Example 7-9. An example implementation for Oracle

```php
<?php
class TableCreatorImp
{
  static public function createTable( $name )
  {
```

Example 7-9. An example implementation for Oracle (continued)

```
    echo( "Oracle version of createTable for $name\n" );
  }
}
?>
```

Running the Hack

Running this code requires some extra command-line parameters, instructing the PHP interpreter to include either the mysql or oracle directory in the include path (and therefore using that database-specific bridge). Here is the version using the MySQL code:

```
% php -d include_path='.:/usr/local/php5/lib/php:mysql' bridge.php
MySQL version of createTable for customer
```

Here is the version using the Oracle code:

```
% php -d include_path='.:/usr/local/php5/lib/php:oracle' bridge.php
Oracle version of createTable for customer
```

It's not rocket science, so you should get the idea pretty quickly. TableCreator actually is implemented by one of several versions of TableCreatorImp, located in platform-specific directories.

Obviously the code here does not create tables; this is merely a framework that would need some additional code to actually work. But the specifics of building tables in different databases aren't germane to teaching the Bridge pattern (that's fancy talk for "You can figure that out on your own").

One big drawback of bridges is that you can't extend your implementation-specific classes. In this case, this isn't an issue, as all the methods in the implementation classes are static. But for regular objects with nonstatic methods, the implementation class derives from the base nonimplementation class. For example, CButtonImp derives from CButton. To extend the behavior, the code would need to derive from CButtonImp, which is hidden. Arguably, however, this is more of a problem in compiled languages like C++.

Build Extensible Processing with Chains

Use the Chain of Responsibility pattern to create a Plug and Play (PnP) processing framework in your code.

Watching football with programmers is fun. Even in the fourth quarter, when the game is 33 to 7 with 1:30 to go, you still get a range of options when you ask who is going to win the game. That's because programmers are trained to think of every potential situation, no matter how unlikely (and generally ludicrous). And I've found that most programmers, including myself, hate closing the door on any question. It's always better to write code that handles 100 possible scenarios, even when your manager swears up and down there will only ever be one.

That's why I think the *Chain of Responsibility pattern* is so appealing. Imagine walking into a room full of people with a box of donuts. You flip open the box and pull out a jelly donut. One by one you ask people, "You want a jelly donut?" until you find someone that does. Then you continue with your varied box of donut flavors until the box is empty.

That's the Chain of Responsibility pattern; each person in the room registers himself in advance with you, the donut vendor. Then, as new donuts come in, you see who wants them by looking through your list of registered people. The advantage is that you, as the vendor, don't care about how many people want donuts; you don't even care what they do with the donuts. You just manage the registry and the vending.

In this hack, I'll write some code that turns URLs into donuts. Actually, it just vends URLs to a bunch of handlers that will potentially remap the URL. If nobody handles the URL, it will just fall through and be ignored.

Figure 7-8 shows how this is going to work. URLMapper is the donut vendor. He has a box full of URLs that he is going to hand to any object that shows up presenting the URLHandler interface. In this case, ImageURLHandler handles mapping image URL requests to an image-handling script. In the same vein, DocumentURLHandler will redirect any document requests to the correct PHP page. This allows the URLs to be sent without any special handling code, but to still be modified as needed by your application.

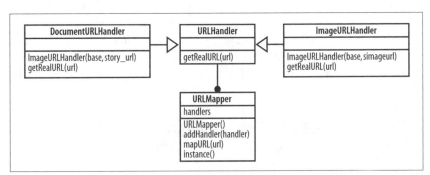

Figure 7-8. The URLHandler interface, the mapper, and two handlers

The Code

Save the code in Example 7-10 as *chain.php*.

Example 7-10. An example of the Chain of Responsibility pattern in PHP

```php
<?php
abstract class URLHandler
{
  abstract function getRealURL( $url );
}

class URLMapper
{
  private $handlers = array( );

  private function URLMapper( )
  {
  }

  public function addHandler( $handler )
  {
    $this->handlers []= $handler;
  }

  public function mapURL( $url )
  {
    foreach( $this->handlers as $h )
    {
      $mapped = $h->getRealURL( $url );
      if ( isset( $mapped ) ) return $mapped;
    }
    return $url;
  }

  public static function instance( )
  {
    static $inst = null;
    if( !isset( $inst ) ) { $inst = new URLMapper( ); }
    return $inst;
  }
}

class ImageURLHandler extends URLHandler
{
  private $base;
  private $imgurl;

  public function ImageURLHandler( $base, $imgurl )
  {
    $this->base = $base;
    $this->imgurl = $imgurl;
  }

  public function getRealURL( $url )
  {
    if ( preg_match( "|^".$this->base."(.*?)$|", $url, $matches ) )
```

Example 7-10. An example of the Chain of Responsibility pattern in PHP (continued)

```php
    {
      return $this->imgurl.$matches[1];
    }
    return null;
  }
}

class StoryURLHandler extends URLHandler
{
  private $base;
  private $story_url;

  public function StoryURLHandler( $base, $story_url )
  {
    $this->base = $base;
    $this->story_url = $story_url;
  }

  public function getRealURL( $url )
  {
    if ( preg_match( "|^".$this->base."(.*?)/(.*?)/(.*?)$|", $url, $matches ) )
    {
      return $this->story_url.$matches[1].$matches[2].$matches[3];
    }
    return null;
  }
}


$ih = new ImageURLHandler( "http://mysite.com/images/",
      "http://mysite.com/image.php?img=" );
URLMapper::instance( )->addHandler( $ih );
$ih = new StoryURLHandler( "http://mysite.com/story/",
      "http://mysite.com/story.php?id=" );
URLMapper::instance( )->addHandler( $ih );

$testurls = array( );
$testurls []= "http://mysite.com/index.html";
$testurls []= "http://mysite.com/images/dog";
$testurls []= "http://mysite.com/story/11/05/05";
$testurls []= "http://mysite.com/images/cat";
$testurls []= "http://mysite.com/image.php?img=lizard";

foreach( $testurls as $in )
{
  $out = URLMapper::instance( )->mapURL( $in );
  print "$in\n --> $out\n\n";
}
?>
```

Running the Hack

Run the *chain.php* script with the command-line PHP interpreter:

```
% php chain.php
http://mysite.com/index.html
--> http://mysite.com/index.html

http://mysite.com/images/dog
--> http://mysite.com/image.php?img=dog

http://mysite.com/story/11/05/05
--> http://mysite.com/story.php?id=110505

http://mysite.com/images/cat
--> http://mysite.com/image.php?img=cat

http://mysite.com/image.php?img=lizard
--> http://mysite.com/image.php?img=lizard

%
```

Each URL that comes in is sent through URLMapper, which returns the mapped URL. In the first case, the URL is not remapped, so it just drops through. In the second case, ImageURLHandler sees that this is an image URL, so it remaps the URL to the *image.php* script. The third URL is recognized by the document mapper, which maps that URL to the *story.php* script.

The great value of the Chain of Responsibility pattern is that you can extend it without changing your core application code. As long as the vendor object has a robust enough API for the registered objects, it can handle almost any situation.

Perhaps the most recognizable instantiation of the Chain of Responsibility pattern is the Apache Web Server. Apache functions as one big donut vendor, delegating various requests to all of its registered handlers.

 This pattern is *not* always easy to use. In fact, this pattern has some serious issues! It's hard to debug, and it's often not very clear how to use the pattern correctly. It also comes in two variants: one where the request stops if a match is found and another where processing continues regardless of a match. It's not always clear which version is being used. Further, the second variation, where all handlers are called on all occasions, can be extremely tricky to debug (even more so than the pattern normally is). Just keep in mind that flexibility in computer programs always comes at a complexity and performance cost.

Break Up Big Classes with Composites

#75 Use the Composite pattern to break megaclasses into small, manageable classes.

I have a curious reaction when I hear news about enormous databases storing everything anyone would ever want to know about me. While most people are immediately concerned about the privacy implications, I think about how poorly designed that system almost certainly is. I'm almost positive there's one awful mega-object in there called `Person`, probably with 4,000 fields and 8,000 methods.

How do I know that? Because I've seen and maintained objects like that before! What that kind of class really needs is the Composite pattern. The *Composite pattern* would retain the `Person` class, but would have groups of those 4,000 fields lumped into contained child objects; the `Person` object would really comprise 100 or so objects, each containing other small objects (which might contain even smaller objects, and so on).

Now, I'm not saying I've seen classes this bad in PHP; but I have seen classes with upward of 100 fields, simply because the objects represent a set of tables that have that many fields related to a single entry. This hack demonstrates how to take a `Customer` class (with far too many fields) and break it up into several smaller classes, but at the end of the process, still have just a single composite `Customer` class.

> Well, in the sample, I'm breaking up only eight or so fields; I'll leave it to you to extrapolate from this to the several hundred fields I've seen on objects before.

The `Customer` construction is shown in Figure 7-9. The `Customer` class contains one of each of the `CustomerName` and `CustomerAddress` objects.

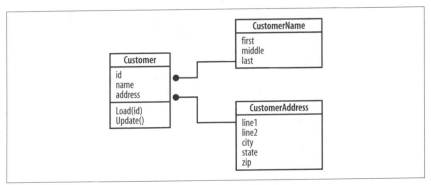

Figure 7-9. The Customer composite class with its child classes

The Code

Save the code in Example 7-11 as *composite.php*.

Example 7-11. A Customer composite object made up of smaller objects

```php
<?php
class CustomerName
{
  public $first = "";
  public $middle = "";
  public $last = "";
}

class CustomerAddress
{
  public $line1 = "";
  public $line2 = "";
  public $city = "";
  public $state = "";
  public $zip = "";
}

class Customer
{
  public $id = null;
  public $name = null;
  public $address = null;

  public function Customer( )
  {
    $this->name = new CustomerName( );
    $this->address = new CustomerAddress( );
  }

  public function Load( $id )
  {
    $this->id = $id;
    $this->name->first = "George";
    $this->name->middle = "W";
    $this->name->last = "Bush";
    $this->address->line1 = "1600 Pennsylvania Ave.";
    $this->address->line2 = "";
    $this->address->city = "Washington";
    $this->address->state = "DC";
    $this->address->zip = "20006";
  }

  public function Update( )
  {
    // Update the record in the database
    // or insert the record if there is no id
  }
```

Example 7-11. A Customer composite object made up of smaller objects (continued)

```
  public function __toString( )
  {
    return $this->name->first." ".$this->name->last;
  }
}

$cust = new Customer( );
$cust->Load( 1 );
print( $cust );
print( "\n" );
?>
```

Running the Hack

You run this script from the command line using the PHP interpreter:

```
% php composite.php
George Bush
```

The code creates a new customer and loads in record #1. I've hardcoded that to be George W. Bush. The code then prints the `Customer` object.

There isn't much to this; the idea is as effective as it is simple. You shouldn't have megaclasses with 100 fields. You should have small grouped classes, such as `CustomerName` and `CustomerAddress`, that you can composite into larger features—in this case, the `Customer` class. Even better, it's possible to reuse a class like `CustomerAddress` in other classes that require postal addresses.

A good clue for when a Composite pattern is required is when the data for an object is spread across multiple database tables. Each related table should be its own object or data structure.

The Composite pattern also allows for database read optimization. Because loading each subobject, such as the address, will require a different query, it's possible to do that lazily. In other words, you can delay the loading of a particular subobject until the data for that object is needed. This avoids your code needing to grab hundreds of fields in multiple tables when all you really need is a person's first and last name.

HACK #76 Simplify APIs Using a Façade

Use the Façade pattern to simplify the API that you present to other programmers.

This is one of the patterns I really wish more programmers would use, and not just because of that fancy squiggle under the c in façade. It's because creating a façade means that some other programmer has thought of me and made sure I have just the information I need (and nothing else that I can screw up).

Take a sample logging API, such as the one shown in Figure 7-10.

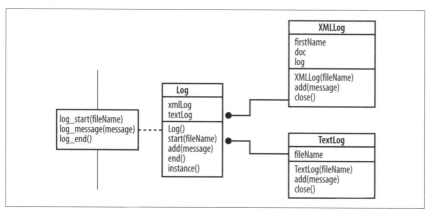

Figure 7-10. The logging API with a simple façade

This API can log to XML, text, or both. Wow. As a peer programmer, I'm impressed with the skill of the coding. There seem to be methods for everything; starting a message, adding text, cleaning up...even handling XML and text easily.

But what I really want to know is which method to use and when to use it. That's precisely what a *façade* does: it ensures that I use the API correctly. The façade in this example is the list of three functions with the line through it on the lefthand side. That line is a sort of theoretical bar that says, "I'll handle the stuff to the right; just call my methods, and I'll take care of the rest."

Not only does the façade simplify APIs, but it also hides implementation details from the client; in fact, the implementation can change without clients even knowing about it. This is at least as important as the simplification that façades bring. Remember, loose coupling means strong and reliable systems.

The Code

Save the code in Example 7-12 as *test.php*.

Example 7-12. The log test code

```php
<?php
require( "log.php" );
```

Example 7-12. The log test code (continued)

```
log_start( "mylog" );
log_message( "Opening application" );
log_message( "Logging a message" );
log_message( "Shutting down" );
log_end();
?>
```

Save the code in Example 7-13 as *log.php*.

Example 7-13. The log façade

```php
<?php
require( "log_impl.php" );

function log_start( $fileName )
{
  Log::instance()->start( $fileName );
}

function log_message( $message )
{
  Log::instance()->add( $message );
}

function log_end()
{
  Log::instance()->end();
}
?>
```

Save the code in Example 7-14 as *log_impl.php*.

Example 7-14. The log library behind the façade

```php
<?php
class XMLLog
{
  private $fileName;
  private $doc;
  private $log;

  public function XMLLog( $fileName )
  {
    $this->fileName = $fileName;

    $this->doc = new DOMDocument();
    $this->doc->formatOutput = true;
    $this->log = $this->doc->createElement( "log" );
    $this->doc->appendChild( $this->log );
  }
```

Example 7-14. The log library behind the façade (continued)

```php
public function add( $message )
{
  $mess_obj = $this->doc->createElement( "message" );
  $text = $this->doc->createTextNode( $message );
  $mess_obj->appendChild( $text );
  $this->log->appendChild( $mess_obj );
}

  public function close()
  {
    $this->doc->save( $this->fileName );
  }
}

class TextLog
{
  private $fh;

  public function TextLog( $fileName )
  {
    $this->fh = fopen( $fileName, "w" );
  }

  public function add( $message )
  {
    fprintf( $this->fh, $message."\n" );
  }

  public function close()
  {
    fclose( $this->fh );
  }
}

class Log
{
  private $xmlLog = null;
  private $textLog = null;

  public function Log()
  {
  }

  public function start( $fileName )
  {
    $this->xmlLog = new XMLLog( $fileName.".xml" );
    $this->textLog = new TextLog( $fileName.".txt" );
  }

  public function add( $message )
  {
```

Example 7-14. The log library behind the façade (continued)

```
    $this->xmlLog->add( $message );
    $this->textLog->add( $message );
  }

  public function end( )
  {
    $this->xmlLog->close( );
    $this->textLog->close( );
  }

  public static function instance( )
  {
    static $inst = null;
    if ( !isset( $inst ) ) $inst = new Log( );
    return $inst;
  }
}
?>
```

Running the Hack

You run this hack from the command line using the PHP command-line interpreter:

```
% php test.php
% cat mylog.txt
Opening application
Logging a message
Shutting down
% cat mylog.xml
<?xml version="1.0"?>
<log>
  <message>Opening application</message>
  <message>Logging a message</message>
  <message>Shutting down</message>
</log>
```

Not much to look at, but it's really the code (and not the output) we are interested in. Beginning with the *test.php* script, the code starts up the log, sends out a few messages, and then shuts down the log. It does that using only the three functions in the façade script, *log.php*. In fact, in an ideal environment, *log.php* is the only script that "outside" programmers would have access to.

The *log.php* file uses the Log singleton object **[Hack #77]** from the *log_impl.php* script to create two logs. It then sends each message to each log and has them output to the corresponding text or XML file.

Create Constant Objects with Singletons

#77

Use the Singleton pattern to create objects that exist as a solitary object in the system.

Of all of the patterns detailed in the Gang of Four's *Design Patterns*, none seems to have been used as often as the Singleton pattern, probably in part because it's so easy to implement. Besides, who can beat coding up a singleton and saying, "There can be only one!" Or maybe that's just a *Highlander* thing.

A *singleton* is an object that can have only one instance at any given time in the system. A great example of a potential singleton is a database handle. For each instance of the PHP interpreter, there should be only one database handle. This hack implements just such a setup, a singleton version of a database handle.

Figure 7-11 shows the UML for the database handle singleton (I told you it was simple!).

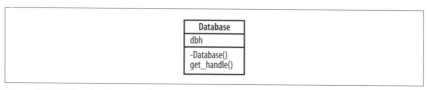

Figure 7-11. The database singleton

Not much to look at, really. The object contains the database handle and has two methods. The first is the constructor, which is private to ensure that nobody outside of the class can create the object. It also contains a static method called get_handle that returns the database handle.

The Code

Save the code in Example 7-15 as *singleton1.php*.

Example 7-15. A database wrapper singleton

```php
<?php
require( 'DB.php' );

class Database
{
  private $dbh;

  private function Database( )
  {
    $dsn = 'mysql://root:password@localhost/test';
```

Example 7-15. A database wrapper singleton (continued)

```
    $this->dbh =& DB::Connect( $dsn, array( ) );
    if (PEAR::isError($this->dbh)) { die($this->dbh->getMessage( )); }
  }

  public static function get_handle( )
  {
    static $db = null;
    if ( !isset($db) ) $db = new Database( );
    return $db->dbh;
  }
}

echo( Database::get_handle( )."\n" );
echo( Database::get_handle( )."\n" );
echo( Database::get_handle( )."\n" );
?>
```

This simple singleton has a constructor that logs into the database and one static accessor that creates an object if one hasn't been created already and returns the database handle from that object. If you use this method to get to database handles, you can rest assured that you will connect to the database only once per page fetch.

Running the Hack

You run this script on the command line using the PHP command-line interpreter:

```
% php singleton1.php
Object id #2
Object id #2
Object id #2
```

This demonstrates that the multiple calls to the get_handle( ) static method are returning the same object time and time again. This means that each time the call was made, the same Database object, and thus the same database handle, was used.

Hacking the Hack

Database handles are one thing, but what about something more complex? Let's try a shared list of states, as shown in Example 7-16.

Example 7-16. A singleton array of states

```
<?php
class StateList
{
  private $states = array( );
```

Example 7-16. A singleton array of states (continued)

```php
  private function StateList( )
  {
  }

  public function addState( $state )
  {
    $this->states []= $state;
  }

  public function getStates( )
  {
    return $this->states;
  }

  public static function instance( )
  {
    static $states = null;
    if ( !isset($states) ) $states = new StateList( );
    return $states;
  }
}

StateList::instance( )->addState( "Florida" );
var_dump( StateList::instance( )->getStates( ) );

StateList::instance( )->addState( "Kentucky" );
var_dump( StateList::instance( )->getStates( ) );
?>
```

This code creates a singleton class, StateList, which contains a list of states. You can add states to the list, as well as getting a listing of the states. To access the single shared instance of this object, you have to use the static instance( ) method (instead of creating an instance directly).

To run this script, use the command-line interpreter:

```
% php singleton2.php
array(1) {
  [0]=>
  string(7) "Florida"
}
array(2) {
  [0]=>
  string(7) "Florida"
  [1]=>
  string(8) "Kentucky"
}
```

The first dump shows that just the first state, Florida, is in the list. The second dump shows the addition of Kentucky to the shared object.

I am a little hesitant to recommend the Singleton pattern too highly. In my experience, it's often overused. In fact, I've seen code that has some rather ugly workarounds to deal with singleton objects; more often than not, these reflect that the Singleton pattern is being used incorrectly. If you're taking significant steps to work with a singleton, it might not be an appropriate use of the pattern.

HACK #78 Ease Data Manipulation with Visitors
Use the Visitor pattern to separate data traversal from data handling.

Early in my career as a programmer, I did a lot of scientific programming with data acquisition systems. These were systems that recorded data at a sampling interval of 3 microseconds—in other words, 333,333 samples per second. That came out to 38 megabytes for every minute of information! For long recording sessions, a file could easily get into gigabytes. Needless to say, we had problems recording and storing that much information without any hiccups.

Another problem had to do with analyzing this data. How do you analyze a multigigabyte file when the machine doing the work has only 128 MB of memory? The answer is to chunk the data. *Chunking* means reading in the file by sections, swapping out the data you don't need and swapping in what you do need.

That said, you'd think that these scientific algorithms were tough enough without worrying about swapping in and out big chunks of data. To solve these problems—and do it elegantly—we used the *Visitor pattern*. One object would handle getting the data in and out of memory, and another object would handle processing the data when it was in memory.

Figure 7-12 shows a RecordList object that contains a list of Records. It has an iterate( ) function that, when given another function, calls the passed-in function on each record.

With this approach, the data processing function—passed in to iterate( )—doesn't have to understand how records are managed in memory. All the function has to do is handle the data it's given.

The Code
Save the code in Example 7-17 as *visitor1.php*.

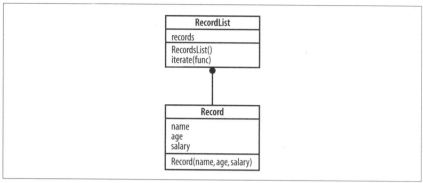

Figure 7-12. A RecordList with an iterate method

Example 7-17. A Visitor pattern moving over database records

```php
<?php
class Record
{
  public $name;
  public $age;
  public $salary;
  public function Record( $name, $age, $salary )
  {
    $this->name = $name;
    $this->age = $age;
    $this->salary = $salary;
  }
}

class RecordList
{
  private $records = array();

  public function RecordList()
  {
    $this->records []= new Record( "Larry", 22, 35000 );
    $this->records []= new Record( "Harry", 25, 37000 );
    $this->records []= new Record( "Mary", 42, 65000 );
    $this->records []= new Record( "Sally", 45, 80000 );
  }

  public function iterate( $func )
  {
    foreach( $this->records as $r )
    {
      call_user_func( $func, $r );
    }
  }
}
```

Example 7-17. A Visitor pattern moving over database records (continued)

```php
$min = 100000;
function find_min_salary( $rec )
{
  global $min;
  if( $rec->salary < $min ) { $min = $rec->salary; }
}

$rl = new RecordList();
$rl->iterate( "find_min_salary", $min );
echo( $min."\n" );
?>
```

Running the Hack

You run this hack on the command line like this:

```
% php visitor1.php
35000
```

This particular algorithm finds the lowest salary of all of the records it sees.

The code in this script is fairly simple. The Record class holds the data for each record. The RecordList class then preloads itself with some dummy data (in a real system, this data might be read from a database or filesystem). In the iterate( ) method, the foreach loop walks through the list of records. call_user_func( ) calls the passed-in data processing function on each record. In this example, that function is find_min_salary( ); it inspects each record to find the lowest salary value.

Hacking the Hack

I find the function-based version of this pattern a little clunky. I would rather specify a visitor object that will receive each record. That way, the object can hold the minimum value that can be accessed later.

Figure 7-13 shows a variant where the iterate( ) method takes an object (of type RecordVisitor) rather than a function.

The updated code is shown in Example 7-18.

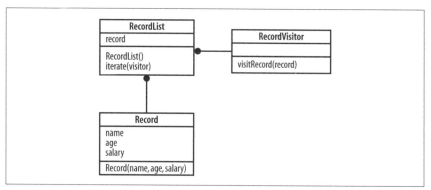

Figure 7-13. A variant where the visitor is an object

Example 7-18. An updated version of the visitor

```php
<?php
class Record
{
  public $name;
  public $age;
  public $salary;
  public function Record( $name, $age, $salary )
  {
    $this->name = $name;
    $this->age = $age;
    $this->salary = $salary;
  }
}

abstract class RecordVisitor
{
  abstract function visitRecord( $rec );
}

class RecordList
{
  private $records = array( );

  public function RecordList( )
  {
    $this->records []= new Record( "Larry", 22, 35000 );
    $this->records []= new Record( "Harry", 25, 37000 );
    $this->records []= new Record( "Mary", 42, 65000 );
    $this->records []= new Record( "Sally", 45, 80000 );
  }
```

Example 7-18. An updated version of the visitor (continued)

```php
  public function iterate( $vis )
  {
    foreach( $this->records as $r )
    {
      call_user_func( array( $vis, "visitRecord" ), $r );
    }
  }
}

class MinSalaryFinder extends RecordVisitor
{
  public $min = 1000000;
  public function visitRecord( $rec )
  {
    if( $rec->salary < $this->min ) { $this->min = $rec->salary; }
  }
}

$rl = new RecordList();
$msl = new MinSalaryFinder();
$rl->iterate( $msl );
echo( $msl->min."\n" );
?>
```

I have added the RecordVisitor abstract class, and implemented it with the
MinSalaryFinder class; this implementation stores a minimum value. The
test code now creates a RecordList, then creates a MinSalaryFinder, and
applies it to the list through the iterate( ) method. Finally, the minimum
value is printed.

A couple of thoughts about this hack are in order before leaving it. First,
PHP is not very good at calling functions dynamically. Specifying a function
by name is weak and prone to error. Python, Perl, Ruby, Java, and C# (and
almost every other language) all have the ability to assign a function pointer
to a value. Then it's easy to invoke a method through that function pointer
(or reference, depending on the language). I like PHP just like everyone else,
but I think this should be cleaned up in the next version of the language.

Testing
Hacks 79–85

Application testing—and squeezing that testing into what are almost always strenuous development cycles—has been a hot topic in recent years. This chapter starts with unit tests, which test an application's individual functions and classes. Then we'll move on and cover automatic generation of unit tests, as well as the testing of an application through alternate means. You'll code up robots that make HTTP requests to a server and tests that use Internet Explorer automation for checking a web interface for problems.

HACK #79 Test Your Code with Unit Tests

Use PHPUnit and PHPUnit2 to test your code continuously.

PHP is quietly becoming a force in enterprise application development. With larger applications come more complexity and requirements for testing in an attempt to make sure that the application is stable. It's a truism that stable applications are built by creating a multitiered structure, with each layer well tested on its own. For example, you might have a self-contained database layer (that is tested) that sits underneath a business logic layer (that is tested), which in turn is used by the user interface layer (that is also tested). Starting to get the idea?

To test each layer, it has become common practice to create *unit tests*. These are tests that are run after any code change and before any code is checked in (you are using version control on your enterprise projects, aren't you?). In fact, it's common to insist that all unit tests *must* pass before code is even a candidate to be checked back into your code repository. Further, when new bugs are found, new unit tests are created that exercise the faulty code and report the error; then, the error is fixed, and the unit tests should pass, ensuring that if the problem reappears, everyone will know about it (through a failing unit test).

This hack shows how to use the PHPUnit2 framework to develop unit tests for PHP 5, available on the PEAR module distribution network [Hack #2].

> For PHP 4, you will want to use the original PHPUnit. This module is also available via PEAR.

The Code

Save the code in Example 8-1 as *Add.php*.

Example 8-1. A simple add function

```php
<?php
function add( $a, $b ) { return $a + $b; }
?>
```

Save the code in Example 8-2 as *TestAdd.php*. This simple script contains two unit tests, test1( ) and test2( ), both which test the add( ) method.

Example 8-2. The add function unit tests

```php
<?php
require_once 'Add.php';
require_once 'PHPUnit2/Framework/TestCase.php';

class TestAdd extends PHPUnit2_Framework_TestCase
{
  function test1() { $this->assertTrue( add( 1, 2 ) == 3 ); }
  function test2() { $this->assertFalse( add( 1, 1 ) == 3 ); }
}
?>
```

As simple as add( ) seems, it is perfectly natural that you would use (at least) two unit tests for testing. Imagine how many unit tests a typical application would need to be thoroughly tested!

Running the Hack

You run this code using the phpunit test runner:

```
% phpunit TestAdd.php
PHPUnit 2.2.1 by Sebastian Bergmann.

..

Time: 0.0028750896453857

OK (2 tests)
%
```

This shows the running of the unit test (represented by the two dots), and the results, which in this case are OK since both unit tests passed.

> Be sure you give phpunit the name of the unit test script, rather than the actual script being tested.

See Also

- "Generate Your Unit Tests" **[Hack #80]**

 HACK **Generate Your Unit Tests**
#80 Use PHP to build your unit tests from code comments.

Unit tests **[Hack #79]** are so critical to the development of a stable application that it's worth going to some effort to create them. However, there's some nice middle ground between writing unit tests completely by hand (including the routine portion of those tests that is the same, over and over again), and automating test creation. This hack shows how to use a script to generate unit test code from comments embedded in your PHP code. The comments are test specific, but this does cut down on the redundant code you have to type in.

The Code

Save the code in Example 8-3 as *Add.php*. Note that several tests are laid out using the == and != operators all in the PHP script comments.

Example 8-3. The code from which to build unit tests

```php
<?php
// UNIT_TEST_START
// ( 1, 2 ) == 3
// ( 1, -1 ) == 0
// ( 1, 1 ) != 3
// ( 1, -1 ) != 1
// UNIT_TEST_END
function add( $a, $b ) { return $a + $b; }

// UNIT_TEST_START
// ( 1, 2 ) == -1
// ( 1, -1 ) == 2
// ( 1, 1 ) != 1
// ( 1, -1 ) != 1
// UNIT_TEST_END
function minus( $a, $b ) { return $a - $b; }
?>
```

Save the code in Example 8-4 as *GenUnit.php*. This script handles generation of tests from another script's comments.

Example 8-4. The unit test generator

```php
<?php
if ( count( $argv ) < 2 )
{
  print "GenUnit.php usage:\n";
  print "   php GenUnit.php <PHP Script>\n";
  exit;
}

$infile = $argv[1];

define( 'STATE_NORMAL', 0 );
define( 'STATE_IN_UNIT_DEF', 1 );
define( 'STATE_WAITING_FOR_FUNC', 2 );

$state = STATE_NORMAL;

$fh = fopen( $infile, "r" );
$tests = array();
$funcs = array();
while( $str = fgets( $fh ) )
{
  if ( $state == STATE_NORMAL )
  {
    if ( preg_match( "|UNIT_TEST_START|", $str ) )
      $state = STATE_IN_UNIT_DEF;
  }
  else if ( $state == STATE_IN_UNIT_DEF )
  {
    if ( preg_match( "|UNIT_TEST_END|", $str ) )
      $state = STATE_WAITING_FOR_FUNC;
    else
    {
      $str = preg_replace( "|^//\s*|", "", $str );
      $str = preg_replace( "|\s*$|", "", $str );
      $tests []= $str;
    }
  }
  else if ( $state == STATE_WAITING_FOR_FUNC )
  {
    if ( preg_match( "|function\s+(.*?)\(|", $str, $out ) )
    {
      $funcs []= array(
        'function' => $out[1],
        'tests' => $tests
      );
```

Example 8-4. The unit test generator (continued)

```
          $state = STATE_NORMAL;
          $tests = array( );
      }
    }
}

fclose( $fh );

ob_start( );

$outfile = "Test".$infile;
$classname = preg_replace( "|[.]php$|i", "", $outfile );

echo( "<?php\n" );
?>
// This code was written by GenUnit.php
//
// Do not alter the code manually or your revisions
// will be lost the next time GenUnit.php is run.

require_once '<?php echo( $infile ); ?>';
require_once 'PHPUnit2/Framework/TestCase.php';

class <?php echo( $classname ); ?> extends PHPUnit2_Framework_TestCase
{
<?php
$id = 1;
foreach( $funcs as $func )
{
    foreach( $func['tests'] as $test ) {
?>
    function test<?php echo($id); ?>() { $this->assertTrue( <?php echo(
$func['function'].$test ) ?> ); }
<?php
    $id+=1;
    }
}
?>
}
<?php
echo( "?>\n" );
$test_php = ob_get_clean( );

print ($id-1)." tests created in $outfile\n";

$fh = fopen( $outfile, "w" );
fwrite( $fh, $test_php );
fclose( $fh );
?>
```

The *GenUnit.php* script is actually pretty interesting. Its job is to read in a PHP script, which it does at the top of the file. It then uses a state machine to parse through each line of the file, looking for the start and end of the special test comment blocks; for each comment, it interprets and stores the tests within the comment blocks into the $funcs array.

> You can easily move from the UNIT_TEST_START and UNIT_TEST_END delimiters to anything you choose by modifying *GenUnit.php*.

The second half of the script then uses the $funcs array to create PHP test code. First, the script buffers the PHP output and creates the test class and each test function. Then it shuts down the text buffer and stores the buffer's output into the PHP test file.

Running the Hack

To run *GenUnit.php*, use the PHP command-line interpreter:

```
% php GenUnit.php Add.php
8 tests created in TestAdd.php
```

The script reads the *Add.php* file and creates *TestAdd.php*. That file (using *Add.php*) looks like this:

```php
<?php
// This code was written by GenUnit.php
//
// Do not alter the code manually or your revisions
// will be lost the next time GenUnit.php is run.

require_once 'Add.php';
require_once 'PHPUnit2/Framework/TestCase.php';

class TestAdd extends PHPUnit2_Framework_TestCase
{
  function test1() { $this->assertTrue( add( 1, 2 ) == 3 ); }
  function test2() { $this->assertTrue( add( 1, -1 ) == 0 ); }
  function test3() { $this->assertTrue( add( 1, 1 ) != 3 ); }
  function test4() { $this->assertTrue( add( 1, -1 ) != 1 ); }
  function test5() { $this->assertTrue( minus( 1, 2 ) == -1 ); }
  function test6() { $this->assertTrue( minus( 1, -1 ) == 2 ); }
  function test7() { $this->assertTrue( minus( 1, 1 ) != 1 ); }
  function test8() { $this->assertTrue( minus( 1, -1 ) != 1 ); }
}
?>
```

You can see that the code that was in the comments is now embedded in test functions. Also note the comment at the top of the file, which tells potential coders that the file was generated (rather than hand-coded); it also clearly lets users know that if they modify the file, their changes will be lost the next time the generator is run.

You can run the generated script just like any other PHP code:

```
% phpunit TestAdd.php
PHPUnit 2.2.1 by Sebastian Bergmann.


........

Time: 0.010335922241211

OK (8 tests)
```

This shows that eight tests were run and that they all worked properly.

See Also

- "Test Your Code with Unit Tests" [Hack #79]

HACK #81 Check for Broken Links

Use output buffering to analyze the current page and CURL to check the links on a page to make sure they point to existing pages.

Broken links are the bane of web administrators; what's worse, a link that works today might not work next week, due to the ever-evolving nature of the Web. To help fix this pesky problem, the script in this hack captures blocks of HTML and checks the links for that section of markup. Then it provides a handy report noting any bad links, allowing you to easily find and repair problems.

The Code

Save the code in Example 8-5 as *index.php*. All this page does is present a link that works and one that doesn't.

Example 8-5. The host page for the link checker

```php
<?php
require_once( "checklinks.php" ); ?>
<html>
<body>
<?php checklinks_start() ?>
<div style="width: 800px" />
```

Example 8-5. The host page for the link checker (continued)

```
<a href="http://www.cnn.com">CNN</a><br/>
<a href="http://badlink">Bad link</a><br/>
<?php checklinks_end( ) ?>
</div>
</body>
</html>
```

Save the script in Example 8-6 as *checklinks.php*.

Example 8-6. The link-checker code

```php
<?php
function checklinks_start( )
{
    ob_start( );
}

function checklinks_end( )
{
  $doc = ob_get_clean( );
  preg_match_all( "/\<a.*?href=[\"|\'](.*?)[\"|\']\>/", $doc, $found );
  print( $doc );

  $badlinks = array( );
  foreach( $found[1] as $link )
  {
    $ch = curl_init( $link );
    ob_start( );
    curl_exec( $ch );
    $out = ob_get_clean( );
    if ( curl_errno( $ch ) != 0 )
       $badlinks []= $link;
    curl_close( $ch );
  }

  if ( count( $badlinks ) > 0 ) {
?>
<br/>
<table style="background: red;" cellspacing="2" cellpadding="2" width="100%">
<tr><td style="white; color: white; text-align:center;">Bad links</td></tr>
<tr><td style="background: white;">
<?php foreach( $badlinks as $link ) { echo( $link."<br/>" ); } ?>
</td></tr>
</table>
<?php } } ?>
```

Running the Hack

Upload both scripts to your server and navigate to the *index.php*page. If you are connected to the Web, you will get a browser display that looks like Figure 8-1.

Figure 8-1. Link checker with a report

The portion of HTML to be checked is bracketed with calls to checklinks_ start( ) and checklinks_end( ). These methods in turn use ob_start( ) and ob_get_clean( ) to buffer the PHP output. The checklinks_end( ) function then uses the CURL functions to request the pages pointed to by the anchor (<a>) tags. As long as the computer is connected to the Internet, the link to the CNN home page should be fine; but the link to *http://badlink* will never be valid. As a result, the checklinks_end( ) function prints out a report detailing which links are broken.

See Also

- "Test Your Application with Simulated Users" [Hack #82]
- "Test Your Application with Robots" [Hack #83]
- "Spider Your Site" [Hack #84]

HACK   **Test Your Application with Simulated Users**
#82   Use the Internet Explorer automation interface to test your application
         through the UI.

You can test the back end of an application by using unit tests for the database and business logic code. You can test a portion of the frontend of your application by using robots [Hack #83] that request pages from the server and submit data. But how do you actually test what users would do? How do you simulate the buttons pushed and the boxes filled in by a typical user?

Particularly with JavaScript-heavy applications, you need something that will actually click on buttons to ensure that your application does what it should.

On Windows, you can use Internet Explorer COM objects to tell the IE browser to navigate to your site and even to hit the appropriate buttons. Figure 8-2 illustrates the relationships among the different PHP files used in this hack. *test.php* and *print.php* are standard PHP web pages. The *testagent.php* script is run on the command line and drives the browser to visit these pages, fill in the forms, and check the results.

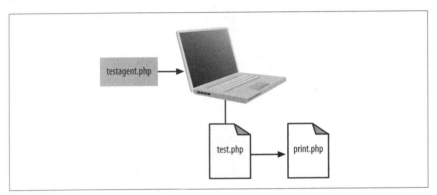

Figure 8-2. The test agent driving the browser

The Code

Save the code in Example 8-7 as *test.php*. This simple web page is used for testing the agent.

Example 8-7. The first page of the test code

```
<html>
<head>
<title>Automated test agent test page</title>
<head>
<body>
<form id="inp_form" action="print.php">
<table cellpadding="2"><tr>
<td>First:</td>
<td><input id="first_name" name="first" type="text"></td>
</tr><tr>
<td>Last:</td>
<td><input id="last_name" name="last" type="text"></td>
</tr>
<tr>
<td colspan="2" align="center">
<input type="submit" />
```

Example 8-7. The first page of the test code (continued)

```
</td>
</tr>
</table>
</form>
</body>
</html>
```

Save the code in Example 8-8 as *print.php*. This is just a form receiver for Example 8-7.

Example 8-8. The second page of the test code

```
<html>
<head>
<title>Automated test agent print page</title>
</head>
<body>
You entered:<br/>
First:
<span id="res_first"><?php echo( $_GET['first'] ); ?></span>
<br/>
Last:
<span id="res_last"><?php echo( $_GET['last'] ); ?></span>
<br/>
</body>
</html>
```

Save the code in Example 8-9 as *testagent.php*.

Example 8-9. The Internet Explorer automation test script

```
<?php
function delay( $ie, $amount )
{
  for( $c = 0; $c < ( $amount / 100 ); $c++ )
    com_message_pump( 100 );
}

function test_page( $ie, $page, $first, $last )
{
  $ie->Navigate( $page );
  delay( $ie, 2000 );

  $fn = $ie->Document->getElementById( "first_name" );
  $fn->Value = $first;
  $ln = $ie->Document->getElementById( "last_name" );
  $ln->Value = $last;
  $inf = $ie->Document->getElementById( "inp_form" );
  $inf->submit();
  delay( $ie, 2000 );
```

Example 8-9. The Internet Explorer automation test script (continued)

```
$rfn = $ie->Document->getElementById( "res_first" );
$rfn = $rfn->innerHTML;
$rln = $ie->Document->getElementById( "res_last" );
$rln = $rln->innerHTML;

if( strcmp( $rfn, $first ) == 0 &&
    strcmp( $rln, $last ) == 0 )
{
  print "Test passed.\n";
  return 0;
}
else
{
  print "Test failed.\n";
  return -1;
}
}

$ie = new COM("InternetExplorer.Application");
$ie->Visible = true;

$result = test_page( $ie,
  "http://localhost:1222/com/test.php",
  "Charles",
  "Herrington" );

$ie->Quit( );

exit( $result );
?>
```

This test script primarily uses the Internet Explorer COM interface via the built-in COM class wrapper. The processing flow starts at the bottom, where the code creates a COM object of type InternetExplorer.Application. The script then runs the test_page( ) function to use Internet Explorer to test the page.

The test_page( ) function navigates IE to the target URL, then fills in the form and submits it. The function waits a little bit, allowing the return page to be loaded. Then, it inspects the <span> tags on the returned page to make sure they contain the right information. The script quits Internet Explorer and sets the exit code to 0 or -1, depending on the result of the test. Finally, a short message about the status of the test is printed out.

> These tests are obviously very specific to a particular site and even a particular page. You won't be able to code generic tests, but this sort of user automation testing is still invaluable.

Running the Hack

Install the *test.php* and *print.php* files in your web server. Alter the *testagent.php* file to use the correct URL for your test page. Then use this command:

```
c:\testagent\> php testagent.php
Test passed.
```

As part of the test, the first thing you should see is the login page (shown in Figure 8-3).

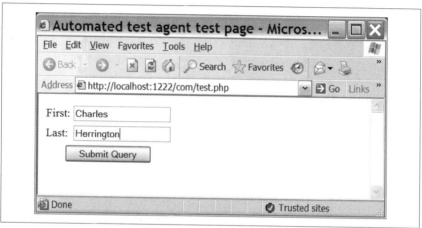

Figure 8-3. The test data-entry page

Then the user agent will fill in the form and click on the Submit Query button. This will take the agent to the next page—Figure 8-4—that simply parrots back what was entered.

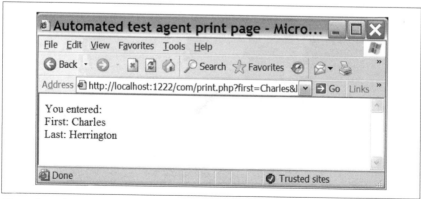

Figure 8-4. The test result page

This *print.php* has span tags that bracket the first and last names that were entered. The user agent uses the innerHTML property of these span tags to ensure that the returned values match those that were input into the form.

 This is exactly what commercial products such as SilkTest (*http://segue.com/*) and TestComplete (*http://automatedqa. com/*) provide for testing web pages. Those products cost a lot of money and this code is, well, free.

See Also

- "Test Your Application with Robots" **[Hack #83]**
- "Spider Your Site" **[Hack #84]**

Test Your Application with Robots

HACK #83

Use the HTTP_Client PEAR module to test your PHP application through the Web.

How do you know that your application is running properly? It's a lot like that little light in your refrigerator; if you can't see it, can you really be sure it's off when you close the door? One way to keep an eye on your application is to build a robot that tests your site. You can run this robot periodically, ensuring the server is always responding properly (and notifying you when it's not).

This hack shows how to use the HTTP_Client PEAR module **[Hack #2]** to test the shopping cart application **[Hack #66]**. Figure 8-5 illustrates the *robot.php* script driving the shopping cart application, all through requests to the web server. The robot checks the contents of each return page in the application, making sure that the process for adding and removing items from the shopping cart works properly.

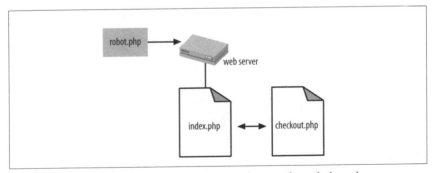

Figure 8-5. The robot testing the shopping cart application through the web server

The Code

Save the code in Example 8-10 as *robot.php*.

Example 8-10. The test robot

```php
<?php
require_once 'HTTP/Client.php';

function check_html( $testname, $client, $values )
{
  $resp = $client->currentResponse( );
  $body = $resp['body'];

  preg_match( "/\<\!\-\- CART \: (.*?) \-\-\>/", $body, $found );

  print "$testname: ";
  print ( $found[1] == join(",", $values ) ) ? "passed" : "failed";
  print "\n";
}

$client = new HTTP_Client( );

$client->get( "http://localhost/phphacks/shopcart/index.php" );

$client->post( "http://localhost/phphacks/shopcart/add.php", array( 'prod_id' =>
    1 ) );
$client->get( "http://localhost/phphacks/shopcart/index.php" );
check_html( "Add one", $client, array( 1 ) );

$client->post( "http://localhost/phphacks/shopcart/add.php", array( 'prod_id' =>
    2 ) );
$client->get( "http://localhost/phphacks/shopcart/index.php" );
check_html( "Add two", $client, array( 1, 2 ) );

$client->post( "http://localhost/phphacks/shopcart/add.php", array( 'prod_id' =>
    3 ) );
$client->get( "http://localhost/phphacks/shopcart/index.php" );
check_html( "Add three", $client, array( 1, 2, 3 ) );

$client->get( "http://localhost/phphacks/shopcart/checkout.php" );
check_html( "Checkout", $client, array( 1, 2, 3 ) );

$client->post( "http://localhost/phphacks/shopcart/delete.php", array( 'ids[]' =>
    2 ) );
$client->get( "http://localhost/phphacks/shopcart/checkout.php" );
check_html( "Remove two", $client, array( 1, 3 ) );
?>
```

The code starts by creating a new HTTP_Client PEAR object. From there it does a series of GET and POST requests that simulate a user's transaction with the system as if there were a browser, but there is no browser. The check_html function is used to check the return page to see the contents of the current shopping cart. The contents of the cart are encoded in a special HTML comment that is embedded in both the *index.php* page and the *checkout.php* page. This comment has a comma-separated list of the IDs of the items in the cart. The robot expects that when it POSTs the ID of a product to the *add.php* page, it will see that ID when it comes back to the *index.php* page, and so on. If the robot doesn't see the cart items it expects, it will signal an error in the test.

Running the Hack

This hack starts with installing and running the shopping cart application [Hack #66]. With the shopping cart installed, you can test it automatically with this robot. Run the robot with the command-line PHP interpreter:

```
% php robot.php
Add one: passed
Add two: passed
Add three: passed
Checkout: passed
Remove two: passed
```

This shows that each step the robot took returned responses that matched what the robot was looking for. It's also worth noting that the pages of the shopping cart are designed to be robot tested; each page has a comment embedded in it that is invisible to the end user, but is picked up by the robot. The robot reads the comment, which contains the current contents of the cart, and compares it to the value it's programmed to expect.

Hacking the Hack

Robots can also be used as unit tests [Hack #79]. Start by installing the PHPUnit2 test framework, available from PEAR [Hack #2]. Then use the code in Example 8-11 for the unit test.

Example 8-11. A PHPUnit version of the robot code

```
<?php
require_once 'HTTP/Client.php';
require_once 'PHPUnit2/Framework/TestCase.php';

class RobotUnit extends PHPUnit2_Framework_TestCase
{
  var $client = null;

  private function check_html( $testname, $values )
  {
    $resp = $this->client->currentResponse( );
```

Example 8-11. A PHPUnit version of the robot code (continued)

```
$body = $resp['body'];

preg_match( "/\<\!\-\- CART \: (.*?) \-\-\>/", $body, $found );

return ( $found[1] == join(",", $values ) );
}

function test1( )
{
  $this->client = new HTTP_Client( );
  $this->client->get( "http://localhost/phphacks/shopcart/index.php" );

  $this->client->post( "http://localhost/phphacks/shopcart/add.php",
      array( 'prod_id' => 1 ) );
  $this->client->get( "http://localhost/phphacks/shopcart/index.php" );
  $this->assertTrue( $this->check_html( "Add one", array( 1 ) ) );
}

function test2( )
{
  $this->client = new HTTP_Client( );
  $this->client->get( "http://localhost/phphacks/shopcart/index.php" );

  $this->client->post( "http://localhost/phphacks/shopcart/add.php",
      array( 'prod_id' => 1 ) );
  $this->client->get( "http://localhost/phphacks/shopcart/index.php" );
  $this->assertTrue( $this->check_html( "Add one", array( 1 ) ) );

  $this->client->post( "http://localhost/phphacks/shopcart/add.php",
      array( 'prod_id' => 2 ) );
  $this->client->get( "http://localhost/phphacks/shopcart/index.php" );
  $this->assertTrue( $this->check_html( "Add two", array( 1, 2 ) ) );
}

function test3( )
{
  $this->client = new HTTP_Client( );
  $this->client->get( "http://localhost/phphacks/shopcart/index.php" );

  $this->client->post( "http://localhost/phphacks/shopcart/add.php",
      array( 'prod_id' => 1 ) );
  $this->client->get( "http://localhost/phphacks/shopcart/index.php" );
  $this->assertTrue( $this->check_html( "Add one", array( 1 ) ) );

  $this->client->post( "http://localhost/phphacks/shopcart/add.php",
      array( 'prod_id' => 2 ) );
  $this->client->get( "http://localhost/phphacks/shopcart/index.php" );
  $this->assertTrue( $this->check_html( "Add two", array( 1, 2 ) ) );

  $this->client->post( "http://localhost/phphacks/shopcart/add.php",
      array( 'prod_id' => 3 ) );
```

Example 8-11. A PHPUnit version of the robot code (continued)

```
    $this->client->get( "http://localhost/phphacks/shopcart/index.php" );
    $this->assertTrue( $this->check_html( "Add three", array( 1, 2, 3 ) ) );


    $this->client->get( "http://localhost/phphacks/shopcart/checkout.php" );
    $this->assertTrue( $this->check_html( "Checkout", array( 1, 2, 3 ) ) );


    $this->client->post( "http://localhost/phphacks/shopcart/delete.php",
        array( 'ids[]' => 2 ) );
    $this->client->get( "http://localhost/phphacks/shopcart/checkout.php" );
    $this->assertTrue( $this->check_html( "Remove two", array( 1, 3 ) ) );
  }
}
?>
```

This new version of the code encapsulates the robot tests into methods within a PHPUnit class. The tests are exactly the same as before, with each test running more and more of the tests until the third method runs the entire test. The reason for the repeats is to check each section of the functionality individually. For example, if the first and second tests pass and the third fails, you know it has something to do with the *checkout.php* page, since that page is checked in the third test.

Run the unit test using the phpunit test runner application:

```
% phpunit RobotUnit.php
PHPUnit 2.2.1 by Sebastian Bergmann.

...

Time: 1.5706360340118

OK (3 tests)
```

The report shows that three tests were run, and they all turned out OK. The three tests—named test1, test2, and test3—each run the robot with an increasing number of requests.

This kind of unit test is ideal for testing a complete system in operation (as opposed to a very small portion of an application). When a system is initialized—after the database is loaded and the pages are in place—you could run this unit test to confirm that all of the pages are responding properly before the system is moved into deployment.

See Also

- "Create a Shopping Cart" [Hack #66]

Spider Your Site

#84 Use the HTTP_Client PEAR module to create a spider that walks all of the
pages on your web site.

This hack demonstrates using PHP to write a spider for checking out the
pages on your site. This is ideal for testing purposes and makes it simple to
ensure that all of the PHP and HTML on your site still responds properly
after an update.

The Code

Save the code in Example 8-12 as *spider.php*.

Example 8-12. A simple spider

```php
<?php
require_once 'HTTP/Client.php';
require_once 'HTTP/Request/Listener.php';

$baseurl = "http://localhost/phphacks/spider/test/index.html";
$pages = array();

add_urls( $baseurl );

while( ( $page = next_page() ) != null )
{
  add_urls( $page );
}

function next_page()
{
  global $pages;
  foreach( array_keys( $pages ) as $page )
  {
    if ( $pages[ $page ] == null )
      return $page;
  }
  return null;
}

function add_urls( $page )
{
  global $pages;

  $start = microtime();
  $urls = get_urls( $page );
  $resptime = microtime() - $start;

  print "$page...\n";
```

Example 8-12. A simple spider (continued)

```
$pages[ $page ] = array( 'resptime' => floor( $resptime * 1000 ), 'url' =>
$page );

  foreach( $urls as $url )
  {
    if ( !array_key_exists( $url, $pages ) )
      $pages[ $url ] = null;
  }
}

function get_urls( $page )
{
  $base = preg_replace( "/\/([^\/]*?)$/", "/", $page );

  $client = new HTTP_Client();
  $client->get( $page );
  $resp = $client->currentResponse();
  $body = $resp['body'];

  $out = array();

  preg_match_all( "/(\<a.*?\>)/is", $body, $matches );
  foreach( $matches[0] as $match )
  {
    preg_match( "/href=(.*?)[\s|\>]/i", $match, $href );
    if ( $href != null )
    {
      $href = $href[1];
      $href = preg_replace( "/^\"/", "", $href );
      $href = preg_replace( "/\"$/", "", $href );
      if ( preg_match( "/^mailto:/", $href ) )
      {
      }
      elseif ( preg_match( "/^http:\/\//", $href ) )
      {
        if ( preg_match( '/^$base/', $href ) )
          $out []= $href;
      }
      else
      {
        $out []= $base.$href;
      }
    }
  }

  return $out;
}

ob_start();
?>
<html>
```

Example 8-12. A simple spider (continued)

```
<head>
<title>Spider report</title>
</head>
<body>
<table width="600">
<tr>
<th>URL</th>
<th>Response Time (ms)</th>
</tr>
<?php foreach( array_values( $pages ) as $page ) { ?>
<tr>
<td><?php echo( $page['url' ] ); ?></td>
<td><?php echo( $page['resptime' ] ); ?></td>
</tr>
<?php } ?>
</table>
</body>
</html>
<?php
$html = ob_get_clean( );
$fh = fopen( "report.html", "w" );
fwrite( $fh, $html );
fclose( $fh );
?>
```

The spider code starts with a single URL and calls add_url( ) on that URL. The add_url( ) function retrieves the specified page and parses out all of the links. It adds the links it finds to the global $pages array. The script then iterates over the $pages array, calling next_page( ) until no more pages remain. Once all of the pages are spidered, the second half of the script outputs the result of each page fetch on the site.

The rest of this hack's examples are test pages for example's sake. Save the first of these, shown in Example 8-13, as *index.html*.

Example 8-13. A sample starting page

```
<html><body>
<a href="test1.html">Test 1</a><br/>
<a href="test2.html">Test 2</a><br/>
<a href="test3.html">Test 3</a><br/>
</body></html>
```

Save the code in Example 8-14 as *test1.html*.

Example 8-14. A second sample page

```
<html><body>
<a href="http://www.cnn.com">CNN</a>
</body></html>
```

Save the code in Example 8-15 as *test2.html*.

Example 8-15. A third sample page

```
<html><body>
</body></html>
```

Save the code in Example 8-16 as *test3.html*.

Example 8-16. A fourth sample page

```
<html><body>
</body></html>
```

Running the Hack

Save the test files (*index.html*, *test1.html*, *test2.html*, and *test3.html*) in a tests subdirectory on your server. Run the spider using the PHP command-line interpreter:

```
% php spider.php
http://localhost/phphacks/spider/test/index.html...
http://localhost/phphacks/spider/test/test1.html...
http://localhost/phphacks/spider/test/test2.html...
http://localhost/phphacks/spider/test/test3.html...
```

The console output of the spider is each URL that it looks at as it spiders the site. In addition, the spider also creates an HTML report of what it spidered, as shown in Figure 8-6.

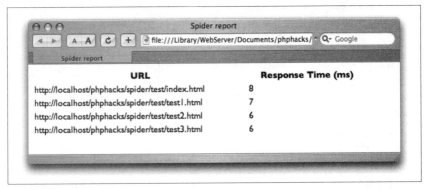

Figure 8-6. The report from the spider

This report shows the time required to fetch the page in milliseconds. That includes the network transit time, and the time the server took to build the page. Because these are static HTML pages, and the web server and spider are both running locally, the fetch times are almost instantaneous; generally, any time under 200 ms is considered a quick response.

This script will *not* find stranded pages, and that's something to watch out for. If users bookmark particular pages that aren't linked to your main site, you can end up with broken pages that this script neither sees nor reports.

See Also

- "Test Your Application with Simulated Users" [Hack #82]
- "Test Your Application with Robots" [Hack #83]

Generate Documentation Automatically

Use PHPDoc comments to document your code, and use the phpDocumentor to build your documentation from code comments.

JavaDoc is the commenting standard for Java, and it is used to generate documentation for Java classes automatically. This comment-to-documentation idea was so popular that now almost every language has a comment markup that can be used to automatically generate documentation.

For PHP, there's PHPDoc; it makes writing programmers' documentation for your classes much easier for everyone involved. phpDocumentor (*http://www.phpdoc.org/*) is an open source tool that parses PHP code, extracts the PHPDoc documentation, and generates HTML from the source, all with a variety of different styles. Figure 8-7 illustrates how PHPDoc takes PHP files as input—in this case, *Author.php*—and creates a set of HTML files as a documentation package.

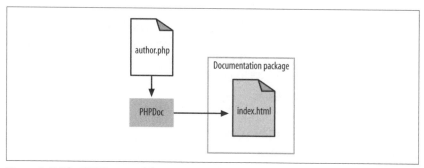

Figure 8-7. The PHPDoc workflow

The Code

Save the code in Example 8-17 as *Author.php*.

Example 8-17. The PHPDoc marked-up Author class

```php
<?php
/**
 * An author class
 */
class Author
{
    /**
     * Gets the name of the author
     */
    function getName( ) { }

    /**
     * Sets the name of the author
     * @param string $name The name of the author
     */
    function setName($name) { }
}
?>
```

Running the Hack

In this case, running the code means running the phpDocumentor command on the PHP files in your project. The *Author.php* file is an example of
a class marked up with PHPDoc comments, which all begin with the distinctive /** syntax and end with */. The text in these special comments then
becomes part of the PHPDoc documentation.

The @param markup element tells the documentation generator that what
follows is the type of parameter, followed by the name of the parameter, followed then by a description of the parameter. For a complete list of these
markup elements, you should reference the phpDocumentor documentation (*http://www.phpdoc.org/*). I'll list a few of the more important ones here:

@author
:   Specifies the author of the code.

@copyright
:   The copyright specification for the code.

@license
:   The license text of the code.

@see

> Cross-links between this class or method and another class or method. The text that follows this tag is the textual identifier of the class or method being referenced.

@param

> Documents a function parameter.

@return

> Documents the return value of the function.

@todo

> Information on what is left to do for this piece of code.

You run the phpDocumentor command this way:

```
phpdoc -t doc -f *.php
```

> The HTML output will be generated in the *doc* directory.

Run the command, and you will see a lot of output as the documentation is generated. Double-click on the *docs/index.html* page in your browser and you will see something that looks like Figure 8-8.

Figure 8-8. The home page of the generated documentation

Using the navigation panel on the lefthand side of the window, click on the Author class link and you will find everything you need to know about the Author class—or at least as much as the programmer commented on—as shown in Figure 8-9.

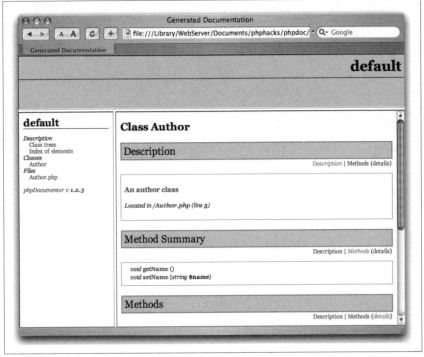

Figure 8-9. The documentation on the Author class

I've used just a few of the basic PHPDoc comment constructs in the *Author.php* class file. Many more PHPDoc documentation keywords allow for cross-linking documentation, hyperlinks, and more.

See Also

- "Generate Your Unit Tests" [Hack #80]

CHAPTER NINE

Alternative UIs
Hacks 86–94

HTML and Dynamic HTML (DHTML) aren't the only user interface technologies that you can take advantage of with PHP. This chapter presents a set of hacks that will get your PHP code producing UIs on a computer desktop—whether it is Linux, Macintosh, Windows, or even PlayStation Portable (PSP). You'll also learn how to communicate with your application using instant messaging.

HACK #86 Create Custom Maps with MapServer

Use MapServer and PHP to build dynamic maps within your web application.

There has been a recent surge in the popularity of digital mapping. Part of this has been fueled by access to open source mapping tools and free geospatial data; it also hasn't hurt to see killer applications like Google Maps and MapQuest come on the scene. These are popular incarnations of some exciting web mapping technology that you too can use. With a few pieces of mapping data, a mapping programming library, and a PHP script, almost anyone can create custom and interactive maps.

Several open source mapping tools are available, from desktop applications to web-enabled mapping services. One of these is the University of Minnesota MapServer (*http://ms.gis.umn.edu/*). With a large user base, active community, and dedicated developers, it is a powerful product for publishing maps over the Web.

MapServer is actively used as the back end to many PHP web page frontends. For example, the Chameleon (*http://maptools.org/*) and Mapbender (*http://mapbender.org/*) products both use PHP extensively. Also available is a powerful implementation of Ajax-based web mapping called ka-Map.

For a tutorial on using ka-Map, see *http://www.xml.com/pub/a/2005/08/10/ka-map.html*.

All of these tools allow PHP programmers to handle maps and mapping data through PHP. MapServer sits on the back end cranking out map images, and PHP controls interaction and brokers requests.

MapServer is commonly used as a CGI application coordinating with a web server. To have ultimate power and flexibility, you can use the MapServer API with one of many programming languages, including PHP, Perl, Python, Ruby, Java, and C#. MapScript provides methods for interacting with mapping data, cartographic styling of map output, and the creation of final map images.

MapServer Concepts

MapServer's core configuration is handled through a text-based runtime configuration file. Referred to as a *map file* (pretty clever, huh?), this file is the core of most MapServer-based applications. The CGI program, or custom MapScript application, reads this configuration file, accesses data, draws a map, and returns a graphic ready for online viewing. The resulting map and graphic can even be run as a standalone command-line program. The examples in this hack use PHP MapScript from the command line. You can take these examples and modify them to suit your particular environment.

The map file has a simple hierarchical object structure, with objects inheriting settings from their parents. This hack uses a very simple map file, intended for use with PHP MapScript. You'll also see how to create a map without having a map file, developing the configuration data totally in memory and rendering the map all within a PHP script.

Getting the PHP MapScript Extension

Before you can start using PHP MapScript, you need to download and set up the MapScript tools. The main PHP MapScript site, *http://maptools.org/php_mapscript/*, has download instructions, as well as an API reference document. There are several other easy ways to get binary distributions of PHP and MapScript preconfigured to work together:

- For Windows, you can use the MapServer for Windows (MS4W) distribution, which is available at *http://maptools.org/ms4w/*. It comes packaged as a base zip file containing all the MapServer basics, as well as PHP MapScript.

- For Linux, you can use the FGS Linux installer at *http://maptools.org/ fgs/*. It includes an installation shell script that you can use to help automate the install. FGS runs as a separate set of libraries, applications, and even a web server, making it easy to get started without having to compile a bunch of external dependencies.

- For other operating systems, you might need to compile your own MapServer from source. When compiling, you can usually set an option to create the PHP MapScript libraries as well.

Hacking Maps with PHP

The following hacks show how to use map files, manipulate those files, and create maps from scratch, all within a simple PHP script.

Step 1: Prepare data. Before you can start creating a map, you will need some basic map information. For these hacks, only one file is required: an image created from global satellite imagery. These images are in a GeoTIFF file format; Figure 9-1 shows an example of the global cloud image data set.

> You can download the sample cloud image dataset from *http://examples.oreilly.com/phphks*.

The TIFF image format might already be familiar to you, but GeoTIFF extends it further, allowing the image to have geographic coordinate information embedded in the image. This makes it possible to use a mapping datafile when you might want to look at a particular geographic area (say, a certain latitude and longitude); GeoTIFFs can quickly make the translation between pixel rows and columns and geographic X and Y coordinates.

> For other data sources, including satellite imagery, country boundary lines, remote web services, etc., see my book, *Web Mapping Illustrated* (O'Reilly), or check out sites such as *http://freegis.org/*.

For these examples, create a folder for your scripts, and then a subfolder called data to store your image file. Unzip the *cloud_image.zip* file into the data folder, and you should see two files: a *.tif* file (the actual image) and a *.tfw* file that stores geographic referencing information.

Step 2: Render a map. A simple MapServer map file and a few bits of PHP code are all you need to create a map. A basic PHP script that loads a map file and renders a map image is shown in Example 9-1.

Example 9-1. A basic MapServer example

```
<?PHP
// ex1_map_basic.php
// Tyler Mitchell, August 2005
// Build a map using a pre-made map file

// Load MapScript extension
if (!extension_loaded("MapScript"))
  dl('php_mapscript.'.PHP_SHLIB_SUFFIX);

// Create a map object.
$oMap = ms_newMapObj("map_points.map");

// Render the map into an image object
$oMapImage = $oMap->draw( );

// Save the map to an image file
$oMapImage->saveImage("worldmap.png");

?>
```

As you can see, it really takes only four lines of PHP code to go through the basic mapping steps:

1. Load the MapScript extension.
2. Open the map file.
3. Render the map image.
4. Save the image to a file.

The result of running the script is a single image, *worldmap.png*. Open the image in your favorite image viewer, and you should see a global image (as already shown in Figure 9-1).

All the map settings are done in the map configuration file. Example 9-2 shows the contents of the map file. It includes a single layer of mapping data, using the global map GeoTIFF image.

This is an extremely simple example that probably won't work outside of the MapScript environment (i.e., using CGI MapServer). For more details on the options and settings in a MapServer configuration file, see the map file reference documentation on the MapServer web site, *http://ms.gis.umn.edu/*.

Example 9-2. A simple map file

```
MAP
  NAME MAP_POINTS
  SIZE 600 300
  EXTENT -180 -90 180 90
  LAYER
    NAME clouds
    TYPE RASTER
    STATUS DEFAULT
    DATA "data/global_clouds.tif"
  END
END
```

Step 3: Modify the map. Of course, the real power of mapping capabilities within a programming language such as PHP is having the ability to control things. Example 9-1 didn't change any settings or add anything to what was already in the map file. The map file is static, but there's a lot more to mapping with PHP than just reading in an existing file and spitting it back out.

For example, you might want to change the geographic extent that the map covers. Instead of using the default EXTENT setting in the map file, you can create your own. All you need to do is set the map object's extent property to use your custom coordinates (via setExtent( )). The extent setting requires two pairs of coordinates: the first pair represents the southwestern corner of the map, and the second pair the northeastern corner. You need to add just one line to your script, as shown in Example 9-3.

Example 9-3. Changing properties on a map

```
<?PHP
// ex3_map_change.php
// Tyler Mitchell, August 2005
// Build a map using a pre-made map file
// and change one property

// Load MapScript extension
if (!extension_loaded("MapScript"))
  dl('php_mapscript.'.PHP_SHLIB_SUFFIX);

// Create a map object
$oMap = ms_newMapObj("ex2_map_basic.map");

// Change the map object's extent property
$oMap->setExtent(-130,20, -70,70);

// Render the map into an image object
$oMapImage = $oMap->draw( );
```

Example 9-3. Changing properties on a map (continued)

```
// Save the map to an image file
$oMapImage->saveImage("worldmap.png");

?>
```

The resulting map image is shown in Figure 9-1 (notice how it is a tighter shot compared to Figure 9-2).

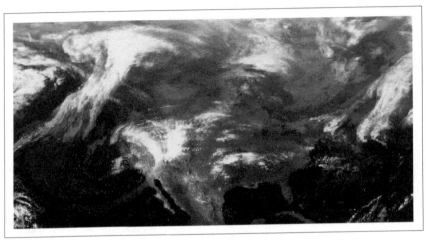

Figure 9-1. Map centered on North American extents

Your script can do much more if you make it interactive for the user. By linking MapScript code into your web applications, you can provide limitless opportunities for zooming in and out on the map, turning layers on and off, adding more data, changing colors, and anything else you can think of. Refer to the PHP MapScript documentation (*http://maptools.org/php_mapscript/index.phtml?page=docs.html*) to get an idea of other methods and properties.

Step 4: Mapping from scratch. You can also create a full PHP MapScript application from scratch without using an existing map file. This can serve two purposes: you can either use the script to create a new map file or use scripts to avoid having external map files to deal with. As you might guess, you will have to create all the objects and set all the properties using PHP code. Your scripts will accordingly be slightly larger than if you simply used a map file, but you get control over all the settings of your maps right in the PHP code.

One common use of PHP MapScript applications is generating dynamic point locations on a map. There are methods for creating what are called *inline features*, where the coordinates of a location (points, lines, or polygonal areas) are entered into the map file. Example 9-4 shows a map file where a single point and an accompanying text label are provided. The map file also includes a symbol object; this tells MapScript how to paint the points on the map. The real work is done in the new layer object at the end.

Example 9-4. Another layer on top of a map

```
MAP
  NAME MAP_POINTS
  SIZE 600 300
  EXTENT -180 -90 180 90

  SYMBOL
    NAME "circle"
    TYPE ELLIPSE
    FILLED TRUE
    POINTS
      1 1
    END
  END

  LAYER
    NAME clouds
    TYPE RASTER
    STATUS DEFAULT
    DATA "data/global_clouds.tif"
  END

  LAYER
    NAME custom_points
    TYPE POINT
    STATUS DEFAULT
    FEATURE # Inline feature definition
      POINTS
        -121 54
      END
      TEXT "My Place"
    END
    CLASS
      COLOR 250 0 0
      OUTLINECOLOR 255 255 255
      SYMBOL "circle"
      SIZE 10
      LABEL
        POSITION AUTO
        COLOR 250 0 0
        OUTLINECOLOR 255 255 255
      END
    END
  END
END
```

The resulting map is shown in Figure 9-2.

Figure 9-2. Map with an inline point and label

 Don't be too distracted by the symbol setting; while it looks obscure, you will likely not need to create additional ones until you start doing more advanced line symbology or area shading.

While handy, a map file is not inherently dynamic; this is where PHP comes in. Example 9-5 is an extensive example showing how to create the same map (from Figure 9-1), but then it overlays on that map a set of graphical "points." This script pulls coordinates from a text file and dynamically adds them to the map when it is rendered. To locate these points, all you need is a simple text file (*points.txt*) containing the longitude/latitude point coordinates and a text label delimited with commas (and with no header line).

 You should save the *points.txt* file in the data subfolder.

Example 9-5. A map example using GeoTIFF

```
<?PHP
// ex5_map_points.php
// Build a map using a single GeoTIFF
// and a text file of coordinates/labels.
// Does not require a mapserver map file to run.
// Tyler Mitchell, August, 2005
```

Example 9-5. A map example using GeoTIFF (continued)

```php
// Load MapScript extension
if (!extension_loaded("MapScript"))
  dl('php_mapscript.'.PHP_SHLIB_SUFFIX);

// Create a map object. Provide empty string if not
// using an existing map file
$oMap = ms_newMapObj("");

// Set size of the output map image
$oMap->setSize(600,300);

// Set the geographic extents of the map.
$oMap->setExtent(-180,-90,180,90);

// Create a map symbol, used as a brush pattern
// for drawing map features (lines, points, etc.)
$nSymbolId = ms_newSymbolObj($oMap, "circle");
$oSymbol = $oMap->getsymbolobjectbyid($nSymbolId);
$oSymbol->set("type", MS_SYMBOL_ELLIPSE);
$oSymbol->set("filled", MS_TRUE);
$aPoints[0] = 1;
$aPoints[1] = 1;
$oSymbol->setpoints($aPoints);

// Create a data layer and associate it with the map.
// This is the raster layer showing some cloud imagery
$oLayerClouds = ms_newLayerObj($oMap);
$oLayerClouds->set( "name", "clouds");
$oLayerClouds->set( "type", MS_LAYER_RASTER);
$oLayerClouds->set( "status", MS_DEFAULT);
$oLayerClouds->set( "data","data/global_clouds.tif");

// Create another layer to hold point locations
$oLayerPoints = ms_newLayerObj($oMap);
$oLayerPoints->set( "name", "custom_points");
$oLayerPoints->set( "type", MS_LAYER_POINT);
$oLayerPoints->set( "status", MS_DEFAULT);

// Open file with coordinates and label text (x,y,label)
$fPointList = file("data/points.txt");

// For each line in the text file
foreach ($fPointList as $sPointItem)
{
   $aPointArray = explode(",",$sPointItem);
   // :TRICKY: Although we are creating points
   // we are required to use a line object (newLineObj)
   // with only one point. I call it a CoordList object
   // for simplicity since we aren't really drawing a line.
   $oCoordList = ms_newLineObj();
   $oPointShape = ms_newShapeObj(MS_SHAPE_POINT);
```

Example 9-5. A map example using GeoTIFF (continued)

```
        $oCoordList->addXY($aPointArray[0],$aPointArray[1]);
        $oPointShape->add($oCoordList);
        $oPointShape->set( "text", chop($aPointArray[2]));
        $oLayerPoints->addFeature($oPointShape);
}

// Create a class object to set feature drawing styles.
$oMapClass = ms_newClassObj($oLayerPoints);

// Create a style object defining how to draw features
$oPointStyle = ms_newStyleObj($oMapClass);
$oPointStyle->color->setRGB(250,0,0);
$oPointStyle->outlinecolor->setRGB(255,255,255);
$oPointStyle->set( "symbolname", "circle");
$oPointStyle->set( "size", "10");

// Create label settings for drawing text labels
$oMapClass->label->set( "position", MS_AUTO);
$oMapClass->label->color->setRGB(250,0,0);
$oMapClass->label->outlinecolor->setRGB(255,255,255);


// Render the map into an image object
$oMapImage = $oMap->draw( );

// Save the map to an image file
$oMapImage->saveImage("worldmap.png");

?>
```

Here's the list of points to add to the map, saved in *points.txt*:

```
    -118.35,34.06,Angie
    -118.40,34.03,Ray
    -111.99,33.52,Alice
    -95.45,29.75,David
    144.85,-37.85,Mark
```

The output of the script is shown in Figure 9-3. To take this example a step further, you could set up the portion of code that draws these points—on any map—as a separate class. Then you could call this class from other PHP scripts—e.g., scripts that take coordinates as user input—and have them drawn on your map.

Learning More

To learn more about MapServer and other open source geospatial technologies, there are many great places to get started. The community actively uses mailing lists and IRC discussion channels and even holds annual conferences.

Figure 9-3. Map showing points and labels taken from a text file

To find other users in your area, ask on a mailing list. The MapServer mailing list tends to be a focal point for many other projects, as they tend to be intertwined, so it might be the best place to look for help.

Web Mapping Illustrated (O'Reilly) covers a wide range of information including MapServer, spatial databases, OGC web services, data conversion, map projections, and much more. Other books on related (open source) subjects include *Mapping Hacks* (O'Reilly), *Beginning MapServer* (Apress), and *Pragmatic GIS* (Pragmatic Bookshelf, not yet released).

—*Tyler Mitchell*

See Also

- "Create Custom Google Maps" **[Hack #95]**

HACK #87 Build GUI Interfaces with GTk

Use GTk to build cross-platform GUIs for your PHP code.

Why limit yourself to web markup, or even tag-based devices? Why not take over the desktop itself with your PHP code? With the GTk toolkit you can do that, and it's really easy. This hack shows how to use GTk to develop a simple regular-expression test application.

The Code

Save the code in Example 9-6 as *retest.php*.

Example 9-6. A GTk regular expression tester

```php
<?php
if( !extension_loaded('gtk')) {
  dl( 'php_gtk.'.PHP_SHLIB_SUFFIX);
}


$start_regex = "/name:\\s*(.*?)\\n/";
$start_text = "name: Jack\nname:Lori\nname:Megan\n";

function delete_event() { return false; }

function shutdown() { gtk::main_quit(); }

function run()
{
  global $rb_regex, $tb_text, $ft;

  $regex = $rb_regex->get_chars(0, -1);
  $text = $tb_text->get_chars(0, -1);

  preg_match_all( $regex, $text, $found );

  $ft->clear();
  $i = 0;
  foreach( $found[1] as $f )
  {
    $ft->insert( $i, array( $f ) );
    $i++;
  }
}

$window = &new GtkWindow();
$window->set_usize( 700, 400 );
$window->set_title( "Regular Expression Tester" );
$window->connect('destroy', 'shutdown');
$window->connect('delete-event', 'delete_event');

$bb = new GtkTable();

$rb = new GtkTable();

$rb_label = new GtkLabel( "Regex:" );
$rb->attach( $rb_label, 0, 1, 0, 1, GTK_SHRINK, GTK_SHRINK, 5, 5 );
$rb_regex = new GtkEntry();
$rb_regex->insert_text( $start_regex, 0 );
$rb->attach( $rb_regex, 1, 2, 0, 1, GTK_FILL, GTK_SHRINK, 5, 5 );
$rb_run = new GtkButton( "Run" );
$rb_run->connect('clicked', 'run');
$rb->attach( $rb_run, 2, 3, 0, 1, GTK_SHRINK, GTK_SHRINK, 5, 5 );

$tb_label = new GtkLabel( "Text:" );
$rb->attach( $tb_label, 0, 1, 1, 2, GTK_SHRINK, GTK_SHRINK, 5, 5 );
```

Example 9-6. A GTk regular expression tester (continued)

```
$tb_text = new GtkText( );
$tb_text->set_editable( true );
$tb_text->insert_text( $start_text, 0 );
$rb->attach( $tb_text, 1, 2, 1, 2, GTK_FILL, GTK_FILL, 5, 5 );

$bb->attach( $rb,0,1,0,1,GTK_SHRINK,GTK_FILL,5,5 );

$ft = new GtkCList( 1 );

$bb->attach( $ft,1,2,0,1 );

$window->add( $bb );

$window->show_all( );

gtk::main( );
?>
```

Most of the code in this hack sets up the GUI interface. That starts with the creation of a new GtkWindow. After that, the controls for the window are created and attached to the original window. The regular expression code is run when the user clicks the Run button; that button is connected to the run( ) function through the connect( ) method on the $rb_run object.

The run( ) function takes the current contents of the $rb_regex variable, as well as the text fields and runs the regular expression. It then clears out the contents of the table and adds all of the regular expression matches into the table using the insert( ) method.

Running the Hack

You run this hack on the command line using a special version of the PHP 4 interpreter that you can download from *http://gtk.php.net/*, which includes support for GTk:

    c:\retest\ > php retest.php

Even though you still run php, you need the GTk version of the interpreter. Otherwise, you're going to get some nasty errors when you try to run *retest.php*.

This launches the window shown in Figure 9-4.

Next, click on the Run button to run the regular expression in the top text box against the text string in the lower, larger text box. The result is shown in Figure 9-5.

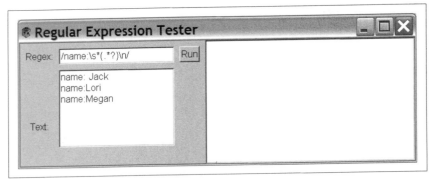

Figure 9-4. The starting point of the interface

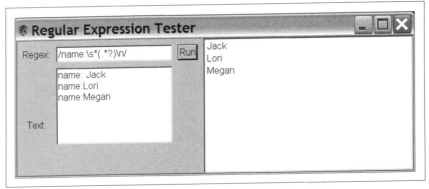

Figure 9-5. After clicking the Run button

This shows that three strings were found: Jack, Lori, and Megan. You can alter the regular expression and the text however you like. This is actually a nifty tool, and it can come in handy when you are just learning the weird world that is regular expressions, perhaps when you're working on your URL rewriting rules [Hack #60].

An in-depth explanation of how GTk functions is beyond the scope of this hack. Suffice it to say that all of the standard Windows controls are there, as well as an option for custom drawing. Even better, the toolkit runs on Windows, Mac, and Linux, giving your PHP script far more portability than other languages provide.

That being said, GTk is not perfect. In general, you have less formatting control than you do when coding directly to the native Windows API with C or C++. But for applications such as this one, or a handy widget that (for example) checks your server status, pixel-perfect positioning is probably not required.

See Also

- "Read XML on the Cheap with Regular Expressions" **[Hack #38]**

HACK #88 Send RSS Feeds to Your IM Application Using Jabber

Use PHP and Jabber to send RSS feeds to your instant messaging application.

Instant messaging is ubiquitous. Some studies have shown that younger Internet users rely more on IM than on email. Unfortunately, because of the proprietary nature of the most popular IM systems and the stateless connections of HTTP, IM hasn't been easily integrated into PHP applications.

The Jabber open source protocol, developed by Jeremie Miller in 1998 (and now called the Extensible Messaging and Presence Protocol [XMPP]), is a native XML streaming protocol and IETF-approved Internet standard for presence and messaging technologies. Important to us, though, is that XMPP allows for PHP scripts to access IM applications. This hack creates a command-line PHP Jabber client that uses the freely available class.jabber. php as a bridge to the XMPP protocol.

Another popular XML protocol called RSS allows a site to syndicate its content as a feed. Newsreaders and web pages poll a feed URL periodically, looking for new content items. The Jabber client we create will poll some existing weather RSS feeds for a new weather alert and send that alert off as an instant message.

The Code

Save the code in Example 9-7 as *client.php*.

Example 9-7. A Jabber client example

```php
<?php

/* CONFIG VARIABLES */

// jabber server you are registed at
$SERVER   = 'yourserver';
//username and password for your special account
$USERNAME = 'yourusername';
$PASSWORD = 'yourpassword';
// jabber id for your personal account
$PERSONAL = 'username@yourserver';
//rss url for the alerts you want
$NOAA     = 'http://www.nws.noaa.gov/alerts/ct.rss';
```

Example 9-7. A Jabber client example (continued)

```
/* END CONFIG */

function send($to, $msg) {
  global $JABBER;
  $JABBER->SendMessage("$to","normal", NULL, array("body" =>
htmlspecialchars($msg)),$payload);
}

//overrides jabber.class.php handler
function Handler_message_normal($message) {
  global $JABBER;
  $from = $JABBER->GetInfoFromMessageFrom($message);
  $body = $JABBER->GetInfoFromMessageBody($message);
  if (substr ($body ,0,3) == SMS) {
      $bodyparts = explode(":", $body);
      $zip = $bodyparts[1];
      weatherize($from, $zip);
  }
}

function Handler_message_chat($message) {
  Handler_message_normal($message);
}
//RSS functions adapted from PHP RSS Reader v1.1 By Richard James Kendall
function startElement($parser, $name, $attrs) {
    global $rss_channel, $currently_writing, $main;
    switch($name) {
    case "RSS":
    case "RDF:RDF":
    case "ITEMS":
        $currently_writing = "";
        break;
    case "CHANNEL":
        $main = "CHANNEL";
        break;
    case "IMAGE":
        $main = "IMAGE";
        $rss_channel["IMAGE"] = array();
        break;
    case "ITEM":
        $main = "ITEMS";
        break;
    default:
        $currently_writing = $name;
        break;
    }
}

function endElement($parser, $name) {
    global $rss_channel, $currently_writing, $item_counter;
    $currently_writing = "";
```

Example 9-7. A Jabber client example (continued)

```
    if ($name == "ITEM") {
        $item_counter++;
    }
}

function characterData($parser, $data) {
    global $rss_channel, $currently_writing, $main, $item_counter;
    if ($currently_writing != "") {
        switch($main) {
        case "CHANNEL":
            if (isset($rss_channel[$currently_writing])) {
                $rss_channel[$currently_writing] .= $data;
            } else {
                $rss_channel[$currently_writing] = $data;
            }
            break;
        case "IMAGE":
            if (isset($rss_channel[$main][$currently_writing])) {
                $rss_channel[$main][$currently_writing] .= $data;
            } else {
                $rss_channel[$main][$currently_writing] = $data;
            }
            break;
        case "ITEMS":
            if (isset($rss_channel[$main][$item_counter][$currently_writing])) {
                $rss_channel[$main][$item_counter][$currently_writing] .= $data;
            } else {
                $rss_channel[$main][$item_counter][$currently_writing] = $data;
            }
            break;
        }
    }
}

function parseXML($url) {
    global $rss_channel, $currently_writing, $main, $item_counter;
    $file = $url;
    $last_item = $_REQUEST['last_item'];
    $rss_channel = array();
    $currently_writing = "";
    $main = "";
    $item_counter = 0;

    $xml_parser = xml_parser_create();
    xml_set_element_handler($xml_parser, "startElement", "endElement");
    xml_set_character_data_handler($xml_parser, "characterData");
    if (!($fp = fopen($file, "r"))) {
        die("could not open XML input");
    }
```

Example 9-7. A Jabber client example (continued)

```
    while ($data = fread($fp, 4096)) {
        if (!xml_parse($xml_parser, $data, feof($fp))) {
            die(sprintf("XML error: %s at line %d",
            xml_error_string(xml_get_error_code($xml_parser)),
            xml_get_current_line_number($xml_parser)));
        }
    }
    xml_parser_free($xml_parser);
}

function NOAA( ) {
    global $rss_channel, $currently_writing, $main, $item_counter;
    global $last_item;
    global $message;
    $message="";
    parseXML($NOAA);
    if (isset($rss_channel["ITEMS"])) {
        if (count($rss_channel["ITEMS"]) > 0) {
            for($i = 0;$i < count($rss_channel["ITEMS"]);$i++) {
                if ($rss_channel["ITEMS"][count($rss_channel["ITEMS"])-
                    1]["TITLE"] == $last_item) { break; } //nothing new
                $message .= $rss_channel["ITEMS"][$i]["TITLE"]."\r\n".$rss_
                    channel["ITEMS"][$i]["LINK"]."\r\n\r\n";
            }
        } else {
            $message = "There are no articles in this feed.";
        }
    }
    $last_item = $rss_channel["ITEMS"][count($rss_channel["ITEMS"])-1]["TITLE"];
    If ($message != '') {
    send($PERSONAL, $message);
    }
}

function weatherize($from, $zip) {
    global $rss_channel, $currently_writing, $main, $item_counter;
    $wunderurl = 'http://www.wunderground.com/cgi-bin/findweather/
getForecast?brand=rss_full&query='.$zip;
    parseXML($wunderurl);
    if (isset($rss_channel["ITEMS"])) {
        if (count($rss_channel["ITEMS"]) > 0) {
            for($i = 0;$i < count($rss_channel["ITEMS"]);$i++) {
                $wunderground .= $rss_channel["ITEMS"][$i]["TITLE"]."\r\n".$rss_
                    channel["ITEMS"][$i]["LINK"]."\r\n".$rss_
                    channel["ITEMS"][$i]["DESCRIPTION"]."\r\n\r\n";
            }
        } else {
            $message = "There are no articles in this feed.";
        }
    }
```

Example 9-7. A Jabber client example (continued)

```
    send($from, $wunderground);
}
//End RSS functions


require("class.jabber.php");
$JABBER = new Jabber;
$JABBER->server        = $SERVER;
$JABBER->port          = "5222";
$JABBER->username      = $USERNAME;
$JABBER->password      = $PASSWORD;
$JABBER->resource      = "client.php";
$JABBER->enable_logging = FALSE;
$JABBER->Connect( )    or die("Couldn't connect!");
$JABBER->SendAuth( )   or die("Couldn't authenticate!");
$JABBER->SubscriptionAcceptRequest($PERSONAL);
while(true) {
    $JABBER->SendPresence(NULL, NULL, "online");
    NOAA( );
    $JABBER->CruiseControl(15 * 60);
}

// may never get here but. . .
$JABBER->Disconnect( );

?>
```

Running the Hack

To complete the hack, you will need at least one new Jabber account, as well as a personal Jabber account to receive the instant message. You have many public servers and Jabber clients to choose from.

> You can find a list of public servers at *http://www.jabber.org/network/* and a list of clients at *http://www.jabber.org/software/clients.shtml*.

Download and install a client if you don't have one already and register an account with one of the Jabber servers. You'll use this account as a web agent (sometimes called a robot, or just bot). If you need a personal Jabber account, register for that as well.

Next, you'll need to download the freely available class.jabber.php, originally written by Carl "Gossip" Zottmann and currently maintained by Nathan "Fritzy" Fritz. The class is available online at *http://cjphp.netflint.net/*. Put the file into the directory in which you'll be putting the rest of this hack's files.

This class greatly simplifies the process of interacting with the XMPP proto-col. Using this class, we are going to create a simple command-line client that will eventually act as a daemonized (that's not *demonized*, for those of you who just got concerned) bridge, giving us access from PHP all the way into an IM client.

Copy the code in Example 9-7 into the file called *client.php*. Modify the con-figuration variables (bolded near the top of the script) to reflect your Jabber accounts and your server information and put the script in the same direc-tory as class.jabber.php. Add the Jabber account you are using to connect with the script to your personal Jabber account contact list (this is essen-tially adding a buddy to your Jabber IM list). Then, from the command line, run the script using the PHP interpreter:

```
php client.php &
```

You should receive an instant message with all the weather alerts currently in effect. Every 15 minutes, the script will check to see if there are any changes. If there are, it will auto-magically send the current alerts again. An example RSS feed is shown in Figure 9-6.

Many thanks go to Richard James Kendall. The RSS parser functions used in the script are adapted from his PHP RSS Reader, which you can find at *http://richardjameskendall.com/*.

Hacking the Hack

I'm sure most people would also be interested in getting their daily weather on demand as well. I was, so I got help from the folks at Weather Under-ground (*http://www.wunderground.com/*). They graciously set up an RSS resource that gets fed a Zip Code and returns the current weather in XML.

The only trick here is that you need to set up the client to be waiting for incoming messages as well. class.jabber.php has a nice feature that lets you define functions to override the default message handlers:

```
function Handler_message_normal($message) {
    global $JABBER;
    $from = $JABBER->GetInfoFromMessageFrom($message);
    $body = $JABBER->GetInfoFromMessageBody($message);
    if (substr ($body ,0,8) == weather:) {
        $bodyparts = explode(":", $body);
        $zip = $bodyparts[1];
        weatherize($from, $zip);
    }
}
```

Figure 9-6. The RSS feed in your instant messenger

```
function Handler_message_chat($message) {
  Handler_message_normal($message);
}
```

We want to respond only to messages requesting weather forecasts here, so we'll use this simple format:

```
weather:zipcode
```

Any incoming message beginning with the word *weather*, followed by a colon will call the function weatherize( ). An example of this is shown in Figure 9-7.

In a similar way, you can add whatever custom functions you want to respond to additional keywords and return custom messages.

—*Matthew Terenzio*

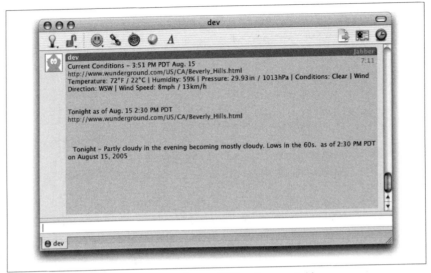

Figure 9-7. Having a conversation with your PHP script over Jabber

See Also

- "IRC Your Web Application" **[Hack #89]**
- "Read RSS Feeds on Your PSP" **[Hack #90]**

IRC Your Web Application

HACK #89

Use Net_SmartIRC to have a conversation with your web application through your web server.

Sometimes a web page is not the most convenient way to talk with an application. A lot of people are using instant messaging and chat systems (like IRC) to converse with each other. So why not allow them to have a conversation with your web application?

Figure 9-8 illustrates the user and a bot having a conversation through an IRC server. The bot is run on the command line as a standalone PHP process. The Net_SmartIRC PEAR module **[Hack #2]** allows your web application to log into an IRC server and respond to commands.

The Code

Save the code in Example 9-8 as *ircbot.php*.

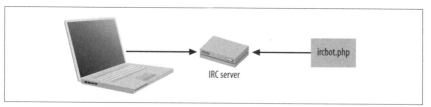

Figure 9-8. The user and the bot talking over IRC

Example 9-8. A simple IRC bot

```php
<?php
include_once('Net/SmartIRC.php');
require_once('DB.php');

$dsn = 'mysql://root:password@localhost/books';
$db =& DB::Connect( $dsn, array() );
if (PEAR::isError($db)) { die($db->getMessage()); }

class dbbot
{
    function listdata(&$irc, &$data)
    {
                global $db;

        $irc->message(SMARTIRC_TYPE_CHANNEL, $data->channel, 'Books: ');

        $res = $db->query( "SELECT name FROM book", array( ) );
        while( $res->fetchInto( $row, DB_FETCHMODE_ASSOC ) )
                {
                $irc->message(SMARTIRC_TYPE_CHANNEL, $data->channel, ' '.
                    $row['name'] );
                }
    }
}

$host = "localhost";
$port = 6667;
$nick = "DBBot";
$chan = "#db";

$bot = &new dbbot( );
$irc = &new Net_SmartIRC( );
$irc->setUseSockets( TRUE );
$irc->registerActionhandler( SMARTIRC_TYPE_CHANNEL, '^list', $bot, 'listdata' );
$irc->connect( $host, $port );
$irc->login( $nick, 'Database bot', 0, $nick );
$irc->join( array( $chan ) );
$irc->listen( );
$irc->disconnect( );
?>
```

Running the Hack

Install the Net_SmartIRC PEAR module **[Hack #2]** and then run the *ircbot.php* script like this:

```
% php ircbot.php
```

Use your IRC client to connect to the IRC server specified in the script. Then join the *#db* channel and type the text "list" into the channel. As you can see in Figure 9-9, the IRC bot responds with a list of records from the *books* database.

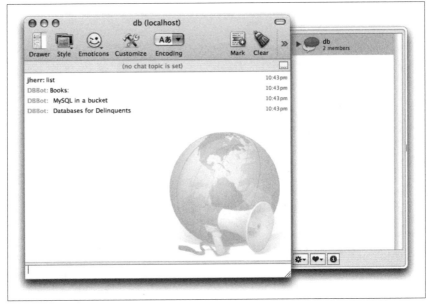

Figure 9-9. Talking with your application through IRC

Your application will undoubtedly reference your own business logic and have a different set of commands and responses. You can add more commands by calling `registerActionHandler( )` with other command handlers.

 We used this mechanism at a prior job to interact with our bug database. IRC used the bug name, which was the same as was used in the bug database. Then, a simple set of commands listed active bugs or the bugs fixed that week, described a bug in detail, marked a bug as fixed, or even downloaded the files associated with the bug.

See Also

- "Send RSS Feeds to Your IM Application Using Jabber" **[Hack #88]**

Read RSS Feeds on Your PSP

Use PHP and the web browser in the PSP's 2.0 system software to read RSS feeds.

The Sony PlayStation Portable (PSP) was a great device even before it got the killer addition of a built-in web browser. But now, with this addition, the game-playing, web-surfing, hip-pocket-size device is simply indispensable.

This hack creates a specially formatted RSS feed data page that displays nicely on a single page of the PSP screen.

The Code

Save the code in Example 9-9 as *index.php*.

Example 9-9. An HTML RSS reader formatted for PSP

```php
<?php
require_once( 'XML/RSS.php' );

function getValue( $node, $name )
{
  $nl = $node->getElementsByTagName( $name );
  return $nl->item(0)->nodeValue;
}

$feeds = array();
$feeds []= array(
  'name' => 'Top Stories',
  'url' => 'http://rss.cnn.com/rss/cnn_topstories.rss'
);
$feeds []= array(
  'name' => 'World',
  'url' => 'http://rss.cnn.com/rss/cnn_world.rss'
);
$feeds []= array(
  'name' => 'U.S.',
  'url' => 'http://rss.cnn.com/rss/cnn_us.rss'
);
$feeds []= array(
  'name' => 'Tech',
  'url' => 'http://rss.cnn.com/rss/cnn_tech.rss'
);

$feed = 0;
if ( isset( $_GET['feed'] ) ) $feed = $_GET['feed'];

ob_start();
$ch = curl_init();
curl_setopt($ch, CURLOPT_URL, $feeds[$feed]['url'] );
curl_setopt($ch, CURLOPT_HEADER, 0);
```

Example 9-9. An HTML RSS reader formatted for PSP (continued)

```php
curl_exec($ch);
curl_close($ch);
$rsstext = ob_get_clean( );

$cols = array( );
$cols []= "";
$cols []= "";
$cols []= "";
$col = 0;

$doc = new DOMDocument( );
$doc->loadXML( $rsstext );
$il = $doc->getElementsByTagName( "item" );
for( $i = 0; $i < $il->length; $i++ )
{
  $item = $il->item( $i );
  $title = getValue( $item, "title" );
  $link = getValue( $item, "link" );
  $description = getValue( $item, "description" );

  $html = "<p class='story'><a href=\"$link\">$title</a></p>";

  $cols[ $col ] .= $html;
  $col++;
  if ( $col >= 3 ) $col = 0;
}
?>
<html>
<head>
<title><?php echo( $feeds[$feed]['name'] ) ?></title>
<style>
body { margin: 0px; padding: 0px; }
.link { font-weight: bold; margin-left: 10px; margin-right: 10px; }
</style>
</head>
<body>
<div style="width:478px;">
<div style="width:478px;border-bottom:1px solid black;margin-bottom: 5px;">
<?php $id = 0; foreach( $feeds as $f ) { ?>
<a class='link' href="index.php?feed=<?php echo($id); ?>">
<?php echo( $f['name'] ); ?></a>
<?php $id++; } ?>
</div>
<table>
<tr>
<td valign="top" width="33%"><?php echo( $cols[0] ); ?></td>
<td valign="top" width="33%"><?php echo( $cols[1] ); ?></td>
<td valign="top" width="33%"><?php echo( $cols[2] ); ?></td>
</tr>
```

Example 9-9. An HTML RSS reader formatted for PSP (continued)

```
</table>
</div>
</body>
</html>
```

The really interesting parts of this script are at the top, where the script finds the currently selected feed and downloads it using CURL. The script then uses the XML DOM system to parse up the RSS XML. Using getElementByTagName( ), it finds all of the item elements in the XML and stores their data into a set of column texts. Each column is specified by one entry in the $cols array.

The second half of the script outputs the list of possible RSS feeds, as well as the columns of article entries for the currently selected RSS feed, in an HTML format that fits nicely on a PSP screen.

Running the Hack

Upload the *index.php* file to the server and try the page first with Firefox. You should see something like Figure 9-10.

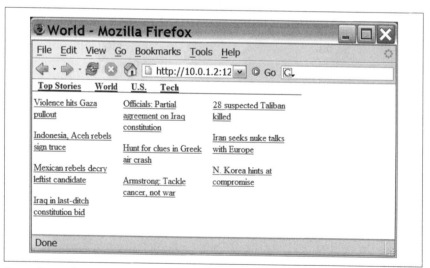

Figure 9-10. The RSS reader in Firefox

OK, that looks pretty good. Let's look at it on the PSP itself. Navigate to the URL by keying it into the address field. Then press the X button to fetch the URL. You should see something like Figure 9-11.

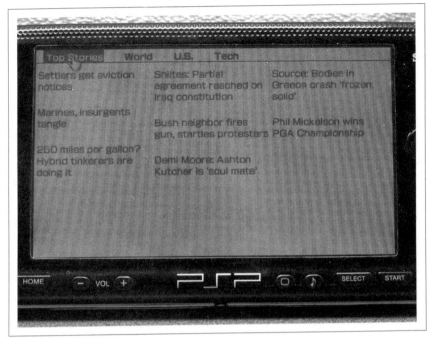

Figure 9-11. The RSS reader on the PSP

You can use the links along the top of the page to select the different categories of CNN news feeds. The links in the middle of the page go to the actual stories from the feed.

See Also

- "Put Wikipedia on Your PSP" [Hack #99]
- "Check Your Network Game with PHP" [Hack #98]

Search Google by Link Graph

Use Google's Web Services API and a Flikr-style link graph to search Google.

Google is a great search engine, but sometimes I find myself looking at the page snippets more than I do the pages themselves. This hack takes the snippets and looks for repeating words around the search term. It's a fascinating way to get more insight into a search phrase.

The Code

Save the code in Example 9-10 as *index.php*.

Example 9-10. A DHTML link graph that uses Google as a data source

```php
<?php
require_once("Services/Google.php");

$ignore = array(
'the','for','and','with','the','new','are','but','its','that','was',
'your', 'yours', 'also', 'all', 'use', 'could', 'would', 'should', 'when',
    'they',
'far', 'one', 'two', 'three', 'you', 'most', 'how', 'these', 'there', 'now',
    'our',
'from', 'only', 'here', 'will' );
$ignorehash = array();
foreach( $ignore as $word ) { $ignorehash[ $word ] = 1; }

$term = "Code Generation";
if( array_key_exists( 'term', $_GET ) )
  $term = $_GET['term'];

$key = "GOOGLE_KEY";

$google = new Services_Google( $key );
$google->queryOptions['limit'] = 50;
$google->search( $term );

$data = array();
foreach($google as $key => $result)
{
  $data []= array(
    'title' => $result->title,
    'snippet' => $result->snippet,
    'URL' => $result->URL
  );
}

function jsencode( $text )
{
  $text = preg_replace( '/\'/', '', $text );
  return $text;
}

function get_words( $text )
{
  $text = preg_replace( '/\<(.*?)\>/', '', $text );
  $text = preg_replace( '/[.]/', '', $text );
  $text = preg_replace( '/,/', '', $text );
  $text = html_entity_decode( $text );
  $text = preg_replace( '/\<(.*?)\>/', '', $text );
  $text = preg_replace( '/[\'|\"|\-|\+|\:|\;|\@|\/|\\\\|\#|\!|\(|\)]/', '',
    $text );
  $text = preg_replace( '/\s+/', ' ', $text );
```

Example 9-10. A DHTML link graph that uses Google as a data source (continued)

```php
  $words = array();
  foreach( split( ' ', $text ) as $word )
  {
    $word = strtolower( $word );
    $word = preg_replace( '/^\s+/', '', $word );
    $word = preg_replace( '/\s+$/', '', $word );
    if( strlen( $word ) > 2 )
      $words []= $word;
  }
  return $words;
}

$found = array();

$id = 0;
foreach( $data as $row )
{
  $row['id'] = $id; $id += 1;

  $words = @get_words( $row['snippet'] );
  foreach( $words as $word )
  {
    if ( !array_key_exists( $word, $found ) )
    {
      $found[$word] = array();
      $found[$word]['word'] = $word;
      $found[$word]['count'] = 0;
      $found[$word]['rows'] = array();
    }
    $found[$word]['count'] += 1;
    $found[$word]['rows'][$row['URL']] = $row;
  }
}

$good = array();

foreach( array_keys( $found ) as $text )
{
  if ( $found[$text]['count'] > 1 && array_key_exists( $text, $ignorehash ) ==
    false )
    $good []= $found[$text];
}

$min = 1000000;
$max = -1000000;

function row_compare( $a, $b ) { return strcmp( $a['word'], $b['word'] ); }

usort( $good, 'row_compare' );
```

Example 9-10. A DHTML link graph that uses Google as a data source (continued)

```
foreach( $good as $row )
{
  if ( $row['count'] < $min ) $min = $row['count'];
  if ( $row['count'] > $max ) $max = $row['count'];
}

$ratio = 10.0 / (float)( $max - $min );
?>
<html>
<head>
<style type="text/css">
.word-link { line-height: 18pt; }
.title { border-bottom: 1px dotted black; margin-top: 5px; }
.snippet { margin-left: 20px; font-size:small; margin-top: 5px; margin-bottom:
5px; }
</style>
<script language="Javascript">
var pages = [
<?php
foreach( $data as $row ) {
?>
{
  url: '<?php echo( $row['URL'] ); ?>',
  snippet: '<?php echo( jsencode( $row['snippet'] ) ); ?>',
  title: '<?php echo( jsencode( $row['title'] ) ); ?>'
},
<?php
}
?>
];

function display( items )
{
  var obj = document.getElementById( 'found' );
  var html = "";
  for( i in items )
  {
    var p = pages[ items[ i ] ];
    html += "<div class=\"title\"><a href=\""+p.url+"\" target=\"_blank\">"+p.
        title+"</a></div>";
    html += "<div class=\"snippet\">"+p.snippet+"</div>";
  }
  obj.innerHTML = html;
}
</script>
</head>
<body>
<table width="600" cellspacing="0" cellpadding="5">
<tr>
<td colspan="2">
<form>
```

Example 9-10. A DHTML link graph that uses Google as a data source (continued)

```
Search term: <input type="text" name="term" value="<?php echo($term); ?>" />
 
<input type="submit" value="Search">
</form>
</td>
</tr>
<tr>
<td width="50%" valign="top">
<?php
foreach( $good as $row )
{
$val = (float)( $row['count'] - $min );
$fontsize = floor( 10.0 + ( $val * $ratio ) );
$row_ids = array();
foreach( $row['rows'] as $r ) { $row_ids []= $r['id']; }
$rows = join(',', $row_ids );
?>
<a class="word-link" href="javascript:display([<?php echo($rows); ?>]);"
style="font-size:<?php echo($fontsize); ?>pt;"><?php echo( $row['word'] ); ?></a>
 
<?php } ?>
</td>
<td width="50%" id="found" valign="top">
</td>
</tr>
</table>
</body>
</html>
```

This script is a combination of PHP and JavaScript. The PHP uses the
Services_Google PEAR module [Hack #2] to download a set of search results. It
then removes the HTML from the results and breaks up the text into words.
It counts the number of hits on each word and stores that number, along
with the related article URLs and descriptions, all via JavaScript arrays on
the page.

After that, it's up to the browser, which displays the found terms on the lefthand side of the display. The JavaScript handles when a user clicks on a
term by setting the inner HTML (innerHTML) on the righthand side of the display to show the found articles.

All of this occurs in the JavaScript display( ) function.

Running the Hack

Edit the file to replace the value of $key with the value that you get when you sign up for Google's Web API access (*http://www.google.com/apis/*). Next, install the Services_Google PEAR module [Hack #2].

The final step is to upload the *index.php* file to the server and browse to it in your browser. The result should look like Figure 9-12.

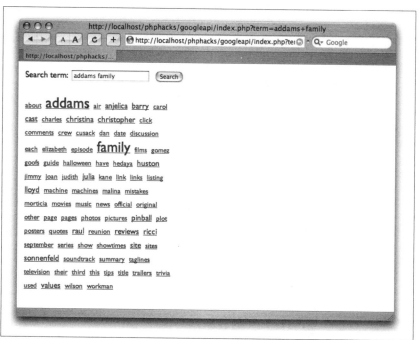

Figure 9-12. Searching for Addams Family

The lefthand column is showing me all of the words that show up several times in the snippet associated with each search result. As you can see, the two most popular are *Addams* and *Family*, which makes perfect sense. But there are some interesting ones as well, such as the names of the other characters in the show, as well as *review*, *cast*, and (surprisingly) *goofs*.

Clicking on any one of these items will list the pages that had that word in the snippet, as shown in Figure 9-13.

I wrote this little page for this book as a test of the Google Web Services API, but it's turned out to be much cooler than that. The link-graph-style visualization [Hack #24] can take this information to a whole new level.

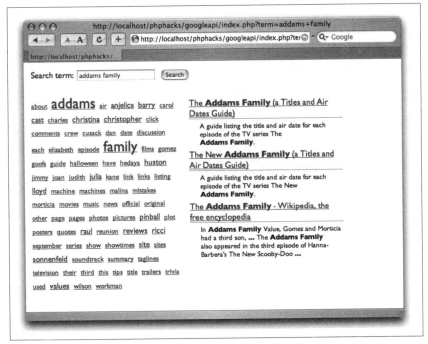

Figure 9-13. Clicking on a snippet term shows the related pages

See Also

- "Create Link Graphs" [Hack #24]

HACK #92   Create a New Interface for Amazon.com

Use Amazon.com's Web Services API to create a new search mechanism for books.

Amazon.com was one of the first major dotcom companies to embrace web services fully. Its API is both extensive and easy to use. For this hack, I'll use just the book search portion of the API to create a search mechanism that shows the results from two searches simultaneously in two columns. Any books that show up in both searches are placed at the top of the page across the two columns. Theoretically, this should show you the highly ranked books that cover both of the topics you are interested in.

The Code

Save the code in Example 9-11 as *index.php*.

Example 9-11. An HTML interface that compares two Amazon book searches

```php
<?php
require_once 'PEAR.php';
require_once 'Services/Amazon.php';

$devtoken = "XXXXXXX";
$userid = "USERID";
$amazon = &new Services_Amazon( $devtoken, $userid );

function list_products( $products )
{
?>
<table width="100%" cellspacing="0" cellpadding="3" border="0">
<?php
foreach( $products as $product ) {
?>
<tr>
<td valign="top" width="10%" valign="middle" align="center">
<a href="<?php echo($product['url']); ?>" target="_new"><img src="<?php
echo($product['imagesmall']); ?>" border="0" /></a>
</td>
<td valign="top" width="90%">
<div class="title"><a href="<?php echo($product['url']); ?>" target="_new"><?php
echo( $product['name'] ); ?></a></div>
<div class="author"><?php echo($product['creator']); ?></div>
<div class="date">Release Date: <?php echo($product['release']); ?></div>
<div class="price">Price: <?php echo($product['price']); ?></div>
</td>
</tr>
<?php } ?>
</table>
<?php
}

function find_books( $keyword  )
{
  global $amazon;

  $out = array();
  $products = $amazon->searchKeyword($keyword, "books", 1);
  if( $products != null )
  {
    foreach($products as $product)
    {
      $creator = 'by ' . implode(', ', $product['authors']);

      $price = '';
      if( $product['listprice'] != $product['ourprice'] )
        $price = '<strike>'.$product['listprice'].'</strike> '.
            $product['ourprice'];
      else
        $price = $product['listprice'];
```

Example 9-11. An HTML interface that compares two Amazon book searches (continued)

```
      if ( strlen( $product['name'] ) > 0 )
        $out[ $product['asin'] ] = array(
          'url' => $product['url'],
          'imagesmall' => $product['imagesmall'],
          'name' => $product['name'],
          'release' => $product['release'],
          'manufacturer' => $product['manufacturer'],
          'asin' => $product['asin'],
          'creator' => $creator,
          'price' => $price
        );
    }
  }
  return $out;
}

$terma = isset( $_GET['terma'] ) ? $_GET['terma'] : 'mysql';
$termb = isset( $_GET['termb'] ) ? $_GET['termb'] : 'php';

$lista = find_books( $terma );
$listb = find_books( $termb );

$overlaps = array( );
$onlya = array( );
$onlyb = array( );

foreach( array_keys( $lista ) as $asin )
{
  if ( array_key_exists( $asin, $listb ) )
    $overlaps[ $asin ] = $lista[$asin];
  else
    $onlya[ $asin ] = $lista[$asin];
}
foreach( array_keys( $listb ) as $asin )
{
  if ( !array_key_exists( $asin, $lista ) )
    $onlyb[ $asin ] = $listb[$asin];
}

?>
<html>
<head>
<title>Amazon Search Compare</title>
<style type="text/css">
th { border-bottom: 1px solid black; background: #eee; margin-bottom: 5px; font-size: small; }
td { font-size: small; }
.title { font-weight: bold; font-size: medium; }
.author { margin-left: 30px; font-style: italic; }
</style>
</head>
```

Example 9-11. An HTML interface that compares two Amazon book searches (continued)

```
<body>
<form>
<div style="width:600px;">

<table width="100%" cellspacing="0" cellpadding="0" border="0">
<tr><th width="50%"><input type="text" name="terma" value="<?php echo( $terma );
?>" /></th>
<th width="50%"><input type="text" name="termb" value="<?php echo( $termb ); ?>"
/><input type="submit" value="Go" /></th></tr>
</table>

<table width="100%" cellspacing="0" cellpadding="0" border="0">
<tr><td><?php list_products( array_values( $overlaps ) ); ?></td></tr>
</table>

<table width="100%" cellspacing="0" cellpadding="0" border="0">
<tr><td valign="top" width="50%"><?php list_products( array_values( $onlya ) );
?></td>
<td valign="top" width="50%"><?php list_products( array_values( $onlyb ) ); ?></
td></tr>
</table>

</div>
</form>
</body>
</html>
```

This hack uses the Services_Amazon PEAR module to search on two separate terms simultaneously. The find_books() function takes a search term and returns all of the books associated with that term. The script creates two of these lists, $lista and $listb, with each of the search results. It then creates three additional lists; those books that appear in both lists are stored in $overlaps, while those that are only in $lista go into $onlya and those only in $listb end up in $onlyb. The rest of the script formats these lists into HTML using standard PHP text templating techniques.

Running the Hack

Edit the code to replace the $devtoken and $userid values with those you get when signing up for Amazon Web Services access (*http://amazon.com/webservices*). Next, install the Services_Amazon PEAR module [Hack #2].

The last step is to upload the *index.php* page to your web site, and navigate to it in your browser. This should give you a page that looks like Figure 9-14.

You can change the terms used in the search by altering the values in the column headings and clicking the Go button.

Figure 9-14. Simultaneously searching for PHP and MySQL

See Also

- "Create a Weather Showdown" [Hack #100]
- "Search Google by Link Graph" [Hack #91]

HACK #93 Send SMS Messages from Your IM Client

Use PHP to send SMS messages to a cell phone from Jabber messages from
your instant messenger client.

One of the most useful features of instant messaging is the availability of
user presence (knowing whether a user is online). Of course, if a user is
unavailable and you really want to get a message to him, it would probably
be really cool if you could send the message to his mobile phone.

While many of the latest mobile phones are beginning to support instant messaging, nearly all of them support SMS text messaging. It would be great to send an instant message to a user's cell phone, and this hack shows how to do just that, by using an email-to-SMS gateway (something almost all major phone providers already have in place).

The Code

Save the code in Example 9-12 as *smsclient.php*.

Example 9-12. An SMS client in PHP

```php
<?php

/* CONFIG VARIABLES */

// jabber server you are registed at
// jabber server you are registed at
$SERVER   = 'yourserver';
//username and password for your special account
$USERNAME = 'yourusername';
$PASSWORD = 'yourpassword';
// jabber id for your personal account
$PERSONAL = 'username@yourserver';
//these values may change
global $cingular;
global $verizon;
global $nextel;
global $tmobile;
global $ATT;
$cingular = '@cingularME.com';
$verizon  = '@vtext.com';
$nextel   = '@messaging.nextel.com';
$tmobile  = '@tmomail.com';
$ATT      = '@mmode.com';
//store any numbers and their carriers here
global $cell;
//put any ten digit number and the carrier corresponding
// to the globals above as name-value pairs here
//e.g "2125551234" => "cingular"
$cell = array(
            "10digitnumber" => "carrier"
            );
/* END CONFIG */

function send($to, $msg) {
  global $JABBER;
  $JABBER->SendMessage("$to","normal", NULL, array("body" =>
htmlspecialchars($msg)),$payload);
}
```

Example 9-12. An SMS client in PHP (continued)

```php
//overrides jabber.class.php handler
function Handler_message_normal($message) {
  global $JABBER;
  $body = $JABBER->GetInfoFromMessageBody($message);
  if (substr ($body ,0,3) == SMS) {
      $bodyparts = explode(":", $body);
      $tokenparts = $bodyparts[1];
      $tokens = explode(" ", $tokenparts, 3);
      $num = $tokens[0];
      $sub = $tokens[1];
      $bod = $tokens[2];
      sms($num, $sub, $bod);
  }
}

function sms($number, $subject, $body) {
    global $cingular;
    global $verizon;
    global $nextel;
    global $tmobile;
    global $ATT;
    global $cell;
    switch($cell[$number]) {
    case "cingular":
        $suffix = $cingular;
        break;
    case "verizon":
        $suffix = $verizon;
        break;
    case "nextel":
        $suffix = $nextel;
        break;
    case "tmobile":
        $suffix = $tmobile;
        break;
    case "ATT":
        $suffix = $ATT;
        break;
    }
    $address = $number.$suffix;
    mail($address, $subject, $body);
    echo $address.$subject.$body;
}

function Handler_message_chat($message) {
  Handler_message_normal($message);
}
```

Example 9-12. An SMS client in PHP (continued)

```
require("class.jabber.php");
$JABBER = new Jabber;
$JABBER->server        = $SERVER;
$JABBER->port          = "5222";
$JABBER->username      = $USERNAME;
$JABBER->password      = $PASSWORD;
$JABBER->resource      = "smsclient.php";
$JABBER->enable_logging = FALSE;
$JABBER->Connect()      or die("Couldn't connect!");
$JABBER->SendAuth()     or die("Couldn't authenticate!");
$JABBER->SubscriptionAcceptRequest($PERSONAL);
while(true) {
    $JABBER->SendPresence(NULL, NULL, "online");
    $JABBER->CruiseControl(15 * 60);
}

// may never get here but. . .
$JABBER->Disconnect();

?>
```

Running the Hack

First, you'll need to have a few Jabber accounts set up and have class.
jabber.php downloaded [Hack #88] and placed inside your hack directory.

Next, edit the configuration variables at the top of the script, which contain
the values of the formats of the email-to-SMS gateways to the major wire-
less providers; these variables are bolded in the code listing. Save the script
as *smsclient.php* and put it in a directory with class.jabber.php.

> The values defined for each cell phone network work at the
> time of this writing, but keep in mind that mergers and other
> changes to the volatile business landscape of wireless carri-
> ers might cause these values to change. You might have to
> retrieve updated information from your carrier's web site.

It is interesting to note that you need to know the carrier in advance. In light
of recent laws allowing users to keep their cell numbers when switching car-
riers, there is really no way to store this information and be even moderately
accurate. You could optionally choose to blast the message out to all carri-
ers; that's kind of a sloppy solution, but then again, this is a hack!

Add the Jabber account you are using to connect with the script to your personal Jabber account contact list. Run the script from the command line:

```
php smsclient.php &
```

Messages sent to a cell phone will take the following format:

```
SMS:10digitnumberSubject Body
```

Just type in your message, and enjoy!

—Matthew Terenzio

See Also

- "IRC Your Web Application" **[Hack #89]**
- "Send RSS Feeds to Your IM Application Using Jabber" **[Hack #88]**

Generate Flash Movies on the Fly

Use Ming to create dynamic Flash movies from PHP.

Have you ever wanted to make a web graphic have a little more pizzazz or zing? We all have at some point. One way to do this is to use the Macromedia Flash format (also known as the SWF format). But how do you do that with just open source tools? Well, there is a PHP module called Ming that saves the day (ironic, isn't it? Ming saves Flash?). It allows you to generate full-blown Flash files on the fly. This hack will show you how to pull that off with a Flash application that dynamically generates charts.

The Code

Save the code in Example 9-13 as *data.php*.

Example 9-13. Some XML to be rendered by Flash

```php
<?php
header("Expires: Mon, 26 Jul 1997 05:00:00 GMT");     // Date in the past
header("Last-Modified: " . gmdate("D, d M Y H:i:s") . " GMT"); // always modified
header("Cache-Control: no-store, no-cache, must-revalidate");  // HTTP/1.1
header("Cache-Control: post-check=0, pre-check=0", false);
header("Pragma: no-cache");                            // HTTP/1.0
header('Content-type: application/xml');
echo("<?xml version=\"1.0\" ?>\n");
?>
<GRAPH TYPE="BAR">
  <TITLE>Revenues 2005</TITLE>

  <YAXIS>Dollars
    <RANGE MIN="0" MAX="50000" />
  </YAXIS>
```

Example 9-13. Some XML to be rendered by Flash (continued)

```
  <XAXIS>Period
  </XAXIS>

<DATA>

<?php
  $colors = array( "0xFF0000", "0xFFFF00", "0xFF00FF", "0x00FFFF", "0x00FF00" );

  srand((double)microtime( )*1000000);

  for ($i = 1; $i < 7; $i++)
  {
    $clr = $colors[ ($i - 1) % count($colors)  ] ;
    $val = rand(10000,45000);
    echo("<D$i>$val<COLOR C=\"$clr\" /></D$i>\n");
  }
  /*
  <D1>20000<COLOR C="0xFF0000" /></D1>
  <D2>25000<COLOR C="0xFFFF00" /></D2>
  <D3>27000<COLOR C="0xFF00FF" /></D3>
  <D4>42000<COLOR C="0x00FFFF" /></D4>
  <D5>48000<COLOR C="0x00FF00" /></D5>
  */
?>

</DATA>
</GRAPH>
```

graph.php, shown in Example 9-14, is the actual PHP script that does the work (with lots of help from Ming).

Example 9-14. Ming and PHP to the rescue

```
<?
  ming_useswfversion(6);     // Important!


  $m = new SWFMovie( );
  $m->setBackground(0x80, 0x80, 0x80);
  $m->setDimension(320, 240);
  $m->setRate(30.0);


  $s = new SWFShape( );
  $f = $s->addFill(0xff, 0xff, 0xff);
  $s->setRightFill($f);

  $s->movePenTo (-5,  0);
  $s->drawLineTo( 5,  0);
  $s->drawLineTo( 5, -10);
```

Example 9-14. Ming and PHP to the rescue (continued)

```
$s->drawLineTo(-5, -10);
$s->drawLineTo(-5,  0);

$p = new SWFSprite( );
$i = $p->add($s);
$i->setDepth(1);
$p->nextFrame( );


$i = $m->add($p);
$i->setDepth(1);
$i->moveTo(-10, -10);
$i->setName("box");

$m->add(new SWFAction("


var data = [];
var heights = [];
var actual  = [];
var timerID;

// Animate the bars to their final position
function anim ( )
{
  var done = true;
  for (var k = 0; k < data.length; k++)
  {
    var n = 'D' + k;

    if (heights[k] != actual[k])
       done = false;
    else
       continue;

    var diff = (heights[k] - actual[k]) / 5;
    actual[k] += diff;
    _root[n]._height = actual[k];
    if (diff < 0.1)
       actual[k] = heights[k];

  }
  if (done)
  {
    clearInterval(timerID);
    stop( );
  }
};
```

Example 9-14. Ming and PHP to the rescue (continued)

```
// Take the XML data transformed into a JavaScript/ActionScript
// object and display it

function doit(o)
{
  // Take the data and draw
  // Draw the axes
  createEmptyMovieClip ('grp', 1);
  with (grp)
  {
  lineStyle (1, 0xFFFFFF, 100);
  // X - Axis
  moveTo (40, 200);
  lineTo (280, 200);
  // Y - Axis
  moveTo (40, 200);
  lineTo (40, 20);

  // Draw the Main Title
  createTextField('title', 1, 100, 00, 100, 100);
  var fmt = new TextFormat( );
  fmt.color = 0xffffff;
  fmt.font = 'Arial';

  title.text = o['TITLE']['_txt'];
  title.setTextFormat(fmt);

  // Draw the X Axis Title
  createTextField('xtitle', 2, 120, 220, 100, 100);
  var fmt = new TextFormat( );
  fmt.color = 0xffffff;
  fmt.font = 'Arial';
  fmt.size = '10';

  xtitle.text = o['XAXIS']['_txt'];
  xtitle.setTextFormat(fmt);

  // Draw the Y Axis Title
  createTextField('ytitle', 3, 0, 100, 100, 100);
  var fmt = new TextFormat( );
  fmt.color = 0xffffff;
  fmt.font = 'Arial';
  fmt.size = '10';

  ytitle.text = o['YAXIS']['_txt'];
  ytitle.setTextFormat(fmt);

  // Draw the Y Axis Labels
  createTextField('ylabeltop', 5, 20, 16, 20, 20);
  var fmt = new TextFormat( );
  fmt.color = 0xffffff;
```

Example 9-14. Ming and PHP to the rescue (continued)

```
fmt.font = 'Arial';
fmt.size = '6';
fmt.align = 'right';
ylabeltop.text = o['YAXIS']['RANGE']['1'];
ylabeltop.setTextFormat(fmt);

createTextField('ylabelbot', 6, 20, 193, 20, 20);
var fmt = new TextFormat( );
fmt.color = 0xffffff;
fmt.font = 'Arial';
fmt.size = '6';
fmt.align = 'right';
ylabelbot.text = '0';
ylabelbot.setTextFormat(fmt);

};    // End with(grp)



// Draw the Data



// Determine how many data items we have
for (var k = 0; k < 10; k++)
{
  if (typeof(o['DATA']['D'+k]) == 'object')
    data.push(o['DATA']['D'+k]);
}

// Draw the Data
// Go through each data item and position a movie there

var increment = 180 / data.length;
var width = increment / 2;
var max = Number(o['YAXIS']['RANGE']['1']);

for (var k = 0; k < data.length; k++)
{
  // dup the box into a new column
  var n = 'D' + k;
  duplicateMovieClip(box, n, 10+k);

  // move to final position
  _root[n]._x = 40 + ((k + 1) * increment);
  _root[n]._y = 199.5;
  _root[n]._width = width;

  // Set heights initially to zero, and animate later
  _root[n]._height = 0;
```

Example 9-14. Ming and PHP to the rescue (continued)

```
    // Get the data value and transform to viewport
    var n2 = 'D' + (k+1);
    var h = 180 / max * Number(o['DATA'][n2]['_txt']);

    heights.push(h);
    actual.push(0);

    var c = new Color(_root[n]);
    c.setRGB(Number(o['DATA'][n2]['COLOR']['1']));
  }

  // We are done, setup an animation timer to refresh
  // the movie clip sizes every 32 millis until they achieve
  // their final height.

  timerID = setInterval(anim, 32);
}

function convertToJS(nodes, o)
{
  if (arguments.length == 1)
    o = {};

  for (var i = 0; i < nodes.length; i++)
  {

    if (nodes[i].nodeType == 1)
    {
    var tmp = convertToJS(nodes[i].childNodes);

    // Add attributes
    var attribs = nodes[i].attributes;
    for (var j in attribs)
        tmp[i] = attribs[j];

      var name = nodes[i].nodeName;

    o[name] = tmp;

  }
  else
  {
    var v = nodes[i].nodeValue;
    o._txt = v;
  }
  }

  return o;
}
```

Example 9-14. Ming and PHP to the rescue (continued)

```
var xml = new XML();
xml.ignoreWhite = true;  // Otherwise lots of blank nodes created

xml.onLoad = function(success)
{
  if (!success)
  {
    // Do a Javascript alert here through a url
    return;
  }
  var o = convertToJS(this.childNodes[0].childNodes);

  doit(o);
};
xml.load('data.php');

"));
$m->nextFrame();

header('Content-type: application/x-shockwave-flash');
$m->output();

?>
```

The process used here is illustrated in Figure 9-15. The file *graph.php* is
called by the web browser to render. The script then uses the Ming library to
generate a movie with some simple off-screen sprites. As the final action of
the movie, it will call some ActionScript to load an XML file from a URL.
This XML file will be dynamically generated by PHP in *data.php*. Currently,
data.php generates random data for a bar chart. Once the data is loaded and
parsed by the Flash player, the bars are animated to display their final values.

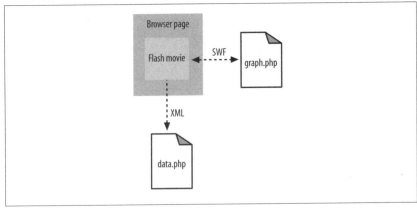

Figure 9-15. The relationship between the player and the PHP scripts

The Ming PHP library is object oriented (OO), which is nice, so it uses classes throughout the process. This makes it easy to see what methods each object supports. The most important class is the SWFMovie class. This is the class that will render the elements into the SWF file with an output( ) call. To see something, though, you need to add display objects to the movie. I created a simple white box sprite that will be placed off-screen and will be used as the prototype for the bars in the chart. Finally, an ActionScript object (SWFAction) is added.

The ActionScript code in the Flash object does the bulk of the work, and demonstrates what customizations you can make in a Flash application.

Technically, you can build a Flash app without an SWFAction, but it would be pretty impractical.

The code defines several functions that will be used later on in the rendering process. Finally, it creates an XML object and does the interesting work, talking over a network to retrieve an XML file (a hack just isn't cool if you aren't talking over a network).

Keep in mind that the XML document has to come from the same web server that the SWF file came from (for security reasons).

Since it can take a while to retrieve and read the XML, this process is done asynchronously. Otherwise, Flash animations would halt, waiting on ActionScript to load in a file from over the Net. When the file is read, the XML object calls the onLoad( ) function to load the data from *data.php*. This starts the chain of events that actually renders the data.

To get the XML object, a simple PHP script was written to generate the XML file needed for the charting. PHP can render XML just as easily as its close relative, HTML. There are a few gotchas, though. Notice the header modifications in Example 9-13. It turns out that without these headers, the Flash XML object will aggressively cache the data (to your chagrin, when that data actually changes). Another thing to note is the echo of the XML prolog. If you don't put this line in—instead of putting out the prolog in the script, along with the rest of the XML—PHP will refuse to run your script.

After the XML file is loaded and parsed, the XML DOM is converted to a hierarchy of ActionScript objects. This makes it much easier for us to get at the data using native ActionScript types. After that, the initial graph is drawn with the doit( ) function. It creates a new movie and adds the axes and labels. Then it iterates through the data sent in from the XML file, and creates the bars for the chart. It does this by duplicating the box sprite and giving the new objects names and depths (a z-order). These objects are then moved (translated) to their proper spot on the graph. Here the squares will be given their new width, height (which is initially zero), and color. Finally, the doit( ) function sets up a timer to call a function called anim( ) every 32 milliseconds. This will cause the bars to grow into their final positions. The anim( ) function uses a simple decaying growth function on the bars to give them a neat, smooth deceleration effect. Once the bars are in their final position, the anim( ) function cancels the timer and the whole process is done.

Not bad for five kilobytes of code, huh?

Running the Hack

To perform this hack, you need to have Ming installed. The official site for Ming is *http://ming.sourceforge.net/*. From there you can get the source to build the library for your PHP platform (it's a simple configuration and install).

 If you are using Windows, you can get prebuilt DLLs in the *http://kromann.info/php.php* PHP distribution.

With Ming installed, all you need to do is pull up your favorite text editor next to your browser window and have at it. You should see something like Figure 9-16.

Hacking the Hack

The hardest challenge with any PHP-Ming-Flash application is just getting something on the screen that resembles what you had in mind. The Flash Player is very resilient to errors, and as a result, it just gracefully drops improper instructions. This is good for the end user, but leaves the programmer (you!) scratching his head wondering when the spinning rectangle is supposed to show up. With this example, you have a base-level Flash application that is a great starting point for more hacks.

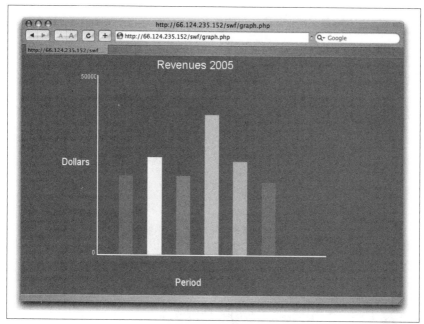

Figure 9-16. The graphing Flash movie

A good additional hack would be to integrate gradient fills into the rendering of the background or the bars. After that, you could do some simple things to give the application a more three-dimensional look. You could add more traditional graph features like grid lines or tick marks, or even add a legend. Flash has tremendous support for other media, such as video and audio formats. You could integrate those as well. Another hack would be to animate every aspect of the graph when it is first displayed. If you really want to hack, you could add support for Flash Version 8 and add some more great things, such as real-time filter effects (blurring, for example). The visual capabilities of Flash are tremendous, and there are many examples of this on the Internet to inspire you.

We're not done yet, though; this covers only the visual side of the hack. I was just displaying random data. With PHP, it should be easy to render the XML file with some real data from a database. Another simple thing to do would be to add a timer to have the graph rerender periodically. You could also pass parameters to the PHP script that generates the graph. If you take that route, you could avoid the XML file altogether and just query for the data to display at render time. If you add UI event handling (buttons, mouse, keyboard), you could even pass different parameters to the XML URL and display data dynamically to the user. There are many, many possibilities.

—Dru Nelson

CHAPTER TEN

Fun Stuff
Hacks 95–100

PHP coding isn't always about writing accounting applications. This chapter contains hacks that cover the fun side of PHP. From creating your own Google maps, to building an MP3 server, to uploading Wikipedia to your PlayStation Portable (PSP), this chapter's all about the frivolous side of PHP.

Create Custom Google Maps

HACK #95 Use the Google Maps API to embed dynamic maps into your application with custom markup, overlays, and interactivity.

In what little spare time I have, I love to hike around my neighborhood in Fremont, California. Thankfully, some of the best hiking in the Bay Area is just a walk away. In particular, the hike up Mission Peak is tremendous, both for its scenic vista and for the great workout.

To illustrate my hikes up Mission Peak, I've always used a wiki page with a bunch of images. But I always wanted something more interactive—and with the advent of Google Maps and its extensible API, I was able to use a combination of PHP and JavaScript to detail my hike up the mountain, using satellite imagery and interactive markers (how's that for technology and nature converging!).

The Code

Start by saving the code in Example 10-1 as *index.php*.

Example 10-1. Setting up latitude and longitude for Google mapping tasks

```
<?php
$images = array(
    array( 'lat' => -121.9033, 'lon' => 37.5029, 'img' => "mp0.jpg" ),
    array( 'lat' => -121.8949, 'lon' => 37.5050, 'img' => "mp1.jpg" ),
    array( 'lat' => -121.8889, 'lon' => 37.5060, 'img' => "mp2.jpg" ),
```

Example 10-1. Setting up latitude and longitude for Google mapping tasks (continued)

```
  array( 'lat' => -121.8855, 'lon' => 37.5076, 'img' => "mp3.jpg" ),
  array( 'lat' => -121.8835, 'lon' => 37.5115, 'img' => "mp4.jpg" ),
  array( 'lat' => -121.8805, 'lon' => 37.5120, 'img' => "mp5.jpg" )
);
?>
<!DOCTYPE html PUBLIC "-//W3C//DTD XHTML 1.0 Strict//EN" "http://www.w3.org/TR/
xhtml1/DTD/xhtml1-strict.dtd">
<html xmlns="http://www.w3.org/1999/xhtml">
<head>
<title>Simple Google Maps Page</title>
<script src="http://maps.google.com/maps?file=api&v=1&key=<mapskey>" type="text/
javascript"></script>
</head>
<body>
<table>
<tr>
<td valign="top">
<div id="map" style="width: 300px; height: 300px"></div>
</td>
<td valign="top">
<img src="mp0.jpg" id="mpimg">
</td>
</tr>
</table>
<script type="text/javascript">
var mp_images = [
<?php $first = true; foreach( $images as $img ) { ?>
<?php if ( $first == false ) { echo( ',' ); } ?>
  { lat: <?php echo( $img['lat'] ) ?>,
    lon: <?php echo( $img['lon'] ) ?>,
    img: "<?php echo( $img['img'] ) ?>" },
<?php $first = false; } ?>
];
var map = new GMap(document.getElementById("map"));
map.addControl(new GSmallMapControl());
map.centerAndZoom(new GPoint(-121.8858, 37.5088), 4);
map.setMapType( G_SATELLITE_TYPE );

var icon = new GIcon();
icon.shadow = "http://www.google.com/mapfiles/shadow50.png";
icon.iconSize = new GSize(20, 34);
icon.shadowSize = new GSize(37, 34);
icon.iconAnchor = new GPoint(9, 34);
icon.infoWindowAnchor = new GPoint(9, 2);
icon.infoShadowAnchor = new GPoint(18, 25);
icon.image = "http://www.google.com/mapfiles/marker.png";

var markers = {};
for( i in mp_images )
{
```

Example 10-1. Setting up latitude and longitude for Google mapping tasks (continued)

```
  markers[i] = new GMarker( new GPoint( mp_images[i].lat, mp_images[i].lon ),
icon );
  GEvent.addListener(markers[i], "click", function( ) {
    for( m in markers ) {
      if ( markers[m] == this ) {
        document.getElementById( "mpimg" ).src = mp_images[m].img;
      }
    }
  } );
  map.addOverlay(markers[i]);
}
</script>
</body>
</html>
```

Running the Hack

Before you run this hack, you need to get yourself a Google Maps API key. Simply visit the Google Maps site at *http://google.com/apis/maps*. You should see something like Figure 10-1.

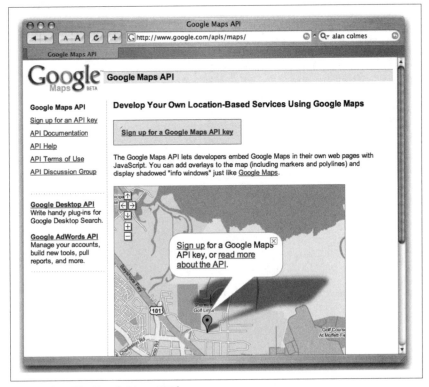

Figure 10-1. The Google Maps API home page

From this site, click on the "Sign up for a Google Maps API key" link. That link takes you to the licensing page, where you can confirm that you've read Google's license agreement. You also need to specify your site's URL, which is of course where you'll display maps. This page is shown in Figure 10-2.

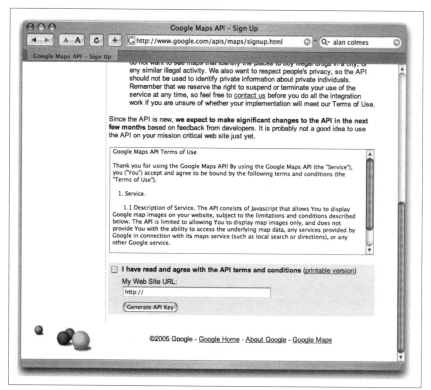

Figure 10-2. Specifying the URL of the page that will host the map

You'll have to be directory-specific as well. If the URL of the maps page will be *http://www.mysite.com/maps/mymap.php*, you should enter *http://www.mysite.com/maps/*.

When you click Generate API Key, you might be asked for a login. If you don't already have a Google login, you will need to create one. Once you have created an account, you will be taken to the page where you can find your maps key. This page is shown in Figure 10-3.

I've blurred out the key here (hey, get your own!). The top box is the API key that you will need to place in the hack code where the <mapskey> placeholder is shown in Example 10-1 (it's highlighted in the code).

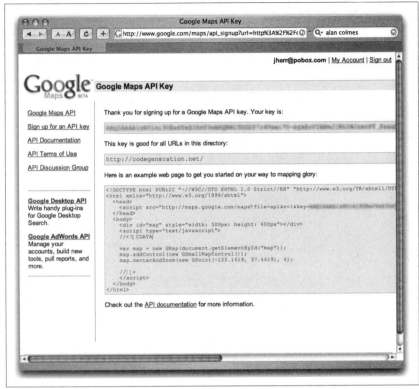

Figure 10-3. The API key and the code fragment for the specified URL

Google also provides some sample code on the bottom of the API key page to help get you started. Isn't Google nice?

Once you have modified the hack code to add your Google key, upload the code and images to the server. Then surf to your PHP page in your web browser (mine is shown in Figure 10-4).

The page shows the map on the lefthand side, and the image from the base of the mountain. When you click on one of the markers on the left, the image on the right changes to the image associated with the selected marker. In Figure 10-5, I've clicked on a marker about halfway up the mountain.

This example shows just how easy it is to create a highly interactive map in your PHP application and to add custom interactivity to that map. I've seen dating-site maps based on this technology, and even a site that graphically overlays the bomb blast radius of various sizes of nuclear devices on any map location! Google, maps [Hack #86], and PHP are everywhere!

Figure 10-4. The home page of the Mission Peak map

Figure 10-5. After clicking on one of the markers

See Also

- "Create Custom Maps with MapServer" [Hack #86]
- "Find Out Where Your Guests Are Coming From" [Hack #63]

Create Dynamic Playlists

#96   Use the XML Simple Playlist Format (XSPF) to create playlists from PHP.

Creating an MP3-playing application for you and your friends is easy with PHP. A new standard for playlists called XSPF (*http://www.xspf.org/*) is available and can be used by a Flash MP3 player movie called Music Player (*http://musicplayer.sf.net*). And, of course, PHP will work with all of this.

Figure 10-6 illustrates how the Flash movie requests the XSPF playlist XML from the *playlist.php* script.

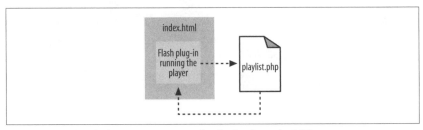

Figure 10-6. The Flash movie requesting the playlist from the PHP script

The Code

Save the code in Example 10-2 as *index.html*.

Example 10-2. Beginning the process of setting up an MP3 player

```
<html>
<body>
<object classid="clsid:d27cdb6e-ae6d-11cf-96b8-444553540000"
  codebase="http://fpdownload.macromedia.com/pub/shockwave/cabs/flash/swflash.
cab#version=7,0,0,0"
  width="400" height="153" id="xspf_player" align="middle">
<param name="allowScriptAccess" value="sameDomain" />
<param name="movie" value="http://localhost/xspf/xspf_player.
swf?autoload=true&playlist_url=http://localhost/xspf/playlist.php" />
<param name="quality" value="high" />
<param name="bgcolor" value="#e6e6e6" />
<embed src="http://localhost/xspf/xspf_player.swf?autoload=true&playlist_
url=http://localhost/xspf/playlist.php"
  quality="high" bgcolor="#e6e6e6" width="400" height="153"
  name="xspf_player" align="middle" allowScriptAccess="sameDomain"
  type="application/x-shockwave-flash"
  pluginspage="http://www.macromedia.com/go/getflashplayer" />
</object>
</body>
</html>
```

Now save the code in Example 10-3 as *playlist.php*.

Example 10-3. A little more PHP for creating an XML playlist

```
<? echo( "<?xml version=\"1.0\" encoding=\"UTF-8\" ?>" ) ?>
<playlist version="1" xmlns="http://xspf.org/ns/0/">
<title>My Radio</title>
<trackList>
<?
$dir = opendir( "." );
while ($file = readdir($dir)) {
if ( preg_match( "/[.]mp3$/i", $file ) ) {
?>
<track>
<location>http://localhost/xspf/<? print($file) ?></location>
<annotation><? print( $file ) ?></annotation>
</track>
<? } } ?>
</trackList>
</playlist>
```

Running the Hack

Upload the PHP and HTML from the preceding code, upload the XSPF Flash movie from the Music Player site (*http://musicplayer.sf.net/*) into the same directory, and upload any MP3 files you want into the same directory. Then navigate to that page with your web browser.

> The directory used in this example is *xspf*. If you change the name of the directory, you will need to change the references in the *index.html* file.

You should see something similar to Figure 10-7.

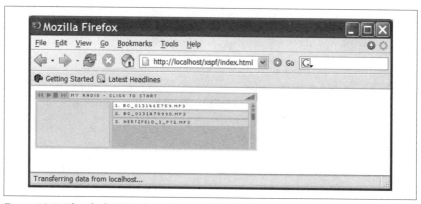

Figure 10-7. The Flash MP3 player showing the playlist

The files you see in the player will be the MP3 files in the same directory as the PHP script. The script looks through the directory, finds the MP3 files, and adds them to the XSPF playlist file.

This can be a very handy script if you are podcasting and you want a page that has a Flash player with all of your blogs. As an example, Figure 10-8 shows the player being used on artist Joshua Armstrong's site (*http://joshuaarmstrong.net/*).

Figure 10-8. Flash player in use on Joshua Armstrong's site

The player is integrated into the home page in the lower-righthand corner over a background image. That presents an all-in-one package: the artist's image, a place to buy the album, and the music from the album, all on the home page.

See Also

- "Create a Media Upload/Download Center" **[Hack #97]**

HACK
#97
Create a Media Upload/Download Center

Allow users to upload and download media files from your application.

Sometimes the customers of your site will want to trade more than just text. They will want to trade media files, images, and who knows what else. The legality of such things aside, this hack will walk you through building a simple media upload/download center for your site.

Figure 10-9 shows the page flow of the upload/download center. The user starts at *index.php*, where he uploads a file through *upload.php*. The *upload.php* script forwards him to the *dir.php* page, which then shows the files that are available as downloads. Clicking on any of the files will download them through the *download.php* script.

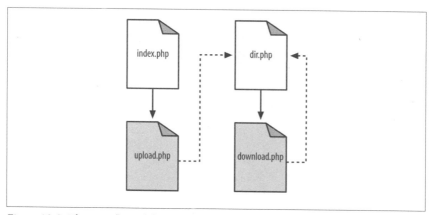

Figure 10-9. The page flow of the media upload/download center

The Code

Save the code in Example 10-4 as *media.sql*. It's a simple little SQL statement to create a new table.

Example 10-4. Creating the media table for file uploads

```
DROP TABLE IF EXISTS media;
CREATE TABLE media (
        id MEDIUMINT NOT NULL AUTO_INCREMENT,
        filename TEXT,
        mime_type TEXT,
        PRIMARY KEY( id )
);
```

Save the HTML in Example 10-5 as *index.php*.

Example 10-5. A form allowing for an upload

```
<html>
<body>
        <form enctype="multipart/form-data" action="upload.php" method="post">
                <input type="hidden" name="MAX_FILE_SIZE" value="2000000" />
                <input type="file" name="file" />
                <input type="submit" value="Upload" />
        </form>
</body>
</html>
```

The PHP in Example 10-6 handles downloads; save it as *download.php*.

Example 10-6. Connecting to a database and allowing for file downloading

```
<?php
require_once( "db.php" );
$db =& DB::connect("mysql://root@localhost/media", array( ));
if (PEAR::isError($db)) { die($db->getMessage( )); }

$res = $db->query( "SELECT filename, mime_type FROM media WHERE id = ?", array(
$_GET['id'] ) );
$res->fetchInto($row);
$filename = $row[0];
$type = $row[1];

$datafile = "media/".$_GET['id'].".dat";

header( "Content-type: $type" );
header( "Content-Length: ".@filesize( $datafile ) );
header( 'Content-Disposition: attachment; filename="'.$filename.'"' );

readfile( $datafile);
?>
```

The PHP in Example 10-7, *dir.php*, handles listing files.

Example 10-7. Listing available files by name

```
<?php
require_once( "db.php" );
$db =& DB::connect("mysql://root@localhost/media", array( ));
if (PEAR::isError($db)) { die($db->getMessage( )); }
?>
<html>
<body>
<?php
$res = $db->query( "SELECT * FROM media" );
while ($res->fetchInto($row)) { ?>
<a href="download.php?id=<?php echo( $row[0] ); ?>">
```

Example 10-7. Listing available files by name (continued)

```
<?php echo( $row[1] ); ?></a><br/>
<?php } ?>
</body>
</html>
```

The code in Example 10-8 is the most complicated of the scripts; it handles file uploads. Save this code as *upload.php*.

Example 10-8. Loading a file into the database

```
<?php
require_once( "db.php" );
$db =& DB::connect("mysql://root@localhost/media", array());
if (PEAR::isError($db)) { die($db->getMessage()); }

if ( $_FILES['file']['tmp_name'] )
{
        $sth = $db->prepare( "INSERT INTO media VALUES ( 0, ?, ? )" );
        $db->execute( $sth, array( $_FILES['file']['name'], $_
FILES['file']['type'] ) );

        $res = $db->query( "SELECT last_insert_id()" );
        $res->fetchInto( $row );

        $newid = $row[0];

        move_uploaded_file( $_FILES['file']['tmp_name'], "media/".$newid.".dat"
);
}

header( "location: dir.php" );
?>
```

Running the Hack

Upload all of these files to the server. Use the `mysql` command to load the schema into a database named *media*:

```
% mysql --user=myusername --password=mypassword media < media.sql
```

After the database is up, you need to create a directory called *media* inside the directory where you added the scripts, used to store the uploaded files. Once that directory is created, surf on over to your *index.php* page. You should see something like Figure 10-10.

Click on the Browse button and pick a file somewhere. A small JPEG file should do the trick. I found a picture of a fish on Google's image search and used that image for testing.

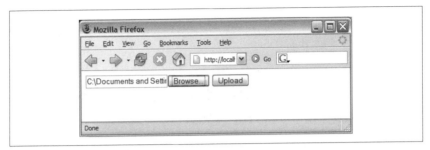

Figure 10-10. The upload form

Click on the Upload button, and you should get a page that looks like Figure 10-11.

Figure 10-11. The directory of uploaded media

This listing lets you know that the file has been uploaded properly and that the database has been updated with the new file. The file has also been copied to the media directory and given the name `<id>.dat` where `<id>` is the record ID in the database.

Next, click on the filename. You should get a pop-up dialog asking you what you want to do with the downloaded file (as shown in Figure 10-12).

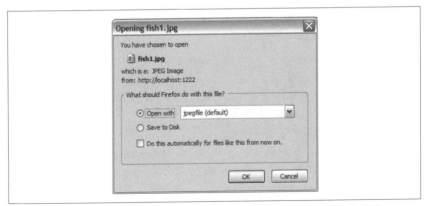

Figure 10-12. The download dialog that comes up when the media link is clicked

I used the "Open with" command to show the file in a JPEG viewer just so that I could make sure the file was uploaded and maintained properly.

The result is Figure 10-13. As you can see, the image came through OK; so start loading some MP3s [Hack #96]!

Figure 10-13. The JPEG viewer on Windows that displays the downloaded file

See Also

- "Create Dynamic Playlists" [Hack #96]

Check Your Network Game with PHP

#98 Use the Net_GameServerQuery PEAR module to check up on your network game, all using PHP.

There is a PEAR module [Hack #2] for almost anything, it seems! Proving that to be true, this hack uses the Net_GameServerQuery module to check up on a *Half Life* server, just to see how many people are playing (and to show off PEAR and yet another cool module).

The Code

Save the code in Example 10-9 as *index.php*.

Example 10-9. Checking the Half Life server as an automated task

```php
<?php
require( 'Net/GameServerQuery.php' );

$protocol = 'halflife';
$ip = '66.159.222.15';

$gsq = new Net_GameServerQuery( );
$gsq->addServer( $protocol, $ip );
```

Example 10-9. Checking the Half Life server as an automated task (continued)

```
$res = $gsq->execute( );
?>
<html>
<head>
<title>Game Server Status</title>
</head>
<style>
body { font-family: arial, verdana, sans-serif; }
th { font-size: xx-small; border-bottom: 1px solid black; }
td { font-size: xx-small; vertical-align: top; }
.num-players { text-align: center; }
.header { font-weight: bold; }
</style>
<body>
<table>
<tr>
<td class="header">Protocol</td>
<td><?php echo($protocol); ?></td>
</tr>
<tr>
<td class="header">IP</td>
<td><?php echo($ip); ?></td>
</tr>
</table>
<table width="100%" cellspacing="0" cellpadding="3">
<tr>
<th width="20%">IP/Port</th>
<th width="20%">Password</th>
<th width="20%">Hostname</th>
<th width="20%">Players</th>
<th width="20%">Mod</th>
</tr>
<?php foreach( $res[0] as $r ) { ?>
<tr>
<td width="20%"><?php echo($r['ip']); ?><br/><?php echo($r['port']); ?></td>
<td width="20%"><?php echo($r['password']); ?></td>
<td width="20%"><?php echo($r['hostname']); ?></td>
<td width="20%" class="num-players">
<?php echo($r['numplayers']); ?> current<br/>
<?php echo($r['maxplayers']); ?> max
</td>
<td width="20%"><?php echo($r['mod']); ?></td>
</tr>
<?php } ?>
</table>
</body>
</html>
```

Running the Hack

First, install the Net_GameServerQuery PEAR module on your PHP installation [Hack #2]. Next, change the $ip and $protocol variables to match your game server's IP address and game type.

> The Net_GameServerQuery module's documentation (*http://pear.php.net/net_gameserverquery*) includes the list of protocols in their package information.

Upload the script to the PHP server and surf to the page using your web browser. You should see something like Figure 10-14.

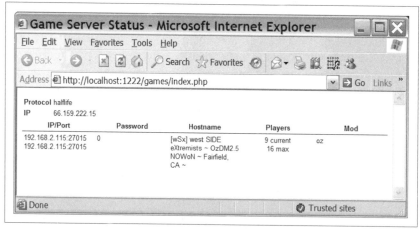

Figure 10-14. The Half Life game server status

You can use data such as this in several ways. You can create a small WML page for your phone to check the games, and you can even build a small page for your PSP. That way, you can know right away when there is a game worth playing! If you're responsible for keeping the server running, you can poll it and restart the server if the game isn't running. That's a lot better than waking up in the middle of the night, isn't it?

See Also

- "Read RSS Feeds on Your PSP" [Hack #90]

Put Wikipedia on Your PSP

#99   Use MySQL and PHP to build a dictionary from Wikipedia that fits in your hip pocket.

Wikipedia (*http://www.wikipedia.org*) is probably the single most informative site on the Internet. It's a user-contributed encyclopedia and dictionary. What's even better is that you can download the entire contents of Wikipedia and use it for your own purposes.

In my case, I wanted the Wikipedia dictionary on my PSP. Being a PHP hacker, of course I had to use PHP and MySQL; I created a set of static pages from Wikipedia and then downloaded those pages to my PSP memory stick. It's not dynamic, but it still impresses my buddies when I can look up *grok* on my PSP.

Figure 10-15 shows the basic flow of the processing in this hack. The Wiktionary contents are loaded into the MySQL database **[Hack #1]**. An elaborate *dict.php* script takes the contents of the database and creates a set of specially formatted HTML pages appropriate to the PSP.

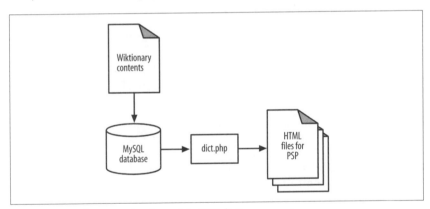

Figure 10-15. The processing flow of the PSP dictionary creator

The Code

Save the code in Example 10-10 as *dict.php*.

Example 10-10. Downloading the current Wikipedia to create static HTML

```php
<?php
require_once( "DB.php" );
require_once( "Text/Wiki.php" );

$g_wiki = new Text_Wiki();
```

Example 10-10. Downloading the current Wikipedia to create static HTML (continued)

```
$g_wiki->enableRule('html');
$g_wiki->enableRule('list');

function wikiToHTML( $text )
{
  global $g_wiki;

  $text = preg_replace( "/\=\=\=\s* Pronunciation.*?\n\=\=\=/is", "\n===", $text
  );
  $text = preg_replace( "/\=\=\=\=\=\s*(.*?)\s*\=\=\=\=\=/", "\n+++++ $1", $text
  );
  $text = preg_replace( "/\=\=\=\=\s*(.*?)\s*\=\=\=\=/", "++++ $1", $text );
  $text = preg_replace( "/\=\=\=\s*(.*?)\s*\=\=\=/", "+++ $1", $text );
  $text = preg_replace( "/\=\=\s*(.*?)\s*\=\=/", "++ $1", $text );
  $text = preg_replace( "/\=\s*(.*?)\s*\=/", "++ $1", $text );
  $text = preg_replace( "/\[\[image:.*?\]\]/i", "", $text );
  $text = preg_replace( "/\[\[it:.*?\]\]/i", "", $text );
  $text = preg_replace( "/\[\[.*?\|(.*?)\]\]/", "$1", $text );
  $text = preg_replace( "/\[\[(.*?)\]\]/", "$1", $text );
  $text = preg_replace( "/\[(.*?)\]/", "$1", $text );
  $text = preg_replace( "/\n\#([^#])/", "\n# $1", $text );
  $text = preg_replace( "/\n\*([^*])/", "\n* $1", $text );
  $text = preg_replace( "/\<\!\-\-.*?\-\-\>/mi", "", $text );
  $text = preg_replace( "/\n\|.*?\|\s*\n/", "", $text );
  $text = preg_replace( "/\n\{\|.*\n/", "", $text );
  $text = preg_replace( "/\n\|\}.*\n/", "", $text );
  $text = preg_replace( "/\n\|\}\n/", "", $text );
  $text = preg_replace( "/\{\{.*?\}\}/", "", $text );
  $text = preg_replace( "/\|\}/", "", $text );
  $text = preg_replace( "/\|.*?\|/", "", $text );
  $text = preg_replace( "/\'\'\'\'\'\'/", "'''\n'''", $text );

  return $g_wiki->transform( $text, 'Xhtml' );
}

function goodWord( $word )
{
  if ( preg_match( "/^[A-Za-z]/", $word ) )
  {
    if ( preg_match( "/[^A-Za-z.-]/", $word ) ) return false;
    if ( preg_match( "/\-$/", $word ) ) return false;
    if ( preg_match( "/\[.]$/", $word ) ) return false;
    if ( preg_match( "/^.-/", $word ) ) return false;
    if ( preg_match( "/^.[.]/", $word ) ) return false;

    $cutword = preg_replace( "/[^A-Za-z]/", "", $word );

    if ( strlen( $cutword ) < 4 ) return false;
    if ( strlen( $cutword ) > 20 ) return false;
```

Example 10-10. Downloading the current Wikipedia to create static HTML (continued)

```
    return true;
  }
  return false;
}

function goodText( $text )
{
  if ( preg_match( "/#REDIRECT/i", $text ) )
    return false;
  return true;
}

$g_words = array( );
$g_wurl = array( );

$dsn = 'mysql://root:password@localhost/wp';
$db =& DB::Connect( $dsn, array( ) );
if (PEAR::isError($db)) { die($db->getMessage( )); }

$blocksize = 100;
$total_html = "";
$block = 0;
$block_id = 0;

function writeBlock( $block, $html )
{
  $fh = fopen( "pages/words/".$block.".html", "w" );
  fwrite( $fh, "<html><head>\n" );
  fwrite( $fh, "<link rel=\"stylesheet\" type=\"text/css\" href=\"../default.css\
    " />\n" );
  fwrite( $fh, "</head><body><div style='width:478px'>\n" );
  fwrite( $fh, $html );
  fwrite( $fh, "</div></body></html>\n" );
  fclose( $fh );
}

$res = $db->query( "SELECT cur_title as word, cur_text as text FROM cur WHERE
cur_namespace=0");
while ( $res->fetchInto( $row, DB_FETCHMODE_ASSOC ) )
{
  $word = $row['word'];
  $text = $row['text'];
  if ( goodWord( $word ) && goodText( $text ) )
  {
    $c1 = strtolower( $word[0] );
    if ( !isset( $g_words[ $c1 ] ) ) $g_words[ $c1 ] = array( );

    $c2 = strtolower( $word[1] );
    if ( !isset( $g_words[ $c1 ][ $c2 ] ) ) $g_words[ $c1 ][ $c2 ] = array( );

    $oword = $word;
    $word = strtolower( $word );
```

Example 10-10. Downloading the current Wikipedia to create static HTML (continued)

```php
    $g_words[ $c1 ][ $c2 ] []= $oword;

    $g_wurl[ $word ] = "../words/".$block_id.".html#".$block;

    print( "$word\n" );

    $total_html .= "<a name=\"".$block."\" />";
    $total_html .= "<div class='word-header'>".$oword."</div>";
    $total_html .= "<table width='100%' cellspacing='0' cellpadding='0'><tr><td>
        ";
    $total_html .= wikiToHTML( $text );
    $total_html .= "</td></tr></table>";

    if ( $block >= $blocksize )
    {
      writeBlock( $block_id, $total_html );
      $block_id++;
      $block = 0;
      $total_html = "";
    }
    else
      $block++;
  }
}
writeBlock( $block_id, $total_html );

ob_start( );
?>
<html><head><title>Index</title>
<link rel="stylesheet" type="text/css" href="default.css" />
</head><body><div style="width:478px;">
<div id="c1-header">
<?php
foreach( array_keys( $g_words ) as $c1 )
{
?>
<a href="lev1/<?php echo( $c1 ); ?>.html"><?php echo( $c1 ); ?></a>
<?php
}
?>
</div></div></body></html>
<?php
$index = ob_get_clean( );
$ih = fopen( "pages/index.html", "w" );
fwrite( $ih, $index );
fclose( $ih );

ob_start( );
foreach( array_keys( $g_words ) as $c1 )
{
?>
<a href="../lev1/<?php echo( $c1 ); ?>.html"><?php echo( $c1 ); ?></a>
```

Example 10-10. Downloading the current Wikipedia to create static HTML (continued)

```php
<?php
}
$c1header = ob_get_clean( );

foreach( array_keys( $g_words ) as $c1 )
{
  ob_start( );
?>
<html><head><title><?php echo( $c1 ); ?></title>
<link rel="stylesheet" type="text/css" href="../default.css" />
</head><body><div style="width:478px;">
<div id="c1-header"><?php echo( $c1header ); ?></div>
<?php foreach( array_keys( $g_words[$c1] ) as $c2 ) { ?>
<a href="../lev2/<?php echo( $c1.$c2 ); ?>.html"><?php echo( $c1.$c2 ); ?></a>
<?php } ?>
</div></body></html>
<?php
  $html = ob_get_clean( );

  $fh = fopen( "pages/lev1/".$c1.".html", "w" );
  fwrite( $fh, $html );
  fclose( $fh );
}

foreach( array_keys( $g_words ) as $c1 )
{

ob_start( );
foreach( array_keys( $g_words[$c1] ) as $c2 )
{
?>
<a href="<?php echo( $c1.$c2 ); ?>.html"><?php echo( $c1.$c2 ); ?></a>
<?php
}
$c2header = ob_get_clean( );

foreach( array_keys( $g_words[$c1] ) as $c2 )
{
  $words = $g_words[ $c1 ][ $c2 ];
  ob_start( );
?>
<html><head><title><?php echo( $c1.$c2 ); ?></title>
<link rel="stylesheet" type="text/css" href="../default.css" />
</head><body><div style="width:478px;">
<div id="c1-header"><?php echo( $c1header ); ?></div>
<div id="c2-header"><?php echo( $c2header ); ?></div>
<?php foreach( $words as $word ) { ?>
<a href="<?php echo( $g_wurl[ strtolower( $word ) ] ); ?>"><?php echo( $word );
?></a>
<?php } ?>
</div></body></html>
<?php
```

Example 10-10. Downloading the current Wikipedia to create static HTML (continued)

```
$html = ob_get_clean( );

$fh = fopen( "pages/lev2/".$c1.$c2.".html", "w" );
fwrite( $fh, $html );
fclose( $fh );
}
}
?>
```

There are four primary sections of this code. The first reads the data from the database. The second section iterates through all of the entries, discarding those it doesn't like and then cleaning up the ones it does like while converting them into HTML.

The HTML for each word entry is created in blocks of 100 words. If the script were to create a file for each word, even though the total size in bytes of the output would be the same, it would exceed the capacity of most memory sticks. So, the script groups words into files of 100 words. The script keeps track of which words are in which file using the g_wurl hash table, which has a URL as the value for each word as the key.

The remaining two sections of the script output the first and second levels of letter pages. The first-level pages have the letters of the alphabet across the top and links to the letter plus a second letter in the row below that. The second-level pages have all of the words that start with a particular two-letter combination. This breakdown into first and second letters was to keep the size of each page manageable.

Running the Hack

This hack requires the Text_Wiki PEAR module **[Hack #2]**. After that, you need to download the most recent English dictionary (Wiktionary) database from Wikipedia (the relevant URLs are *http://download.wikipedia.org/* and *http://download.wikipedia.org/wiktionary/*).

The next step is to load the dictionary into your MySQL database:

```
mysqladmin --user=root --password=password create wp
mysql --user=root --password=password create wp < 20050623_cur_table.sql
```

> The name of the file will change based on when you download the dictionary from Wikipedia.

With your dictionary in place, run the *dict.php* script:

```
% php dict.php
aant
aave
```

```
abta
acas
acats
aclu
acme
acronym
...
zygapophysial
zygapophysis
zygote
zymurgy
zythum
zyzzyva
%
```

Grab some coffee; the script will take a while to finish. The Wikipedia databases are very large, and processing them takes a while. For example, on my G4 PowerBook, it took about an hour to create all of the HTML files.

Next, download the HTML files to your PSP memory stick. Put your PSP into USB mode and then attach it to your computer.

Bring up the PSP browser and surf to *file://common/index.html*. You should see something like Figure 10-16.

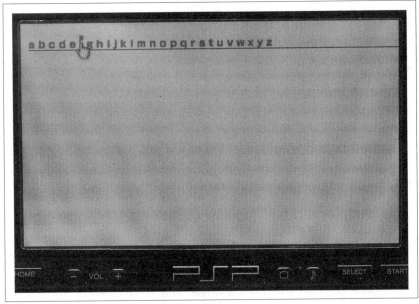

Figure 10-16. The home page of the dictionary

From here, you can select an initial letter and then a second letter (to be more specific and selective). That brings up a page of words that start with the first two letters that you selected. This page is shown in Figure 10-17.

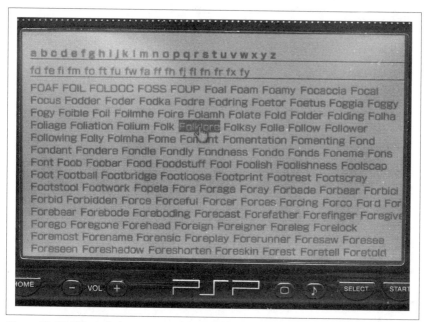

Figure 10-17. The drill-down page after selecting the first and second characters

Now, find a word that interests you and click on it. That will take you to the detail page, which defines the word. This page is shown in Figure 10-18.

Pretty sweet!

As Wikipedia keeps growing, the size of the dictionary will change depending on when you run this process. When I ran this script, the dictionary HTML was around 30 MB in size, which fit easily onto even the smallest memory stick.

See Also

- "Read RSS Feeds on Your PSP" [Hack #90]

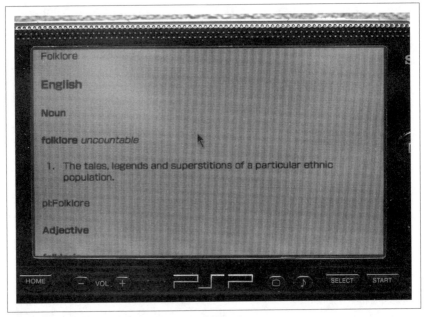

Figure 10-18. The display after selecting "folklore"

HACK 100   Create a Weather Showdown

Use Weather.com's web service to build a weather showdown page that will help you decide where you want to be this week (and what to pack).

The Services_Weather PEAR module [Hack #2] makes it easy to integrate weather forecast information into your web application. This hack uses the information from the Weather.com web service through the Services_Weather PEAR module to find the weekly temperature range in two different cities. It then compares those temperatures against a desired value and tells you which city is closer to your desired climate.

The Code

Save the code in Example 10-11 as *index.php*.

Example 10-11. PHP checking the weather forecast

```php
<?php
require_once( "Services/Weather.php" );

$weather = new Services_Weather();
$wdc = $weather->service( 'Weatherdotcom' );

function get_average( $zip )
{
```

Example 10-11. PHP checking the weather forecast (continued)

```php
  global $wdc;

  $fc = $wdc->getForecast( $zip, 7 );
  $dayavg = 0;
  foreach ( $fc['days'] as $day )
  {
    $high = $day['temperatureHigh'];
    $low = $day['temperatureLow'];
    $dayavg += $high;
    $dayavg += $low;
  }
  return floor(($dayavg/14));
}

$zipa = isset( $_GET['zipa'] ) ? $_GET['zipa'] : '94587';
$zipb = isset( $_GET['zipb'] ) ? $_GET['zipb'] : '19081';
$desired = isset( $_GET['desired'] ) ? $_GET['desired'] : '65';

$tempa = get_average( $zipa );
$tempb = get_average( $zipb );

$da = abs( $desired - $tempa );
$db = abs( $desired - $tempb );
$victor = ( $da < $db ) ? 1 : 2;
$stylea = ( $victor == 1 ) ? "background: #bbb;" : "";
$styleb = ( $victor == 2 ) ? "background: #bbb;" : "";
?>
<html>
<head>
<title>Average Temperature Showdown</title>
<style type="text/css">
td { text-align: center; }
</style>
</head>
<body>
<form>
<table width="600">
<tr>
<th>Desired</th>
<th style="<?php echo($stylea); ?>"><input type="text" name="zipa" value="<?php
echo( $zipa ); ?>" size="6" /></th>
<th style="<?php echo($styleb); ?>"><input type="text" name="zipb" value="<?php
echo( $zipb ); ?>" size="6" /></th>
</tr>
<tr>
<td><input type="text" name="desired" value="<?php echo( $desired ); ?>" size="3"
    /></td>
<td style="<?php echo($stylea); ?>"><?php echo( $tempa ); ?></td>
<td style="<?php echo($styleb); ?>"><?php echo( $tempb ); ?></td>
</tr>
<tr>
<td colspan="3"><input type="submit" value="Compare" /></td>
```

Example 10-11. PHP checking the weather forecast (continued)

```
<tr>
</table>
</form>
</body>
</html>
```

The weather service that is exposed through the Services_Weather PEAR module provides a structure of forecast results in response to a Zip Code that is provided. The structure isn't very elaborate. There is an array of days, each day containing a hash table that has the predicted temperature. This page averages the temperature across the days to give a comparison between the two locations.

Running the Hack

Download and install the Services_Weather PEAR module [Hack #2] on your server and then upload the *index.php* file. Navigate to the page in your web browser; you should see something like Figure 10-19.

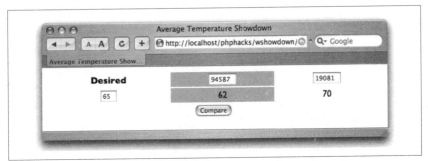

Figure 10-19. Comparing the temperature in Union City, California to that in Swarthmore, Pennsylvania

Change the values in the column headers to your local Zip Codes and click the Compare button to see which town is the temperature victor for this coming week. If you want to get fancy, add some Google maps [Hack #95] and really make this a killer application.

See Also

- "Search Google by Link Graph" [Hack #91]
- "Create a New Interface for Amazon.com" [Hack #92]

Index

We'd like to hear your suggestions for improving our indexes. Send email to *index@oreilly.com*.

D

G

games, checking network game with
PHP, 419–421
GD imagint functions, 103
geographical location for IP
addresses, 271
geospatial technologies, open
source, 364
GeoTIFF, 357, 358
map example using, 362–364
getNames( ) method (JavaScript), 75
GNU Public License (GPL), 47
Google
searching by link graph, 382–388
Web API access, 387
Google Maps
creating custom, 406–411
scrolling effect, creating, 93–99
web site, 93
graphics, 101–141
accessing iPhoto pictures, 126–141
arrows, 60
creating with SVG, 104–107
image overlays, 123–126
merging images, 117–120
simplifying with objects, 107–115
splitting an image into multiple
images, 115–117
thumbnail images, creating, 101–104
vector, adding with PHP, 79–81
graphics modules, PHP on Mac OS X, 6
GraphicSpace class, 112
graphing in PHP, xix
graphs
adapter example using text
graph, 304–307
building with DHTML, 52–58
creating with PHP, 120–122
dynamic generation by Flash
application, 396–405
link graphs, creating, 85–88
grid control (ActiveWidgets), 44–47
GTk, building GUI interfaces, 365–368
limitations, 368
PHP 4 interpreter with GTk
support, 367
GUIs (graphical user interfaces) (see UIs)

H

Half Life server, checking, 419–421
has_role( ) function, 247
head tag, 63
header function, 206
hiding JavaScript code, 67–69
hints, pop-up, 47–48
HSB( ) function, 84
HSB color values, 81–84
hsb2hex( ) function, 84
htdocs directory, 3
HTML
alternative interface comparing two
Amazon searches, 388–391
broken links, checking for, 335–337
drag-and-drop lists, 49–52
formatted for PSP
Wikipedia, 422–427
RSS reader formatted for
PSP, 379–382
use in PHPReports system, 236
HTML, Dynamic (see DHTML)
HTMLBuilder class (example), 297, 299
HTTP requests, forcing new for
redirects, 255
HTTP transfer requests, Ajax and, 73
HTTP_Client module, 342–344,
347–351
installing, 13
httpd executable, Apache, 8
httpd.conf file
editing for Mac OS X, 6
editing for Windows, 3
HttpRequest object, 75
hue, saturation, and brightness (see HSB
color values)

I

IGN gaming site, 258
IIS server, installing PHP, 3
IM (instant messaging)
sending RSS feeds to
application, 369–376
sending SMS messages from
client, 392–396
image display, PHP script for, 76–78
image resizing (scale.php), 78
image scaling (see scaling images)
image scroller design, 94

R

Rails framework, Ruby, 154
ranges, 257
$rb_run object, 367
readRecords( ) method, 295
Record class, 290
    RecordReader class and, 294
RecordFactory class, 290
RecordList class, 324
RecordReader class, 294
    readRecords( ) method, 295
records, inserting into orders table, 264
redirections
    basic, 255
    regular expressions, using, 255–258
redirector for ads, 258–261
refreshing pages, avoiding, 99
regular expressions
    GTk test application, 365–368
    reading XML, 165–167
    scraping web pages for
        data, 184–189
    used by mod_rewrite, 255–258
relational databases, 144–146
RenderItem class, 112
RenderQueue class, 112
reporting engines, 235
reports, user-customizable, 234–237
REST requests, in Ajax, 73
rewriting URLs, 253–258
RGB values, conversion to and from
    HSB, 82–84
RLIB (reporting engine), 235
robots, testing applications
    with, 342–346
    robots as unit tests, 344–346
roles, 241–249
    database library for, 242
    home page for logged-in users, 246
    login page, 243
    login processor, 243
    logout processor, 244
    management page, 244
    security library functions, 245
    SQL code for users database, 245
RSS feeds
    reading on your PSP, 379–382
    sending to IM application, 369–376

RTF (Rich Text Format) documents,
    creating dynamically, 202
Ruby, Rails framework, 154
run( ) function, 367
run_queue( ) function, 215

S

sales
    tracking, 263
    verifying, 264, 267–269
saveXML( ) method, 229
Scalable Vector Graphics (SVG), 79
scaling images, 78
    Google Maps scrolling effect, 97
    image overlay, 125
    merged images, 120
    viewport scaling, 112
schema tag, 169
screen scraping, 184–189
    technical and legal problems
        with, 188
scrolling effect (Google Maps),
    creating, 93–99
scrolling panorama, 117
sectioning page content with
    spinners, 58–61
security
    database access control, 147
    improving, xviii
    roles, 241–249
Services_Google module, 386, 387
Services_Weather module, 430–432
_ _set method, 154
setCalendarText( ) function, 93
set_clock( ) function, 72
set_state( ) function, 72
shopping cart, 277–285
    adding items, 280
    checkout page, 280
    database library, 278
    database schema, 277
    processing with prepared
        statements, 270
    product page, 279–280
    removing items, 282
    testing with HTTP_Client, 342–344
SimpleListener class, 226
simulated users, testing
    application, 337–342

Colophon

Our look is the result of reader comments, our own experimentation, and feedback from distribution channels. Distinctive covers complement our distinctive approach to technical topics, breathing personality and life into potentially dry subjects.

The image on the cover of *PHP Hacks* is a propeller beanie. The hat's name is thought to come from the early 20th-century slang term "bean," meaning "head," and it was first worn by blue-collar laborers during that time, presumably to keep their hair out of their eyes as they worked. Later, wearing beanies became a fad for young boys, and the propeller beanie is now a popular symbol of science fiction fans in comic art. This association is thought to have originated in 1948 when Ray Nelson, who would later become a science fiction author and cartoonist, supposedly suggested that the members of his science fiction club wear these hats to a science fiction convention so that they would stand out. Since Ray was a teenager in high school at the time, his father would not allow him to attend the convention, but at least one of his fellow club members, George Young, is thought to have worn his beanie to the convention. While the beanie has become an icon of geekdom, it eventually evolved into the more sporty baseball cap.

Reba Libby was the production editor and the proofreader for *PHP Hacks*. Audrey Doyle copyedited the book. Sanders Kleinfeld and Marlowe Shaeffer provided quality control. Ellen Troutman Zaig wrote the index.

Marcia Friedman designed the cover of this book, based on a series design by Edie Freedman. The cover image comes from Metaphorically Speaking, CVCD Library. Karen Montgomery produced the cover layout with Adobe InDesign CS using Adobe's Helvetica Neue and ITC Garamond fonts.

David Futato designed the interior layout. This book was converted by Keith Fahlgren to FrameMaker 5.5.6 with a format conversion tool created by Erik Ray, Jason McIntosh, Neil Walls, and Mike Sierra that uses Perl and XML technologies. The text font is Linotype Birka; the heading font is Adobe Helvetica Neue Condensed; and the code font is LucasFont's TheSans Mono Condensed. The illustrations that appear in the book were produced by Robert Romano, Jessamyn Read, and Lesley Borash using Macromedia FreeHand MX and Adobe Photoshop CS. This colophon was written by Reba Libby.

Better than e-books

Buy *PHP Hacks* and access the digital
edition FREE on Safari for 45 days.

Go to www.oreilly.com/go/safarienabled
and type in coupon code WYD6-HLSE-1UZL-FKDI-7YC8

Search
thousands of
top tech books

Download
whole chapters

Cut and Paste
code examples

Find
answers fast

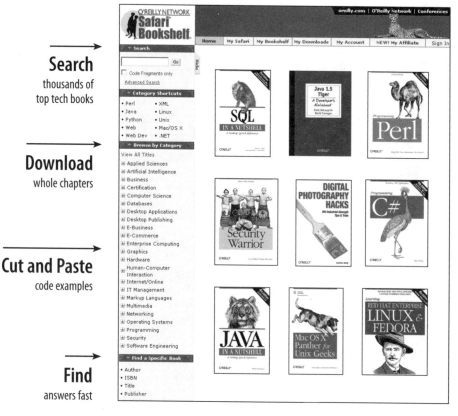

Search Safari! The premier electronic reference
library for programmers and IT professionals.

Related Titles from O'Reilly

Web Programming

ActionScript Cookbook

ActionScript for Flash MX: The
Definitive Guide, *2nd Edition*

Dynamic HTML: The Definitive
Reference, *2nd Edition*

Flash Hacks

Essential PHP Security

Google Hacks, *2nd Edition*

Google Pocket Guide

HTTP: The Definitive Guide

JavaScript & DHTML
Cookbook

JavaScript Pocket Reference,
2nd Edition

JavaScript: The Definitive
Guide, *4th Edition*

Learning PHP 5

PayPal Hacks

PHP Cookbook

PHP in a Nutshell

PHP Pocket Reference,
2nd Edition

PHPUnit Pocket Guide

Programming ColdFusion MX,
2nd Edition

Programming PHP

Upgrading to PHP 5

Web Database Applications
with PHP and MySQL, *2nd
Edition*

Webmaster in a Nutshell,
3rd Edition

Web Authoring and Design

Ambient Findability

Cascading Style Sheets: The
Definitive Guide, *2nd Edition*

Creating Web Sites:
The Missing Manual

CSS Cookbook

CSS Pocket Reference,
2nd Edition

Dreamweaver 8:
The Missing Manual

Essential ActionScript 2.0

Flash 8: The Missing Manual

Flash Hacks, *2nd Edition*

Flash Out of the Box

FrontPage 2003:
The Missing Manual

Head First HTML with CSS
& XHTML

HTML & XHTML: The
Definitive Guide, *5th Edition*

HTML Pocket Reference,
2nd Edition

Information Architecture
for the World Wide Web,
2nd Edition

Learning Web Design,
2nd Edition

Programming Flash
Communication Server

Web Design in a Nutshell,
3rd Edition

Web Site Measurement Hacks

Web Administration

Apache Cookbook

Apache Pocket Reference

Apache: The Definitive Guide,
3rd Edition

Perl for Web Site Management

Squid: The Definitive Guide

Web Performance Tuning,
2nd Edition

29.95